T0334648

Convenience Dynamics and White-Collar Crime

This book introduces a dynamic perspective to study white-collar crime. It argues that as personal motives change over time, so too do organizational opportunities, and willingness for deviant behavior.

The work contends that the extent of white-collar crime is dependent on the extent of crime convenience perceived and preferred by potential offenders. It discusses how potential white-collar offenders expand organizational opportunities for financial crime over time. The dynamics are illustrated here by system dynamics models to capture cause and effect relationships. The book also presents a new structural model illustrating the elements of convenience theory along with a new dynamic model illustrating the evolution of white-collar crime. The practical aspects are illustrated with a number of case studies.

The book will be of interest to researchers, academics and professionals working in the areas of Criminal Justice, Criminology, Criminal Law and Business Studies.

Petter Gottschalk is a professor in the Department of Leadership and Organizational Behavior at BI Norwegian Business School in Oslo, Norway. Dr. Gottschalk has published extensively on knowledge management, intelligence strategy, police investigations, white-collar crime, and fraud examinations.

Convenience Dynamics and White-Collar Crime

Petter Gottschalk

Routledge
Taylor & Francis Group

LONDON AND NEW YORK

First published 2021
by Routledge
2 Park Square, Milton Park, Abingdon, Oxon OX14 4RN

and by Routledge
605 Third Avenue, New York, NY 10017

First issued in paperback 2022

Routledge is an imprint of the Taylor & Francis Group, an informa business

© 2021 Petter Gottschalk

The right of Petter Gottschalk to be identified as author of this work has been asserted by him in accordance with sections 77 and 78 of the Copyright, Designs and Patents Act 1988.

All rights reserved. No part of this book may be reprinted or reproduced or utilised in any form or by any electronic, mechanical, or other means, now known or hereafter invented, including photocopying and recording, or in any information storage or retrieval system, without permission in writing from the publishers.

Trademark notice: Product or corporate names may be trademarks or registered trademarks, and are used only for identification and explanation without intent to infringe.

Publisher's Note
The publisher has gone to great lengths to ensure the quality of this reprint but points out that some imperfections in the original copies may be apparent.

British Library Cataloguing-in-Publication Data
A catalogue record for this book is available from the British Library

Library of Congress Cataloging-in-Publication Data
A catalog record for this book has been requested

ISBN: 978-0-367-54407-2 (pbk)
ISBN: 978-0-367-54404-1 (hbk)
ISBN: 978-1-003-08915-5 (ebk)

DOI: 10.4324/9781003089155

Typeset in Galliard
by Apex CoVantage, LLC

Contents

Introduction

White-collar crime is financial crime committed by individuals in privileged positions in business and public organizations (Sutherland, 1983). White-collar crime is unlawful conduct that elites and the powerful commit without fear of coming into contact with the criminal justice system. White-collar offenders commit and conceal their crime in a professional setting where they have legitimate access to premises, resources and systems (Logan et al., 2019). White-collar crime includes all categories of financial crime, such as fraud, corruption, manipulation and theft (Piquero, 2018).

For too long, greed has been the dominating explanation for white-collar crime (Friedrichs, 2010: 479):

> Arguably the simplest, most direct explanation for white-collar crime is captured by a single word: greed.

Greed implies that the offender is never satisfied, as he, she or the organization always wants more profit (Goldstraw-White, 2012). Greed represents socially constructed needs and desires that can never be completely covered or contended. There is a strong preference to maximize wealth for the corporation, possibly at the expense of violating the laws, rules, and guidelines. Economic greed is a strong motive for financial crime (Bucy et al., 2008; Hamilton and Micklethwait, 2006).

This book argues that the extent of white-collar crime is dependent on the extent of crime convenience perceived and preferred by potential offenders. Convenience is the state of being able to proceed with something with little effort or difficulty, avoiding pain and strain (Mai and Olsen, 2016). Convenience is savings in time and effort (Farquhar and Rowley, 2009), as well as avoidance of pain and obstacles (Higgins, 1997). Convenience is a relative concept concerned with the efficiency in time and effort as well as reduction in pain and solution to problems (Engdahl, 2015). Convenience is an advantage in favor of a specific action to the detriment of alternative actions. White-collar offenders choose the most convenient path to reach their goals (Wikstrom et al., 2018).

The potential offender faces the alternatives of legal versus illegal means, where the relative convenience determines whether or not law-abiding versus law-breaking behavior is most convenient and thus chosen. Convenience addresses the time and effort exerted before, during, and after an action or avoidance of action (Collier and Kimes, 2012). Blickle et al. (2006) found that if the rationally expected utility of an action by a white-collar offender clearly outweighs the expected disadvantages resulting from the action, thereby leaving some net material advantage, then the offender would commit the offense in question.

A convenient individual is not necessarily bad or lazy. On the contrary, the person can be seen as smart and rational (Sundström and Radon, 2015). Convenience orientation varies among individuals, as some are more concerned than others are about time saving, effort reduction, and pain avoidance.

Convenience theory is emerging as a possible multi-dimensional explanation for white-collar and corporate offending. This perspective, which is composed of three interrelated concepts, including motivation, opportunity, and willingness, suggests that individuals more likely to commit white-collar crime are differently oriented to convenience as a factor in the choice to engage in illegal behavior. Individuals become more oriented towards convenience as motive becomes stronger, as opportunity improves, and as willingness to engage in deviant behavior become more intense. Thus, perceptions of convenience should differ between those who view white-collar crime as more acceptable and those who view it as less acceptable.

The theory of convenience suggests that white-collar misconduct and crime occurs when there is a financial motive benefiting the individual or the organization, an organizational opportunity to commit and conceal crime, and a personal willingness for deviant behavior (Braaten and Vaughn, 2019; Chan and Gibbs, 2020; Hansen, 2020; Kireenko et al., 2019; Vasiu and Podgor, 2019). There cannot be a crime without an opportunity for one to occur. While deviance generally is purposeful behaviors that violate organizational norms and is intended to harm someone or something, this book applies the term deviance in the meaning of crime, where crime is violation of the law.

The theory of convenience is an umbrella term for many well-known perspectives from criminology, strategy, psychology, and other schools of thought. Motive, opportunity and willingness are the three dimensions in convenience theory. Since convenience is a relative concept, convenience theory is a crime-as-choice theory. Shover et al. (2012) suggest that it is a conscious choice among alternatives that leads to law violation.

This book argues that perceived and preferred convenience changes dynamically over time. Dynamics simply mean variations over time (Kocagil, 2004), and white-collar crime itself is often a dynamic phenomenon (Leap, 2007; Li and Ouyang, 2007). The offender's financial motive can become stronger or weaker over time. Perceived organizational opportunity can become larger or smaller over time. The offender's personal willingness for deviant behavior can become higher or lower over time. In addition, motive, opportunity, and willingness can dynamically influence each other.

For example, a chief financial officer (CFO) in Norway became divorced and his financial motive became stronger. The growing motive caused him to search for opportunity expansion in the organization. One of his actions was to take control over the auditing process, where he succeeded in controlling that what the auditor presented to the chief executive officer (CEO) and the board of directors. He was thus able to make the organizational opportunity larger. As he noticed that he succeeded in organizational opportunity expansion, his willingness for deviant behavior became higher than it was before.

Opportunity expansion represents an increase in white-collar convenience over time. Therefore, opportunity in convenience theory is a dynamic rather than a static condition. By collecting decision rights, by controlling information flows, and by authoritarian leadership styles a potential offender develops an opportunity space that grows over time. Whether intentional or not, the opportunity space changes over time as a reaction to the potential offender's behavior. In a dynamic perspective, an offender can thus improve the organizational convenience for financial crime (Schnatterly et al., 2018). For example, by taking on a personal project of selling some business activities for the organization, the offender can make sure that he or she is alone in handling the case. When making sure that nobody else is involved, some of the income can be diverged to private accounts.

In addition to convenience dynamics from changes in motive, opportunity and willingness over time, as well as interdependencies among these three dimensions, changes in convenience orientation among actors will also create convenience dynamics. A less conveniently oriented person might not feel disturbed by a legitimate path that has some obstacles and delays, while a more conveniently oriented person might always look for the shortest way out of trouble and the shortest path to exploit and explore possibilities that emerge. A convenience-oriented person is one who seeks to accomplish a task in the shortest time with the least expenditure of human energy (Berry et al., 2002).

Chapter 1 presents all supporting concepts in convenience theory, where the purpose is to integrate a number of theoretical approaches to understand and explain the white-collar crime phenomenon. Chapter 2 introduces convenience dynamics in white-collar crime. It takes the conceptual structure in the previous chapter into a behavioral mode of dynamics where motive, opportunity, and willingness change over time.

Chapter 3 focuses on the organizational dimension of convenience dynamics in white-collar crime. The organization is the arena where offenders can commit as well as conceal financial crime. Offenders have high social status in privileged positions, and they have legitimate access to crime resources. There might be disorganized institutional deterioration occurring, there might be lack of over-sight and guardianship, and there might be criminal market structures.

Chapter 4 treats convenience dynamics in white-collar crime in a historical evolution perspective. The question here is whether white-collar crime has become more or less convenient over time. The purpose of this chapter is to discuss how convenience in white-collar crime has a role in business history as the extent of convenience influences the magnitude of financial crime among privileged individuals in the course of their professions. Motive, opportunity and willingness in convenience theory represent criteria to evaluate the extent of historical convenience in white-collar crime.

Chapter 5 presents possible operationalization of elements in the financial motive, the organizational opportunity, and the personal willingness. These elements represent themes that explored in Chapter 6.

Chapter 7 discusses the discrepancy between high-end financial crime in the form of white-collar crime and low-end financial crime in the form of social security fraud.

Chapters 8 and 10 present two case studies of convenience theory, while Chapter 9 in between presents the challenge of filling the gap in public and private policing of white-collar crime. Finally, Chapters 11 and 12 present more perspectives on convenience dynamics. In Chapter 11, a white-collar offender may develop along a stage model into a more serious deviant behavior. In Chapter 12, a business hit by a white-collar crime scandal may develop their crisis-response match by varying accounts over time.

References

Berry, L.L., Seiders, K. and Grewal, D. (2002). Understanding service convenience, *Journal of Marketing*, 66, 1–17.

Blickle, G., Schlegel, A., Fassbender, P. and Klein, U. (2006). Some personality correlates of business white-collar crime, *Applied Psychology: An International Review*, 55 (2), 220–233.

Braaten, C.N. and Vaughn, M.S. (2019). Convenience theory of cryptocurrency crime: A content analysis of U.S. federal court decisions, *Deviant Behavior*, published online, https://doi.org/10.1080/01639625.2019.1706706.

Bucy, P.H., Formby, E.P., Raspanti, M.S. and Rooney, K.E. (2008). Why do they do it? The motives, mores, and character of white collar criminals, *St. John's Law Review*, 82, 401–571.

Chan, F. and Gibbs, C. (2020). Integrated theories of white-collar and corporate crime, in: Rorie, M.L. (editor), *The Handbook of White-Collar Crime*, Hoboken, NJ: Wiley & Sons, chapter 13, pages 191–208.

Collier, J.E. and Kimes, S.E. (2012). Only if it is convenient: Understanding how convenience influences self-service technology evaluation, *Journal of Service Research*, 16 (1), 39–51.

Engdahl, O. (2015). White-collar crime and first-time adult-onset offending: Explorations in the concept of negative life events as turning points, *International Journal of Law, Crime and Justice*, 43 (1), 1–16.

Farquhar, J.D. and Rowley, J. (2009). Convenience: A services perspective, *Marketing Theory*, 9 (4), 425–438.

Friedrichs, D.O. (2010). Integrated theories of white-collar crime, in: Cullen, F.T. and Wilcox, P. (editors), *Encyclopedia of Criminological Theory*, Volume 1, Los Angeles, CA: Sage Publications, pages 479–486.

Goldstraw-White, J. (2012). *White-Collar Crime: Accounts of Offending Behavior*, London, UK: Palgrave Macmillan.

Hamilton, S. and Micklethwait, A. (2006). *Greed and Corporate Failure: The Lessons from Recent Disasters*, Basingstoke, UK: Palgrave Macmillan.

Hansen, L.L. (2020). Review of the book "Convenience Triangle in White-Collar Crime: Case Studies of Fraud Examinations", *ChoiceConnect*, vol. 57, no. 5, Middletown, CT: Association of College and Research Libraries.

Higgins, E.T. (1997). Beyond pleasure and pain, *American Psychologist*, 52, 1280–1300.

Kireenko, A.P., Nevzorova, E.N. and Fedotov, D.Y. (2019). Sector-specific characteristics of tax crime in Russia, *Journal of Tax Reform*, 5 (3), 249–264.

Kocagil, A.E. (2004). Optionality and daily dynamics of convenience yield behavior: An empirical analysis, *The Journal of Financial Research*, 27 (1), 143–158.

Leap, T.L. (2007). *Dishonest Dollars: The Dynamics of White-Collar Crime*, Ithaca, NY: Cornell University Press.

Li, S. and Ouyang, M. (2007). A dynamic model to explain the bribery behavior of firms, *International Journal of Management*, 24 (3), 605–618.

Logan, M.W., Morgan, M.A., Benson, M.L. and Cullen, F.T. (2019). Coping with imprisonment: Testing the special sensitivity hypothesis for white-collar offenders, *Justice Quarterly*, 36 (2), 225–254.

Mai, H.T.X. and Olsen, S.O. (2016). Consumer participation in self-production: The role of control mechanisms, convenience orientation, and moral obligation, *Journal of Marketing Theory and Practice*, 24 (2), 209–223.

Piquero, N.L. (2018). White-collar crime is crime: Victims hurt just the same, *Criminology & Public Policy*, 17 (3), 595–600.

Schnatterly, K., Gangloff, K.A. and Tuschke, A. (2018). CEO wrongdoing: A review of pressure, opportunity, and rationalization, *Journal of Management*, 44 (6), 2405–2432.

Shover, N., Hochstetler, A. and Alalehto, T. (2012). Choosing white-collar crime, in: Cullen, F.T. and Wilcox, P. (editors), *The Oxford Handbook of Criminological Theory*, Oxford, UK: Oxford University Press.

Sundström, M. and Radon, A. (2015). Utilizing the concept of convenience as a business opportunity in emerging markets, *Organizations and Markets in Emerging Economies*, 6 (2), 7–21.

Sutherland, E.H. (1983). *White Collar Crime: The Uncut Version*, New Haven, CT: Yale University Press.

Vasiu, V.I. and Podgor, E.S. (2019). Organizational opportunity and deviant behavior: Convenience in white-collar crime, in: *Criminal Law and Criminal Justice Books*, New Brunswick, NJ: Rutgers, the State University of New Jersey, July, www.clcjbooks.rutgers.edu.

Wikstrom, P.O.H., Mann, R.P. and Hardie, B. (2018). Young people's differential vulnerability to criminogenic exposure: Bridging the gap between people- and place-oriented approaches in the study of crime causation, *European Journal of Criminology*, 15 (1), 10–31.

1 Deviant convenience structure

This chapter introduces all perspectives that are included in the theory of convenience, which consists of three dimensions: economical white-collar crime motive, organizational white-collar crime opportunity, and personal white-collar crime willingness. The motive is dichotomous in possibilities and threats, the opportunity is dichotomous in committing crime and concealing crime, and the willingness is dichotomous in choice and innocence.

Vasiu and Podgor (2019) argue that the theory of convenience provides a new landscape for evaluating white-collar offenses. Hansen (2020) suggests that the theory of convenience is based on a new theoretical paradigm. Braaten and Vaughn (2019) found support for convenience theory when studying cryptocurrency crime. Convenience theory suggests that rather than losing material enrichment, power and not climbing further up in prestige, a white-collar offender chooses an illegitimate alternative that is convenient. Increased inconvenience of responding in legal ways under financial incentives and pressures and increased convenience in responding in illegal ways to financial incentives and pressures lead to a greater risk of white-collar criminal behavior. Therefore, responsible agents must make white-collar crime less convenient by establishing more severe criminal consequences such as increased likelihood of detection by identifying the higher-ups that are in the sweetest spots to turn to convenient alternatives.

Vasiu and Podgor (2019) suggest that a distinction exists between deliberate conveniences versus negligent conveniences on the part of offenders. The negligent convenience perspective finds support when sliding on the slippery slope (Arjoon, 2008; Welsh et al., 2014).

Development of convenience theory

Theory is a necessary part of research in organization sciences (Ashkanasy, 2016), and convenience theory emphasizes the organizational opportunity to commit and conceal white-collar crime. Theory is a systematic, interrelated set of concepts that explain a body of data. In convenience theory, three main concepts explain the occurrence of white-collar crime: financial motive, organizational opportunity, and personal willingness. These concepts are all interrelated as organizational opportunity interacts with financial motive and personal willingness. Interactions between motive, opportunity, and willingness determine the extent of convenience perceived by a potential white-collar crime offender.

Theory is a way of imposing conceptual order on the empirical complexity of the phenomenal world. Convenience theory offers a conceptual order on financial crime by members in the elite in society who certainly do not need to commit crime for their own survival. Theory offers a statement of relations between concepts within a set of boundary assumptions and constraints. Convenience theory makes assumptions about human behavior, such as individuals' motives and desires as well as individuals' behaviors in organizational contexts. A theory reflects the magnitude of a discipline's knowledge base. Convenience theory reflects and builds on a knowledge base from criminology, psychology, management, strategy and many other disciplines.

As argued by Thornberry (1989: 52), theory is a set of logically interrelated propositions designed to explain a particular phenomenon:

> From this perspective, therefore, the two most fundamental characteristics of a theory are its propositional form and its explanatory purpose.

In line with this argument, convenience theory integrates a number of perspectives that propose influence on the extent of white-collar crime. By directing these perspectives towards more or less crime, they provide possible explanations of crime occurrence.

Theory does more than abstracting and organizing knowledge. It also signals the values upon which we build knowledge (Suddaby, 2014). In white-collar crime research, a number of values are at stake. For example, not all are equal to the law. Some are simply too powerful to jail (Pontell et al., 2014). Ever since Sutherland (1939) coined the term white-collar crime, researchers in the field have emphasized the value of preventing and detecting elite crime. Therefore, an important value signaled by convenience theory is that white-collar crime is just as bad as – and maybe even much worse than – traditional street crime including rape, murder and theft, since offenders' motive is found in their choice of convenience with no regard to harm and victims (Dodge, 2020b). This signal from white-collar crime research is controversial still today. Many seem to consider white-collar criminals as individuals who were unlucky, who made a mistake that was not intentional, who made a short cut in a stressed job situation, and who are not really crooks. According to Leap (2007), white-collar crime imposes a degree of physical and emotional trauma on its victims that far exceeds the trauma inflicted by street criminals. Victims "suffer from something terrible that 'happens' to them or is deliberately done to them" (Cohen, 2001: 14).

Developing theory is neither easy nor ever completed. Weick (1989) defines theory development as disciplined imagination, where theory is an ordered set of assertions about a generic behavior or structure assumed to hold throughout a significantly broad range of specific instances. Offenders can find the generic behavior in white-collar crime in the abuse of power, influence and trust, and the generic structure is visible in the organizational context among convicted offenders.

As suggested by Barney (2018), a theoretical contribution like this book on the theory of convenience is part of an ongoing conversation in the literature. The conversation is concerned with white-collar crime as a phenomenon and its occurrences in different situations. One unresolved theoretical issue related to white-collar crime is its convenience relative to legal means of reaching desired states for privileged individuals and organizations. This unresolved issue is important, as both prevention and detection of white-collar crime rests on a relevant understanding of its motives, opportunities, and behaviors.

As suggested by Haveman et al. (2019: 241), "it is theory that gives meaning to empirical results". Insights into white-collar crime occurrences are dependent on theory that guides us to what questions to ask and tells us why they are important. Theory provides a discipline of reasoning about occurrences that otherwise would end up as special cases of practice in the minds of observers.

There are a number of interactions between dimensions in the theory of crime convenience. For example, opportunity enhances temptation (Steffensmeier and Allan, 1996: 478):

> An illegitimate enterprise, being able tends to make one more willing, just as being willing increases the prospects for being able.

Thus, the organizational dimension of opportunity influences the desire for financial gain in the economical dimension. Opportunity also influences the behavioral willingness, while the behavioral willingness in turn influences abilities in terms of organizational opportunities.

The theory of convenience finds its base in reasoning by analogy where the core analogy is that the organization is an arena for individual motives, opportunities, and behaviors with varying convenience options. Many of the supporting perspectives find their basis in analogies as well. For example, the principal-agent perspective derives from the analogy that the organization is a nexus of contracts, as explained later in this book. Ketokivi et al. (2017) argue that theoretical reasoning by analogy provides a link between two domains of meaning: the source and the target domains. The source domain in convenience theory is convenience orientation experienced among people, while the target domain is the organization where white-collar crime can occur.

The convenience perspective suggests that motivation (personal and organizational ambitions), opportunity (offense and concealment in an organizational context), as well as behavior (lack of control and neutralization of guilt) make financial crime a convenient option to avoid threats and to exploit opportunities.

Convenience theory makes statements about relationships between motive, opportunity, and behavior. The primary goal of the theory is to answer the questions of how, when, and why white-collar crime. The question of how is answered in the organizational context where there is an opportunity to commit white-collar crime. The question of when is answered in the behavioral context where the offender finds it relevant to apply deviant behavior. The question of why is answered in the economical dimension where the motive is profit to avoid threats and to exploit possibilities.

The key components of convenience theory are similar to Felson and Boba's (2017) problem triangle analysis in routine activity theory. Routine activity theory suggests three conditions for crime to occur: a motivated offender, an opportunity in terms of a suitable target, and the absence of a capable or moral guardian. Moral wrongfulness includes cheating, deception, stealing, coercion, exploitation, disloyalty, promise-breaking, and disobedience. The existence or absence of a likely guardian represents an inhibitor or facilitator for crime. The premise of routine activity theory is that crime is to a minor extent affected by social causes such as poverty, inequality and unemployment. Motivated offenders are individuals who are not only capable of committing criminal activity, but are willing to do so. Suitable targets can be something that offenders recognize as particularly attractive.

When introducing routine activity theory, Cohen and Felson (1979) concentrated upon the circumstances in which offenders carry out predatory criminal acts. Most criminal acts require convergence in space and time of (1) likely offenders, (2) suitable targets, and (3) the absence of capable guardians against crime. The lack of any of these elements is sufficient to prevent the successful completion of a crime. Though guardianship is implicit in everyday life, it usually is invisible by the absence of violations and is therefore easy to overlook. Guardians are not only protective tools, weapons and skills, but also mental models in the minds of potential offenders that stimulate self-control to avoid criminal acts.

When compared to convenience theory, routine activity theory's three conditions do not cover all three dimensions. The likely offenders occur in the behavioral dimension, while both suitable targets and absence of capable guardians occur in the organizational dimension. While routine activity theory defines conditions for crime to occur, convenience theory defines situations where crime occurs. White-collar crime only occurs when there is a financial motive in the economical dimension.

Another traditional theory is worthwhile to compare to convenience theory. Fraud theory with the fraud triangle suggests three conditions for fraud (Cressey, 1972): (1) incentives and pressures, (2) opportunities, and (3) attitudes and rationalization. Incentives and pressures belong in the economical dimension; opportunities belong in the organizational dimension, while attitudes and rationalization belong in the behavioral dimension. As such, the fraud triangle covers all dimensions of convenience theory. However, at the core of convenience theory is convenience in all three dimensions as well as opportunity found in the organizational setting based on professional role and trust by others. Furthermore, convenience theory emphasizes the relative importance of convenience, where offenders have alternative legitimate actions available to respond to incentives and pressures, but they choose illegitimate actions since these actions subjectively emerge as more convenient. We return to this theme when we compare Cressey's (1972) fraud triangle with the convenience triangle.

Some have suggested that there is nothing as practical as a good theory. Ployhart and Bartunek (2019: 495) suggest the opposite, that there is nothing as theoretical as good practice:

> In other words, we should start with the phenomena unveiled in practice situations.

The public has for too long explained the phenomenon of white-collar crime by greed. However, as we dive into cases of the white-collar phenomenon, we find a number of elements in practice that rather point at convenience in situations of alternative avenues. A phenomenon-driven theory such as convenience theory calls for more phenomenon-driven research, where the practice is a basis for theorizing. As Krogh et al. (2012: 278) explained:

> Phenomena can be defined as regularities that are unexpected, that challenge existing knowledge (including the extant theory) and that are relevant to scientific discourse. Thus, the aim of phenomenon-based research is to capture, describe and document, as well as conceptualize, a phenomenon so that appropriate theorizing and the development of research designs can proceed.

More than two decades ago, there was an important debate about what theory is and is not, where the main contributors were DiMaggio (1995), Sutton and Staw (1995), and Weick (1995, Weick et al., 2005).

Sutton and Staw (1995: 378) define theory in the following way:

> Theory is about the connections among phenomena, a story about why acts, events, structure, and thoughts occur. Theory emphasizes the nature of causal relationships, identifying what comes first as well as the timing of such events. Strong theory, in our view, probes underlying processes so as to understand the systematic reasons for a particular occurrence or nonoccurrence. It often burrows deeply into microprocesses, laterally into neighboring concepts, or in an upward direction, tying itself to broader social phenomena. It usually is laced with a set of convincing and logically interconnected arguments. It can have implications that we have not seen with our naked (or theoretically unassisted) eye. It may have implications that run counter to our common sense.

Corley and Gioia (2011: 12) provide a short definition of theory:

> Theory is a statement of concepts and their interrelationships that shows how and/or why a phenomenon occurs.

Various disciplines such as criminology, sociology, psychology, strategy, marketing, and management have developed a number of theories with the aim of explaining how and why individuals involve themselves in crime, and how they get involved in crime. Some of the theories are individualistic and look at risk factors in personality traits and family conditions (Listwan et al., 2010). Other theories emphasize ideology and culture, which represent the environment in terms of economy, society and structures.

Sociological theories of white-collar crime, for example, postulate that managers who commit economic offenses live in a social setting, i.e. culture, in which a very high value associates with material success and individual wealth. Both economic theories and sociological theories are of the opinion that strong striving for wealth and enjoyment in some way contributes to economic crime committed by managers (Blickle et al., 2006).

It is difficult to overstate the importance of theory to preventive understanding of white-collar crime. Theory allows analysts to understand and predict outcomes on a basis of probability (Colquitt and Zapata-Phelan, 2007). Theory also allows analysts to describe and explain a process or sequence of events. Theory prevents analysts from avoiding confusion by the complexity of the real world by providing a linguistic tool for organizing a coherent understanding of the real world.

Theory acts as an educational tool, which researchers use to develop insights into criminal phenomena such as financial crime in general and white-collar crime in particular. A theory is an undocumented explanation of a phenomenon or relationship. The opposite of theory is not practice. The opposite of theory is empirical findings. Both theory and empirical study are concerned with practice. While theory presents thoughts about practice, empirical study presents facts about practice.

In this book, we apply the following definition of theory as summarized by Løkke and Sørensen (2014): A series of logical arguments that specifies a set of relationships among concepts. Specifically, we first introduce the main concept of convenience and describe convenience orientation. Next, we introduce three concepts as dimensions in convenience theory: desire for profit caused by threats and possibilities, organizational opportunity to commit and conceal, and personal willingness for deviant behavior. Finally, a set of relationships can link motive, opportunity and willingness. Convenience theory suggests that there are mutual influences among all three concepts. For example, greater opportunity can cause greater willingness, and greater willingness can lead to greater opportunity. The purpose of convenience theory is to explain why white-collar crime occurs, which again explains how white-collar crime takes place.

Theoretical elements in convenience theory

Table 1.1 lists all theoretical elements derived from the research literature in criminology, management, psychology, sociology and related fields. The literature review identified 15 perspectives on financial motive, 21 perspectives on opportunity, and 24 perspectives on willingness for white-collar crime. In addition, there are eight references to general perspectives on convenience, where convenience is similar to comfort that focuses on relief and ease (Carrington and Catasus, 2007).

Table 1.1 Theoretical elements in convenience theory from the literature review

ECONOMICAL WHITE-COLLAR CRIME MOTIVE	ORGANIZATIONAL WHITE-COLLAR CRIME OPPORTUNITY	PERSONAL WHITE-COLLAR CRIME WILLINGNESS	GENERAL PERSPECTIVES ON CONVENIENCE
1. Climb the hierarchy of needs for status and success (Maslow, 1943)	1. Executive language that people do not understand (Ferraro et al., 2005)	1. Acceptable for the elite from social conflict (Petrocelli et al., 2003)	1. A convenient individual is not necessarily bad or lazy. On the contrary, the person can be seen as smart and rational (Sundström and Radon, 2015)
2. Realize the American dream of prosperity (Schoepfer and Piquero, 2006)	2. Elite members too big to fail and too powerful to jail (Pontell et al., 2014)	2. Narcissistic identification with the organization (Galvin et al., 2015)	2. Savings in time and effort is a desire for all individuals (Farquhar and Rowley, 2009)
3. Satisfy the need for acclaim as a narcissist (Chatterjee and Pollock, 2017)	3. Blame game by misleading attribution to others (Eberly et al., 2011)	3. Professional deviant identity (Obodaru, 2017)	3. Relief and ease characterizes comfort (Carrington and Catasus, 2007)
4. Restore the perception of equity and equality (Leigh et al., 2010)	4. Offender humor distraction from deviant behavior (Yam et al., 2018)	4. Personality trait of narcissism expecting preferential treatment (Zvi and Elaad, 2018)	4. Convenience is the state of being able to proceed with something with little effort or difficulty, avoiding pain and strain (Mai and Olsen, 2016)
5. Satisfy the desire to help others as social concern (Agnew, 2014)	5. Power inequality between elite members and others (Patel and Cooper, 2014)	5. Reputation adaption to individual labels (Bernburg et al., 2006)	5. People will avoid pain and obstacles (Higgins, 1997) and accomplish a task in the shortest time (Berry et al., 2002)
6. Reach business objectives that justify means (Jonnergård et al., 2010)	6. Legitimate access to premises and systems (Benson and Simpson, 2018)	6. Social ties dwindle with age (Sampson and Laub, 1993)	6. A convenient individual prefers efficiency in time and effort as well as reduction in pain and solution to problems (Engdahl, 2015)

ECONOMICAL WHITE-COLLAR CRIME MOTIVE	ORGANIZATIONAL WHITE-COLLAR CRIME OPPORTUNITY	PERSONAL WHITE-COLLAR CRIME WILLINGNESS	GENERAL PERSPECTIVES ON CONVENIENCE
7. Satisfy greed where nothing is ever enough (Goldstraw-White, 2012)	7. Opportunity creation by entrepreneurship (Ramoglou and Tsang, 2016)	7. Deviant identity labeling (Mingus and Burchfield, 2012)	7. Convenience addresses the time and effort exerted before, during, and after an action or avoidance of action (Collier and Kimes, 2012)
8. Enjoy mutual benefits in exchange relationships (Huang and Knight, 2017)	8. Specialized access in routine activity (Cohen and Felson, 1979)	8. Perception of benefits exceeding costs as rational choice (Pratt and Cullen, 2005)	8. There is decision convenience, access convenience, benefit convenience, transaction convenience, and post benefit convenience (Seiders et al., 2007)
9. Make as much profit as possible since it is the only goal (Naylor, 2003)	9. Legitimate access to strategic resources (Adler and Kwon, 2002)	9. Behavioral reinforcement of deviance over time (Benartzi et al., 2017)	
10. Avoid loss of self-esteem after organizational failure (Crosina and Pratt, 2019)	10. Institutional deterioration based on external legitimacy (Rodriguez et al., 2005)	10. Undesirable impulses in self-regulation (Mawritz et al., 2017)	
11. Remove strain, pain, and uncertainty (Langton and Piquero, 2007)	11. Inability to control because of social disorganization (Hoffmann, 2002)	11. No risk of detection perceived and thus no deterrence effect (Comey, 2009)	
12. Avoid falling from position in the privileged elite (Piquero, 2012)	12. Interference and noise in crime signals (Karim and Siegel, 1998)	12. Work-related stress self-determined (Olafsen et al., 2017)	
13. Avoid corporate collapse and bankruptcy (Blickle et al., 2006)	13. Misrepresentation in accounting (Qiu and Slezak, 2019)	13. Sensation seeking to experience adventure (Craig and Piquero, 2017)	

(Continued)

Table 1.1 (Continued)

ECONOMICAL WHITE-COLLAR CRIME MOTIVE	ORGANIZATIONAL WHITE-COLLAR CRIME OPPORTUNITY	PERSONAL WHITE-COLLAR CRIME WILLINGNESS	GENERAL PERSPECTIVES ON CONVENIENCE
14. Adapt to profitable criminal market forces (Leonard and Weber, 1970)	14. Auditors reporting to management (Hurley et al., 2019)	14. Learning from others by differential association (Sutherland, 1983)	
15. Join profitable criminal networks and cartels (Goncharov and Peter, 2019)	15. Lack of control in principal-agent relationships (Bosse and Phillips, 2016)	15. Action according to authority as obedience (Baird and Zelin, 2009)	
	16. Sensemaking of actions difficult for outsiders (Weick, 1995)	16. Collectivist value orientations (Bussmann et al., 2018)	
	17. Costs exceed benefits for whistleblowers (Keil et al., 2010)	17. The act of wrongdoing is morally justifiable (Schnatterly et al., 2018)	
	18. Ethical climate conflict (Victor and Cullen, 1988)	18. Upper echelon information selection (Gamache and McNamara, 2019)	
	19. Rule complexity preventing compliance (Lehman et al., 2019)	19. Disappointing work context cause entitlement (Nichol, 2019)	
	20. Participation in crime networks such as cartels (Nielsen, 2003)	20. Negative life events have occurred (Engdahl, 2015)	
	21. Usual way of business in markets with crime forces (Chang et al., 2005)	21. Peer pressure (Gao and Zhang, 2019)	
		22. Application of neutralization techniques (Sykes and Matza, 1957)	
		23. Sliding on the slippery slope (Welsh et al., 2014)	
		24. Lack of self-control (Gottfredson and Hirschi, 1990)	

Structural model of white-collar convenience

A combination of motive, opportunity and willingness determine the extent of white-collar crime convenience as illustrated in the structural model in Figure 1.1.

In the financial motive, profit might be a goal in itself or an enabler to exploit possibilities and to avoid threats. Possibilities and threats exist both for individual members of the organization as well as for the corporation. It is convenient to exploit possibilities and to avoid threats by financial means.

In the organizational opportunity, convenience can exist both to commit white-collar crime and to conceal white-collar crime. Offenders have high social status in privileged positions, and they have legitimate access to crime resources. Disorganized institutional deterioration causes decay, lack of oversight and guardianship cause chaos, while criminal market structures cause collapse.

The personal willingness for deviant behavior focuses on offender choice and perceived innocence. The choice of crime can be caused by deviant identity, rational consideration, or learning from others. Justification and neutralization

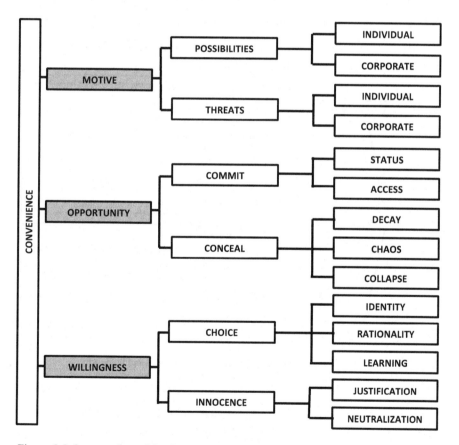

Figure 1.1 Structural model of convenience theory

cause the perceived innocence at crime. Identity, rationality, learning, justification, and neutralization all contribute to making white-collar crime action a convenient behavior for offenders.

Structural model of financial motive

The economical dimension of convenience theory focuses on financial motives that the offender has to exploit and explore possibilities, and to reduce and avoid threats. Possibilities and threats are motives both for individuals and for the organization, as illustrated in Figure 1.2.

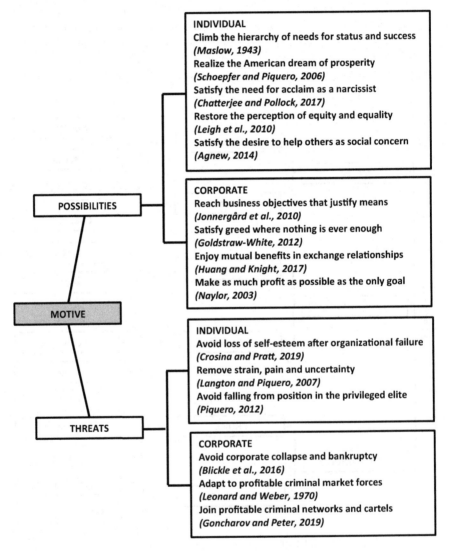

Figure 1.2 Structural model of motive in convenience theory

Possibilities for the individual include climbing the hierarchy of needs for status and success (Maslow, 1943). A privileged member of the elite has already satisfied all basic needs in the hierarchy, such as food and clothes, as well as advanced needs such as power and influence. Yet the offender would like to climb higher in the pyramid, into characteristics such as self-realization, admiration by others, fame and improved reputation, recognition and status (Cleff et al., 2013; Hirschi and Gottfredson, 1987). To the extent that the offender has a strong motive where financial resources can help climbing, while legitimate means are inconvenient, then white-collar crime might be a convenient option (Pillay and Kluvers, 2014; Welsh et al., 2014). High-status individuals strive for fulfillment, self-esteem and esteem from others. As Agnew (2014: 2) formulates it: "crime is often the most expedient way to get what you want" and "fraud is often easier, simpler, faster, more exciting, and more certain than other means of securing one's ends".

The American dream suggests that the greatest and most satisfying experience in life is to become economically rich, and that everyone can indeed become rich if he or she works hard enough and smart enough (Schoepfer and Piquero, 2006). It is a one-dimensional emphasis on the desirability of material success and individual achievement in life. The American dream is a set of cultural beliefs telling that in the United States, everyone can be economically successful. It instructs all Americans to strive for material success, suggesting that hard work will bring high rewards (Cullen, 2010: 170):

> The American dream has positive effects, because it creates strong desires for upward mobility and allows some people who might otherwise have been mired in the bottom of society to achieve enormous wealth. But this dream also has a dark side. The difficulty is that the American dream preaches universal success – that is, that it tells everyone that economic mobility not only is to be cherished but also is within reach. But this dream confronts harsh reality: the unequal American class structure. Opportunities for success are not universal but differentially available.

If the belief in the American dream is strong, then financial resources can help directly. The dark side of the American dream implies that if legal means seem inconvenient then white-collar crime might be a convenient option (Pratt and Cullen, 2005; Trahan et al., 2005).

Some high-status individuals have a need for acclaim as narcissists (Chatterjee and Pollock, 2017; Zhu and Chen, 2015). If illegal financial gain can help achieve desired acclaim, narcissists might feel entitled to crime (Nichol, 2019). Narcissists exhibit an unusual trust in themselves, believing that they are uniquely special and entitled to more benefits than are legitimately available to them (Galvin et al., 2015; Ouimet, 2010; Zvi and Elaad, 2018).

A financial crime motive is the desire to restore the perception of equity and equality (Leigh et al., 2010). The equity perspective suggests that an executive or other privileged person compares his or her work efforts to another person or group of persons chosen as reference. A situation evaluated being without equity, will initiate behavior to remove the feeling of discomfort (Huseman et al., 1987; Kamerdze et al., 2014; Martin and Peterson, 1987; Roehling et al., 2010). The equity perspective is linked to the social exchange perspective, where there is a norm of reciprocity. Social exchange considers executives and other trusted employees as partners with the employer, who exchange valued contributions. The organization provides trusted employees material and socio-emotional rewards in exchange for their work effort and loyalty (Cropanzano and Mitchell, 2005). If a trusted employee perceives that the norm of reciprocity is violated, then the retaliation principles implies that the emphasis is placed both on the return of benefits and on the return of injuries (Caesens et al., 2019). Disloyalty is to defect from supporting someone. A trusted individual who feels mistreated might reciprocate by behaving in a manner that harms the source of this mistreatment (Gibney et al., 2009). Restoring the perception of equity and equality might also be a matter of responding to dehumanization, which is a feeling of being a tool or an instrument based on a perception of a treatment as lesser than or different from others (Bell and Khoury, 2016; Väyrynen and Laari-Salmela, 2015).

Agnew (2014) introduced the motive of social concern and crime, where there is a desire to help others, and thus moving beyond the assumption of simple self-interest. However, as argued by Paternoster et al. (2018), helping others can be a self-interested, rational action that claims social concern.

Possibilities for the corporation include reaching business objectives by ignoring whether or not means are legitimate or illegitimate (Campbell and Göritz, 2014; Jonnergård et al., 2010; Kang and Thosuwanchot, 2017). Ends simply justify means that might represent crime. It may be so important to have a bottom line in accounting that satisfies investors and others that crime emerges as potentially acceptable. Welsh and Ordonez (2014) found that high performance goals cause unethical behavior. Dodge (2009: 15) suggests that tough rivalry among executives make them commit crime to attain goals: "The competitive environment generates pressures on the organization to violate the law in order to attain goals".

Corporate greed implies that the organization is never satisfied, as it always wants more profit (Goldstraw-White, 2012). Greed reflects needs and desires that are socially constructed, and the needs and desires can never be completely covered or contended. There is a strong preference to maximize wealth for the corporation, possibly at the expense of violating the laws, rules, and guidelines. Economic greed is a strong motive for financial crime (Bucy et al., 2008; Hamilton and Micklethwait, 2006).

Corporations enter into exchange relationships with suppliers, customers, banks, consultants and others. Exchanges can be thought of as discrete events nested within continuous relationships that are developing and changing over the course of time. Reciprocity such as kickbacks might be natural according to expectations in an exchange relationship to secure future business possibilities (Huang and Knight, 2017).

Finally, in the motive of possibilities for corporations, making as much profits as possible might be the ultimate goal (Naylor, 2003). Rather than viewing profits as an enabler to invest and expand, profits as such might be the final goal in itself. Financial crime can be an attractive strategic decision (Lopez-Rodriguez, 2009; Menon and Siew, 2012). Financial crime is a rational decision where advantages exceed disadvantages (Barry and Stephens, 1998; Hefendehl, 2010; Lyman and Potter, 2007).

Moving down in Figure 1.2 to threats, there are again theoretical perspectives on motives at the individual as well as the corporate level. As argued by Crosina and Pratt (2019), organizations can foster deep bonds among their members, whether in the form of person-organization fit, organizational commitment, organizational identification, or some other type of attachment. Organizational failure in the form of bankruptcy is not only a threat to personal income and status. Failure can also cause organizational mourning that is negative feelings following the loss of the organization. Fighting for the survival of the organization can become a strong motive for financial crime to avoid loss of self-esteem after organizational failure.

The strain perspective has become one of the leading theoretical explanations for crime (Agnew, 2005, 2012; Cleff et al., 2013; Froggio and Agnew, 2007; Hoffmann, 2002; Langton and Piquero, 2007; Ngo and Paternoster, 2016). The strain perspective emphasizes the frustration of not succeeding with a task, such as the inability to achieve economic prosperity. Strains tend to generate negative emotions, such as anger, depression, and despair. These negative emotions create pressures for corrective action to reduce the gap between the desired and the actual situation, with crime being one possible response. A range of factors influence whether individuals cope with strains through crime (Thaxton and Agnew, 2018: 888):

> Criminal coping is said to be most likely among those with poor coping skills and resources, little social support, low social control, beliefs favorable to crime, and criminal associates, and opportunities for crime.

Strain is linked to anomie, which refers to confusion without moral guidance (Benson and Simpson, 2018). Anomie is the lack of social or ethical norms that places a strain on individuals. To the extent rules exist, anomie means a low commitment to such rules where the guiding power of normative standards is undermined (Schoepfer and Piquero, 2006).

Many top executives and other members of the elite in society have a fear of falling from their positions (Piquero, 2012). The fear of falling perspective suggests that the motivation for financial crime by white-collar offenders is the fear of losing what one has worked so hard to achieve (Benson and Chio, 2020). The desire to maintain one's standard of living can motivate criminal behavior as it relates specifically to the position in the class system. The fear of losing and falling from grace can stimulate illegal behavior to survive as member of the elite in society (Kouchaki and Desai, 2015; Wood and Alleyne, 2010).

The threat of corporate collapse and bankruptcy might cause exploration and exploitation of illegal avenues to survive, where moral panic can occur

(Chattopadhyay et al., 2001; Kang and Thosuwanchot, 2017). The survival of the corporation can become so important that no means come across as unacceptable in the current situation (Blickle et al., 2006). Sometimes, fraud and corruption are considered temporary measures to recover from a crisis (Geest et al., 2017), where the measures will be terminated when the crisis is over. A crisis is a fundamental threat to the organization, which is often characterized by ambiguity of cause, effect, and means of resolution (König et al., 2020).

Financial balance is a strong motive for corporate economic crime (Brightman, 2009). In some markets, the only way to survive is to implement financial practices similar to the ones applied by competitors (Leonard and Weber, 1970). If corruption is the name of the game, every participant on the market has to provide bribes to stay in business (Berghoff, 2018; Bradshaw, 2015). Threats from monopolies are a strong motive for financial crime (Chang et al., 2005).

Similarly, if a cartel is the name of the game, the only way to survive might be to join the cartel, where cartel members divide markets among themselves (Freiberg, 2020; Goncharov and Peter, 2019).

Structural model of organizational opportunity

The opportunity dimension of convenience theory focuses on opportunities that the offender has to commit and conceal white-collar crime. Opportunity is any "potential course of action, made possible by a particular set of social conditions, which has been symbolically incorporated into an actor's repertoire of behavioral possibilities" (Coleman, 1987: 409). Aguilera and Vadera (2008: 434) describe a criminal opportunity as "the presence of a favorable combination of circumstances that renders a possible course of action relevant". An opportunity is attractive as a means of responding to desires, wishes and ambitions.

Committing financial crime might be convenient because of the offender's status and legitimate access to resources. Concealing financial crime might be convenient because of decay, chaos and collapse. Disorganized institutional deterioration causes decay, lack of oversight and guardianship causes chaos, and criminal market structures cause external collapse. External market collapse creates similar opportunities to internal decay and chaos, as offenders and others face laws and rules with ignorance without anyone noticing or reacting. Figures 1.3 and 1.4 illustrate perspectives on opportunity to commit and conceal financial crime.

Executives and others in the elite may use language that followers do not necessarily understand. Followers nevertheless trust executive messages. Language shapes what people notice and ignore (Ferraro et al., 2005), and language is a window into organizational culture (Holt and Cornelissen, 2014; Srivastava and Goldberg, 2017; Weick, 1995). Offender language can cause obedience among followers (Mawritz et al., 2017).

Some offenders know that they are too big to fail and too powerful to jail (Pontell et al., 2014; Schnatterly et al., 2018). They are too important to blame (Eberly et al., 2011; Slyke and Bales, 2012). They enjoy high social status in

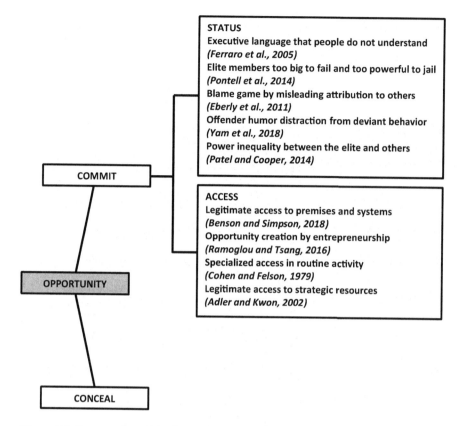

STATUS
Executive language that people do not understand
(Ferraro et al., 2005)
Elite members too big to fail and too powerful to jail
(Pontell et al., 2014)
Blame game by misleading attribution to others
(Eberly et al., 2011)
Offender humor distraction from deviant behavior
(Yam et al., 2018)
Power inequality between the elite and others
(Patel and Cooper, 2014)

ACCESS
Legitimate access to premises and systems
(Benson and Simpson, 2018)
Opportunity creation by entrepreneurship
(Ramoglou and Tsang, 2016)
Specialized access in routine activity
(Cohen and Felson, 1979)
Legitimate access to strategic resources
(Adler and Kwon, 2002)

COMMIT

OPPORTUNITY

CONCEAL

Figure 1.3 Structural model of opportunity in convenience theory (part 1:2)

privileged positions. White-collar offenders "are now regarded as the untouch-ables, too well-heeled and powerful to lock up" (Hausman, 2018: 381). Katz (1979) found that financial crime higher up in the organization will be ignored to a larger extent than lower down in the organization, or blame is allocated elsewhere (Keaveney, 2008; Lee and Robinson, 2000; Sonnier, 2015). Campbell and Göritz (2014) found that leaders in corrupt organizations might argue that corruption is normal.

Linked to the blame game is shaming, where suspected elite members express social disapproval of innocent individuals in the organization, thereby attempting to gain social control on perceptions of criminality. Shaming implies stigmatiza-tion (Braithwaite, 1989). Social control is based on attachment, commitment, involvement, and belief, where a control mechanism is informal punishment in the appearance of shaming.

White-collar offenders can use humor to distract attention from their crime. Offender humor distraction as suggested by Yam et al. (2018) implies that

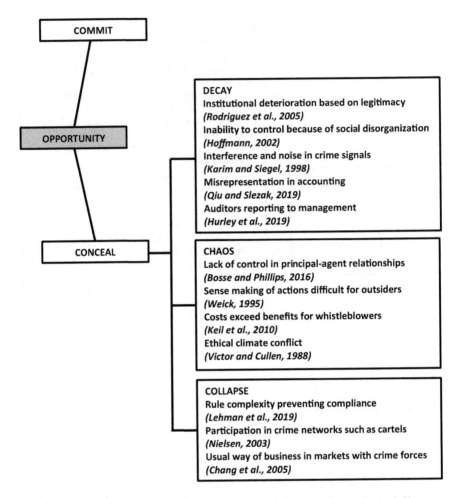

Figure 1.4 Structural model of opportunity in convenience theory (part 2:2)

potential white-collar offenders can influence the organizational opportunity structure by aggressive humor. Aggressive humor is a negatively directed style of humor that an individual carries out at the expense and detriment of one's relationships with others.

The perspective of power inequality suggests that, for example, family members in family firms wield significant influence in their firms. Family members often have legitimate access to firm resources that nonfamily executives in the firm cannot question (Patel and Cooper, 2014). Kempa (2010) found that white-collar offenders have unlimited authority to get it the way they want.

White-collar crime can be distinguished from ordinary crime ("street crime") based on the status of offenders, their access to legitimate professions, the common presence of an organizational form, and the extent of the costs and harmfulness of such crime (Cullen et al., 2020). While street criminals hide themselves after an offense, white-collar criminals hide the offense while staying in the same positions (Michel, 2016). This is because they have legitimate access to premises and systems to commit financial crime (Benson and Simpson, 2018).

High social status in privileged positions is sometimes associated with entrepreneurship, where an entrepreneurial individual can create opportunities for deviant behavior (Ramoglou and Tsang, 2016). The entrepreneurship perspective emphasizes that entrepreneurs discover and create innovative and entrepreneurial opportunities (Smith, 2009; Tonoyan et al., 2010; Welter et al., 2017). Criminal entrepreneurs actualize illegal opportunities in the shadow economy (McElwee and Smith, 2015).

Specialized access in the routine activity perspective suggests that crime is convenient since there is an absence of a capable or moral guardian at the workplace, where white-collar crime "directly arises out of the routines of everyday life" (Huisman and Erp, 2013: 1179). The absence of a likely guardian represents a facilitator for crime. The routine activity theory focuses on the convenient victimization by offenders (Dodge, 2020b). Routines in activities are consequences of lifestyles, where lifestyle is routine daily activities including occupational activities and leisure activities. Movement through time and space exposes potential victims to varying numbers and varieties of potentially motivated offenders (Cohen and Felson, 1979; Williams et al., 2019).

A white-collar offender has typically legitimate and convenient access to resources to commit crime (Adler and Kwon, 2002; Füss and Hecker, 2008; Huisman and Erp, 2013; Lange, 2008; Pinto et al., 2008; Reyns, 2013). A resource is an enabler applied and used to satisfy human and organizational needs. A resource has utility and limited availability. According to Petrocelli et al. (2003), access to resources equates access to power. Other organizational members are losers in the competition for resources (Wheelock et al., 2011). In the conflict perspective suggested by Petrocelli et al. (2003), the upper class in society exercises its power and controls the resources. Valuable resources are typically scarce, unique, not imitable, not transferrable, combinable, exploitable, and not substitutable.

Moving to Figure 1.4 addressing concealment of financial crime, the first topic is decay in the form of institutional deterioration (Barton, 2004; Donk and Molloy, 2008). Institutions are the patterned, mutually shared ways that people develop for living together. Institutional deterioration improves conditions of convenience for corruption and other forms of financial crime (Kostova et al., 2008; Pinto et al., 2008; Rodriguez et al., 2005). Institutional deterioration can occur conveniently, resulting from external legitimacy where deviance is the norm. An offender's actions have a superficial appearance of legitimacy also internally, since both legal and illegal actions in the company occur in a manner characterized by disorganization (Benson and Simpson, 2018). Conventional mechanisms of social control are weak and unable to regulate the behavior within the organization (Pratt and Cullen, 2005). Concealment of crime occurs conveniently by simply disappearing among other seemingly legitimate transactions.

Social disorganization is the inability of an organization to realize common values of its members and maintain effective social control. Social disorganization implies that the ability of social bonds to reduce delinquent behavior is absent (Forti and Visconti, 2020; Hoffmann, 2002; Onna and Denkers, 2019). Differential reinforcement of crime convenience develops over time as individuals become vulnerable to various associations and definitions conducive to delinquency. Social disorganization occurs because the human nature is selfish, and people are unwilling to share a common culture. In the perspective of life-courses with age-graded determinants of crime, it is interesting to notice that white-collar crime represents adult-onset offending. White-collar offenders are people who live more or less conventional law-abiding lives until they are adults and who then commit crime. Moving into the elite as an adult reduces social controls through social bonds (Benson and Chio, 2020).

Misconduct and crime can be hard to detect, because signals of deviant behavior drown or disappear in noise. Karim and Siegel (1998) define four possible outcomes in the decision matrix of an observer. First, the observer notices a noise signal when it is a crime signal (called a miss). Second, the observer notices a crime signal when it is a crime signal (called a hit). Third, the observer notices a noise signal when it is a noise signal (called a correct identification). Finally, the observer notices a crime signal when it is a noise signal (called a false alarm). The more false alarms and misses, the greater the opportunity is successfully to conceal white-collar crime. Szalma and Hancock (2013) found that control functions typically have low signal alertness, and that such functions lack the ability to recognize and interpret patterns in signals. One reason might be that control functions have dysfunctional cognitive style and achievement motivation (Martinsen et al., 2016).

Misreporting in accounting is often a convenient way of concealing illegal transactions (Qiu and Slezak, 2019). Lack of transparency makes concealment in accounting convenient (Davidson et al., 2019; Goncharov and Peter, 2019). Managers can withhold bad news in accounting misrepresentation (Bao et al., 2019). Balakrishnan et al. (2019) found that reduced corporate transparency in accounting is associated with increased corporate tax aggressiveness. Accounting fraud in terms of account manipulation is lacking transparency (Toolami et al., 2019).

Concealing illegal transactions also results from the failure of auditors to do their job. Auditors are supposed to serve as gatekeepers to protect shareholders and other stakeholders, but deviant corporate management tend to hire and control auditors instead of letting auditors report to the board of directors or the supervisory board (Hurley et al., 2019). Reporting fraud to public authorities will also harm auditors (Mohliver, 2019: 316):

> As organizations, audit firms are often severely penalized for client malfeasance. Yet the individual auditors working for these firms are susceptible to "motivated blindness" stemming from conflicts of interest that bias their moral judgment toward choices that help their clients.

Shadnam and Lawrence (2011) found that morale collapse increases the tendency to financial crime. In fact, repetition of criminal actions might institutionalize such actions (Hatch, 1997). Dion (2008) found that the larger the corporation, the less deterrence effect from laws on financial crime, which may have to do with increased convenience in concealing crime.

Lack of oversight and guardianship causes chaos. The agency perspective suggests that a principal is often unable to control an agent who does work for the principal. The agency perspective assumes narrow self-interest among both principals and agents. The interests of principal and agent tend to diverge, they may have different risk willingness or risk aversion, there is knowledge asymmetry between the two parties, and the principal has imperfect information about the agent's contribution (Bosse and Phillips, 2016; Chrisman et al., 2007; Pillay and Kluvers, 2014; Williams, 2008). According to principal-agent analysis, exchanges can encourage illegal gain for both principal and agent, as explained later in this book.

Concealing crime is convenient also because others than the offender are incapable of making sense of actions that have occurred (Weick, 1995). People tend to trust what an elite member does, based on the authority position occupied by the offender. Sense making links to crime signal detection by the challenge of perceiving and understanding a crime signal versus a noise signal, as discussed previously. People without experience are unable to make sense of weak signals from white-collar offenders. They are not able to frame or categorize through words what the signal is about (Holt and Cornelissen, 2014).

Even when an observer believes to have noticed a crime signal, the observer can be reluctant to report the observation (Bjørkelo et al., 2011; Bussmann et al., 2018; Mpho, 2017). In most countries, there are no benefits from reporting misconduct and crime in the organization (Brown et al., 2016; Keil et al., 2010). Rather, retaliation and reprisals can be the result for the observer (Mesmer-Magnus and Viswesvaran, 2005; Park et al., 2020; Rehg et al., 2009; Shawver and Clements, 2019). Therefore, white-collar crime can remain conveniently concealed even when others have noticed and observed it (Bussmann et al., 2018). Lack of trust in the legitimacy, capacity, and competence of the police and the criminal justice system in general causes a further reduction in the willingness to blow the whistle on observed wrongdoing (Tankebe, 2019).

The ethical climate can be another element of the opportunity structure for white-collar crime. The ethical climate perspective defines five distinct climate types within organizations, among them the instrumental climate (Victor and Cullen, 1988). The instrumental climate is where Murphy and Free (2015) believe fraud is most likely to occur. Instrumental means that executives and other privileged individuals in the organization tend to prioritize decisions that either provide personal benefits or serve the organization's interests with little or no regard for ethical considerations. The climate can encourage corruption and fraudulent behavior as normal and acceptable (Murphy and Dacin, 2011; Tankebe, 2019).

The final topic in Figure 1.4 is collapse from rule complexity preventing compliance (Lehman et al., 2019), participation in crime networks such as cartels (Nielsen, 2003), and financial crime as the usual way of business in markets with crime forces (Chang et al., 2005). Collapse represents a convenient situation for everybody ready to commit white-collar crime.

Rule complexity can create a situation where nobody is able to tell whether an action represented a criminal offense. It is impossible to understand what is right and what is wrong. Some laws, rules and regulations are so complex that compliance becomes random, where compliance is the action of complying with laws, rules and regulations. The regulatory legal environment is supposed to define the boundaries of appropriate organizational conduct. However, legal complexity is often so extreme that even specialist compliance officers struggle to understand what to recommend to business executives in the organizations (Lehman et al., 2019). Then regulatory inspection does not work for compliance (Braithwaite, 2020). Business executives can thus find the large grey zone in legal matters a convenient space for misconduct and crime.

When rule complexity is linked to anomie in the sense of low commitment to mainstream rules in the organization (Schoepfer and Piquero, 2006) then the organizational opportunity for financial crime is further enhanced. The organization is reluctant to follow mainstream rules that are too complicated. The reluctance becomes stronger when mainstream rules will harm business performance. Trying to follow the law may result in inefficient business practices that depress organizational results and hurt careers of organizational members. Noncompliance might allow the corporation to be more profitable than competitors who follow the rules.

Monopolies, cartels and crime networks do not only represent threats in the motivational dimension of convenience theory (Chang et al., 2005; Geest et al., 2017). For deviant members of the elite, monopolies, cartels and crime networks can represent attractive avenues for extra profits (Freiberg, 2020; Goncharov and Peter, 2019; Leonard and Weber, 1970). Participation in criminal networks can be attractive (Nielsen, 2003), especially if criminogenic market symptoms cause markets with crime forces to be the usual way of doing business (Chang et al., 2005).

The final topic of collapse in Figure 1.4 is concerned with organizational opportunity for white-collar crime from interactions with the external environment. Rule complexity, crime networks, and deviance by other actors externally are all factors that can enhance the convenience for white-collar offenders internally. An additional perspective here is situational action suggesting that crime is a social and behavioral outcome of interactions between human beings and their environments. Interaction with the external situation might enable a potential offender to perceive more deviant alternatives for action (Kroneberg and Schulz, 2018). The situational action perspective addresses how environments shape crime opportunities and, subsequently, how modifications in environments can increase criminal opportunities (Huisman and Erp, 2013). When the situational action perspective by Wikstrom et al. (2018) distinguishes between three stages, (1) perception of action alternatives (legal alternatives, illegal alternatives), (2) process of choice (habit, rational deliberation), and (3) action, then Kroneberg and Schulz (2018) conceptualize lack of self-control as well as lack of deterrence on the axis from (2) to (3). The latter items belong in the willingness dimension of convenience. The situational action perspective aims to integrate personal and environmental explanatory perspectives within the framework of a situation.

As cited previously, Aguilera and Vadera (2008: 434) describe a criminal opportunity as "the presence of a favorable combination of circumstances that renders a possible course of action relevant". Coleman (1987: 409) describes an opportunity as any "potential course of action, made possible by a particular set of social conditions, which has been symbolically incorporated into an actor's repertoire of behavioral possibilities". Figures 1.3 and 1.4 illustrate circumstances and conditions, such as status and access to commit crime; and decay, chaos, and collapse to conceal crime.

Structural model of personal willingness

The personal willingness dimension of convenience theory focuses on the willingness for deviant behavior among white-collar offenders. Personal willingness for deviant behavior implies a positive attitude towards violating social norms, including formally enacted laws, rules and regulations (Aguilera et al., 2018). Deviance is a term to describe behavior that contravenes accepted norms, values, and ethical standards (Smith and Raymen, 2018). Deviance is "the failure to obey group rules" (Becker, 1963: 8). Deviance is "a form of behavior that violates organizational norms and that consequently negatively impacts the well-being of the organization and its members" (Michalak and Ashkanasy, 2013: 20). Deviance is detrimental to organizational performance in several ways, including damaged reputation, exposure to lawsuits, and financial loss (Dilchert et al., 2007).

The willingness derives either from an active choice to commit and conceal crime, or from the perception of personal innocence when committing and concealing crime. Figure 1.5 lists theoretical contributions supporting the choice perspective by identity, rationality and learning, while Figure 1.6 lists theoretical contributions supporting the innocence perspective by justification and neutralization.

The powerful and wealthy in the upper class of society define their own identity in terms of what is right and what is wrong for them, sometimes in a state-corporate alignment (Bernat and Whyte, 2020; Rothe, 2020; Rothe and Medley, 2020; Tombs and Whyte, 2020; Zysman-Quirós, 2020). If they themselves break their own laws, then there is a need to change the laws rather than punish law violators (Petrocelli et al., 2003).

Forbes magazine reported, "Trump's pardons are meant to normalize white-collar crime" (Sarkis, 2020). White (2019: 59) wrote,

> One vital marker of an ethical culture is whether there really is a zero-tolerance policy for wrongdoing. Many companies claim to have one, but when high producers or senior people break the rules, leaders may go easy on them, either for business reasons or out of loyalty.

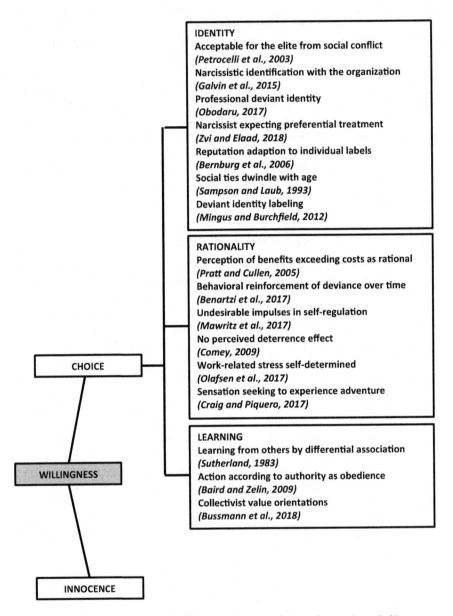

Figure 1.5 Structural model of willingness in convenience theory (part 1:2)

The rich and mighty people can behave like robber barons, because they make the laws and because they control law enforcement. White-collar offenders argue that laws are there to protect the powerful (Schwendinger and Schwendinger, 2014). The ruling class does not consider white-collar offenses as regular crime, and certainly not similar to street crime. Rather, the conflict perspective suggests that the upper class defines laws that the lower classes are to obey.

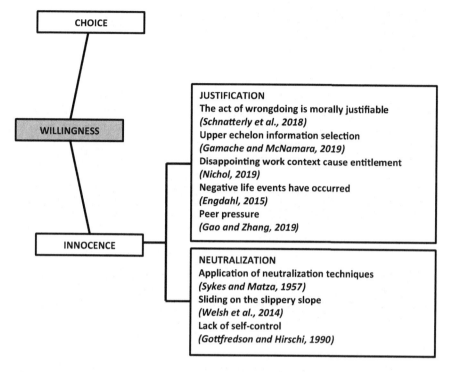

Figure 1.6 Structural model of willingness in convenience theory (part 2:2)

The personality trait of narcissism expects preferential treatment. A pervasive pattern of grandiosity, a need for admiration, and an empathy deficit characterize narcissism. Narcissistic identification is a special type of narcissism, where the offender sees little or no difference between self and the corporation. The company money is personal money that can be spent whatever way the narcissist prefers (Galvin et al., 2015). While grandiosity and admiration belong to the motivational dimension of convenience theory, empathy deficit belongs to the willingness dimension of convenience theory where the offender possesses a sense of entitlement (Nichol, 2019). The offender shows unreasonable expectations to receive and obtain preferential treatments (Zvi and Elaad, 2018).

In addition to narcissism, a research suggestion is that white-collar offenders may have psychopathic traits. However, Piquero et al. (2019) found no support for this suggestion, since individuals with adverse, antisocial behavior are unlikely to be able to climb to and stay in positions of power and trust. Pusch and Holtfreter (2020) found that negative personality traits, negative personal morality, lack of positive personality traits, and lack of self-control significantly and negatively predict white-collar offending. Dark personality traits exist in many forms among elite members in society (Kholin et al., 2020).

Some white-collar offenders take on a professional deviant identity (Obodaru, 2017). The identity perspective suggests that individuals develop professional identities where they commit to a chosen identity. Misbehavior finds an anchor in a person's professional identity (Blickle et al., 2020). The deviant identity person is increasingly likely to become involved in social groups that consist of social deviants and unconventional others without feeling any doubt or regret since the behavior is in accordance with the identity label glued to the person also by others (Bernburg et al., 2006).

Social ties to the corporation can dwindle with age, making the offender reluctant to consider the welfare of the organization or its members. The age-graded perspective of informal social control assumes that social ties can dwindle in later stages of life (Sampson and Laub, 1993). There is a lack or absence of severity in obligations and restraints, so the only relevant choice to make is what benefits the offender.

Deviant identity labeling implies that the label of deviant, and the stigma that comes with such a label, may cause the person to act in accordance with that label (Mingus and Burchfield, 2012). The offender accepts a deviant identity and acts accordingly (Crank, 2018).

The choice perspective of rationality in Figure 1.5 addresses offenders' comparison of benefits from crime with costs of crime. The rational choice assumption about offending is based on a normative foundation where advantages and disadvantages are subjectively compared (Müller, 2018). Offenders consider it rational to commit crime if benefits exceed costs. Individual preferences thus determine whether crime is committed (Pratt and Cullen, 2005). The greater benefits of crime and the less costs of crime, the more attractive it is to commit criminal acts. According to Berghoff and Spiekermann (2018: 293), potential white-collar offenders "act on cost-benefit calculations involving the expected utility, the likelihood of being caught, and punishment costs". The assumption of rational choice is that every crime is chosen and committed for specific reasons. Individuals consciously and deliberately choose criminal behavior of their own free will. However, the choice can be bounded and constrained by personal and situational factors.

Offenders can reinforce their deviant behavior over time, as they perceive misconduct and crime as normal and thus acceptable. The nudge perspective by Benartzi et al. (2017) suggests that behavioral reinforcement of deviance over time alters individuals' behavior in a voluntary manner.

Mawritz et al. (2017) argue that the choice of crime might happen as the result of undesirable impulses in self-regulation. Individuals possess varying and limited self-regulatory resources that inhibit certain responses, while allowing for other responses. Inhibiting or allowing certain responses may arise from physiological processes, habit, learning, or the unacceptability of being in the situation. When individuals deplete resources that regulate normal self-control and judgment, they may replace such resources with the choice of listening to their own urges and engage in behavior almost unwittingly, using quick, thoughtless responses.

White-collar offenders have typically no fear of coming in contact with the criminal justice system. There is thus no perceived deterrence effect from possible incarceration to prevent offenses (Comey, 2009). Rather, as part of the opportunity structure, the choice of crime seems like a safe avenue for the rich and powerful. Deterrence would come from whether or not an offender has to go to prison, rather than the severity of sanction in terms of prison length. Generally, the severity of punishment has shown to have no effect (Mears and Cochran, 2018). Deterrence is a process in which threatened or actual sanctions discourage criminal acts.

The notion of general deterrence holds that crime rates increase as the threat of generalized punishments decrease. The probability of such punishments includes those based on perceptions and reality. Given that the subjectively perceived detection likelihood is microscopically small, a benefit-cost analysis of white-collar crime might quickly conclude with crime.

Disappointed executives and employees can feel entitled to deviant behaviors (Nichol, 2019). This is in line with the self-determination perspective, which suggests that awareness and attention facilitate the choice of behaviors that coincide with the offender's values, needs, and interests (Olafsen, 2017; Olafsen et al., 2017). Work contexts that individuals do not find supportive of basic psychological needs are leading to disloyal executives and employees.

The choice of crime might derive from sensation seeking. Craig and Piquero (2017) suggest that the willingness to commit financial crime by some white-collar offenders has to do with their inclination for adventure and excitement.

Offenders are not only seeking new, intense, and complicated experiences and sensations, as well as exciting adventures, they are also accepting the legal, physical, financial and social risks associated with these adventures. They attempt to avoid boredom by replacing repetitive activities such as regular meetings with thrill and adventures. They search risky and exciting activities and have distaste for monotonous situations.

The final theme in Figure 1.5 is learning, where learning from others by differential association was introduced by Sutherland (1983), who coined the term white-collar crime several decades earlier. The differential association perspective suggests that offenders associate with those who agree with them, and distance themselves from those who disagree. The choice of crime is thus caused by social learning from others with whom offenders associate (Akers, 1985).

The choice of crime can also be the consequence of obedience, where the offender has learned that obedience is more preferable than disobedience. Obedience in human behavior is a form of social influence receipt in which a person learns how to adhere to instructions or orders from a person of authority (Baird and Zelin, 2009; Hollow, 2014).

The final choice perspective in Figure 1.5 is collectivist value orientations, where offenders do what they think others are doing. Bussmann et al. (2018: 256) argue that studies have shown a significant relationship between the collectivist value orientations in a country and its degree of corruption: "Such values encourage patronage along with the formation and stabilization of exclusive and corrupt networks".

Figure 1.6 illustrates the innocence theme in personal willingness for deviant behavior. While Figure 1.5 lists perspectives where offenders make the choice of crime, Figure 1.6 lists perspectives where offenders justify what they have done and neutralize their own guilt feelings. By neutralizing guilt feelings, offenders do not feel accountable, ashamed or responsible (Chen and Moosmayer, 2020). Schnatterly et al. (2018) found that offenders might explain their acts of wrongdoing as morally justifiable. They found that deviant chief executive officers (CEOs) in particular can refer to pressures and other circumstances that justify their white-collar crime. Pressure to engage in wrongdoing can originate from forces outside of the organization, such as competition and active investors. External forces that provide justification to commit or facilitate wrongdoing include industry cultures and norms.

A focus on risk taking increases the scope of potential results, while at the same time allowing for more freedom with regard to means (including wrongful means) to reach desired goals.

Individuals have different perspectives on their own past, present and future time dispositions. Gamache and McNamara (2019: 923) suggest that offenders in the upper echelon who mainly focus on their present time dispositions in their information selection are more inclined to justify their wrongdoing since they have "the proclivity to act impulsively, move quickly with current opportunities, and consider current issues when making decisions". A future time focus tends to increase the mental time span and reduce the perception of urgency.

A white-collar offender can justify wrongdoing by claiming entitlement to action because of a disappointing work context (Nichol, 2019). As discussed previously, entitlement to illegal gain also influences the motive dimension of convenience theory, as offenders with narcissistic traits might feel entitled to crime, as well as the choice perspective in the willingness dimension caused by an identity of narcissistic identification. Here in the innocence perspective of the willingness dimension by justification, the disappointing work context that does not support psychological and material needs is leading to disloyal executives and disloyalty from other members of the elite. Especially in the perspective of loss aversion, the disutility of giving up an object is greater than the utility of acquiring one. In turbulent times, an offender can justify deviant action by claiming loss of privileges enjoyed in the past.

Engdahl (2015) suggests that negative life events can serve as justification of white-collar crime. The perspective of negative life events implies that events such as divorce, accident, lack of promotion, and sudden cash problems can cause offenders to consider financial crime as a convenient solution. They may perceive being victims of unfortunate circumstances that they have to compensate in some ways.

The opinion of innocence can be justified by peer pressure, where the offender claims that the offense had to take place because a person with authority had told the offender to do so (Gao and Zhang, 2019). In the perspective of leader and follower, a follower has a belief in the leader's pressure as morally right that can make the follower experience shame and guilt if failing to support the leader (Fehr et al., 2015). Glasø and Einarsen (2008) studied emotion regulation in leader-follower relationships (Gottfredson et al., 2020). They found that followers typically suppress negative emotions such as disappointment, uncertainty, and annoyance, while they typically express or fake positive emotions such as enthusiasm, interest, and calmness.

The final theme in Figure 1.6 is concerned with the lack of guilt feeling by means of neutralization. White-collar offenders deny a guilty mind (Benson, 1985). Sykes and Matza (1957) introduced a number of neutralization techniques that have been expanded in recent years (Jordanoska, 2018; Kaptein and Helvoort, 2019; Schoultz and Flyghed, 2019; Siponen and Vance, 2010). Offenders disclaim responsibility for crime, refuse damage from crime, refuse victim from crime, condemn those who criticize, apologize by higher loyalties, claim blunder quota, claim legal mistake, claim normality of action, claim entitlement to action, claim solution to dilemma, argue necessity of crime, claim role in society, perceive being victim of incident, gather support for behavior, and claim rule complexity. Successful application of neutralization techniques enables offenders to experience no guilt or shame for engaging in the act or for being caught doing so. White-collar offenders may also suffer from self-deception, which is the practice of allowing oneself to believe that a false idea or thought about circumstances is true. Self-deception provides survival and reproductive benefits to those who employ it (Chan and Gibbs, 2020). Deception, on the other hand, occurs when one person misleads another by making things appear other than as they really are. Cohen (2001: 38) finds the concept of self-deception problematic:

> What can it mean to "lie to yourself" – the conventional (and bizarre) meaning of self-deception? A lie is a statement intended to deceive a dupe about the state of the world, including the intentions and attitudes of the liar. The liar, that is, intends to cause the dupe to adopt an understanding about the world and/or the mind of the liar that the liar believes to be false. The distinction between truth and deceit, Barnes reminds us, refers to the intentions of the liar, not the nature of the world. . . . The notion of self-deception, though, must suppose inner dialogues or man-sided conversations just like these: the roles of the liar and dupe are indeed played or thought out by the same person. . . . Self-deception is a way to keep secret from ourselves the truth we cannot face.

Sliding on the slippery slope can make the offender feel innocent, as the offender did not notice ending up on the wrong side of the law (Welsh et al., 2014). Arjoon (2008: 78) explains slippery slope in the following way: "As commonsense experience tells us, it is the small infractions that can lead to the larger ones". A series of small infractions gradually increase over time. Committing small indiscretions over time gradually lead people to complete larger unethical acts that they otherwise would have judged impermissible (Murphy and Dacin, 2011; Pettigrew, 2018).

Lack of self-control is the final innocence perspective in Figure 1.6. As argued by Gottfredson and Hirschi (1990), human behavior finds innocence in the self-centered quest for satisfaction and avoidance of suffering. Self-control is the blockade that stands between the individual and criminal activity. Lack of self-control is lack of such a blockade, making the short-term pleasure seeking dominate the mind. Lack of self-control implies that the offender lacks the ability and tendency to consider potential implications of a deviant action (Kroneberg and Schulz, 2018), as they are impulsive and unstable (Craig and Piquero, 2016; Jones et al., 2015). Those lacking self-control will typically have a short-term focus and be adventuresome, risk-willing and indifferent.

Integrated deductive theory of convenience

The theory of convenience is an integrated deductive theory explaining white-collar crime offenders. It is a combination of many preexisting perspectives, which are relevant for selection based on their perceived commonalities. To integrate is to form, coordinate, or blend into a functioning or unified whole. Integration is to add perspectives and propositions that improve the validity, generalizability, and utility of a theory to explain a phenomenon and to predict potential outcomes (Fried and Slowik, 2004; Hambrick and Lovelace, 2018).

The theory of convenience integrates various perspectives on convenience into a single theory with greater comprehensiveness and explanatory value than any one of its component perspectives. As such, convenience theory attempts to explain white-collar crime by bringing together several different theories and invoking multiple levels of analysis at the individual, organizational, as well as societal levels as suggested by Friedrichs (2010: 479):

> The number of different theories or levels, and the formality, with which the relationship between the theories or variables on different levels of analysis is posited, varies.

Deductive reasoning is the process of reasoning from one or more statements (premises) to reach a logically certain conclusion. A conclusion results reductively by applying general rules, which hold over the entirety of a closed domain of discourse. Pratt et al. (2019) argue that most management scholars employ deductive and quantitative methods in positivistic testing of hypotheses.

Krohn and Eassey (2014) argue that up-and-down integration – also referred to as deductive integration – might be considered the classic form of theoretical integration (Liska et al., 1989: 5):

> Up-and-down integration refers to identifying a level of abstraction or generality that encompasses much of the conceptualization of the constituent theories.

There are two types of up-and-down integration. In one type, integrated propositions in an up-and-down manner use the premise of one theory to derive the propositions of constituent theories. In particular, if theory A contains a more abstract or more general proposition from which theory B can be specified, then it is possible to integrate B with theory A, resulting in a single theory. Alternatively, if both theories A and B are able to be elaborated using assumptions more general than either theory individually, then it could be possible to synthesize the theories together in order to create a new theory C, which contains parts of both constituent theories. The former approach often involves theoretical reduction, while the latter involves theoretical synthesis.

The theory of convenience is a result of deductive integration by theoretical synthesis where a large number of theoretical perspectives blend into a unified whole to explain the main dimensions of motive, opportunity, and willingness. Some scholars argue that deductive integration is the only true type of theoretical integration. It is also the most difficult to do (Krohn and Eassey, 2014).

The theory of convenience also applies another kind of up-and-down integration by including different units of analysis. Some perspectives are at the individual level of the offender (e.g., personal neutralization and personal strain). Some perspectives are at the group level of the organization (e.g., lack of guardianship and institutional deterioration), while some perspectives are at the level of society (e.g., criminogenic market structures and resource scarcity).

The integrated deductive theory of convenience results from a synthesis of perspectives in three dimensions:

- *Convenience in motive.* It is convenient to use illegitimate financial gain to explore possibilities and avoid threats. Climb the hierarchy of needs for status and success (Maslow, 1943), realize the American dream of prosperity (Schoepfer and Piquero, 2006), satisfy the need for acclaim as a narcissist (Chatterjee and Pollock, 2017), and restore the perception of equity and equality (Leigh et al., 2010) are some of the perspectives integrated in the motive dimension of convenience theory. In addition, goal setting is a common practice in the field of organizational behavior, where high performance goals tend to encourage unethical behavior (Welsh et al., 2019). The extra profit from financial crime enables the offender to handle desired possibilities and potential threats. It is mainly the convenience of extra profit, rather than the convenience of illegal profit, that is important in the motive dimension of convenience theory. However, under certain circumstances, there might be some extra benefits from illegal extra profit rather than extra profit in general, since illegal funds avoid the attention of external and internal control mechanisms, including compliance functions (Kawasaki, 2020). Illegitimate financial gain can thus find its ways into exploring possibilities and avoiding threats that recorded funds cannot.
- *Convenience in opportunity.* There is convenient access to resources to commit and conceal financial crime. Legitimate access to premises and systems (Benson and Simpson, 2018), specialized access in routine activity (Cohen and Felson, 1979), blame game by misleading attribution to others (Eberly et al., 2011), and institutional deterioration (Rodriguez et al., 2005) are some of the perspectives integrated in the opportunity dimension of convenience theory. A typical white-collar offender does not go into hiding as

many street criminals do. Rather, the offender conceals financial crime among legal transactions to make illegal transactions seem legitimate, or the offender conceals financial crime by removing certain activities from the books. A typical white-collar offender who has convenient legitimate access to commit crime might spend most of the energy on concealing crime in the professional context.

- *Convenience in behavior.* Offenders can conveniently justify crime and neutralize guilt feelings. By neutralizing guilt feelings, offenders do not feel accountable, ashamed or responsible (Chen and Moosmayer, 2020). Application of neutralization techniques (Sykes and Matza, 1957), sliding on the slippery slope (Welsh et al., 2014), lack of self-control (Gottfredson and Hirschi, 1990), narcissistic identification with the organization (Galvin et al., 2015), learning from others by differential association (Sutherland, 1983), and professional deviant identity (Obodaru, 2017) are some of the perspectives integrated in the willingness dimension of convenience theory. When a white-collar offender justifies crime, then it is obvious to him and her that wrongdoing occurred. However, the offender can claim that the act of wrongdoing is morally justifiable (Schnatterly et al., 2018), and that a negative life event has occurred (Engdahl, 2015). When a white-collar offender denies a guilty mind, then the offender applies neutralization techniques. When a white-collar offender makes crime as a choice, it is convenient based on identity (Galvin et al., 2015), rationality (Pratt and Cullen, 2005), and learning from others (Sutherland, 1983).

The integrated deductive theory of convenience results from synthesis within each of these three dimensions as well as among these three dimensions. According to Liska et al. (1989), theoretical synthesis requires that the postulation of abstract or general principles that will allow at least fractions of merging theories to be subsumed and interrelated. Effective synthesis can generate additional predictive power not made by the merging theories individually.

Themes identified in convenience theory derive from discourse analysis of the research literature (Chan and Gibbs, 2020; Garcia-Rosell, 2019). Chan and Gibbs (2020) argue that criminological theorizing is typically discursive in nature. Discourse can describe a group of statements that provides a language for talking and producing a particular type of knowledge about a topic (Garcia-Rosell, 2019: 1019):

> Thus, discourses provide the frames for forming and articulating ideas concerning our relationships to nature and other members of society in a particular space at a particular time.

While the theory of convenience is an integrated deductive theory, there are other kinds of integrated theories such as cross-level sequential theory and cross-level parallel theory of white-collar crime. Cross-level sequential theory is sequential end-to-end integration that specifies the propositions of one theory as sequentially following the propositions of another. As such, end-to-end integration implies a temporal ordering among the causal variables in which the first set of variables influences the next set (Krohn and Eassey, 2014), the next set influences the following set, and so on, and in turn leading to the predicted outcome (Liska et al., 1989: 5):

> End-to-end (sequential) integration refers to specifying the temporal order between causal variables, so that the dependent variables of some theories constitute the independent variables of others.

Cross-level integration is combination of micro and macro perspectives. For example, convenience theory has micro elements such as neutralization techniques applied by individuals and macro elements such as criminal market structures in society. Cross-level integration is perhaps the most difficult type of integration and perhaps the most necessary type.

An example of cross-level theory of white-collar crime is Rorie's (2015) integrated theory of corporate environmental compliance and overcompliance. She integrates the license framework's emphasis on corporate-level factors with a rational choice framework that models how individual perceptions and attitudes mediate or moderate corporate-level concerns.

Cross-level parallel theory is parallel side-by-side integration by partitioning the subject matter of interest into distinct categories and using different theories to explain each (Liska et al., 1989: 5):

> Side-by-side (horizontal) integration refers to the partitioning of the subject matter of crime and deviance into cases that are explained by different theories.

As a result, much attention in side-by-side integration focuses on the criteria used to partition the subject matter, and only then focuses on the theories, which can best explain each category (Krohn and Eassey, 2014). The theory of convenience does partition the subject matter of interest into distinct categories of motive, opportunity, and willingness. However, the main form of integration in convenience theory is up-and-down, rather than side-by-side or end-to-end.

One way of partitioning the subject matter is into occupational and corporate crime (Kennedy, 2020). Self-interested individuals commit occupational crime in their profession against their employers (e.g., embezzlement or receipt of bribes) and other victims (Baird and Zelin, 2009; Benson and Chio, 2020; Shepherd and Button, 2019). Occupational crime is an offense committed by an individual using the skills, knowledge and access granted to him or her by the legitimate occupation, to obtain some financial gain (Kennedy, 2020). Organizational officials commit corporate crime in the larger interest of an organization, such as bribing potential customers, avoiding taxes by evasion, and misrepresenting accounting to get unjustified government subsidies (Craig and Piquero, 2016, 2017; Dodge, 2020a). Corporate crime may ultimately provide an individual with some tangible benefit, such as a promotion, bonus pay, or gifts for exceptional performance (Kennedy, 2020: 178):

> Yet, the primary purpose of committing a corporate crime is to provide a benefit to the corporation. Accordingly, corporate crimes have a distinctly organizational focus irrespective of whether they are committed by one person or 100 persons.

Another way of partitioning the subject matter is into different genders. Steffensmeier et al. (2013) studied how gendered focal concerns can inhibit criminal behaviors in females in the corporate context. Generally, the fraction of females who might exploit opportunity structures for white-collar crime is increasing, and it is thus an interesting kind of partitioning to study whether female offending is changing in response to changes in opportunities.

The integrated deductive theory of convenience is parsimonious, where the principle of parsimony dictates that a theory should provide the simplest possible (viable) explanation for a phenomenon. Parsimonious means the simplest theory with the least assumptions and variables but with greatest explanatory power. The parsimony principle is basic to all science and tells us to choose the simplest scientific explanation that fits the evidence. The opposite would be that the more assumptions you have to make, the more unlikely an explanation for the phenomenon being studied.

Chan and Gibbs (2020) suggest that convenience theory unifies concepts from macro-economic, meso-organizational, and micro-behavioral theories under the construct of convenience. Meso-level analysis means detailed examination of a specific group, a community, an organization, or parts of society, where outcomes may focus on phenomena between levels of individual, organization, and society. While both the motive dimension and the willingness dimension are mainly at the individual level of an offender or at the group level of offenders, the opportunity dimension is mainly at the organizational and society level. The opportunity can derive from lack of controls and guardianship in the organization; and it can derive from criminal market structures in society as well. Meso-level analysis is sometimes labeled network analysis, where the researcher examines the patterns of social ties among people in a group and how those patterns affect the overall group. While not obvious and visible in convenience theory, the opportunity structure can reflect a pattern of social ties among people in the organization.

Some perspectives in the theory of convenience are not necessarily compatible because of their diverging assumptions about human nature. For example, a reviewer of this manuscript has suggested that this book brings together multiple (and sometimes rival) theoretical traditions, including strain/anomie, differential association/learning, control/bonding/rational choice/techniques of rationalization, and even conflict. However, as long as the integration is mainly concerned with accumulation and synthesis of perspectives that influence the extent of convenience, then perspectives do not need to be compatible. If perspectives are competing, then theoretical synthesis is possible by changing the polarity of causality. For example, Hirschi (1989) argues that social control theory was developed in explicit opposition to strain theory. While social control can prevent crime, strain theory can cause crime. When integrating social control and strain into convenience, the polarity of social control is negative while the polarity of strain is positive: Less social control increases criminogenity, while more stress increases criminogenity.

While the theory of convenience is an integrated and at the same time general theory of white-collar crime occurrence, there might be cases of white-collar crime where the theory does not apply. State-corporate crime might be an example (Bernat and Whyte, 2020; Rothe, 2020; Rothe and Medley, 2020; Tombs and Whyte, 2020; Zysman-Quirós, 2020).

One-dimensional and multi-dimensional theories

Historically, most criminological theories have focused on relatively specific factors or processes that presumably explain either criminal behavior or the distribution of crime (Messner et al., 1989). Friedrichs (2010: 479) describe such theories as frequently one-dimensional:

> Most of the attempts to explain crime, including white-collar crime, are not integrated theories, and some of the most widely discussed criminological theories are best described as one-dimensional. Some such theories, as general theories, claim to explain both conventional forms of crime and white-collar crime. A one-dimensional general theory of crime, which can be empirically tested, has considerable appeal to many criminologists. It is compatible with the view that criminologists should function as social scientists, and should provide clear, useful answers to the enduring question of why crime occurs, and what can be done about it. But proponents of integrated theories of white-collar crime – especially in its corporate form – hold that such crime is complex, and that as theorists our principal objective should be to put forth theories that advance us toward a sophisticated understanding of such crime. Furthermore, one-dimensional general theories of crime, as applied to white-collar crime, promote limited and ineffective policy responses to such crime, as opposed to the multidimensional policies and practices that might have a real impact.

An example of a one-dimensional, yet widely discussed and applied theory of white-collar crime is differential association theory that focuses on the interaction of people with their primary groups to describe the process by which they learned perspectives favorable to the violation of the law, which in turn would lead to criminal behavior (Krohn and Eassey, 2014). Crime is a behavioral outcome of social interactions between a person and his or her environment. The theory of differential association suggested by Sutherland (1939, 1983) is thus an individual-level theory that the theory of convenience integrates in the willingness dimension. As an individual-level theory, differential association theory provides a psycho-sociological explanation for offending, whereby individuals learn criminal behavior from those who already practice it. Criminal behavior is absorbed in association with those who already practice it, and those individuals who learn distance themselves from other individuals who do not want to learn (Jordanoska and Schoultz, 2020: 7):

> The first method of socialization into white-collar crime is when more junior employees are ordered by their managers to do things, which they regard as unethical or illegal; the second method is when employees learn from peers how to get ahead in business. In this way, individuals learn both specific techniques of violations of the law and a particular type of criminal ideology.

In addition to differential association, Severson et al. (2020) discuss a number of other one-dimensional individual level theories such as rational choice theory including techniques of neutralization, strain theory, and subculture theory.

Sutherland's (1939, 1983) research on white-collar offenders focused on theorizing the role of the corporation (Jordanoska and Schoultz, 2020: 8):

> Corporations enable individuals to have legitimate and respectable careers (notably of corporate managers) in occupations that rely on trust. Sutherland considered that the violation of this occupational delegated or implied trust is the key trait of white-collar crime. Corporations also perpetuate violations of law by: enabling the socialization of employees into criminogenic business cultures, creating anonymity that impedes or clouds the location of responsibility, and increasing rationality in managers' behavior.

The next chapter introduces a dynamic perspective in convenience theory to understand cause-and-effect relationships in white-collar crime. This is in line with the cross-level sequential perspective mentioned previously. For example, Chan and Gibbs (2020) suggest that white-collar crime might occur from the confluence of motivation and opportunity. If this were the case, then willingness would follow because of motivation and opportunity. In an end-to-end integration, willingness would be the end, where it starts with motivation and opportunity.

The cross level-sequential perspective suggested by Krohn and Eassey (2014) could imply that perspectives might be temporarily ordered in a sequence. For example, in the status box in Figure 1.3, one might suggest that elite members are considered too big to fail and too powerful to jail (Pontell et al., 2014), and there is power inequality between the elite and others (Patel and Cooper, 2014). Therefore, subordinates accept executive language that they do not really understand (Ferraro et al., 2005), and they get distracted from observing deviant behavior by offender humor (Yam et al., 2018). A consequence of strange language and offender humor might be an acceptance of blame game by misleading attribution to others (Eberly et al., 2011).

Similarly, there might be a causal chain from A to E in the decay perspective of opportunity to conceal white-collar crime:

A. Institutional deterioration based on legitimacy (Rodriguez et al., 2005)
B. Interference and noise in crime signals (Karim and Siegel, 1998)

C. Inability to control because of social disorganization (Hoffmann, 2002)
D. Safe misrepresentation in accounting (Qiu and Slezak, 2019)
E. Auditors reporting and loyal to deviant management (Hurley et al., 2019)

Friedrichs (2010: 480) argues that all theories of crime must adopt some definition of crime:

> Many criminological theories explicitly or implicitly have adopted relatively narrow – often legalistic – definitions of crime. Since the legalistic definitions lend themselves most readily to measurement, they are especially attractive to those promoting some form of positivistic theory.

The theory of convenience is a positivist theory that researchers might empirically test by case studies, t-statistics and regression analysis. It applies implicitly the legal definition of crime being violations of the law. However, the theory expands easily to a wider set of crime, where crime is harmful acts that should be punished, independent of whether or not there is a legal statute. Crime is then wrongdoing that requires punishment, while law is statutory principles, which may or may not cover the specific wrongdoing. Friedrichs (2020: 19) mentions humanistic definition of crime:

> A humanistic definition of crime focuses on demonstrable harm, more often than not coming from powerful elements of society, rather than legal status as the basis for something being designated a crime.

In this book, however, crime is simply violation of the law, because we study offenders who have to go to jail or to prison. This legal definition of crime is problematic since it does not provide "a stable reference point for distinguishing criminal acts from noncriminal acts because laws change from one society to another and across time" (DiCristina, 2017: 298). For example, providing a bribe in a corrupt situation was in many jurisdictions considered an expense that was deductible from revenues in corporate accounting some decades ago. Criminal laws can vary to great degrees over time, and they can vary dramatically across societies. Generally, a crime is a harmful action to somebody that deserves punishment, but this research sticks to the definition of crime as breaches of rules of conduct stated in law (Wikstrom et al., 2018).

The legal definition of crime applied in this book is in line with Berghoff and Spiekermann (2018: 292):

> Crime is a category created by legislatures, and, with the increasing complexity of economic transactions, the number and the intricacies of laws and regulations swell. New offences are invented with high speed and in large numbers, and the rules of the game that determine the relative payoffs to different entrepreneurial activities do change dramatically from one time and place to another. The ever-growing jungle of accounting

and taxation rules, along with the proliferation and differentiation of health and safety laws are drastic examples. Indeed, according to the Economist, there were about 300 000 regulatory statutes carrying criminal penalties in the USA in the early 1990s, a number that can only have grown since then. For financial crime especially, there are now so many laws, and they are so complex that enforcing them is becoming discretionary. . . . As legal risks escalate the chances of becoming a white-collar criminal by accident or negligence have increased enormously. . . . At the same time, potential white-collar offenders may have entrepreneurial skills to discover loopholes in the law and grey areas of unclear legal status. . . . A growing army of business lawyers in large law firms help entrepreneurial executives and wealthy individuals to find ways of avoiding obvious law violations.

In a historical perspective, "most crimes were regarded as private matters, and it was therefore the responsibility of injured parties to prosecute" (Taylor, 2018: 347). Therefore, the legal definition of crime applied in this book influences the scope of our study in the sense that what made white-collar crime convenient in the past will differ from what makes white-collar crime convenient presently. For example, Berghoff and Spiekermann (2018: 298) state in this context of changing times for criminal justice and control mechanisms that "whether this has led to a marked reduction in economic crime is unknown but unlikely".

This book makes no distinction between words such illegal, illegitimate, and illicit. Illegal applies to what the current law has sanctioned. Illegitimate may apply to a legal right or status but also, in extended use, to abuse of someone else's rights. Illicit applies to a strict disconformity to the provisions of the law (Huisman, 2020). This book also stays away from the endless discussion of what white-collar crime is and is not (Galvin, 2019).

References

Adler, P.S. and Kwon, S.W. (2002). Social capital: Prospects for a new concept, *Academy of Management Review*, 27 (1), 17–40.

Agnew, R. (2005). *Pressured into Crime: An Overview of General Strain Theory*, Oxford, UK: Oxford University Press.

Agnew, R. (2012). Reflection on "A Revised Strain Theory of Delinquency", *Social Forces*, 91 (1), 33–38.

Agnew, R. (2014). Social concern and crime: Moving beyond the assumption of simple self-interest, *Criminology*, 52 (1), 1–32.

Aguilera, R.V. and Vadera, A.K. (2008). The dark side of authority: Antecedents, mechanisms, and outcomes of organizational corruption, *Journal of Business Ethics*, 77, 431–449.

Aguilera, R.V., Judge, W.Q. and Terjesen, S.A. (2018). Corporate governance deviance, *Academy of Management Review*, 43 (1), 87–109.

Akers, R.L. (1985). *Deviant Behavior: A Social Learning Approach*, 3rd edition, Belmont, CA: Wadsworth.

Arjoon, S. (2008). Slippery when wet: The real risk in business, *Journal of Markets & Morality*, Spring, 11 (1), 77–91.

Ashkanasy, N.M. (2016). Why we need theory in the organization sciences, *Journal of Organizational Behavior*, 37 (8), 1126–1131.

Baird, J.E. and Zelin, R.C. (2009). An examination of the impact of obedience pressure on perceptions of fraudulent acts and the likelihood of committing occupational fraud, *Journal of Forensic Studies in Accounting and Business*, 1 (1), 1–14.

Balakrishnan, K., Blouin, J.L. and Guay, W.R. (2019). Tax aggressiveness and corporate transparency, *The Accounting Review*, 94 (1), 45–69.

Bao, D., Kim, Y., Mian, G.M. and Su, L. (2019). Do managers disclose or withhold bad news? Evidence from short interest, *The Accounting Review*, 94 (3), 1–26.

Barney, J. (2018). Editor's comments: Positioning a theory paper for publication, *Academy of Management Review*, 43 (3), 345–348.

Barry, B. and Stephens, C.U. (1998). Objections to an objectivist approach to integrity, *Academy of Management Review*, 23 (1), 162–169.

Barton, H. (2004). Cultural reformation: A case for intervention within the police service, *International Journal of Human Resources Development and Management*, 4 (2), 191–199.

Becker, H.S. (1963). *Outsiders: Studies in the Sociology of Deviance*, New York, NY: The Free Press.

Bell, C.M. and Khoury, C. (2016). Organizational powerlessness, dehumanization, and gendered effects of procedural justice, *Journal of Managerial Psychology*, 31, 570–585.

Benartzi, S., Beshears, J., Milkman, K.L., Sunstein, C.R., Thaler, R.H., Shankar, M., Tucker-Ray, W., Congdon, W.J. and Galing, S. (2017). Should governments invest more in nudging? *Psychological Science*, 28 (8), 1041–1055.

Benson, M.L. (1985). Denying the guilty mind: Accounting for involvement in a white-collar crime, *Criminology*, 23 (4), 583–607.

Benson, M.L. and Chio, H.L. (2020). Who commits occupational crimes, in: Rorie, M. (editor), *The Handbook of White-Collar Crime*, Hoboken, NJ: John Wiley & Sons, chapter 7, pages 97–112.

Benson, M.L. and Simpson, S.S. (2018). *White-Collar Crime: An Opportunity Perspective*, 3rd edition, New York, NY: Routledge.

Berghoff, H. (2018). "Organised irresponsibility?" The Siemens corruption scandal of the 1990s and 2000s, *Business History*, 60 (3), 423–445.

Berghoff, H. and Spiekermann, U. (2018). Shady business: On the history of white-collar crime, *Business History*, 60 (3), 289–304.

Bernat, I. and Whyte, D. (2020). State-corporate crimes, in: Rorie, M.L. (editor), *The Handbook of White-Collar Crime*, Hoboken, NJ: Wiley & Sons, chapter 9, pages 191–208.

Bernburg, J.G., Krohn, M.D. and Rivera, C.J. (2006). Official labeling, criminal embeddedness, and subsequent delinquency, *Journal of Research in Crime and Delinquency*, 43 (1), 67–88.

Berry, L.L., Seiders, K. and Grewal, D. (2002). Understanding service convenience, *Journal of Marketing*, 66, 1–17.

Bjørkelo, B., Einarsen, S., Nielsen, M.B. and Matthiesen, S.B. (2011). Silence is golden? Characteristics and experiences of self-reported whistleblowers, *European Journal of Work and Organizational Psychology*, 20 (2), 206–238.

Blickle, G., Kückelhaus, B.P., Kranefeld, I., Schütte, N., Genau, H.A., Gansen-Ammann, D.N. and Wihler, A. (2020). Political skill comouflages Machiavellianism: Career role performance and organizational misbehavior at short and long tenure, *Journal of Vocational Behavior*, 118, https://doi.org/10.1016/j.jvb.2020.103401.

Blickle, G., Schlegel, A., Fassbender, P. and Klein, U. (2006). Some personality correlates of business white-collar crime, *Applied Psychology: An International Review*, 55 (2), 220–233.

Bosse, D.A. and Phillips, R.A. (2016). Agency theory and bounded self-interest, *Academy of Management Review*, 41 (2), 276–297.

Braaten, C.N. and Vaughn, M.S. (2019). Convenience theory of cryptocurrency crime: A content analysis of U.S. federal court decisions, *Deviant Behavior*, published online, https://doi.org/10.1080/01639625.2019.1706706.

Bradshaw, E.A. (2015). "Obviously, we're all oil industry": The criminogenic structure of the offshore oil industry, *Theoretical Criminology*, 19 (3), 376–395.

Braithwaite, J. (1989). *Crime, Shame and Reintegration*, Cambridge, UK: Cambridge University Press.

Braithwaite, J. (2020). Regulatory mix, collective efficacy, and crimes of the powerful, *Journal of White Collar and Corporate Crime*, 1 (1), 62–71.

Brightman, H.J. (2009). *Today's White-Collar Crime: Legal, Investigative, and Theoretical Perspectives*, New York, NY: Routledge, Taylor & Francis Group.

Brown, J.O., Hays, J. and Stuebs, M.T. (2016). Modeling accountant whistleblowing intentions: Applying the theory of planned behavior and the fraud triangle, *Accounting and the Public Interest*, 16 (1), 28–56.

Bucy, P.H., Formby, E.P., Raspanti, M.S. and Rooney, K.E. (2008). Why do they do it? The motives, mores, and character of white collar criminals, *St. John's Law Review*, 82, 401–571.

Bussmann, K.D., Niemeczek, A. and Vockrodt, M. (2018). Company culture and prevention of corruption in Germany, China and Russia, *European Journal of Criminology*, 15 (3), 255–277.

Caesens, G., Nguyen, N. and Stinglhamber, F. (2019). Abusive supervision and organizational dehumanization, *Journal of Business and Psychology*, 34, 709–728.

Campbell, J.L. and Göritz, A.S. (2014). Culture corrupts! A qualitative study of organizational culture in corrupt organizations, *Journal of Business Ethics*, 120 (3), 291–311.

Carrington, T. and Catasus, B. (2007). Auditing stories about discomfort: Becoming comfortable with comfort theory, *European Accounting Review*, 16 (1), 35–58.

Chan, F. and Gibbs, C. (2020). Integrated theories of white-collar and corporate crime, in: Rorie, M.L. (editor), *The Handbook of White-Collar Crime*, Hoboken, NJ: Wiley & Sons, chapter 13, pages 191–208.

Chang, J.J., Lu, H.C. and Chen, M. (2005). Organized crime or individual crime? Endogeneous size of a criminal organization and the optimal law enforcement, *Economic Inquiry*, 43 (3), 661–675.

Chatterjee, A. and Pollock, T.G. (2017). Master of puppets: How narcissistic CEOs construct their professional worlds, *Academy of Management Review*, 42 (4), 703–725.

Chattopadhyay, P., Glick, W.H. and Huber, G.P. (2001). Organizational actions in response to threats and opportunities, *Academy of Management Journal*, 44 (5), 937–955.

Chen, Y. and Moosmayer, D.C. (2020). When guilt is not enough: Interdependent self-construal as moderator of the relationship between guilt and ethical consumption in a Confucian context, *Journal of Business Ethics*, 161, 551–572.

Chrisman, J.J., Chua, J.H., Kellermanns, F.W. and Chang, E.P.C. (2007). Are family managers agents or stewards? An exploratory study in privately held family firms, *Journal of Business Research*, 60 (10), 1030–1038.

Cleff, T., Naderer, G. and Volkert, J. (2013). Motives behind white-collar crime: Results of a quantitative study in Germany, *Society and Business Review*, 8 (2), 145–159.

Cohen, L.E. and Felson, M. (1979). Social change and crime rate trends: A routine activity approach, *American Sociological Review*, 44, 588–608.

Cohen, S. (2001). *States of Denial: Knowing about Atrocities and Suffering*, Cambridge, UK: Polity Press.

Coleman, J. (1987). Toward an integrated theory of white-collar crime, *American Journal of Sociology*, 93 (2), 406–439.

Collier, J.E. and Kimes, S.E. (2012). Only if it is convenient: Understanding how convenience influences self-service technology evaluation, *Journal of Service Research*, 16 (1), 39–51.

Colquitt, J.A. and Zapata-Phelan, C.P. (2007). Trends in theory building and theory testing: A five-decade study of the Academy of Management Journal, *Academy of Management Journal*, 50 (6), 1281–1303.

Comey, J.B. (2009). Go directly to prison: White collar sentencing after the Sarbanes-Oxley act, *Harvard Law Review*, 122, 1728–1749.

Corley, K.G. and Gioia, D.A. (2011). Building theory about theory building: What constitutes a theoretical contribution? *Academy of Management Review*, 36 (1), 12–32.

Craig, J.M. and Piquero, N.L. (2016). The effects of low self-control and desire-for-control on white-collar offending: A replication, *Deviant Behavior*, 37 (11), 1308–1324.

Craig, J.M. and Piquero, N.L. (2017). Sensational offending: An application of sensation seeking to white-collar and conventional crimes, *Crime & Delinquency*, 63 (11), 1363–1382.

Crank, B.R. (2018). Accepting deviant identities: The impact of self-labeling on intentions to desist from crime, *Journal of Crime and Justice*, 41 (2), 155–172.

Cressey, D. (1972). *Criminal Organization: Its Elementary Forms*, New York, NY: Harper and Row.

Cropanzano, R. and Mitchell, M.S. (2005). Social exchange theory: An interdisciplinary review, *Journal of Management*, 31 (6), 874–900.

Crosina, E. and Pratt, M.G. (2019). Toward a model of organizational mourning: The case of former Lehman Brothers bankers, *Academy of Management Journal*, 62 (1), 66–98.

Cullen, F.T. (2010). Cloward, Richard A., and Lloyd E. Ohlin: Delinquency and opportunity, in: Cullen, F.T. and Wilcox, P. (editors), *Encyclopedia of Criminological Theory*, Volume 1, Los Angeles, CA: Sage Publications, pages 170–174.

Cullen, F.T., Chouhy, C. and Jonson, C.L. (2020). Public opinion about white-collar crime, in: Rorie, M.L. (editor), *The Handbook of White-Collar Crime*, Hoboken, NJ: Wiley & Sons, chapter 14, pages 211–228.

Davidson, R.H., Dey, A. and Smith, A.J. (2019). CEO materialism and corporate social responsibility, *The Accounting Review*, 94 (1), 101–126.

DiCristina, B. (2017). Criminology and the "essence" of crime: The views of Garofalo, Durkheim, and Bonger, *International Criminal Justice Review*, 26 (4), 297–315.

Dilchert, S., Ones, D.S., Davis, R.D. and Rostow, C.D. (2007). Cognitive ability predicts objectively measured counterproductive work behaviors, *Journal of Applied Psychology*, 92, 616–627.

DiMaggio, P.J. (1995). Comments on 'what theory is not', *Administrative Science Quarterly*, 40, 391–397.

Dion, M. (2008). Ethical leadership and crime prevention in the organizational setting, *Journal of Financial Crime*, 15 (3), 308–319.

Dodge, M. (2009). *Women and white-collar crime*, Saddle River, NJ: Prentice Hall.

Dodge, M. (2020a). Who commits corporate crime? in: Rorie, M. (editor), *The Handbook of White-Collar Crime*, Hoboken, NJ: John Wiley & Sons, chapter 8, pages 113–126.

Dodge, M. (2020b). A black box warning: The marginalization of white-collar crime victimization, *Journal of White Collar and Corporate Crime*, 1 (1), 24–33.

Donk, D.P. van and Molloy, E. (2008). From organizing as projects, to projects as organizations, *International Journal of Project Management*, 26, 129–137.

Eberly, M.B., Holley, E.C., Johnson, M.D. and Mitchell, T.R. (2011). Beyond internal and external: A dyadic theory of relational attributions, *Academy of Management Review*, 36 (4), 731–753.

Engdahl, O. (2015). White-collar crime and first-time adult-onset offending: Explorations in the concept of negative life events as turning points, *International Journal of Law, Crime and Justice*, 43 (1), 1–16.

Farquhar, J.D. and Rowley, J. (2009). Convenience: A services perspective, *Marketing Theory*, 9 (4), 425–438.

Fehr, R., Yam, K.C. and Dang, C. (2015). Moralized leadership: The construction and consequences of ethical leader perceptions, *Academy of Management Review*, 40 (2), 182–209.

Felson, M. and Boba, R.L. (2017). Chapter 12: White-collar crime, in: *Crime and Everyday Life*, Thousand Oaks, CA: Sage Publications.

Ferraro, F., Pfeffer, J. and Sutton, R.I. (2005). Economics language and assumptions: How theories can become self-fulfilling, *Academy of Management Review*, 30 (1), 8–24.

Forti, G. and Visconti, A. (2020). From economic crime to corporate violence: The multifaceted harms of corporate crime, in: Rorie, M.L. (editor), *The Handbook of White-Collar Crime*, Hoboken, NJ: John Wiley & Sons, chapter 5, pages 64–80.

Freiberg, A. (2020). Researching white-collar crime: An Australian perspective, in: Rorie, M.L. (editor), *The Handbook of White-Collar Crime*, Hoboken, NJ: Wiley & Sons, chapter 26, pages 418–436.

Fried, Y. and Slowik, L.H. (2004). Enriching goal-setting theory with time: An integrated approach, *Academy of Management Review*, 29 (3), 404–422.

Friedrichs, D.O. (2010). Integrated theories of white-collar crime, in: Cullen, F.T. and Wilcox, P. (editors), *Encyclopedia of Criminological Theory*, Volume 1, Los Angeles, CA: Sage Publications, pages 479–486.

Froggio, G. and Agnew, R. (2007). The relationship between crime and "objective" versus "subjective" strains, *Journal of Criminal Justice*, 35, 81–87.

Füss, R. and Hecker, A. (2008). Profiling white-collar crime. Evidence from German-speaking countries, *Corporate Ownership & Control*, 5 (4), 149–161.

Galvin, B.M., Lange, D. and Ashforth, B.E. (2015). Narcissistic organizational identification: Seeing oneself as central to the organization's identity, *Academy of Management Review*, 40 (2), 163–181.

Galvin, M.A. (2019). Substance or semantics? The consequences of definitional ambiguity for white-collar research, *Journal of Research in Crime and Delinquency*, published online, pages 1–31, https://doi.org/10.1177/0022427819888012.

Gamache, D.L. and McNamara, G. (2019). Responding to bad press: How CEO temporal focus influences the sensitivity to negative media coverage of acquisitions, *Academy of Management Journal*, 62 (3), 918–943.

Gao, P. and Zhang, G. (2019). Accounting manipulation, peer pressure, and internal control, *The Accounting Review*, 94 (1), 127–151.

Garcia-Rosell, J.C. (2019). A discursive perspective on corporate social responsibility education: A story co-creation exercise, *Journal of Business Ethics*, 154, 1019–1032.

Geest, V.R., Weisburd, D. and Blokland, A.A.J. (2017). Developmental trajectories of offenders convicted of fraud: A follow-up to age 50 in a Dutch conviction cohort, *European Journal of Criminology*, 14 (5), 543–565.

Gibney, R., Zagenczyk, T.J. and Masters, M.F. (2009). The negative aspects of social exchange: An introduction to perceived organizational obstruction, *Group and Organization Management*, 34, 665–697.

Glasø, L. and Einarsen, S. (2008). Emotion regulation in leader-follower relationships, *European Journal of Work and Organizational Psychology*, 17 (4), 482–500.

Goldstraw-White, J. (2012). *White-Collar Crime: Accounts of Offending Behavior*, London, UK: Palgrave Macmillan.

Goncharov, I. and Peter, C.D. (2019). Does reporting transparency affect industry coordination? Evidence from the duration of international cartels, *The Accounting Review*, 94 (3), 149–175.

Gottfredson, M.R. and Hirschi, T. (1990). *A General Theory of Crime*, Stanford, CA: Stanford University Press.

Gottfredson, R.K., Wright, S.L. and Heaphy, E.D. (2020). A critique of the leader-member exchange construct: Back to square one, *The Leadership Quarterly*, https://doi.org/10.1016/j.leaqua.2020.101385.

Hambrick, D.C. and Lovelace, J.B. (2018). The role of executive symbolism in advancing new strategic themes in organization: A social influence perspective, *Academy of Management Review*, 43 (1), 110–131.

Hamilton, S. and Micklethwait, A. (2006). *Greed and Corporate Failure: The Lessons from Recent Disasters*, Basingstoke, UK: Palgrave Macmillan.

Hansen, L.L. (2020). Review of the book "Convenience Triangle in White-Collar Crime: Case Studies of Fraud Examinations", *ChoiceConnect*, vol. 57, no. 5, Middletown, CT: Association of College and Research Libraries.

Hatch, M.J. (1997). *Organizational Theory: Modern, Symbolic, and Postmodern Perspectives*, Oxford, UK: Oxford University Press.

Hausman, W.J. (2018). Howard Hopson's billion dollar fraud: The rise and fall of associated gas & electric company, *Business History*, 60 (3), 381–398.

Haveman, H.A., Mahoney, J.T. and Mannix, E. (2019). Editors' comments: The role of theory in management research, *Academy of Management Review*, 44 (2), 241–243.

Hefendehl, R. (2010). Addressing white collar crime on a domestic level, *Journal of International Criminal Justice*, 8, 769–782.

Higgins, E.T. (1997). Beyond pleasure and pain, *American Psychologist*, 52, 1280–1300.

Hirschi, T. (1989). Exploring alternatives to integrated theory, in: Messner, S.F., Krohn, M.D. and Liska, A.E. (editors), *Theoretical Integration in the Study of Deviance and Crime*, Albany, NY: State University of New York Press, chapter 2, pages 37–50.

Hirschi, T. and Gottfredson, M. (1987). Causes of white-collar crime, *Criminology*, 25 (4), 949–974.

Hoffmann, J.P. (2002). A contextual analysis of differential association, social control, and strain theories of delinquency, *Social Forces*, 81 (3), 753–785.

Hollow, M. (2014). Money, morals and motives, *Journal of Financial Crime*, 21 (2), 174–190.

Holt, R. and Cornelissen, J. (2014). Sensemaking revisited, *Management Learning*, 45 (5), 525–539.

Huang, L. and Knight, A.P. (2017). Resources and relationships in entrepreneurship: An exchange theory of the development and effects of the entrepreneur-investor relationship, *Academy of Management Review*, 42 (1), 80–102.

Huisman, W. (2020). Blurred lines: Collusions between legitimate and illegitimate organizations, in: Rorie, M.L. (editor), *The Handbook of White-Collar Crime*, Hoboken, NJ: Wiley & Sons, chapter 10, pages 139–158.

Huisman, W. and Erp, J. (2013). Opportunities for environmental crime, *British Journal of Criminology*, 53, 1178–1200.

Hurley, P.J., Mayhew, B.W. and Obermire, K.M. (2019). Realigning auditors' accountability: Experimental evidence, *The Accounting Review*, 94 (3), 233–250.

Huseman, R.C., Hatfield, J.D. and Miles, E.W. (1987). A new perspective on equity theory: The equity sensitivity construct, *Academy of Management Review*, 12 (2), 222–234.

Jones, S., Lyman, D.R. and Piquero, A.R. (2015). Substance use, personality, and inhibitors: Testing Hirschi's predictions about the reconceptualization of self-control, *Crime & Delinquency*, 61 (4), 538–558.

Jonnergård, K., Stafsudd, A. and Elg, U. (2010). Performance evaluations as gender barriers in professional organizations: A study of auditing firms, *Gender, Work and Organization*, 17 /6), 721–747.

Jordanoska, A. (2018). The social ecology of white-collar crime: Applying situational action theory to white-collar offending, *Deviant Behavior*, 39 (11), 1427–1449.

Jordanoska, A. and Schoultz, I. (2020). The "discovery of white-collar crime": The legacy of Edwin Sutherland, in: Rorie, M. (editor), *The Handbook of White-Collar Crime*, Hoboken, NJ: John Wiley & Sons, chapter 1, pages 3–15.

Kamerdze, S., Loughran, T., Paternoster, R. and Sohoni, T. (2014). The role of affect in intended rule breaking: Extending the rational choice perspective, *Journal of Research in Crime and Delinquency*, 51 (5), 620–654.

Kang, E. and Thosuwanchot, N. (2017). An application of Durkheim's four categories of suicide to organizational crimes, *Deviant Behavior*, 38 (5), 493–513.

Kaptein, M. and Helvoort, M. (2019). A model of neutralization techniques, *Deviant Behavior*, 40 (10), 1260–1285.

Karim, K.E. and Siegel, P.H. (1998). A signal detection theory approach to analyzing the efficiency and effectiveness of auditing to detect management fraud, *Managerial Auditing Journal*, 13 (6), 367–375.

Katz, J. (1979). Concerted ignorance: The social construction of cover-up, *Urban Life*, 8 (3), 295–316.

Kawasaki, T. (2020). Review of comparative studies on white-collar and corporate crime, in: Rorie, M.L. (editor), *The Handbook of White-Collar Crime*, Hoboken, NJ: Wiley & Sons, chapter 27, pages 437–447.

Keaveney, S.M. (2008). The blame game: An attribution theory approach to marketer-engineer conflict in high-technology companies, *Industrial Marketing Management*, 37, 653–663.

Keil, M., Tiwana, A., Sainsbury, R. and Sneha, S. (2010). Toward a theory of whistle-blowing intentions: A benefit-cost differential perspective, *Decision Sciences*, 41 (4), 787–812.

Kempa, M. (2010). Combating white-collar crime in Canada: Serving victim needs and market integrity, *Journal of Financial Crime*, 17 (2), 251–264.

Kennedy, J.P. (2020). Organizational and macro-level corporate crime theories, in: Rorie, M.L. (editor), *The Handbook of White-Collar Crime*, Hoboken, NJ: Wiley & Sons, chapter 12, pages 175–190.

Ketokivi, M., Mantere, S. and Cornelissen, J. (2017). Reasoning by analogy and the progress of theory, *Academy of Management Review*, 42 (4), 637–658.

Kholin, M., Kückelhaus, B. and Blickle, G. (2020). Why dark personalities can get ahead: Extending the toxic career model, *Personality and Individual Differences*, 156, https://doi.org/10.1016/j.paid2019.109792.

König, A., Graf-Vlachy, L., Bundy, J. and Little, L.M. (2020). A blessing and a curse: How CEOs' trait empathy affects their management of organizational crises, *Academy of Management Review*, 45 (1), 130–153.

Kostova, T., Roth, K. and Dacin, M.T. (2008). Institutional theory in the study of multinational corporations: A critique and new directions, *Academy of Management Review*, 33 (4), 994–1006.

Kouchaki, M. and Desai, S.D. (2015). Anxious, threatened, and also unethical: How anxiety makes individuals feel threatened and commit unethical acts, *Journal of Applied Psychology*, 100 (2), 360–375.

Krogh, G., Rossi-Lamastra, C. and Haefliger, S. (2012). Phenomenon-based research in management and organization science: When is it rigorous and does it matter? *Long Range Planning*, 45, 277–298.

Krohn, M.D. and Eassey, J.M. (2014). Integrated theories of crime, in: Miller, J.M. (editor), *The Encyclopedia of Theoretical Criminology*, Chichester, UK: John Wiley & Sons, pages 458–463.

Kroneberg, C. and Schulz, S. (2018). Revisiting the role of self-control in situational action theory, *European Journal of Criminology*, 15 (1), 56–76.

Lange, D. (2008). A multidimensional conceptualization of organizational corruption control, *Academy of Management Journal*, 33 (3), 710–729.

Langton, L. and Piquero, N.L. (2007). Can general strain theory explain white-collar crime? A preliminary investigation of the relationship between strain and select white-collar offenses, *Journal of Criminal Justice*, 35 (1), 1–15.

Leap, T.L. (2007). *Dishonest dollars: The dynamics of white-collar crime*, Ithaca, NY: Cornell University Press.

Lee, F. and Robinson, R.J. (2000). An attributional analysis of social accounts: Implications of playing the blame game, *Journal of Applied Social Psychology*, 30 (9), 1853–1879.

Lehman, D.W., Cooil, B. and Ramanujam, R. (2019). The effects of rule complexity on organizational noncompliance and remediation: Evidence from restaurant health inspections, *Journal of Management*, published online, pages 1–33, https://doi.org/10.1177/0149206319842262.

Leigh, A.C., Foote, D.A., Clark, W.R. and Lewis, J.L. (2010). Equity sensitivity: A triadic measure and outcome/input perspectives, *Journal of Managerial Issues*, 22 (3), 286–305.

Leonard, W.N. and Weber, M.G. (1970). Automakers and dealers: A study of criminogenic market forces, *Law & Society Review*, 4 (3), 407–424.

Liska, A.E., Krohn, M.D. and Messner, S.F. (1989). Strategies and requisites for theoretical integration in the study of crime and deviance, in: Messner, S.F., Krohn, M.D. and Liska, A.E. (editors), *Theoretical Integration in the Study of Deviance and Crime*, Albany, NY: State University of New York Press, pages 1–20.

Listwan, S.J., Piquero, N.L. and Voorhis, P.V. (2010). Recidivism among a white-collar sample: Does personality matter? *Australian and New Zealand Journal of Criminology*, 43 (1), 156–174.

Løkke, A.K. and Sørensen, P.D. (2014). Theory testing using case studies, *The Electronic Journal of Business Research Methods*, 12 (1), 66–74, www.ejbrm.com.

Lopez-Rodriguez, S. (2009). Environmental engagement, organizational capability and firm performance, *Corporate Governance*, 9 (4), 400–408.

Lyman, M.D. and Potter, G.W. (2007). *Organized Crime*, 4th edition, Upper Saddle River, NJ: Pearson Prentice Hall.

Mai, H.T.X. and Olsen, S.O. (2016). Consumer participation in self-production: The role of control mechanisms, convenience orientation, and moral obligation, *Journal of Marketing Theory and Practice*, 24 (2), 209–223.

Martin, J. and Peterson, M.M. (1987). Two-tier wage structures: Implications for equity theory, *Academy of Management Journal*, 30 (2), 297–315.

Martinsen, Ø.L., Furnham, A. and Hærem, T. (2016). An integrated perspective on insight, *Journal of Experimental Psychology*, 145 (10), 1319–1332.

Maslow, A.H. (1943). A theory of human motivation, *Psychological Review*, 50 (4), 370–396.

Mawritz, M.B., Greenbaum, R.L., Butts, M.M. and Graham, K.A. (2017). I just can't control myself: A self-regulation perspective on the abuse of deviant employees, *Academy of Management Journal*, 60 (4), 1482–1503.

McElwee, G. and Smith, R. (2015). Towards a nuanced typology of illegal entrepreneurship: A theoretical and conceptual overview, in: McElwee, G. and Smith, R. (editors), *Exploring Criminal and Illegal Enterprise: New Perspectives on Research, Policy & Practice: Contemporary Issues in Entrepreneurship Research*, Volume 5, Bingley, UK: Emerald.

Mears, D.P. and Cochran, J.C. (2018). Progressively tougher sanctioning and recidivism: Assessing the effects of different types of sanctions, *Journal of Research in Crime and Delinquency*, 55 (2), 194–241.

Menon, S. and Siew, T.G. (2012). Key challenges in tackling economic and cyber-crimes – Creating a multilateral platform for international co-operation, *Journal of Money Laundering Control*, 15 (3), 243–256.

Mesmer-Magnus, J.R. and Viswesvaran, C. (2005). Whistleblowing in an organization: An examination of correlates of whistleblowing intentions, actions, and retaliation, *Journal of Business Ethics*, 62 (3), 266–297.

Messner, S.F., Krohn, M.D. and Liska, A.E. (1989). *Theoretical Integration and the Study of Deviance and Crime: Problems and Prospects*, Albany, NY: State University of New York Press.

Michalak, R. and Ashkanasy, N.M. (2013). Emotions and deviances, in: Elias, S.M. (editor), *Deviant and Criminal Behavior in the Workplace*, New York, NY: NYU Press.

Michel, C. (2016). Violent street crime versus harmful white-collar crime: A comparison of perceived seriousness and punitiveness, *Critical Criminology*, 24, 127–143.

Mingus, W. and Burchfield, K.B. (2012). From prison to integration: Applying modified labeling theory to sex offenders, *Criminal Justice Studies*, 25 (1), 97–109.

Mohliver, A. (2019). How misconduct spreads: Auditors' role in the diffusion of stock-option backdating, *Administrative Science Quarterly*, 64 (2), 310–336.

Mpho, B. (2017). Whistleblowing: What do contemporary ethical theories say? *Studies in Business and Economics*, 12 (1), 19–28.

Müller, S.M. (2018). Corporate behavior and ecological disaster: Dow Chemical and the Great Lakes mercury crisis, 1970–1972, *Business History*, 60 (3), 399–422.

Murphy, P.R. and Dacin, M.T. (2011). Psychological pathways to fraud: Understanding and preventing fraud in organizations, *Journal of Business Ethics*, 101, 601–618.

Murphy, P.R. and Free, C. (2015). Broadening the fraud triangle: Instrumental climate and fraud, *Behavioral Research in Accounting*, 28 (1), 41–56.

Naylor, R.T. (2003). Towards a general theory of profit-driven crimes, *British Journal of Criminology*, 43, 81–101.

Ngo, F.T. and Paternoster, R. (2016). Toward an understanding of the emotional and behavioral reactions to stalking: A partial test of general strain theory, *Crime & Delinquency*, 62 (6), 703–727.

Nichol, J.E. (2019). The effects of contract framing on misconduct and entitlement, *The Accounting Review*, 94 (3), 329–344.

Nielsen, R.P. (2003). Corruption networks and implications for ethical corruption reform, *Journal of Business Ethics*, 42 (2), 125–149.

Obodaru, O. (2017). Forgone, but not forgotten: Toward a theory of forgone professional identities, *Academy of Management Journal*, 60 (2), 523–553.

Olafsen, A.H. (2017). The implications of need-satisfying work climates on state mindfulness in a longitudinal analysis of work outcomes, *Motivation and Emotion*, 41 (1), 22–37.

Olafsen, A.H., Niemiec, C.P., Halvari, H., Deci, E.L. and Williams, G.C. (2017). On the dark side of work: A longitudinal analysis using self-determination theory, *European Journal of Work and Organizational Psychology*, 26 (2), 275–285.

Onna, J.H.R. and Denkers, A.J.M. (2019). Social bonds and white-collar crime: A two-study assessment of informal social controls in white-collar offenders, *Deviant Behavior*, 40 (10), 1206–1225.

Ouimet, G. (2010). Dynamics of narcissistic leadership in organizations, *Journal of Managerial Psychology*, 25 (7), 713–726.

Park, H., Bjørkelo, B. and Blenkinsopp, J. (2020). External whistleblowers' experiences of workplace bullying by superiors and colleagues, *Journal of Business Ethics*, 161, 591–601.

Patel, P.C. and Cooper, D. (2014). Structural power equality between family and nonfamily TMT members and the performance of family firms, *Academy of Management Journal*, 57 (6), 1624–1649.

Paternoster, R., Jaynes, C.M. and Wilson, T. (2018). Rational choice theory and interest in the "fortune of others", *Journal of Research in Crime and Delinquency*, 54 (6), 847–868.

Petrocelli, M., Piquero, A.R. and Smith, M.R. (2003). Conflict theory and racial profiling: An empirical analysis of police traffic stop data, *Journal of Criminal Justice*, 31 (1), 1–11.

Pettigrew, W.A. (2018). The changing place of fraud in seventeenth-century public debates about international trading corporations, *Business History*, 60 (3), 305–320.

Pillay, S. and Kluvers, R. (2014). An institutional theory perspective on corruption: The case of a developing democracy, *Financial Accountability & Management*, 30 (1), 95–119.

Pinto, J., Leana, C.R. and Pil, F.K. (2008). Corrupt organizations or organizations of corrupt individuals? Two types of organization-level corruption, *Academy of Management Review*, 33 (3), 685–709.

Piquero, N.L. (2012). The only thing we have to fear is fear itself: Investigating the relationship between fear of falling and white-collar crime, *Crime and Delinquency*, 58 (3), 362–379.

Piquero, N.L., Piquero, A.R., Narvey, C., Boutwell, B. and Farrington, D.P. (2019). Are there psychopaths in white-collar jobs? *Deviant Behavior*, published online https://doi.org/10.1080/01639625.2019.1708537.

Ployhart, R.E. and Bartunek, J.M. (2019). Editors' comments: There is nothing so theoretical as good practice – A call for phenomenal theory, *Academy of Management Review*, 44 (3), 493–497.

Pontell, H.N., Black, W.K. and Geis, G. (2014). Too big to fail, too powerful to jail? On the absence of criminal prosecutions after the 2008 financial meltdown, *Crime, Law and Social Change*, 61 (1), 1–13.

Pratt, M.G., Kaplan, S. and Whittington, R. (2019). Editorial essay: The tumult over transparency: Decoupling transparency from replication in establishing trustworthy qualitative research, *Administrative Science Quarterly*, published online, pages 1–19, https://doi.org/10.1177/0001839219887663.

Pratt, T.C. and Cullen, F.T. (2005). Assessing macro-level predictors and theories of crime: A meta-analysis, *Crime and Justice*, 32, 373–450.

Pusch, N. and Holtfreter, K. (2020). Individual and organizational predictors of white-collar crime: A meta-analysis, *Journal of White-Collar and Corporate Crime*, published online, pages 1–19, https://doi.org/10.1177/2631309X19901317.

Qiu, B. and Slezak, S.L. (2019). The equilibrium relationships between performance-based pay, performance, and the commission and detection of fraudulent misreporting, *The Accounting Review*, 94 (2), 325–356.

Ramoglou, S. and Tsang, E.W.K. (2016). A realist perspective of entrepreneurship: Opportunities as propensities, *Academy of Management Review*, 41, 410–434.

Rehg, M.T., Miceli, M.P., Near, J.P. and Scotter, J.R.V. (2009). Antecedents and outcomes of retaliation against whistleblowers: Gender differences and power relationships, *Organization Science*, 19 (2), 221–240.

Reyns, B.W. (2013). Online routines and identity theft victimization: Further expanding routine activity theory beyond direct-contact offenses, *Journal of Research in Crime and Delinquency*, 50, 216–238.

Rodriguez, P., Uhlenbruck, K. and Eden, L. (2005). Government corruption and the entry strategies of multinationals, *Academy of Management Review*, 30 (2), 383–396.

Roehling, M.V., Roehling, P.V. and Boswell, W.R. (2010). The potential role of organizational setting in creating "entitled" employees: An investigation of the antecedents of equity sensitivity, *Employee Responsibilities & Rights Journal*, 22, 133–145.

Rorie, M. (2015). An integrated theory of corporate environmental compliance and overcompliance, *Crime, Law and Social Change*, 64 (2–3), 65–101.

Rothe, D.L. (2020). Moving beyond abstract typologies? Overview of state and state-corporate crime, *Journal of White-Collar and Corporate Crime*, 1 (1), 7–15.

Rothe, D.L. and Medley, C. (2020). Beyond state and state-corporate crime typologies: The symbiotic nature, harm, and victimization of crimes of the powerful and their continuation, in: Rorie, M. (editor), *The Handbook of White-Collar Crime*, Hoboken, NJ: John Wiley & Sons, chapter 6, pages 81–94.

Sampson, R.J. and Laub, J.H. (1993). *Crime in the Making: Pathways and Turning Points Through Life*, Cambridge, MA: Harvard University Press.

Sarkis, S. (2020). Trump's pardons are meant to normalize white-collar crime, *Forbes*, www.forbes.com, published February 18.

Schnatterly, K., Gangloff, K.A. and Tuschke, A. (2018). CEO wrongdoing: A review of pressure, opportunity, and rationalization, *Journal of Management*, 44 (6), 2405–2432.

Schoepfer, A. and Piquero, N.L. (2006). Exploring white-collar crime and the American dream: A partial test of institutional anomie theory, *Journal of Criminal Justice*, 34 (3), 227–235.

Schoultz, I. and Flyghed, J. (2019). From "we didn't do it" to "we've learned our lesson": Development of a typology of neutralizations of corporate crime, *Critical Criminology*, published online doi.org/10.1007/s10612-019-09483-3.

Schwendinger, H. and Schwendinger, J. (2014). Defenders of order or guardians of human rights? *Social Justice*, 40 (1/2), 87–117.

Seiders, K., Voss, G.B., Godfrey, A.L. and Grewal, D. (2007). SERVCON: Development and validation of a multidimensional service convenience scale, *Journal of the Academy of Marketing Science*, 35, 144–156.

Severson, R.E., Kodatt, Z.H. and Burruss, G.W. (2020). Explaining white-collar crime: Individual-level theories, In: Rorie, M.L. (editor), *The Handbook of White-Collar Crime*, Hoboken, NJ: Wiley & Sons, chapter 11, pages 159–174.

Shadnam, M. and Lawrence, T.B. (2011). Understanding widespread misconduct in organizations: An institutional theory of moral collapse, *Business Ethics Quarterly*, 21 (3), 379–407.

Shawver, T. and Clements, L.H. (2019). The impact of value preferences on whistle-blowing intentions of accounting professionals, *Journal of Forensic and Investigative Accounting*, 11 (2), 232–247.

Shepherd, D. and Button, M. (2019). Organizational inhibitions to addressing occupational fraud: A theory of differential rationalization, *Deviant Behavior*, 40 (8), 971–991.

Siponen, M. and Vance, A. (2010). Neutralization: New insights into the problem of employee information security policy violations, *MIS Quarterly*, 34 (3), 487–502.

Slyke, S.V. and Bales, W.D. (2012). A contemporary study of the decision to incarcerate white-collar and street property offenders, *Punishment & Society*, 14 (2), 217–246.

Smith, O. and Raymen, T. (2018). Deviant leisure: A criminological perspective, *Theoretical Criminology*, 22 (1), 63–82.

Smith, R. (2009). Understanding entrepreneurial behavior in organized criminals, *Journal of Enterprising Communities: People and Places in the Global Economy*, 3 (3), 256–268.

Sonnier, B.M., Lassar, W.M. and Lassar, S.S. (2015). The influence of source credibility and attribution of blame on juror evaluation of liability of industry specialist auditors, *Journal of Forensic & Investigative Accounting*, 7 (1), 1–37.

Srivastava, S.B. and Goldberg, A. (2017). Language as a window into culture, *California Management Review*, 60 (1), 56–69.

Steffensmeier, D. and Allan, E. (1996). Gender and crime: Toward a gendered theory of female offending, *Annual Review of Sociology*, 22, 459–487.

Steffensmeier, D., Schwartz, J. and Roche, M. (2013). Gender and twenty-first-century corporate crime: Female involvement and the gender gap in Enron-era corporate frauds, *American Sociological Review*, 78 (3), 448–476.

Suddaby, R. (2014). Editor's comments: Why theory? *Academy of Management Review*, 39 (4), 407–411.

Sundström, M. and Radon, A. (2015). Utilizing the concept of convenience as a business opportunity in emerging markets, *Organizations and Markets in Emerging Economies*, 6 (2), 7–21.

Sutherland, E.H. (1939). White-collar criminality, *American Sociological Review*, 5 (1), 1–12.

Sutherland, E.H. (1983). *White Collar Crime: The Uncut Version*, New Haven, CT: Yale University Press.

Sutton, R.I. and Staw, B.M. (1995). What theory is not, *Administrative Science Quarterly*, 40, 371–384.

Sykes, G. and Matza, D. (1957). Techniques of neutralization: A theory of delinquency, *American Sociological Review*, 22 (6), 664–670.

Szalma, J.L. and Hancock, P.A. (2013). A signal improvement to signal detection analysis: Fuzzy SDT on the ROCs, *Journal of Experimental Psychology: Human Perception and Performance*, 39 (6), 1741–1762.

Tankebe, J. (2019). Cooperation with the police against corruption: Exploring the roles of legitimacy, deterrence and collective action theories, *British Journal of Criminology*, 59, 1390–1410.

Taylor, J. (2018). White-collar crime and the law in nineteenth-century Britain, *Business History*, 60 (3), 343–360.

Thaxton, S. and Agnew, R. (2018). When criminal coping is likely: An examination of conditioning effects in general strain theory, *Journal of Quantitative Criminology*, 34, 887–920.

Thornberry, T.P. (1989). Reflections on the advantages and disadvantages of theoretical integration, in: Messner, S.F., Krohn, M.D. and Liska, A.E. (editors), *Theoretical Integration in the Study of Deviance and Crime*, Albany, NY: State University of New York Press, chapter 3, pages 51–60.

Tombs, S. and Whyte, D. (2020). The shifting imaginaries of corporate crime, *Journal of White-Collar and Corporate Crime*, 1 (1), 16–23.

Tonoyan, V., Strohmeyer, R., Habib, M. and Perlitz, M. (2010). Corruption and entrepreneurship: How formal and informal institutions shape small firm behavior in transition and mature market economies, *Entrepreneurship: Theory & Practice*, 34 (5), 803–831.

Toolami, B.N., Roodposhti, F.R., Nikoomaram, H., Banimahd, B. and Vakilifard, H. (2019). The survey of whistleblowing intentions for accounting frauds based on demographic individual differences among accounting staff, *International Journal of Finance and Managerial Accounting*, 4 (14), 1–13.

Trahan, A., Marquart, J. and Mullings, J. (2005). Fraud and the American dream: Toward an understanding of fraud victimization, *Deviant Behavior*, 26 (6), 601–620.

Vasiu, V.I. and Podgor, E.S. (2019). Organizational opportunity and deviant behavior: Convenience in white-collar crime, in: *Criminal Law and Criminal Justice Books*, New Brunswick, NJ: Rutgers, the State University of New Jersey, July, www.clcjbooks.rutgers.edu.

Väyrynen, T. and Laari-Salmela, S. (2015). Men, mammals, or machines? Dehumanization embedded in organizational practices, *Journal of Business Ethics*, 147, 1–19.

Victor, B. and Cullen, J.B. (1988). The organizational bases of ethical work climates, *Administrative Science Quarterly*, 33, 101–125.

Weick, K.E. (1989). Theory construction as disciplined imagination, *Academy of Management Review*, 14 (4), 516–531.

Weick, K.E. (1995). *Sensemaking in Organizations*, Sage, CA: Thousand Oaks.

Weick, K.E., Sutcliffe, K.M. and Obstfeld, D. (2005). Organizing and the process of sensemaking, *Organization Science*, 16 (4), 409–421.

Welsh, D., Bush, J., Thiel, C. and Bonner, J. (2019). Reconceptualizing goal setting's dark side: The ethical consequences of learning versus outcome goals, *Organizational Behavior and Human Decision Processes*, 150, 14–27.

Welsh, D.T. and Ordonez, L.D. (2014). The dark side of consecutive high performance goals: Linking goal setting, depletion, and unethical behavior, *Organizational Behavior and Human Decision Processes*, 123, 79–89.

Welsh, D.T., Ordonez, L.D., Snyder, D.G. and Christian, M.S. (2014). The slippery slope: How small ethical transgressions pave the way for larger future transgressions, *Journal of Applied Psychology*, 100 (1), 114–127.

Welter, F., Baker, T., Audretsch, D.B. and Gartner, W.B. (2017). Everyday entrepreneurship: A call for entrepreneurship research to embrace entrepreneurial diversity, *Entrepreneurship: Theory and Practice*, 41 (3), 323–347.

Wheelock, D., Semukhina, O. and Demidov, N.N. (2011). Perceived group threat and punitive attitudes in Russia and the United States, *British Journal of Criminology*, 51, 937–959.

White, M.J. (2019). What I've learned about white-collar crime, *Harvard Business Review*, July-August, 58–59.

Wikstrom, P.O.H., Mann, R.P. and Hardie, B. (2018). Young people's differential vulnerability to criminogenic exposure: Bridging the gap between people- and place-oriented approaches in the study of crime causation, *European Journal of Criminology*, 15 (1), 10–31.

Williams, J.W. (2008). The lessons of Enron: Media accounts, corporate crimes, and financial markets, *Theoretical Criminology*, 12 (4), 471–499.

Williams, M.L., Levi, M., Burnap, P. and Gundur, R.V. (2019). Under the corporate radar: Examining insider business cybercrime victimization through an application of routine activities theory, *Deviant Behavior*, 40 (9), 1119–1131.

Wood, J. and Alleyne, E. (2010). Street gang theory and research: Where are we now and where do we go from here? *Aggression and Violent Behavior*, 15, 100–111.

Yam, K.C., Christian, M.S., Wei, W., Liao, Z. and Nai, J. (2018). The mixed blessing of leader sense of humor: Examining costs and benefits, *Academy of Management Journal*, 61 (1), 348–369.

Zhu, D.H. and Chen, G. (2015). CEO narcissism and the impact of prior board experience on corporate strategy, *Administrative Science Quarterly*, 60 (1), 31–65.

Zvi, L. and Elaad, E. (2018). Correlates of narcissism, self-reported lies, and self-assessed abilities to tell and detect lies, tell truths, and believe others, *Journal of Investigative Psychology and Offender Profiling*, 15, 271–286.

Zysman-Quirós, D. (2020). White-collar crime in South and Central America: Corporate-state crime, governance, and the high impact of the Odebrecht corruption case, in: Rorie, M.L. (editor), *The Handbook of White-Collar Crime*, Hoboken, NJ: Wiley & Sons, chapter 23, pages 363–380.

2 Deviant convenience dynamics

While Chapter 1 presented the deviant convenience structure for white-collar crime, this chapter presents a model for dynamic analysis of white-collar convenience. Convenience for a potential offender is not static, but rather dynamic, as convenience changes over time in all three dimensions. The motive can become stronger or weaker, the opportunity can become greater or smaller, and the willingness can become higher and lower. Furthermore, a change in one of the three dimensions can cause change in the remaining two dimensions, which this chapter illustrates through six case studies.

Dynamic model of white-collar convenience

Figure 2.1 presents the dynamic model of convenience theory. The model has the same elements as the structural model of convenience theory in Figure 1.1. Just like in Figure 1.1, Figure 2.2 breaks down the financial motive into individual and corporate possibilities as well as individual and corporate threats. The model breaks down organizational opportunity into committing crime and concealing crime, where the convenience to commit crime is dependent on privileged status and access to resources, while the convenience to conceal crime is dependent on functional decay, oversight chaos and external collapse. The model breaks down personal willingness into crime choice and crime innocence, where crime choice is dependent on deviant identity, rational decision, and deviant learning, while crime innocence is dependent on justification and neutralization.

Figure 2.1 illustrates causal relationships in the dynamic model. An arrow represents a cause-and-effect relationship. For example, a stronger financial motive can cause initiatives for organizational opportunity expansion. On the other hand, a greater organizational opportunity for white-collar crime can make the financial motive stronger. Similarly, when the personal willingness for deviant behavior is higher, then organizational opportunity expansion might occur. On the other hand, a greater organizational opportunity can cause a higher personal willingness. Motive might be stronger or weaker; opportunity might be greater or smaller, while willingness might be higher or lower.

All causal relationships in Figure 2.1 are positive in the system dynamics sense of the word, which means that one increase causes another increase, while one

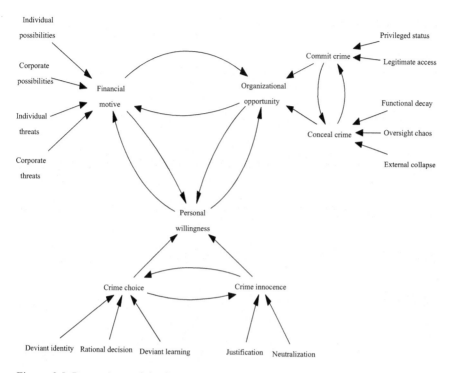

Figure 2.1 Dynamic model of convenience theory

decrease causes another decrease (Randers, 2019; Sterman, 2018). It is thus a change in the same direction from the cause to the effect in the relationship. For example, as stated previously, an increase in financial motive can cause an increase in organizational opportunity, while a decrease in financial motive can cause a decrease in organizational opportunity. Similarly, an increase in personal willingness can cause an increase in organizational opportunity, while a decrease in personal willingness can cause a decrease in organizational opportunity.

In the system dynamics terminology (Randers, 2019; Sterman, 2018), financial motive, organizational opportunity, and personal willingness are endogenous variables, as they influence and are influenced by other variables in the dynamic model. In addition, to commit crime and to conceal crime is endogenous variables in the model, as the convenience to commit crime might increase the convenience to conceal crime, and vice versa. Similarly, crime choice and crime innocence are endogenous variables in the model, as a stronger willingness to choose crime can influence the ability to justify crime, while the ability to justify crime can influence crime as a choice. All other themes in the model in Figure 2.1 are endogenous variables, as they only influence other variables without other variables influencing them.

It is possible to follow causal paths in Figure 2.1. For example, a change in the privileged status of potential offenders causes change in the convenience to commit crime, which in turn represents a change in organizational opportunity, which in turn causes a change in personal willingness, and so forth. If the privileged position of a potential offender increases, for example by enjoying sole and exclusive access to all financial transactions, then the organizational opportunity to commit crime increases, which in turn might strengthen the personal willingness to become an offender.

The dynamic model of convenience theory in Figure 2.1 has several causal loops. Either a causal loop can be reinforcing as a positive feedback loop, or it can be stabilizing as a negative feedback loop. All loops in the figure are positive loops. For example, when the financial motive becomes stronger, then the organizational opportunity increases, which causes the motive to become even stronger. Another example is the loop including all three dimensions: the financial motive strengthens, the organizational opportunity increases, the personal willingness becomes higher, and the financial motive becomes even stronger. Furthermore, in Figure 2.1 there is a positive loop involving committing crime and concealing crime, as well as a positive loop between crime choice and crime convenience. The assumption is that increased convenience in committing crime will link to an increased convenience in concealing crime, while an increased willingness to choose crime will link to an increased ability to feel innocent.

In the model in Figure 2.1, several factors are modeled as exogenous variables, while they might in themselves represent dynamics if modeled as endogenous variables. An example is oversight chaos created by social disorganization. The social disorganization perspective argues that crime is a function of people dynamics in the organization and between organizations, especially weak social controls, and not necessarily a function of each individual within such organizations (Forti and Visconti, 2020; Hoffmann, 2002; Pratt and Cullen, 2005).

In a detection perspective, individual motives, organizational opportunities, as well as personal willingness make observation and monitoring more or less impossible. However, over time the extent of trust versus controls of executives and others in privileged positions might change. Reduction in trust implies that vulnerability receives minor acceptance based on positive expectations of the motives and actions of another (Dearden, 2016, 2017, 2019). Abuses of trust are easier to detect when the level of trust decreases and the level of suspicion increases.

Dynamic influence from financial motive

Changes in the strength of financial motive can influence both the magnitude of organizational opportunity as well as the level of personal willingness for deviant behavior to commit white-collar crime. The first case is concerned with opportunity expansion resulting from a stronger desire for illegal profit to cover personal or organizational needs. Offenders have access to resources for opportunity expansion. Over time, an offender can expand opportunities for white-collar crime. Earlier research has emphasized that opportunity is dependent on the social capital available to the criminal, as well as the structure and quality of social ties in hierarchical and transactional relationships that shape opportunity structures (e.g., Adler and Kwon, 2002; Pontell et al., 2014). In a dynamic perspective, an offender can improve the organizational convenience of white-collar crime.

The case of a chief financial officer (CFO) in a Norwegian enterprise who received a prison sentence for embezzlement in the organization can illustrate the dynamic perspective. The district court in Gjøvik is located north of the capital Oslo in Norway. On August 8, 2014, district court judge Håkon Schei Mentzoni announced a verdict of four years and six months in prison for the former CFO. The average prison sentence for white-collar criminals in Norway is two years and four months, so the judge passed a severe sentence to the former CFO. His conviction included to pay back the embezzled amount of 18 million Norwegian kroner (about US $2.2 million) to his former employer HRB (Gjøvik tingrett, 2014).

The former CFO was divorced and had a strong desire to impress his children with cars, houses, and travels. He had a new girlfriend with whom he enjoyed expensive wine and restaurant visits. His income was not sufficient to cover all his expenses.

The former CFO had the task to develop and implement a new system for accounting generally and money transfer procedures for bank accounts specifically. This is where his first opportunity expansion occurred. He designed procedures with single approval requirements where approval rights rested with people in the accounting function. Before taking on the CFO position at HRB, he had worked in the parent company. This is where his second opportunity expansion occurred. He kept professional and social ties to executives in the parent company, so that the other executives at HRB never dared questioning his performance or behavior. He was a friendly person who everyone seemed to like, although he never talked about work. The chief executive officer (CEO) at HRB later told fraud examiners from global auditing firm PwC (2014) that he simply felt he had no other choice but to trust the man.

The external auditor later told fraud examiners from PwC (2014) that the cooperation with the CFO went so smoothly since the CFO always provided large volumes of records for review. The auditor never felt a need to ask for more information. This is where the third opportunity expansion occurred. The CFO made sure that the auditor received an overload of information so that the auditor would not ask for more.

Hestnes (2017) asked the question in his study of the CFO case: Why did the auditor fail in detecting embezzlement at HRB? Normally in a Norwegian context, the auditor is to report annually to the board in the business where the auditor has reviewed accounts. Since the cooperation between the auditor and the CFO went so smoothly, the CEO did not invite the auditor anymore to board meetings. This is where the fourth opportunity expansion occurred. The CFO became the actual person to report external audit results to the board. The CFO's fifth and final opportunity expansion was to separate flows of money for current expenses from flows of money for investments. He embezzled mainly investment money. This separation enabled him to present results where the bottom line had no signs of his financial crime.

Changes in the strength of financial motive can influence the level of personal willingness for deviant behavior to commit white-collar crime. The second case is thus concerned with higher willingness resulting from a stronger desire for illegal profit to cover personal or organizational needs.

Procurement officers in public office can be an attractive target for vendors who are willing to bribe officials. When officials have a stronger desire for a bribe, then their willingness will increase and corruption is more likely to occur. The German bus manufacturer MAN bribed more than nine procurement officers at the bus operating company Unibuss in Oslo, Norway.

There were a large number of offenders identified in the Unibuss case, where nine persons ended up in prison, and more persons were waiting for their trials in Oslo district court. The Unibuss scandal started in Germany where bus manufacturer MAN was systematically bribing public transportation companies to make them buy MAN busses. For example, MAN made procurement officials specify the need for busses of exactly 18 meters and 75 centimeters in length. The only bus manufacturer supplying exactly that length was MAN. Corruption did not only occur towards procurement officers but also executives at Oslo city transportation company Unibuss (Haugan, 2014).

All of the bribed Norwegians were on public salaries, which is significantly lower than salaries in the private sector. Their strong desire for a better standard of living seems to be the case since their spending of bribes mainly ended up in home expansions and better private cars. They obviously felt they deserved more than they earned, which influenced their willingness to accept bribes.

When Unibuss procurement officials and executives from Norway visited MAN sales executives in Germany, they received envelopes with euros in cash during social events. However, some years later, a Unibuss employee was on vacation in Munich in Germany when he read a local newspaper. He read that MAN sales executives faced prosecution in Germany in a corruption scandal. In the newspaper in German, the article mentioned that several countries might be involved in the bribery scandal, including Norway. When the Unibuss employee returned home from his vacation, he went to his superior, whom he trusted, and told about the media story.

Fraud examiners at local law firm Wiersholm (2012) found that some of the Norwegians at Unibuss had asked for bribes, while others had waited for MAN to offer them bribes. All payments used only cash from the firm MAN Nutz-fahrzeuge AG, where payments registered as mediation commission.

A technical executive received a sentence of five years and nine months in prison, while a procurement executive received a sentence of five years in prison by Oslo district court in 2014. Other sentences were two or three years in prison for the chief executive officer (CEO) and seven more top executives at Unibuss.

The difficulty of blowing the whistle can illustrate the convenience in this MAN-Unibuss case (Nisar et al., 2019). As mentioned in the chapter on deviant convenience structure, even when an observer believes to have noticed a crime signal, the observer can be reluctant to report the observation (Bjørkelo et al., 2011; Bussmann et al., 2018; Mpho, 2017). In Norway like in most other countries, there are no benefits from reporting misconduct and crime in the organization (Brown et al., 2016; Keil et al., 2010). Rather, retaliation and reprisals can be the result for the observer (Mesmer-Magnus and Viswesvaran, 2005; Park et al., 2020; Rehg et al., 2009; Shawver and Clements, 2019).

Nevertheless, a whistleblower attempted to blow the whistle at Unibuss long before the Unibuss employee on vacation in Munich read the local newspaper. He told us about his experiences as a whistleblower. Whistleblower Jan Erik Skog repeatedly gave information on censurable circumstances. The case ended with conviction of betrayal and corruption of ten people more than a decade after the first warning from Skog (Slettholm, 2016). Final terms of punishment were determined in the Supreme Court for three of the convicted (NTB, 2016). The Unibuss case is one of the larger legal proceedings against bribery in Norway (NTB, 2014).

Jan Erik Skog worked as an electrician in Unibuss, an Oslo-based public bus company, where he also held the role as craft union representative. Skog had reactions on purchasing routines, gave statements on high prices and the fact that tenders were not invited. Initially, Skog informed his concern to the corporation, but there was no response to his anxiety. When Skog blew the whistle again, it was to the Oslo office of the city auditor. However, neither politicians nor corporate management showed any interest in or took Skog's allegations and documentation seriously. Thus, investigation was not seen a necessary action, it was merely viewed as a waste of taxpayers' money (Tømmerås, 2014). If someone had followed up Skog's concerns, both the amount of money spent and the personal tragedies of this case would have been less wide-ranging. Over the years, the case grew in size and complexity resulting in a huge clean-up operation (Folkvord, 2015).

Jan Erik Skog was one of two whistleblowers sharing The Freedom of Expression Foundations prize for 2015. Even though he expresses difficult times of adversity and having to fight strong and powerful forces, he recommends raising a voice when you witness something suspicious (Fritt ord, 2015).

Skog also became a member of a government-appointed expert group, focusing on better conditions for whistleblowers (Mortensen and Grimsrud, 2016).

Our interview with Skog focused on each of five stages in the whistleblowing process, and the following description presents his response.

Stage 1: signal detection by observer

I was absolutely sure right away. A new procurement manager was hired, but we knew him from before. You had to count your fingers after shaking his hand. We were not allowed anymore to buy as cheap as possible. He demanded to have his people in, his network should deliver, the price was not important. We should not complain to vendors when parts did not work. I thought it was crime right away. I am in general suspicious and skeptical, and I do not accept what executives tell me is the truth. I analyze on my own, and draw my own conclusions. I might have been a reasonably qualified detective. I see patterns and notice things that others do not recognize. It is indeed stressful to be this way, since I am unable to sleep at night before I see some kind of light in the end of the tunnel.

Stage 2: signal registration by observer

I was a union representative on the board, but I worked on the floor. My fellow union members believed me, and they joined me in my thoughts. Without the union, I would be lost. We became especially suspicious towards the new procurement manager, when we learned that he had been fired from a similar position in a different company some years ago. He had received kickbacks, and he had hired his son-in-law. We were convinced it was corruption. For example, he suddenly got a new private car from a vendor, who was our main supplier of tires for our buses. I got up in the middle of the night to make notes, and I could hardly sleep afterwards. All accusations could be documented, any saw it, but were uncertain how it could be exposed.

Stage 3: signal interpretation by whistleblower

I was rational and wrote a report about my observations. I discussed it with other union members and colleagues. I also discussed it with a left-wing politician who had discovered corruption in the municipality in the past. My signal awareness was strong based on my experience in the organization for many years. I considered myself qualified to identify patterns in criminal activities. Yet nobody else in the organization wanted to talk loud about it, maybe because surprisingly many of my colleagues had minor fringe benefits that they were reluctant to lose. For example, writing overtime without being at work was granted to many of my colleagues informally. Some were allowed to use company cars privately. I ended up sending my report to the chief executive officer. I had never blown the whistle before.

Stage 4: signal reception by responsible

I was called to a meeting with the chief executive, where another executive also was present. I told the corruption story, but they did not want to believe it. Instead, they presented all kinds of reasons why what I had observed was quite normal, and that I had obviously misunderstood what was going on. They had only good things to say about the procurement manager, and they offered normal explanations for observed deviance. I asked, "Why did he buy tires from a friend, from whom he privately bought or got a car?" They responded; "He knows everyone in the tire business". The meeting lasted for an hour. I had raised several issues, but they were all ignored. I went on to notify the chairperson of the board. He simply said that we all should be friends and look ahead.

Nobody wanted to listen to me at the board meeting. They started to suspect me. I became an issue, not my message. They searched for my motives to accuse someone of bribery. They knew that I as a union representative on the board was opposing and resisting much of what was going on in the organization. Little did I know that the chief executive later was to be convicted of corruption – that was together with a number of other business executives, who had received favors from major vendors. At one point, the chief executive discovered that I had communicated an allegation that was not completely true. He asked me to regret my allegation in writing. Therefore, I did, and he said he hoped I had learned from my mistake. It was obviously a way of trying to silence me.

Stage 5: signal knowledge by responsible

The chief executive was extremely good at talking, everyone on the board listened to him. Almost hallelujah every time he was speaking. Board members made me look like a fool when I presented my critical comments at board meetings. However, the left-wing politician in the municipality had asked the control committee to tell the audit function to investigate rumors of corruption in the public company. Then the matter became serious also for the company board. However, the signal knowledge was not complete with the whistleblowing and the audit report. Politicians and board members still tried to ignore the emerging stream of information. The ice first really broke when a journalist reported in the media about a court case in Germany involving bus manufacturer MAN and the Norwegian customer Unibuss. Then the snowball really started to roll very fast. People were arrested, and I was exposed in the media as a whistleblower for the first time. I was not called as a witness in court, but I attended all court hearings. Information that originated from me was used in court, in addition to findings from the municipal audit. Some evidence I knew existed was never presented in court. I do not know why.

Dynamic influence from organizational opportunity

Changes in organizational opportunity can influence both motive and willingness. The first case is concerned with greed expansion resulting from an emerging ample organizational opportunity for financial crime. A priest in the Methodist church appointed chief executive officer (CEO) in the religious Betanien Foundation in Bergen in Norway. He lived a modest lifestyle while successfully expanding foundation business. He did very well in negotiations with the Municipality of Bergen Hordaland County and the government, and he had a genuine interest in achieving the best possible deals for Betanien. On several occasions, people honored and admired him for having brought Betanien to successful expansion and profitability. Soon Betanien ran several hospitals, nursing homes, and kindergartens.

The district court of Drammen is located west of the capital Oslo in Norway. On February 2, 2015, the former CEO was sentenced to prison for three years because of embezzlement in the Methodist foundation Betanien (Drammen tingrett, 2015). He admitted to embezzlement of 16 million Norwegian kroner (about US $2 million) that he later agreed to pay back based on future income and heritage.

Fleckenstein and Bowes (2002) phrased the question: Do members often betray trust in terms of white-collar crime in religious institutions? According to Owens and Shores (2010), most white-collar crime incidents are exploitations of trust, where trust may originate from a shared religious identity between the victim and the perpetrator. Shores (2010) phrased the questions: Are social religious networks an attractive arena for white-collar criminals? Is the morale of not acting illegally blinded from a chance perspective when an attractive opportunity arises? Alternatively, as suggested by Corcoran et al. (2012): Do shared religious beliefs lead to less acceptability of white-collar crime?

Fundacion Betanien opened in the autumn of 2001 in Alfaz del Pi in Spain. The institution in Spain is part of Betanien's rehabilitation and nursing home. Betanien Foundation in Bergen owned and operated the home. The CEO initiated and successfully established Fundacion Betanien. He told accountants in Bergen whenever they had to transfer money from Norway to Spain.

The CEO experienced complete trust from all involved. He had authority both as a business leader and as a religious leader. When he made a mistake, nobody noticed. He was managing large sums of money all by himself. The auditor in Norway believed that Spanish auditors would audit accounts in Spain, while accountants in Spain believed the audit took place in Norway.

In Spain, the CEO developed a drinking problem. While always sober in Norway, he became a heavy drinker in Spain. He enjoyed drinking, and he could afford it at the expense of the foundation. Soon he expanded his local lifestyle in Spain to include parties with prostitutes that he paid with money from the foundation. His embezzlement of funds from the foundation enabled him to live a double life, where he was modest at home, while living like a playboy in Spain. He abused the money that he controlled on behalf of the foundation to enjoy a lifestyle in Spain that he could never do at home as a priest and as a family man.

After much pressure and threats from two whistleblowers, the chairperson at the foundation hired BDO (2014) to conduct an internal investigation, where fraud examiners detected large sums of money embezzled by the CEO over a period of several years.

Changes in organizational opportunity can influence willingness. The second case is concerned with willingness expansion caused by emerging ample organizational opportunity for financial crime. One brother was in charge of property management and maintenance within the municipality while two other brothers were in the maintenance business. When they discovered the mutual interest in doing business with each other, they ignored public procurement regulations. A court of appeals convicted all three brothers to prison for several years. The court found them guilty of corruption and organized crime (Borgarting, 2011).

Five and a half years in prison for corruption and organized crime became the verdict of the former property manager in the municipality. This ruling from a district court in 2009 received confirmation in the court of appeals in 2011 (Borgarting, 2011). Together with his brothers, he caused a loss for the municipality of 20 million Norwegian kroner (about US $2.5 million). They cheated by lack of competition and systematically overbilling maintenance services. The convicts shared the profits via craft services, building materials, boats, motorcycles and cash (Gedde-Dahl, 2011).

Benson and Simpson (2018) argue that many white-collar offenses manifest the following opportunity properties: (1) the offender has legitimate access to the location in which the crime is committed (2) the offender is spatially separate from the victim, and (3) the offender's actions have a superficial appearance of legitimacy. Situation-focused perspectives explain crime in terms of opportunity structures. Piquero and Benson (2004) proposed a middle-ground explanation of white-collar crime, which they call the punctuated situational theory of offending. This theory assumes that white-collar criminals start offending when they reach their forties. Opportunities that result from a certain occupational status may explain crime. Situational factors – such as a more influential job and a growing number of important contacts – provide access to legitimate means to obtain desirable goals.

Willingness driven by opportunity implies that an opportunity is attractive as a means of responding to desires. The presence of a favorable combination of circumstances can stimulate willingness (Aguilera and Vadera, 2008). Fraud examiners at G-Partner (2007) found that the property manager had convenient opportunity to order services from whomever he liked, since he was empowered to do it on his own, and no control mechanisms or audit procedures were in place.

Dynamic influence from personal willingness

Changes in personal willingness for deviant behavior can influence both motive and opportunity. The first case here is concerned with motive expansion caused by a stronger willingness for deviant behavior. Narcissistic organizational identification by some CEOs is one of several perspectives on potential criminal behavior (Galvin et al., 2015). If a CEO says and believes in the statement – "I am the company" – then the organization can be up for trouble. Narcissism here means seeing oneself as central to the organization's identity. It is a self-centered form of organizational identification. The CEO may lose his or her independent sense of self and engage in questionable behaviors. Narcissistic organizational identification implies domination of individual identity over organizational identity. CEOs with narcissistic organizational identification feel a strong affinity for their organizations' identities, but as an expression of themselves. They see their own identity as the main reference for understanding what the organization is doing and how it is structured. Removing the separation between the individual and the organization can cause the CEO to think of company money as personal money.

While there is considerable variance in narcissistic tendencies across CEOs, many CEOs have narcissistic personality traits such as self-focus, self-admiration, a sense of entitlement, and a sense of superiority (Zhu and Chen, 2015). Galvin et al. (2015: 163) found that:

> It is not uncommon to learn of individuals in positions of power and responsibility, especially CEOs, who exploit and undermine their organizations for personal gain. A circumstance not well explained in the literature, however, is that some of those individuals may highly identify with their organizations, meaning that they see little difference between their identity and the organization's identity – between their interests and the organization's interest. This presents a paradox, because organizational identification typically is not noted for its adverse consequences on the organization.

The CEO in Norway received a sentence of seven years in prison. He had spent company money on a variety of projects that had nothing to do with the business. As suggested by Zhu and Chen (2015), the convicted CEO favored bold actions that could cause external recognition. For example, he built a water fountain in front of a nursing home since one of the company's business areas was water supply.

The CEO bought from company money a hunting farm in South Africa. He argued in court that this was an investment according to his new business model for the company. Similarly, a number of other money flows he claimed in court as business investments resulting from his expanded business model. He told the court that they did not understand his business ideas.

The convicted CEO was very much in line with a description presented by Zhu and Chen (2015: 35):

> Narcissistic CEOs tend to favor bold actions, such as large acquisitions, that attract attention. They are less responsive than other CEOs to objective indicators of their performance and more responsive to social praise. For instance, while narcissistic CEOs tend to aggressively adopt technological discontinuities, they are especially likely to do so when such behavior is expected to garner attention and admiration from external audiences.

The convicted CEO had received an honor from the King of Norway for his good deeds in his local community, including the water fountain in front of a nursing home. Fraud examiners from Distriktsrevisjonen (2007) found that several causal factors had worked together to enable the CEO to carry out his systematic pouring and emptying of resources from the company. Among the factors were his personal commitment, willingness and motivation to work in untraditional ways.

Changes in personal willingness for deviant behavior can influence opportunity. The second case is concerned with opportunity expansion caused by a stronger willingness for deviant behavior. Two employees in the city of Drammen outside Oslo found building regulations too strict, and therefore started to approve construction applications that represented violations of the law. They disagreed with the law, and were thus willing to break it. To enable law violation, they cooperated in the receipt of new applications. Normally, there should be random assignment of new applications to one of several officers in the construction branch department in the municipality. The two employees expanded their organizational opportunity by manipulating the system so that one of them always got a case from the other one whom applicants had been contacting personally. For each successful application, the two officers received a bribe of 20 or 30,000 Norwegian kroner (approximately US\$ 3,000).

In March 2018, both employees received prison sentences of six years and three and a half years respectively in Drammen district court. The defendants were a woman age 59 years and a man age 46 years. The sentence was more severe than suggested by the prosecutor in court (Kommandantvold and Bjerkeseth, 2018).

In their fraud examination, Deloitte (2017: 4) draws the following conclusion:

> The investigation shows that the department has not had a framework or system that ensures adequate control in the construction application work. Deficiencies are revealed that relate to the control structure and culture in the department, including lack of formal delegation of authority to relevant personnel and lack of overview of responsibilities and authorizations. The department has no management system, and there are shortcomings associated with access to functions in the case processing system, which contributes to a lack of overview and control.

Deloitte's (2017) review originated from the control committee's mandate, which essentially deals with organizational conditions. Fraud examiners at Deloitte had to take into account that there was a police investigation going on in parallel. Investigators from Deloitte collected data through document analysis, interviews and review of 58 building cases, which all received favorable outcomes in the municipality building permit department.

Personal willingness can in itself be a dynamic phenomenon that develops over time. Cleff et al. (2013: 149) define six phases for such a development:

> In the first phase, the delinquents initially try to achieve their professional and private goals through legally acceptable means. In the second phase, they realize that they have not accomplished what they set out to do while remaining within the law: the anticipated success and strived-for satisfaction of perceived needs fail to materialize, paving the way for negative emotions such as the fear of failure or loss, or even anxiety about their livelihood. On a search for solutions for these problems, the individual begins to sound out areas at the margins of legality during the third phase – and to consider even illegal means for achieving his ends. If he now meets with success, his criminal behavior has been positively confirmed and reinforced: the fourth phase. This feeds the desire for further success, overriding the fear of

possible repercussions and ultimately culminating in the fifth phase: the "point of no return". In this situation, the offender's "personal sense of right and wrong" is adapted to fit his own criminal behavior, enabling him to continue to rationalize his actions to himself. Those affected increasingly lose touch with reality, becoming entangled more and more deeply in illegal actions that preclude any turning back to the state of affairs before the crime. With the discovery of the deed, the sixth phase then begins – the shock of reality.

Similarly, Benartzi et al. (2017) suggest behavioral reinforcement of deviance over time. Their nudge perspective emphasizes reinforcement and indirect suggestions to try to influence motives, incentives and decision-making of groups and individuals. A nudge is an influence that alters people's behavior in a voluntary manner. Nudges can influence individuals to perceive misconduct and crime as normal and thus acceptable.

Changes in personal willingness in phases as suggested by Cleff et al. (2013) can expand to the group level in terms of absorptive capacity. Absorptive capacity is a dynamic capability of processing knowledge about goal achievement among participants (Joshi et al., 2010), where knowledge from others is identified, assimilated, transformed, and applied. Absorptive capacity depends on prior related knowledge (Roberts et al., 2012). Among participants moving down a delinquent path, there can be a number of forces, including dynamics between tacit knowledge and explicit knowledge (Garrick and Chan, 2017), dynamics of market perceptions (Kocagil, 2004), dynamics of narcissism (Ouimet, 2010), and dynamics of the CEO-board relationship (Shen, 2003). In addition, there are variations in convenience orientation among participants, where some prefer convenient solutions to problems and challenges even when the solutions imply breaking the law.

In their article on organizational dynamics to understand causes and effects of top management fraud, Zahra et al. (2005: 128) emphasize organization-level pressures:

> Without stockholder monitoring, some executives may act opportunistically and enrich themselves while foregoing stockholder-desired, long-term value creating activities for their firms.

Autobiography by a chairman of the board

Some members of the upper echelon in society violate laws whenever they feel necessary. They have access to resources to commit and conceal financial crime while they deny the guilty mind. Autobiographies by convicted white-collar offenders are an interesting source of information to understand motives, opportunities, and willingness for deviant behaviors.

This research applies the theory of convenience to study the autobiography of a convicted chairperson of the board in Norway. While claiming corporate crime for the benefit of the business, he actually carried out occupational crime to benefit himself (Benson and Chio, 2020; Shepherd and Button, 2019). As an entrepreneur, he felt entitled to do whatever he considered necessary. He suffered from narcissistic identification, where there is little difference between personal money and company money.

Based on his autobiography (Olav, 2014, 2015), the court document (Oslo tingrett, 2015), as well as media reports (e.g., Bjørklund, 2018), this research was able to identify Olav's motive for white-collar crime, his opportunity for white-collar crime in an organizational setting, as well as his willingness for deviant behavior. The dynamic nature of white-collar crime convenience evolves in the case as the business moves closer to bankruptcy.

Financial motive

Officially, his motive was corporate crime to save the business. Corporate crime is white-collar offenses that benefit the organization, while occupational crime is white-collar offenses that benefit the individual (Craig and Piquero, 2016, 2017; Dodge, 2020). Actually, Olav's motive was occupational crime where he exploited the economic situation to acquire funds from the company before a potential bankruptcy. He had seen that the company was heading for possible bankruptcy and tried to secure money as a replacement and compensation for all the struggle and stress he felt exposed to in difficult times. The difficult economic situation that Thule Drilling experienced, led to stress for Olav. The fact that the company was in a pressured situation in relation to having the rig Thule Power completed, contributed to Olav as chairperson of the board becoming more inclined to find convenient solutions to the difficult situation. In case Thule Drilling would go bankrupt and thus his hard work for many years would become worthless, he was motivated to help himself to money that could help him keep his position as a wealthy man.

Olav's claim is that his sole motive was to rescue Thule Drilling from collapse by transferring money in different channels and make funds available to people who could enable completion of Thule Power. Maybe he followed a dual strategy, where he could keep the funds in his own firms if a rescue operation would seem hopeless. Eventually, he saw the opportunity to enrich himself, although he denies it completely in his books (Olav, 2014, 2015). However, the judge believes he intended to enrich himself already at the time of money transfer to his own firms (Oslo tingrett, 2015). Olav argues in his books that he was motivated to rescue Thule Drilling also because he wanted to rescue his own position as chairperson of the board. While he claims to have made his dispositions to save Thule's business, it seems that personal goal achievement, status, respect, admiration, success and esteem high up in Maslow's (1943) pyramid were the driving forces behind his actions. During the Thule crisis that emerged as a scandal, Olav bought himself a new leisure boat for US $100,000 and lithography by the painter Edvard Munch for US $50,000.

Organizational opportunity

Olav's opportunity for white-collar crime in an organizational setting is evident in a series of financial transactions. Accountants at Thule Drilling did what they were told, when Olav asked them urgently to transfer sums of money without documentation. He was the chairperson, and they could not object to his dispositions. He made people first transfer significant sums from the company's account to another account, which after several transactions ended up in one of his accounts in Switzerland, on Malta, or in Monaco. As chairperson of the board, he had the authority to decide on the execution of money transfer. Money transferred seemed to be legal acts and thus had superficial appearance of legitimacy (Benson and Simpson, 2018). Legitimacy is an assessment of the appropriateness of an individual's actions (Bundy and Pfarrer, 2015).

Both board members and management had blind faith in Olav's ability to get Thule Drilling out of trouble. Olav lied to Thule's administration that transactions had to happen immediately, as a problem had arisen in Dubai that money could solve. At that time, Olav tried to influence rig work in Saudi Arabia through contacts in Dubai.

Through his position and power at Thule Drilling, Hans Eirik Olav had access to strategic resources to perform and cover criminal acts. A white-collar offender has typically legitimate access to resources to commit and conceal crime (Adler and Kwon, 2002). A resource enables satisfaction of human and organizational needs. A resource has utility and limited availability. A white-collar offender has usually access to resources that are valuable (application provides appreciated outcome), unique (very few have access), not imitable (resources cannot be copied), not transferrable (resource cannot be released from context), combinable (results in better outcome), exploitable (possible to apply in criminal activities), and not substitutable (cannot be replaced). According to Petrocelli et al. (2003), access to resources equates access to power. Olav thus had many opportunities to find creative and convenient solutions to conceal his illegalities.

Access to resources combined with poor routines in the company meant that he could carry out transactions without any likelihood of negative consequences. If Thule Drilling had avoided bankruptcy, nobody would probably ever detect Olav's illegal transactions. When bankruptcy proceedings revealed his embezzlement of corporate funds, he had access to resources in terms of Norway's most skilled defense lawyer. In addition to a publicly appointed defense lawyer, the defendant can pay for additional defense. Even with self-paid additional defense, his two books (Olav, 2014, 2015), and active defense in the media, the verdict in Oslo district court (Oslo tingrett, 2015) became enforceable, and Olav ended up in prison. He was not as successful as other white-collar defendants where skilled attorneys help defendants to get the case acquitted based on the attorneys' relative knowledge superiority compared to the prosecutor and the judge (Galvin and Simpson, 2020).

Hans Eirik Olav had created a situation where nobody kept an overview of all financial transactions by impulsively ordering people in the administration to change accounting. External auditors withdrew from their assignments due to the company's lack of proper accounting and delayed submission of annual accounts. This may also indicate that there has been a lack of ethics and rules in the organization, which created the opportunity to commit financial crime. In the absence of an audit, which had the potential ability to detect financial crime, a required control regime was absent, which in turn made it easier to carry out illegal actions by the chairperson of the board.

Personal willingness

Olav's willingness for deviant behavior seems partly based on his ability to apply neutralization techniques (Sykes and Matza, 1957). He applied defense of necessity as one of his neutralizations. Defense of necessity implies justification that if rule breaking seems necessary, one should feel no guilt when carrying out the action. It is sometimes a required behavior in this position, so the offender can claim entitlement to action. The offender claims to be in his right to do what he did, often because of a very stressful situation. Olav tried to convince people that his actions resulted from his dedication to save Thule from going bankrupt and help the company complete the rig that would secure them good income in the future. He did what he did for Thule's best interest. At the same time, he argues that he was entitled to carry out the money transfers to receive funds for the work he had done for the company already. Besides, it was natural that he had an account in a tax haven when he ran business through another company there.

Another neutralization technique applied by Olav was claiming legal mistake. What actions he completed should not receive the label illegal. The offender argues that the law is wrong, and what the person did should receive a negative characteristic from nobody. One may therefore break the law since the law is unreasonable. The offender may argue that lawmakers sometimes criminalize behaviors and sometimes decriminalize the same behaviors more or less randomly over time (Haines, 2014). For example, money involved in bribing people were treated as legal expenses in accounting some decades ago, while corruption today is considered a misconduct and therefore criminalized. Similar to the speed limit that car drivers on the street often consider wrong, white-collar offenders consider economic laws reflecting lack of business and industry insights.

In his explanation in court, Olav said the money had a business purpose, and that the transfers were indeed necessary to rescue the company. In the period before illegal money transfers, the company was close to bankruptcy, and the situation was difficult. His explanation gives the impression of transfers being legitimate, so the money transfers were an attempt to save the company, which he himself might have believed.

Olav describes himself as a victim after the public prosecutor charged him with financial crime. This is a third neutralization technique where the offender perceives being a victim of an incident. Others have ruined the offender's life. The incident leads to police investigation, prosecution, and a possible prison sentence. The media prints pictures of the offender on the front page, and public authorities retrieve gains from crime away from the offender. Previous colleagues and friends have left, and so has the family. The offender thus perceives being a loser and made victim of those who reacted to his crime after disclosure. On YouTube, Olav posted a video of himself entitled "justice murder".

Olav claims injustice, and that the prosecuting authority treated him unfairly. This is his fourth neutralization technique where he condemns his condemners. The offender tries to accuse his or her critics of questionable motives for criticizing him. According to this technique of condemning the condemners, one neutralizes one's own guilt feeling by deflecting moral condemnation onto those ridiculing the misbehavior by pointing out that they engage in similar disapproved behavior. In addition, the offender condemns procedures of the criminal justice system, especially police investigation with interrogation, as well as media coverage of his case. Olav claims that the court convicted him even when he is innocent, and that the prosecuting authority treated him unfairly.

Olav condemns investigators and prosecutors as well as the Norwegian state and the judicial system in general. He claims that they did not allow him sufficient insight into the evidence against him. He claims that the prosecution deliberately has failed to use important evidence that would prove that he is completely innocent of financial crime. Police investigators deliberately and systematically have avoided investigating tracks that could clean his name. His attempts to get the police to investigate circumstances that speak to his advantage, law enforcement personnel consistently rejected to look into.

Olav seems to have suffered from narcissistic identification with Thule Drilling. The offender sees little or no difference between self and the business. Then company money is personal money that can be spent whatever way the narcissist prefers (Galvin et al., 2015). A pervasive pattern of grandiosity, need for admiration, and empathy deficits typifies narcissism. While grandiosity and admiration belong to the motivational dimension of convenience theory, empathy deficits belong to the willingness dimension of convenience theory where the offender possesses a sense of entitlement. The offender shows unreasonable expectations to receive and obtain preferential treatments (Zvi and Elaad, 2018). Olav was an entrepreneur who played a key role in establishing Thule Drilling, and he continued to be a key person in the business. His self-confidence and way of approaching opportunities indicate that he has narcissistic features. Writing an autobiography might result from a tendency of narcissism for a convicted white-collar offender.

Olav seems to have moved down the slippery slope. The slippery slope perspective suggests that a person can slide over time from legal to illegal activities without really noticing. The small infractions can lead to the larger ones. An organization that overlooks the small infractions of its employees creates a culture of acceptance that may lead to its own demise (Welsh et al., 2014). Arjoon (2008: 78) explains slippery slope in the following way:

> As commonsense experience tells us, it is the small infractions that can lead to the larger ones. An organization that overlooks the small infractions of

its employees creates a culture of acceptance that may lead to its own demise. This phenomenon is captured by the metaphor of the slippery slope. Many unethical acts occur without the conscience awareness of the person who engaged in the misconduct. Specifically, unethical behavior is most likely to follow the path of a slippery slope, defined as a gradual decline in which no one event makes one aware that he or she is acting unethically. The majority of unethical behaviors are unintentional and ordinary, thus affecting everyone and providing support for unethical behavior when people unconsciously lower the bar over time through small changes in their ethical behavior.

Welsh et al. (2014) argue that many recent scandals seem to result from a slippery slope in which a series of small infractions gradually increase over time. Committing small indiscretions over time may gradually lead people to complete larger unethical acts that they otherwise would have judged to be impermissible. In the case of Olav, it started with convenient solutions to initiate measures to save Thule from financial problems and other difficulties, then gradually to enrich himself at Thule's expense. Olav more and more slipped into financial crime. He slipped through corporate crime to occupational crime.

It seems that Olav suffered from lack of self-control. He was attracted to convenient solutions to problems, where violations of law were less important. For example, he applied inappropriate accounting and failed payments of public fees in his own firm Juno Finance.

Lack of self-control is a frequent explanation for executive deviance and crime in general (Gottfredson and Hirschi, 1990). While many might be tempted, only those lacking self-control will actually do it. Self-regulation monitors self-control, where self-regulation represents a process of using self-regulatory resources to control undesirable impulses and override subsequent behavioral responses. As argued by Mawritz et al. (2017), individuals possess varying and limited self-regulatory resources that inhibit responses that may arise from physiological processes, habit, learning, or the strain of the situation. When resources that regulate self-control are depleted, individuals struggle to constrain their urges and engage in behavior almost unwittingly, using quick, thoughtless responses. They move down the slippery slope from the right side of the law to the wrong side of the law (Arjoon, 2008). Self-control processes deplete self-regulatory resources and impair one's ability to control subsequent inappropriate responses.

The grand self-deception

Already on the cover of his book entitled "The Grand Self-Deception", Olav (2015) formulates a number of rhetoric and provocative questions:

> What if we no longer accept the government's actions that would be deemed morally reprehensible and/or criminal if they were to be done by you and

me? What if we showed determination and courage and pushed back against a system that has made us morally impotent? We have to take our freedom back because freedom is unilaterally positive in all interpersonal relationships. Freedom will create a better, more sustainable, and happier society. If we don't do something fundamentally different before it's too late, it will be a betrayal to future generations.

Olav labels his book a libertarian manifesto against the deep state.

Rather than admitting that he himself might have suffered from self-deception, Olav suggests that society at large suffers from self-deception. Self-deception is the action or practice of allowing oneself to believe that a false or unvalidated feeling, idea, or situation is true. Self-deception originates from the evolutionary need to deceive, which provides survival and reproductive benefits to those who comply with it (Chan and Gibbs, 2020).

Olav as a suspect at this stage takes on a role of not only defending himself, but also defending society. Benson (2013) finds that narcissistic self-confidence when coupled with drive, ambitiousness, and insensitivity to others may enable some people successfully to undertake risky business endeavors that more prudent and introspective individuals would never attempt. An ambitious and convenient mindset may also permit if not drive these individuals in the single-minded pursuit of their goals to engage in financial crime.

Olav (2015: 21) portrays himself as a victim of police arrest:

> Early in the morning of 15 June 2011, both my family and I were brutally dragged out of our beds in our home by Økokrim (Norway's Criminal Police). With my wife and loved ones as incredulous spectators, I was pushed and dragged out of my house by two big men towards a waiting police car, which subsequently drove me down to the police headquarters in Oslo for questioning. Afterwards, I was jailed and thrown into a stripped down isolation cell where I was held for two days longer than what is permitted in the torture clause of the European Convention of Human Rights. Later on, the prosecution authority and the judge lied in court about these events ever having taken place.

Very different from other autobiographies, such as Belfort (2008), Bogen (2008), Kerik (2015) and Middelhoff (2017), Olav (2015) does not really tell his own story. Rather, he focuses on institutional collapse in society of which he has become a victim. It is all about denying the guilty mind in various ways (Benson, 1985).

Punishment inconvenience dynamics

The theory of convenience suggests that white-collar offenders find it convenient to use illegitimate gain to explore possibilities and avoid threats. Furthermore, there is convenient access to resources to commit and financial crime, and offenders can conveniently justify crime and neutralize guilt feelings. This chapter section extends the concept of convenience into the concept of inconvenience when white-collar offenders face detection, investigation, conviction, and incarceration. The extent of inconvenience is dependent on a number of issues such as public opinion about seriousness of wrongdoing, fraud examinations versus police investigations, symbolic defense by attorneys, and the special sensitivity hypothesis versus the special resilience hypothesis. While facing the criminal justice system is never convenient for the offender, the extent of inconvenience might limit itself and partly find compensation by a number of circumstances on the way from crime detection to release from prison.

The theory of convenience for white-collar crime is concerned with financial possibilities and threats, organizational opportunity to commit and conceal financial crime, as well as personal willingness for deviant behavior (Braaten and Vaughn, 2019; Chan and Gibbs, 2020; Hansen, 2020). White-collar offenders commit financial crime in the course of their occupations (Craig, 2019; Craig and Piquero, 2016; Jordanoska, 2018; Onna and Denkers, 2019). Convenience theory suggests that the financial motive in white-collar crime is to explore possibilities and avoid threats; the organizational opportunity is to commit as well as conceal crime;, while the willingness is deviant behavior by justification and neutralization. The theory of convenience is an integrated and deductive theory based on a synthesis of individual-level, organization-level and nation-level perspectives (Chan and Gibbs, 2020).

Research shows that very few white-collar offenders are detected (Andresen and Button, 2019; Gottschalk and Gunnesdal, 2018; Huff et al., 2010; Wall-Parker, 2020). Among those few detected, convenience does not necessarily disappear completely when a white-collar offender faces detection, investigation, prosecution, conviction, and incarceration – at least not in the form of relative convenience or relative inconvenience compared to other criminals. While being investigated, prosecuted, convicted, and incarcerated is not particularly convenient, it might nevertheless not be particularly inconvenient either. It depends on public opinion about seriousness and other factors. Inconvenience is the state or fact of being troublesome or difficult with regard to one's personal requirements and comfort. Inconvenience is simply the opposite of convenience.

This section extends the idea of convenience in white-collar crime into the concept of inconvenience during investigation, prosecution, conviction, and incarceration. Just as convenience was a core concept when it was first introduced to white-collar criminology, inconvenience is another core concept of importance to white-collar criminology.

Crime seriousness

When detection of crime occurs, an issue of public opinion about seriousness emerges. Cullen et al. (2020) studied public opinion about white-collar crime, and they found public willingness to punish white-collar offenders. However, they found that public opinion about inflicting punishment on white-collar criminals varies depending on clarity of culpability, typical harm, violation of trust, and need to show equity. If a detected offender is successful in disclaiming responsibility for crime by not being culpable, then the preference for punitive action declines. The offender can claim one or more of the conditions of responsible agency did not occur. Using this technique, the offender rationalizes that the action in question is beyond his or her control. The offender might present himself or herself as a billiard ball, helplessly propelled through different situations (Craig and Piquero, 2017; Engdahl, 2015; Pratt and Cullen, 2005; Sutherland, 1983; Sykes and Matza, 1957).

It there is no evidence of typical harm – or the offender was successful in hiding evidence of typical harm – then public desire for punitive action might be low. People consider economic harm serious compared to physical harm. When people perceive no damage, harm or victim from the offender's action, then people consider the offense less serious (Michel, 2016). The offense is thus not very serious because there is no emerging evidence of any party suffering directly or visibly because of it (Jordanoska, 2018; Kaptein and Helvoort, 2019; Schoultz and Flyghed, 2019; Siponen and Vance, 2010).

Violation of trust is the third factor of seriousness identified by Cullen et al. (2020: 223), "often compounded by purposeful deception and concealment of injury". Public opinion about inflicting punishment on white-collar criminals depends thus on the extent of violation of trust. Dearden (2016) argues that violation of trust is at the core of white-collar crime. Trust implies that vulnerability seems accepted based upon positive expectations of the motives and actions of another. By successfully playing the blame game, the offender will attribute blame for wrongdoing to someone else (Eberly et al., 2011; Keaveney, 2008; Lee and Robinson, 2000; Sonnier et al., 2015), thereby reducing the perceived violation of trust.

Need to show equity is the fourth and final factor by Cullen et al. (2020: 223):

> The norm of equity demands that white-collar offenders, especially those who enjoy a privileged life, should be treated as harshly as poor, minority criminals are treated. We argue that in comparison to Americans in the 1940s and 1950s, the norm of equity is strong among today's citizenry and will fuel punitiveness when called into play.

However, the norm of equity can change in consequence by the special sensitivity hypothesis suggested for white-collar offenders. The special sensitivity hypothesis implies a relatively tougher life for white-collar offenders when investigated, prosecuted, convicted, and incarcerated (Dhami, 2007; Logan, 2015; Stadler et al., 2013). Therefore, the equity perspective can imply that treatment of elite level criminals should not be as harsh as treatment of street level criminals. White-collar offenders and their attorneys can stress the special sensitivity hypothesis and deny the special resilience hypothesis, which suggests that white-collar offenders are able to adapt to prison life more successfully than other inmates are (Logan et al., 2019). Logan and Olma (2020) label the common belief in the special sensitivity hypothesis a myth different from empirical reality:

> Little is known about the prison experiences of white-collar offenders, despite the fact that the number of individuals incarcerated for white-collar crimes

in the United States has precipitously increased over the past three decades. Indeed, much of what is considered "common knowledge" about incarcerated white-collar offenders is influenced by stereotypes about who they are as people before entering the correctional system. By virtue of their socioeconomic status, white-collar offenders are thought to be particularly susceptible to negative outcomes upon entering the prison system – a belief that has influenced judicial decisions with respect to the sentences they mete out. Although empirical research in this area is scant, there is a growing body of evidence to suggest that this view of white-collar inmates is misguided.

By symbolic defense, rather than substance defense, white-collar attorneys use the media and other channels to present the client as a victim rather than as a potential offender. The purpose of symbolic defense is to communicate information and legal opinions by means of symbols. Examples of attorney opinions are concerns about unacceptable delays in police investigations, low-quality detective work, or other issues related to police and prosecution work. Complaining about delays in police investigations is not substance defense, as the complaint is not expressing a meaning about the crime and possible punishment. Complaining is symbolic defense, where the objective is to mobilize sympathy for the white-collar client. The ambition of a clever white-collar attorney is to stop the public shaming of the client in the media, and to portray the client as a victim for whom everyone should have sympathy.

The less serious an offender is able to make his or her offense in the public domain, the less willingness to punish the offender. An offender can create dynamics reducing punishment inconvenience by causing cloudiness of culpability, by blurring harm, by restoring trust, and by claiming sensitivity. In addition, an offender can question the legitimacy of the police and the criminal justice system in general, and create doubts about objectivity, integrity, accountability, competence, and capacity in police investigations (Tankebe, 2019).

Crime investigation

White-collar crime investigation is the reconstruction of past events and sequences of events without drawing legal conclusions. The objective is to collect information and develop knowledge to answer questions regarding what happened, how it happened, when it happened, who did what to make it happen or not happen, and why it happened (Brooks and Button, 2011; Button, Frimpong et al., 2007; Button, Johnston et al., 2007; Nilsen et al., 2018). Investigators are interested in information regarding people, locations, activities, timing, capabilities, motives, opportunities, and behaviors. Investigators explore a number of information sources such as witnesses, suspects, whistleblowers, documents, and databases.

When a white-collar offender is detected, the organization may first attempt to initiate an internal investigation without the involvement of law enforcement agencies such as the police (Brooks et al., 2009; Button and Gee, 2013; Fitzgibbon and Le, 2018). There is a growing business of local law firms and global auditing firms, which conduct fraud examination for their clients (Schneider,

2006; Williams, 2005a, 2005b, 2014). Internal investigation is more convenient than police investigation (Brooks and Button, 2011; Button, 2019; Button, Frimpong et al., 2007; Button, Johnston et al., 2007; Nilsen et al., 2018), as the organization can control the mandate and thus the direction of the investigation (Gottschalk and Tcherni-Buzzeo, 2017), as well as avoid public attention (Meerts, 2019: 5):

> Organizations are disinclined to report to law enforcement agencies as a result of, first, a low level of trust in the capabilities and expertise of law enforcement agencies and, second, expected negative effects of a report to the authorities (e.g., reputational damage or loss of productivity).

Surprisingly often, fraud examiners conclude in their investigation reports with wrongdoings, but no crime, even though they are not supposed to draw legal conclusions (Button et al., 2018). Frequently, law enforcement agencies seem happy with such private conclusions by staying away from the case. Examples include Lehman Brothers in the United States (Jenner Block, 2010), NNPC in Nigeria (PwC, 2015), Danske Bank in Denmark (Bruun Hjejle, 2018), Nordea in Sweden (Mannheimer Swartling, 2016), and Telenor in Norway (Deloitte, 2016). The inconvenience of detection becomes in this way partly compensated by the convenience of controlling the investigation and often keeping the report of investigation secret (Gottschalk and Tcherni-Buzzeo, 2017).

In cases where law enforcement agencies take on the matter and conduct investigations, white-collar suspects and their organizations quickly hire skilled defense lawyers to protect their interests. A white-collar defense lawyer does not limit efforts to substance defense, using interpretations of laws and previous court rulings to argue that the client has done nothing that justifies police investigation or court proceedings. Defense lawyers in white-collar crime cases tend to take charge of information control at an early stage. Instead of being at the receiving end of documents from the police or prosecution, the attorney is in a position where the flow of information can be monitored.

In addition to substance defense and information control, white-collar attorneys also apply symbolic defense strategies. A symbol is an object or phrase that represents an idea, belief, or action. The purpose of symbolic defense is to communicate information and legal opinions by means of symbols. The objective might be to portray the client as a victim rather than as an offender. For example, the client might be a victim of massive media coverage (Burns and Meitl, 2020: 288):

> White-collar defense attorneys often suggest that the publicity surrounding the alleged crime is already enough punishment for a formally upstanding member of the business community.

The less obvious evidence police investigators are able to collect, the more reluctant they are to suggest prosecution. Based on substance defense, information control, and symbolic defense, white-collar lawyers can succeed in helping the client avoid the inconvenience of prosecution. In fact, inconvenience can turn into a kind of convenience, as failing investigations in many jurisdictions make suspects entitled to claim financial recovery and compensation from the state.

Criminal prosecution

As argued by Burns and Meitl (2020: 284), prosecutors face difficult dilemmas in the decision of who to charge with what kinds of crime:

> In white-collar cases, this decision is often complicated by a variety of factors. Because white-collar crimes often require that the prosecutor prove the specific intent of the defendant (that is, that the defendant knew what they were doing was corrupt of illegal at the time they performed the alleged criminal act), the prosecutor must carefully examine the actions of a variety of individuals in each white-collar context.

What Podgor (2007) found to be the most interesting aspect of Sutherland's (1983) work is that a scholar needed to proclaim that crime committed by a member of the upper socioeconomic class was in fact crime that should be prosecuted. When prosecuted in court, white-collar defendants have defense lawyers who tend to be specialists in financial crime, while prosecutors and judges tend to be generalists.

In their classic book on local prosecutors at work in combating white-collar crime, Benson and Cullen (1998) discuss knowledge and discretionary decision making by legal actors as a central and unavoidable component of the law in action. Prosecutors have authority to attain broad legislative goals. The process of rule into action is dependent upon legal actors who interpret and make choices. In this perspective, prosecutors are powerful actors in criminal justice.

However, white-collar crime often represents a prosecutorial problem. Benson and Cullen (1998: 25) argue that most illegal white-collar conduct does not result in criminal prosecution:

> Scholars differ over why this is so. One school of thought stresses the political and economic power of corporations; the other emphasizes the practical difficulties of applying the criminal law to corporate offenders. These views represent recurrent themes in research on corporate crime but are not necessarily mutually exclusive. Undoubtedly, both have merit.

Galvin and Simpson (2020: 391) stress the importance of collecting reliable evidence:

> Due to the complexity, difficulty of gathering evidence, and the relative rarity of these cases, it seems probable that white-collar cases should be more likely to result in favorable plea agreements.

Since plea bargain in the United States is "largely unknown to German (and continental) system of criminal law" (Walburg, 2020: 341), prosecutors in continental Europe tend to be reluctant to prosecute white-collar cases lacking complete and convincing evidence. As argued by Galvin and Simpson (2020), a number of factors can influence prosecutorial perceptions of case strength, such as evidentiary load, victim behavior, and offender characteristics.

The less satisfying such factors are to the prosecution, the more reluctant they are to bring a case to the court. Again, based on substance defense, information control, and symbolic defense, white-collar lawyers can succeed in helping the client avoid the inconvenience of court hearings. Again, based on dynamic developments, inconvenience can turn into a kind of convenience, where terminated prosecution in many jurisdictions make potential defendants entitled to claim financial recovery and compensation from public authorities in the country.

Criminal proceedings

While there are differences between court systems throughout the world, legal courts in democratic societies have some common characteristics. A court is an institution for finding solutions and making decisions in conflicts (Christensen and Szmer, 2012). In a small nation such as Norway, the district court is the basic level in the judiciary system for both criminal and civil law. Court of appeal is the second level in the system, where district court decisions can be overruled. The third and final level is the Supreme Court in the capital Oslo. While court proceedings for traditional street crime tend to last for some days, court proceedings for white-collar crime tend to last for some months.

One of the reasons for this tremendous difference is the difference in challenge for the prosecution. While street crime cases are concerned with evidence linking the crime to the defendant, white-collar crime cases are concerned with evidence of the crime itself. At the investigation stage, police detectives were looking for offenders in street crime cases, while they were looking for offenses in white-collar crime cases.

An advantage of the months-long proceedings for white-collar defendants is the knowledge rivalry that takes place in court. The rule is that if there is any reasonable doubt, the court has to dismiss the case. Defense attorneys as clever knowledge workers thus compete with prosecutors about the truth to create doubt about guilt (Burns and Meitl, 2020).

If white-collar defendants are convicted in court, the sentencing tends to be more lenient compared to street crime defendants. An explanation for differential treatment is the status advantage for white-collar criminals, including the extent of technical and vocational training. In the United States, "due to the complexity, difficulty of gathering evidence, and the relative rarity of these cases, it seems probable that white-collar cases should be more likely to result in favorable plea agreements" (Galvin and Simpson, 2020: 391).

A comparison in Norway between social security fraud and white-collar fraud indicates significant differential treatment. While social security fraudsters go to jail for a year for fraud of less than the equivalent of US $100,000, white-collar fraudsters receive the same jail sentence for fraud of more than US $1 million (Gottschalk and Gunnesdal, 2018). On average, convicted white-collar offenders have to go to jail for two years and two months, where the average amount of money involved in the financial scam is the equivalent of US $5 million.

The more doubt that occurs during criminal proceedings, the less likely the defendant is facing conviction. The inconvenience of being a defendant for weeks or month might turn into a kind of convenience, as a case dismissal represents a verdict of innocence where the innocent is entitled to claim financial recovery and compensation from the state, in addition to a role of complaining about the criminal justice system privately and in the public.

Criminal incarceration

If convicted to jail or prison, white-collar offenders end up in low-security institutions. Minimum-security institutions have dormitory housing, a relatively low staff-to-inmate ratio, and limited or no perimeter fencing. These institutions in Norway have regular hotel standard with units for each inmate with individual bathrooms. A white-collar offender who received a conviction of nine years in prison for serious bank fraud served his sentence in Hassel prison in Norway. He was into bike riding, and he organized a cycling team among inmates. He was excited about the Tour de France bike ride, and suggested to team members to bike from Norway to France. A team of ten Hassel inmates got on their bikes and reached the border between Norway and Sweden. Norwegian police stopped them at the border, as someone had found out that inmates could not to leave the country while in prison. They returned to Hassel prison. Some years later, when the prison had released them all, the cycling team made the bike ride from Hassel in Norway to Paris in France (Røkeberg, 2012).

Hunter (2020) addressed the correctional experiences of white-collar offenders, where the underlying assumption is that white-collar offenders do experience punishment differently to their non-white-collar criminal peers. Overall, he found that white-collar offenders adjust more easily to prison. This is in line with Dhami (2007), who found that white-collar inmates adjusted to prison life because they felt that their high status and the assumption that they had significant financial resources gave them respect from other prisoners and from prison staff. White-collar offenders tended to find new friends more conveniently, and they were able to sleep all night, while most other inmates had trouble sleeping and making friends in prison (Stadler et al., 2013).

As mentioned earlier, white-collar offenders and their attorneys can stress the special sensitivity hypothesis and deny the special resilience hypothesis, which suggests that white-collar offenders are able to adapt to prison life more successfully than other inmates are. However, recent research suggests that there is more support for the special resilience hypothesis than the special sensitivity hypothesis (Logan et al., 2019). The theory of convenience provides a basis for the special resilience hypothesis, because white-collar offenders tend to have a strong convenience orientation to avoid pain and waste of energy.

After release from jail or prison, "the experience of punishment is likely to last beyond any formal sentence" (Hunter, 2020: 304):

> As with most offenders, white-collar offenders are likely to find themselves in a position of needing to reestablish their lives once punishment has ended. The specifics of this are likely to differ, but we might broadly suggest that this involves some financial independence and acceptance back into the wider community. Many white-collar offenders are pessimistic about their ability to manage this, however, fearing that a conviction is too much of an obstacle to allow them to successfully resettle.

Based on anecdotal evidence from Norway, it seems that reestablishing lives is an issue in several dimensions and depending on several circumstances. Reestablishing professional life seems more challenging than reestablishing private life with family. The circumstance of being a capitalist owning the company or being self-employed as a consultant makes it less troublesome getting back to work.

Conclusion

Crime is a wrongful act that should be punished, independent of whether or not there is a legal statute. Crime is then wrongdoing that requires punishment, while law is statutory principles, which may or may not cover specific wrongdoing (Friedrichs, 2020). This definition is at the core of white-collar crime seriousness as discussed in this section. Many cases of white-collar wrongdoing are not obvious crime in the sense of law violations. Only evidence-based violations of the law are relevant the criminal justice system. Public opinions about seriousness versus the punishment of white-collar offenders might be a matter of whether or not violation of law has occurred.

To make it even more complicated, Benson and Simpson (2018: 49) distinguish between crime and criminality:

> They are conceptually distinct. A crime is an event, something that happens at a particular time and place. Criminality, on the other hand, is a characteristic of a person or an organization. It refers to the likelihood that a person or entity will participate in a criminal act. Most criminological theories focus on criminality, but it is possible to think theoretically about crimes themselves as objects of study separate from criminals.

Hirschi (1989: 47) makes the same distinction by claiming that criminality "refers to stable differences across individuals in the propensity to commit criminal or theoretically equivalent acts". The text in this book makes no such distinction. When the text in this book repeatedly mentions the term crime, the meaning is always a violation of the criminal law as an action by a person.

Punishing white-collar offenders becomes also troublesome because the facts are often missing, misleading or incomplete. This kind of uncertainty creates many opportunities for suspects and their helpers to create ambiguity concerning punishment. The uncertain and thus almost random outcome develops from detection via investigation, prosecution, and conviction to possible incarceration. The result of all these blurring lines between guilt and innocence reduces the inconvenience for white-collar offenders as discussed in this section.

References

Adler, P.S. and Kwon, S.W. (2002). Social capital: Prospects for a new concept, *Academy of Management Review*, 27 (1), 17–40.

Aguilera, R.V. and Vadera, A.K. (2008). The dark side of authority: Antecedents, mechanisms, and outcomes of organizational corruption, *Journal of Business Ethics*, 77, 431–449.

Andresen, M.S. and Button, M. (2019). The profile and detection of bribery in Norway and England & Wales: A comparative study, *European Journal of Criminology*, 16 (1), 18–40.

Arjoon, S. (2008). Slippery when wet: The real risk in business, *Journal of Markets & Morality*, Spring, 11 (1), 77–91.

BDO (2014). *Gransking av Stiftelsen Betanien i Bergen (Examination of the Foundation Betanien in Bergen) – Anonymisert og revidert sammendrag (Anonymised and Revised Summary)*, auditing firm BDO, Oslo, Norway.

Belfort, J. (2008). *The Wolf of Wall Street: How Money Destroyed a Wall Street Superman*, London, UK: Hodder & Stoughton.

Benartzi, S., Beshears, J., Milkman, K.L., Sunstein, C.R., Thaler, R.H., Shankar, M., Tucker-Ray, W., Congdon, W.J. and Galing, S. (2017). Should governments invest more in nudging? *Psychological Science*, 28 (8), 1041–1055.

Benson, M.L. (1985). Denying the guilty mind: Accounting for involvement in a white-collar crime, *Criminology*, 23 (4), 583–607.

Benson, M.L. (2013). Editor's introduction – White-collar crime: Bringing the offender back in, *Journal of Contemporary Criminal Justice*, 29 (3), 324–330.

Benson, M.L. and Chio, H.L. (2020). Who commits occupational crimes, in: Rorie, M. (editor), *The Handbook of White-Collar Crime*, Hoboken, NJ: John Wiley & Sons, chapter 7, pages 97–112.

Benson, M.L. and Cullen, F.T. (1998). *Combating Corporate Crime: Local Prosecutors at Work*, Boston, MA: Northeastern University Press.

Benson, M.L. and Simpson, S.S. (2018). *White-Collar Crime: An Opportunity Perspective*, 3rd edition, New York, NY: Routledge.

Bjørkelo, B., Einarsen, S., Nielsen, M.B. and Matthiesen, S.B. (2011). Silence is golden? Characteristics and experiences of self-reported whistleblowers, *European Journal of Work and Organizational Psychology*, 20 (2), 206–238.

Bjørklund, I. (2018). Må betale over 137 mill i erstatning (Must pay over 137 million in compensation), daily Norwegian business newspaper *Dagens Næringsliv*, www.dn.no, published January 19.

Bogen, T. (2008). *Hvor var du, historien om mitt liv (Where Were You, the Story of My Life)*, Oslo, Norway: Schibsted Publishing.

Borgarting (2011). Case number LB-2009-48300, *Borgarting lagmannsrett (Borgarting Court of Appeals)*, Oslo, Norway, March 18.

Braaten, C.N. and Vaughn, M.S. (2019). Convenience theory of cryptocurrency crime: A content analysis of U.S. federal court decisions, *Deviant Behavior*, published online, https://doi.org/10.1080/01639625.2019.1706706.

Brooks, G. and Button, M. (2011). The police and fraud investigation and the case for a nationalized solution in the United Kingdom, *The Police Journal*, 84, 305–319.

Brooks, G., Button, M. and Frimpong, K. (2009). Policing fraud in the private sector: A survey of the FTSE 100 companies in the UK, *International Journal of Police Science and Management*, 11 (4), 493–504.

Brown, J.O., Hays, J. and Stuebs, M.T. (2016). Modeling accountant whistleblowing intentions: Applying the theory of planned behavior and the fraud triangle, *Accounting and the Public Interest*, 16 (1), 28–56.

Bruun Hjejle (2018). *Report on the Non-Resident Portfolio at Danske Bank's Estonian Branch*, law firm Bruun Hjejle, https://danskebank.com/-/media/danske-bank-com/file-cloud/2018/9/report-on-the-non-resident-portfolio-at-danske-banks-estonian-branch.pdf, published September 19, downloaded September 25.

Bundy, J. and Pfarrer, M.D. (2015). A burden of responsibility: The role of social approval at the onset of a crisis, *Academy of Management Review*, 40 (3), 345–369.

Burns, R.G. and Meitl, M.B. (2020). Prosecution, defense, and sentencing of white-collar crime, in: Rorie, M.L. (editor), *The Handbook of White-Collar Crime*, Hoboken, NJ: Wiley & Sons, chapter 18, pages 279–296.

Bussmann, K.D., Niemeczek, A. and Vockrodt, M. (2018). Company culture and prevention of corruption in Germany, China and Russia, *European Journal of Criminology*, 15 (3), 255–277.

Button, M. (2019). The "new" private security industry, the private policing of cyberspace and the regulatory questions, *Journal of Contemporary Criminal Justice*, published online https://doi.org/10.1177/1043986219890194.

Button, M. and Gee, J. (2013). *Countering Fraud for Competitive Advantage: The Professional Approach to Reducing the Last Great Hidden Cost*, Chichester, UK: John Wiley & Sons.

Button, M., Frimpong, K., Smith, G. and Johnston, L. (2007). Professionalizing counter fraud specialists in the UK: Assessing progress and recommendations for reform, *Crime Prevention and Community Safety*, 9, 92–101.

Button, M., Johnston, L., Frimpong, K. and Smith, G. (2007). New directions in policing fraud: The emergence of the counter fraud specialists in the United Kingdom, *International Journal of the Sociology of Law*, 35, 192–208.

Button, M., Shepherd, D. and Blackbourn, D. (2018). "The iceberg beneath the sea", fraudsters and their punishment through non-criminal justice in the "fraud justice network" in England and Wales, *International Journal of Law, Crime and Justice*, 53, 56–66.

Chan, F. and Gibbs, C. (2020). Integrated theories of white-collar and corporate crime, in: Rorie, M.L. (editor), *The Handbook of White-Collar Crime*, Hoboken, NJ: Wiley & Sons, chapter 13, pages 191–208.

Christensen, R.K. and Szmer, J. (2012). Examining the efficiency of the U.S. courts of appeals: Pathologies and prescriptions, *International Review of Law and Economics*, 32, 30–37.

Cleff, T., Naderer, G. and Volkert, J. (2013). Motives behind white-collar crime: Results of a quantitative study in Germany, *Society and Business Review*, 8 (2), 145–159.

Corcoran, K.E., Pettinicchio, D. and Robins, B. (2012). Religion and the acceptability of white-colar crime: A cross-national analysis, *Journal of the Scientific Study of Religion*, 51 (3), 542–567.

Craig, J.M. (2019). Extending situational action theory to white-collar crime, *Deviant Behavior*, 40 (2), 171–186.

Craig, J.M. and Piquero, N.L. (2016). The effects of low self-control and desire-for-control on white-collar offending: A replication, *Deviant Behavior*, 37 (11), 1308–1324.

Craig, J.M. and Piquero, N.L. (2017). Sensational offending: An application of sensation seeking to white-collar and conventional crimes, *Crime & Delinquency*, 63 (11), 1363–1382.

Cullen, F.T., Chouhy, C. and Jonson, C.L. (2020). Public opinion about white-collar crime, in: Rorie, M.L. (editor), *The Handbook of White-Collar Crime*, Hoboken, NJ: Wiley & Sons, chapter 14, pages 211–228.

Dearden, T.E. (2016). Trust: The unwritten cost of white-collar crime, *Journal of Financial Crime*, 23 (1), 87–101.

Dearden, T.E. (2017). An assessment of adults' views on white-collar crime, *Journal of Financial Crime*, 24 (2), 309–321.

Dearden, T.E. (2019). How modern psychology can help us understand white-collar criminals, *Journal of Financial Crime*, 26 (1), 61–73.

Deloitte (2016). *Review Ownership VimpelCom*, www.telenor.com/wp-content/uploads/2016/04/Deloitte-Report_Telenor_290416_FINAL.pdf, downloaded October 21, 2018.

Deloitte (2017). *Granskning – Byggesaksavdelingen – Drammen kommune (Investigation – Construction Case Department – Drammen Municipality)*, auditing firm Deloitte, Oslo, Norway, January 24.

Dhami, M.K. (2007). White-collar prisoners' perceptions of audience reaction, *Deviant Behavior*, 28, 57–77.

Distriktsrevisjonen (2007). *Rapport etter granskingsoppdrag fra styrene (Report after Investigation Assignment from the Boards)*, local auditing firm Nedre Romerike Distriktsrevisjon, Lillestrøm, Norway, May 30.

Dodge, M. (2020). Who commits corporate crime? in: Rorie, M. (editor), *The Handbook of White-Collar Crime*, Hoboken, NJ: John Wiley & Sons, chapter 8, pages 113–126.

Drammen tingrett (2015). Dom avsagt 02.02.2015 i Drammen tingrett med saksnummer 15-002674ENE-DRAM (Sentence announced on February 2, 2015 in Drammen district court with case number 15-002674ENE-DRAM), *Drammen tingrett (Drammen District Court)*, Drammen, Norway.

Eberly, M.B., Holley, E.C., Johnson, M.D. and Mitchell, T.R. (2011). Beyond internal and external: A dyadic theory of relational attributions, *Academy of Management Review*, 36 (4), 731–753.

Engdahl, O. (2015). White-collar crime and first-time adult-onset offending: Explorations in the concept of negative life events as turning points, *International Journal of Law, Crime and Justice*, 43 (1), 1–16.

Fitzgibbon, W. and Lea, J. (2018). Privatization and coercion: The question of legitimacy, *Theoretical Criminology*, 22 (4), 545–562.

Fleckenstein, M.P. and Bowes, J.C. (2002). When trust is betrayed: Religious institutions and white collar crime, *Journal of Business Ethics*, 23 (1), 111–115.

Folkvord, E. (2015). Unibuss: De som slapp unna (Unibuss: Those who escaped), daily Norwegian newspaper *Dagsavisen*, www.dagsavisen.no, published December 1.

Forti, G. and Visconti, A. (2020). From economic crime to corporate violence: The multifaceted harms of corporate crime, in: Rorie, M.L. (editor), *The Handbook of White-Collar Crime*, Hoboken, NJ: John Wiley & Sons, chapter 5, pages 64–80.

Friedrichs, D.O. (2020). White collar crime: Definitional debates and the case for a typological approach, in: Rorie, M. (editor), *The Handbook of White-Collar Crime*, Hoboken, NJ: John Wiley & Sons, chapter 2, pages 16–31.

Fritt ord (2015). *Freedom of Expression Foundation Prize for 2015 Awarded to Robin Schaefer and Jan Erik Skog*, www.frittord.no, published May 7.

Galvin, B.M., Lange, D. and Ashforth, B.E. (2015). Narcissistic organizational identification: Seeing oneself as central to the organization's identity, *Academy of Management Review*, 40 (2), 163–181.

Galvin, M.A. and Simpson, S.S. (2020). Prosecuting and sentencing white-collar crime in US federal courts: Revisiting the Yale findings, in: Rorie, M.L. (editor), *The Handbook of White-Collar Crime*, Hoboken, NJ: Wiley & Sons, chapter 24, pages 381–397.

Garrick, J. and Chan, A. (2017). Knowledge management and professional experience: The uneasy dynamics between tacit knowledge and performativity in organizations, *Journal of Knowledge Management*, 21 (4), 872–884.

Gedde-Dahl, S. (2011). Streng dom for malermestre (Severe sentence for painting masters), daily Norwegian newspaper *Aftenposten*, Wednesday, March 30, Økonomi (Business section), page 3.

Gjøvik tingrett (2014). Case 14-134676ENE-GJOV, *Gjøvik tingrett (Gjøvik District Court)*, Gjøvik, Norway, August 27.

Gottfredson, M.R. and Hirschi, T. (1990). *A General Theory of Crime*, Stanford, CA: Stanford University Press.

Gottschalk, P. and Gunnesdal, L. (2018). *White-Collar Crime in the Shadow Economy: Lack of Detection, Investigation, and Conviction compared to Social Security Fraud*, London, UK: Springer Publishing/Palgrave Pivot, Palgrave Macmillan.

Gottschalk, P. and Tcherni-Buzzeo, M. (2017). Reasons for gaps in crime reporting: The case of white-collar criminals investigated by private fraud examiners in Norway, *Deviant Behavior*, 38 (3), 267–281.

G-Partner (2007). *Gransking av eiendomsforvaltningen i Bærum kommune (Review of Property Management in Bærum Municipality)*, local Norwegian fraud examination firm G-Partner, February 5, Oslo, Norway.

Haines, F. (2014). Corporate fraud as misplaced confidence? Exploring ambiguity in the accuracy of accounts and the materiality of money, *Theoretical Criminology*, 18 (1), 20–37.

Hansen, L.L. (2020). Review of the book "Convenience Triangle in White-Collar Crime: Case Studies of Fraud Examinations", *ChoiceConnect*, vol. 57, no. 5, Middletown, CT: Association of College and Research Libraries.

Haugan, B. (2014). Unibuss-sjefen legger alle kortene på bordet: -Det var dumt (Unibuss chief executive puts all cards on the table: -It was foolish), web-based Norwegian newspaper *E24*, www.e24.no, published June 25.

Hestnes, M. (2017). *Hvorfor avdekket ikke revisor underslaget i Hadeland og Ringerike Bredbånd? (Why Did the Auditor Not Detect the Embezzlement at Hadeland and Ringerike Broadband?)*, Master of Science thesis, BI Norwegian Business School, Oslo, Norway.

Hirschi, T. (1989). Exploring alternatives to integrated theory, in: Messner, S.F., Krohn, M.D. and Liska, A.E. (editors), *Theoretical Integration in the Study of Deviance and Crime*, Albany, NY: State University of New York Press, chapter 2, pages 37–50.

Hoffmann, J.P. (2002). A contextual analysis of differential association, social control, and strain theories of delinquency, *Social Forces*, 81 (3), 753–785.

Huff, R., Desilets, K. and Kane, J. (2010). *The National Public Survey on White Collar Crime*, Fairmont, WV: National White Collar Crime Center, www.nw3c. org.

Hunter, B. (2020). The correctional experiences of white-collar offenders, in: Rorie, M.L. (editor), *The Handbook of White-Collar Crime*, Hoboken, NJ: Wiley & Sons, chapter 19, pages 297–313.

Jenner Block (2010). *In regard Lehman Brothers Holdings Inc. to United States Bankruptcy Court in Southern District of New York*, law firm Jenner & Block, A.R. Valukas, https://jenner.com/lehman/VOLUME%203.pdf, downloaded September 23, 2018.

Jordanoska, A. (2018). The social ecology of white-collar crime: Applying situational action theory to white-collar offending, *Deviant Behavior*, 39 (11), 1427–1449.

Joshi, K.D., Chi, L., Datta, A. and Han, S. (2010). Changing the competitive landscape: Continuous innovation through IT-enabled knowledge capabilities, *Information Systems Research*, 21 (3), 472–495.

Kaptein, M. and Helvoort, M. (2019). A model of neutralization techniques, *Deviant Behavior*, 40 (10), 1260–1285.

Keaveney, S.M. (2008). The blame game: An attribution theory approach to marketer-engineer conflict in high-technology companies, *Industrial Marketing Management*, 37, 653–663.

Keil, M., Tiwana, A., Sainsbury, R. and Sneha, S. (2010). Toward a theory of whistle-blowing intentions: A benefit-cost differential perspective, *Decision Sciences*, 41 (4), 787–812.

Kerik, B.B. (2015). *From Jailer to Jailed: My Journey from Correction and Police Commissioner to Inmate #84888-054*, New York, NY: Threshold Editions.

Kocagil, A.E. (2004). Optionality and daily dynamics of convenience yield behavior: An empirical analysis, *The Journal of Financial Research*, 27 (1), 143–158.

Kommandantvold, M. and Bjerkeseth, A.W. (2018). *Dømt for grov korrupsjon mot Drammen kommune (Convicted of Gross Corruption against Drammen Municipality)*, Norwegian public broadcasting NRK, www.nrk.no, published March 21.

Lee, F. and Robinson, R.J. (2000). An attributional analysis of social accounts: Implications of playing the blame game, *Journal of Applied Social Psychology*, 30 (9), 1853–1879.

Logan, M.W. (2015). *Coping with Imprisonment: Testing the Special Sensitivity Hypothesis for White-Collar Offenders*, A dissertation to the Graduate School of the University of Cincinnati in partial fulfillment of the requirements for the degree of Doctor of Philosophy in the Department of Criminal Justice, Cincinnati, Ohio.

Logan, M.W., Morgan, M.A., Benson, M.L. and Cullen, F.T. (2019). Coping with imprisonment: Testing the special sensitivity hypothesis for white-collar offenders, *Justice Quarterly*, 36 (2), 225–254.

Mannheimer Swartling (2016). *Report on Investigation of Nordea Private Banking in Relation to Offshore Structures*, www.nordea.com/Images/33-125429/Report-on-investigation-of-Nordea-Private-Banking-in-relation-to-offshore-structures. pdf, downloaded October 20, 2018.

Maslow, A.H. (1943). A theory of human motivation, *Psychological Review*, 50 (4), 370–396.

Mawritz, M.B., Greenbaum, R.L., Butts, M.M. and Graham, K.A. (2017). I just can't control myself: A self-regulation perspective on the abuse of deviant employees, *Academy of Management Journal*, 60 (4), 1482–1503.

Meerts, C. (2019). Corporate investigations: Beyond notions of public-private relations, *Journal of Contemporary Criminal Justice*, published online, https://doi.org/10.1177/1043986219890202.

Mesmer-Magnus, J.R. and Viswesvaran, C. (2005). Whistleblowing in an organization: An examination of correlates of whistleblowing intentions, actions, and retaliation, *Journal of Business Ethics*, 62 (3), 266–297.

Michel, C. (2016). Violent street crime versus harmful white-collar crime: A comparison of perceived seriousness and punitiveness, *Critical Criminology*, 24, 127–143.

Middelhoff, T. (2017). *Der Sturz: Die Autobiografie von Thomas Middelhoff (The Fall: The Autobiography of Thomas Middelhoff)*, Stuttgart, Germany: LangenMuller in der F.A. Herbig Verlagsbuchhandlung.

Mortensen, Y. and Grimsrud, S.A. (2016). Jan Erik varslet om grov korrupsjon på sin arbeidsplass – Nå er han med i varslerutvalget (Jan Erik blew the whistle on serious corruption at work – Now he is a member of the whistleblowing committee), union magazine *FriFagbevegelse*, www.frifagbevegelse.no, published November 11.

Mpho, B. (2017). Whistleblowing: What do contemporary ethical theories say? *Studies in Business and Economics*, 12 (1), 19–28.

Nilsen, J.A., Aaserud, T. and Filstad, C. (2018). Learning how to lead police investigations, *International Journal of Police Science and Management*, 20 (3), 185–195.

Nisar, T.M., Prabhakar, G. and Torchia, M. (2019). Whistleblowing: When do employees act to 'blow the whistle'? *Organizational Dynamics*, 48, 44–49.

NTB (2014). Unibuss-saken i kjerneområdet for korrupsjon (The Unibuss case is at the core of corruption), web-based newspaper *E24*, www.e24.no, published September 19.

NTB (2016). Unibuss-saken til Høyesterett (The Unibuss case to the Supreme Court), web-based newspaper *E24*, www.e24.no, published August 14.

Olav, H.E. (2014). *Det store selvbedraget: Hvordan statsmakt ødelegger menneskeverd og velferd (The Grand Self-Deception: How State Power Harms Human Dignity and Welfare)*, Oslo, Norway: Kolofon Publishing.

Olav, H.E. (2015). *The Grand Self-Deception: A Libertarian Manifesto Against the Deep State – The Failed Welfare-Taxation Model of Norway*, Kindle Edition, printed in Great Britain by Amazon.

Onna, J.H.R. and Denkers, A.J.M. (2019). Social bonds and white-collar crime: A two-study assessment of informal social controls in white-collar offenders, *Deviant Behavior*, 40 (10), 1206–1225.

Oslo tingrett (2015). Verdict 14-067448MED-OTIR/06, judge Bjørn Feyling, *Oslo tingrett (Oslo District Court)*, January 12.

Ouimet, G. (2010). Dynamics of narcissistic leadership in organizations, *Journal of Managerial Psychology*, 25 (7), 713–726.

Owens, E.G. and Shores, M. (2010). *Informal Networks and White Collar Crime: Evidence from the Madoff Scandal*, Social Science Research Network, www.pars.ssm.com, 54 pages.

Park, H., Bjørkelo, B. and Blenkinsopp, J. (2020). External whistleblowers' experiences of workplace bullying by superiors and colleagues, *Journal of Business Ethics*, 161, 591–601.

Petrocelli, M., Piquero, A.R. and Smith, M.R. (2003). Conflict theory and racial profiling: An empirical analysis of police traffic stop data, *Journal of Criminal Justice*, 31 (1), 1–11.

Piquero, N.L. and Benson, M.L. (2004). White collar crime and criminal careers: Specifying a trajectory of punctuated situational offending, *Journal of Contemporary Criminal Justice*, 20, 148–165.

Podgor, E.S. (2007). The challenge of white collar sentencing, *Journal of Criminal Law and Criminology*, 97 (3), 1–10.

Pontell, H.N., Black, W.K. and Geis, G. (2014). Too big to fail, too powerful to jail? On the absence of criminal prosecutions after the 2008 financial meltdown, *Crime, Law and Social Change*, 61 (1), 1–13.

Pratt, T.C. and Cullen, F.T. (2005). Assessing macro-level predictors and theories of crime: A meta-analysis, *Crime and Justice*, 32, 373–450.

PwC (2014). *Hadeland og Ringerike Bredbånd. Rapport – Gransking (Hadeland and Ringerike Broadband. Report – Investigation)*, auditing firm PwC, June 10, Oslo, Norway.

PwC (2015). *Auditor-General for the Federation. Investigative Forensic Audit into the Allegations of Unremitted Funds into the Federation Accounts by the NNPC*, engagement leader Pedro Omontuemhen, PricewaterhouseCoopers, Lagos, Nigeria, www.premiumtimesng.com/docs_download/Full%20report – 20billion%20 dollars%20missing%20oil%20money.pdf?cf=1, downloaded September 2, 2018.

Randers, J. (2019). The great challenge for system dynamics on the path forward: Implementation and real impact, *System Dynamics Review*, 35 (2), 19–24.

Rehg, M.T., Miceli, M.P., Near, J.P. and Scotter, J.R.V. (2009). Antecedents and outcomes of retaliation against whistleblowers: Gender differences and power relationships, *Organization Science*, 19 (2), 221–240.

Roberts, N., Galluch, P.S., Dinger, M. and Grover, V. (2012). Absorptive capacity and information systems research: Review, synthesis, and directions for future research, *MIS Quarterly*, 36 (2), 625–648.

Røkeberg, M.W. (2012). -Finansskandalen reddet livet mitt (-The finance scandal saved my life), Norwegian public broadcasting *NRK*, www.nrk.no, published June 28.

Schneider, S. (2006). Privatizing economic crime enforcement: Exploring the role of private sector investigative agencies in combating money laundering, *Policing & Society*, 16 (3), 285–312.

Schoultz, I. and Flyghed, J. (2019). From "we didn't do it" to "we've learned our lesson": Development of a typology of neutralizations of corporate crime, *Critical Criminology*, published online doi.org/10.1007/s10612-019-09483-3.

Shawver, T. and Clements, L.H. (2019). The impact of value preferences on whistleblowing intentions of accounting professionals, *Journal of Forensic and Investigative Accounting*, 11 (2), 232–247.

Shen, W. (2003). The dynamics of the CEO-board relationship: An evolutionary perspective, *Academy of Management Review*, 28 (3), 466–476.

Shepherd, D. and Button, M. (2019). Organizational inhibitions to addressing occupational fraud: A theory of differential rationalization, *Deviant Behavior*, 40 (8), 971–991.

Shores, M. (2010). *Informal Networks and White Collar Crime: An Extended Analysis of the Madoff Scandal*, www.dspace.library.cornell.edu.

Siponen, M. and Vance, A. (2010). Neutralization: New insights into the problem of employee information security policy violations, *MIS Quarterly*, 34 (3), 487–502.

Slettholm, A. (2016). Unibuss-saken vil gå inn i historien som en av Oslos store korrupsjonssaker (The Unibuss case will go into history as one of Oslo's major corruption cases), daily Norwegian newspaper *Aftenposten*, www.aftenposten.no, published August 17.

Sonnier, B.M., Lassar, W.M. and Lassar, S.S. (2015). The influence of source credibility and attribution of blame on juror evaluation of liability of industry specialist auditors, *Journal of Forensic & Investigative Accounting*, 7 (1), 1–37.

Stadler, W.A., Benson, M.L. and Cullen, E.T. (2013). Revisiting the special sensitivity hypothesis: The prison experience of white-collar inmates, *Justice Quarterly*, 30 (6), 1090–1114.

Sterman, J.D. (2018). System dynamics at sixty: The path forward, *System Dynamics Review*, 34 (1), 5–47.

Sutherland, E.H. (1983). *White Collar Crime: The Uncut Version*, New Haven, CT: Yale University Press.

Sykes, G. and Matza, D. (1957). Techniques of neutralization: A theory of delinquency, *American Sociological Review*, 22 (6), 664–670.

Tankebe, J. (2019). Cooperation with the police against corruption: Exploring the roles of legitimacy, deterrence and collective action theories, *British Journal of Criminology*, 59, 1390–1410.

Tømmerås, O. (2014). Han varslet om korrupsjon i Unibuss i årevis (He blew the whistle on corruption at Unibuss for years), union magazine *Fagbladet*, www.fagbladet.no, published October 30.

Walburg, C. (2020). White-collar and corporate crime: European perspectives, in: Rorie, M.L. (editor), *The Handbook of White-Collar Crime*, Hoboken, NJ: Wiley & Sons, chapter 21, pages 337–346.

Wall-Parker, A. (2020). Measuring white collar crime, in: Rorie, M.L. (editor), *The Handbook of White-Collar Crime*, Hoboken, NJ: John Wiley & Sons, chapter 3, pages 32–44.

Welsh, D.T., Ordonez, L.D., Snyder, D.G. and Christian, M.S. (2014). The slippery slope: How small ethical transgressions pave the way for larger future transgressions, *Journal of Applied Psychology*, 100 (1), 114–127.

Wiersholm (2012). Rapport til styret i Unibuss (Report to the board at Unibuss), law firm *Wiersholm*, May 24.

Williams, J.W. (2005a). Reflections on the private versus public policing of economic crime, *British Journal of Criminology*, 45, 316–339.

Williams, J.W. (2005b). Governability matters: The private policing of economic crime and the challenge of democratic governance, *Policing & Society*, 15 (2), 187–211.

Williams, J.W. (2014). The private eyes of corporate culture: The forensic accounting and corporate investigation industry and the production of corporate financial security, in: Walby, K. and Lippert, R.K. (editors), *Corporate Security in the 21st Century: Theory and Practice in International Perspective*, Palgrave Macmillan, UK: Hampshire, Houndmills, pages 56–77.

Zahra, S.A., Priem, R.L. and Rasheed, A.A. (2005). The antecedents and consequences of top management fraud, *Journal of Management*, 31, 803–828.

Zhu, D.H. and Chen, G. (2015). CEO narcissism and the impact of prior board experience on corporate strategy, *Administrative Science Quarterly*, 60 (1), 31–65.

Zvi, L. and Elaad, E. (2018). Correlates of narcissism, self-reported lies, and self-assessed abilities to tell and detect lies, tell truths, and believe others, *Journal of Investigative Psychology and Offender Profiling*, 15, 271–286.

3 Negative organizational dynamics

The previous chapter described influences from one dimension on other dimensions in convenience theory. Stronger financial motive for illegal gain can create over time greater organizational opportunity for white-collar crime and higher personal willingness for deviant behavior. Greater organizational opportunity for white-collar crime can create over time stronger financial motive for illegal gain and higher personal willingness for deviant behavior. Higher personal willingness for deviant behavior can create over time stronger financial motive for illegal gain and greater organizational opportunity for white-collar crime. The previous chapter illustrated these mechanisms by a number of case studies.

This chapter focuses on the organizational dimension of convenience dynamics in white-collar crime where situational dynamics cause changes over time (Holt and Kennedy, 2020). The organization is the arena where offenders can commit and conceal financial crime. Offenders have high social status in privileged positions, they have legitimate access to crime resources, there might be disorganized institutional deterioration occurring, there might be lack of oversight and guardianship, and there might be criminal market structures. Offenders are employees or otherwise associated with organizations in public administration, local or national politics, corporate businesses, non-government organizations, religious institutions, and other organized activities. An organization is a system of coordinated actions among individuals and groups with boundaries and goals (Puranam, 2014). An organization can be a hierarchy, a matrix, or a network, or any other kind of relationship between people in a professional work environment (Dion, 2008).

Organizational dynamics is an interesting perspective on white-collar crime. Organizational dynamics can cause a downward spiral, leading to misconduct and crime. In the downward spiral, the tendency to commit white-collar crime increases. It becomes more convenient to commit crime in comparison to alternative legitimate actions when crises or opportunities emerge. Perspectives such as institutional deterioration and social disorganization explain negative organizational dynamics.

Organizational dynamics may thus over time create a culture for misconduct and crime (Zahra et al., 2005: 129):

> Over time, some organizations can develop deviant cultures in which wrongdoing is rationalized and institutionalized. These organizations are often

led by leaders who tolerate unethical behavior and conceal corrupt practices. These leaders might also encourage gamesmanship and political maneuvering as a means of getting ahead.

Professional organizational characteristics

Ahrne and Brunsson (2011) argue membership, hierarchy, monitoring and sanctions characterize an organization. Organizations decide about membership, about who is eligible to join the organization as employees. Membership brings a certain identity with it, an identity that differs from that of non-members. Organizations include a hierarchy, a duty to oblige others to comply with decisions. Hierarchy entails a form of organized power. Organizations can issue commands, and they can decide upon rules that its members are expected to follow in their actions. An organization has the right to monitor compliance with its commands and rules (Kawasaki, 2020; Rooij and Fine, 2020). Organizations have the right to decide about sanctions, both positive and negative. They can decide to change a member's status by using promotions, grading systems, awards, diplomas and medals.

Organizational members have different roles that lead to different extent of power and influence. Some organizational members have to do what they receive as orders from above in the hierarchy. Other members decide what they and subordinates should do. Power and influence are associated with level in the organizational hierarchy, tasks to needing execution, as well as individual freedom. A few members enjoy substantial individual freedom although they work at lower levels of the organization.

Privileged individuals in the elite commit white-collar crime. They do typically enjoy substantial individual freedom in their professions with little or no control. A typical example is the chief executive officer (CEO). The CEO is the only person at that hierarchical level in the organization. Below the CEO, there are a number of executives at the same hierarchical level. Above the CEO, there are a number of board members at the same hierarchical level. However, the CEO is alone at his or her level. The CEO is supposed to face control by the board, but the board only meets occasionally to discuss business cases. Executives below the CEO are typically appointed by the CEO and typically loyal to the CEO.

Power, influence and freedom are typical professional characteristics not only of CEOs. Some politicians, government officials, heads of religious organizations and other leading figures in society enjoy trust without control. Some independent professions, such as lawyers and medical doctors, enjoy the same kind of freedom.

The organizational anchoring may cause some revealed white-collar criminals to avoid investigation, prosecution and conviction (Burns and Meitl, 2020). The business may be too powerful or important to collapse (such as banks), and the criminals may be too powerful to jail. After the downturn in the US economy in 2008, many expected bank executives would face prosecution, but they were not. Pontell et al. (2014: 10) explain why it did not happen:

> From a criminological standpoint, the current financial meltdown points to the need to unpack the concept of status when examining white-collar and

corporate offenses. The high standing of those involved in the current scandal has acted as a significant shield to accusations of criminal wrongdoing in at least three ways. First, the legal resources that offenders can bring to bear on any case made against them are significant. This would give pause to any prosecutor, regardless of the evidence that exists. Second, their place in the organization assures that the many below them will be held more directly responsible for the more readily detected offenses. The downward focus on white-collar and corporate crimes is partly a function of the visibility of the offense and the ease with which it can be officially pursued. Third, the political power of large financial institutions allows for effective lobbying that both distances them from the criminal law and prevents the government from restricting them from receiving taxpayer money when they get into trouble.

Similar lack of prosecution and punishment often result from private fraud investigations. For example, Valukas (2010) identified executive misconduct as the reason for the bankruptcy at Lehman Brothers, but the investigation nevertheless concluded that executives were legally not to blame. Therefore, they faced no prosecution as defendants in court.

The organizational setting focuses on profession and position associated with a business or other kind of entity that makes it possible to carry out criminal acts. A profession is an occupation where a person is eligible by virtue of education and experience. In a narrow sense, a profession is a group of professionals with the exclusive right to perform certain work because they have completed a special education. Examples are medical doctors and attorneys. This definition is too narrow in our context. Profession is a qualified occupational practice based on knowledge and experience.

Dion (2009) argues that organizational culture makes it possible to adopt organizational purposes and objectives that are deviant in comparison to social norms, yet in line with the competition. Deviant purposes become relevant when business corporations seem trapped by doubtful, immoral or disloyal means that competitors seem to be using. Deviant purposes can also derive from the business milieu as a social institution. Furthermore, deviant purposes can result from their own sector-based morality, which is oriented towards profit maximization.

Organizational white-collar crime opportunity

Organizational opportunity is a distinct characteristic of white-collar crime that varies with the persons who are involved in crime. An opportunity is attractive as a way to respond to needs (Bucy et al., 2008). The organizational dimension gives white-collar criminals the opportunity to commit economic crime and hide it in seemingly legal activities in the business.

Aguilera and Vadera (2008: 434) describe a criminal opportunity as "the presence of a favorable combination of circumstances that renders a possible course of action relevant". Opportunities for crime occur when individuals and groups can engage in illegal and unethical behavior and expect, with a certain confidence (Haines, 2014), that they will avoid detection and punishment.

Opportunity to commit white-collar crime exists at the community level, the business level, and the individual level. At the community level, control regimes might be absent, and entire industries may be available for financial crime. An example here could be the construction industry, where one can find instances of both cartels and undeclared work. Another example could be tax collection authorities that are unable to trace and control accounting figures from businesses, thereby opening up for tax evasion with minimal risk of detection and punishment.

Huisman and Erp (2013) argue that a criminal opportunity has the following five characteristics: (1) the effort required to carry out the offense, (2) the perceived risks of detection, (3) the rewards to gainable from the offense, (4) the situational conditions that may encourage criminal action, and (5) the excuse and neutralization of the offense.

At the business level, ethics and rules can be absent, while economic crime is a straightforward business practice. An example here is subsidy fraud, where ferry companies report lower traffic number to ensure greater government transfers. Another example is internal invoice fraud, where the accounting department lacks overview over who has permission to approve what invoices.

At the individual level, greed can dominate, where the business does not have any relevant reaction to economic crime. An example here might be law firms where partners abuse money in client accounts. Another example is corruption, where the bribed person receives money from the bribing person, without anybody noticing on either side.

Benson and Simpson (2018) write that the organizational opportunity to commit white-collar manifests itself through the following three characteristics: (1) the offender has lawful and legitimate access to the premises and systems where crime is committed, (2) the offender has no physical contact with the victim, and (3) criminal acts appear to be legitimate business.

This is very different from street crime such as violence and burglary, where the offender has no legal access, the offender is at the same place as his victim, and the offense does not appear to be legal. A fundamental difference between white-collar crime and street crime is that while white-collar people conceal their crime but do not hide themselves, street criminals do not conceal their crime but hide themselves (Huisman, 2020: 139):

> In traditional crime investigations, the police are searching for the criminal, but in cases of white-collar crime they are searching for the crime.

Street crime is often evident in terms of physical harm or material damage, while street criminals are not always easy to find. White-collar crime usually lacks physical harm and material damage, while white-collar criminals are easy to find.

White-collar crime does not take place privately; it takes place on the job. The organization is the venue for crime. McKenndall and Wagner (1997) describe the opportunity by context and environmental conditions that facilitate rather than prevent the carrying out of criminal activities. For example, in the case of corruption, both the briber and the bribed are linked to a job context. The briber typically uses company money to pay, while the bribed receives the money personally because his organization is attractive to the bribing company.

The organizational dimension through work represents the offender's scope for crime. By virtue of employment, ownership, position, relations and knowledge, the offender can explore and exploit his association with the organization to commit financial crime. As sales executive, the person can pay bribes, and as procurement executive, the person can receive bribes. As finance executive, the person may safely commit embezzlement by fixing accounting figures, and as chief accountant, the person can manipulate accounting resulting in tax evasion. As chief executive, the person can sign fake contracts or order fraudulent appraisals that open up for bank fraud by asking the bank to finance future income based on fake promises from contract partners or fake value assessments at sale of real estate. There are many opportunities for economic crime by executives and others linked to enterprises. Examples of others include administrative managers, attorneys, auditors, bank managers, board members, boat dealers, car dealers, concert organizers, council members, management consultants, district managers, entrepreneurs, and investors, as well as members of parliament, medical doctors, nursery owners, property developers, real estate agents, shipbrokers, stockbrokers, surveyors, and mayors.

White-collar crime opportunities occur through the three characteristics described by Benson and Simpson (2018). The opportunities are greatest for top executives and other members of the elite in society. In relation to convenience theory, the three characteristics make it comfortable, easy and convenient to commit financial crime to solve a problem or answer to a challenge. It may be relatively simple and thus convenient for white-collar elite members to hide criminal activities in the stream of legal activities, and thus give crime an outer semblance of credibility in a respectable business (Pickett and Pickett, 2002).

It sometimes stated in the public that opportunity makes a thief. If the availability of legal opportunities to solve problems and exploit possibilities deteriorates, while illegal opportunities flourish and seem convenient, then white-collar individuals will become less law-abiding. If fraud, theft, manipulation and corruption embedded in the enterprise seems convenient, while law-abiding alternatives are invisible or hard to implement, then opportunity creates an offender.

Organizational opportunity for economic crime depends on intellectual and social capital that is available to the potential white-collar offender. Intellectual capital is knowledge in terms of understanding, insight, reflection, ability and skill. Social capital is relations in hierarchical and transactional exchanges. Social capital is the sum of actual and potential resources available for white-collar individuals by virtue of his or her position in formal and informal hierarchies, networks, and matrices (Adler and Kwon, 2002). Formal as well as informal power means influence over resources that one potentially allocates to crime.

White-collar offenders are often not alone when committing financial crime. They may cooperate with people internally as well as with people externally. If there is internal crime cooperation, then it may be more convenient for each individual to participate. An environment where crime is accepted strengthens the organizational opportunity. If there is external crime cooperation, then it may again be more convenient for each individual to participate. External actors, who for example, submit fake invoices or receive bribes, enter into a relationship with the internal actor in a code of silence.

The organizational dimension of white-collar offenses is particularly evident when crime is committed on behalf of the business. A distinction is relevant between white-collar criminals who commit financial crime for personal gain and white-collar criminals who do it for their employer (Trahan et al., 2005). The first carries the label occupational crime (Benson and Chio, 2020), while the second receives the label corporate crime (Dodge, 2020). Examples of corporate crime include manipulation of financial figures for tax evasion and unjustified government subsidies, bribery to obtain contracts, false loan applications to obtain credit in banks, and money laundering in tax havens to recruit securities clients. The organizational anchoring of crime is evident in corporate offenses as crime takes place within the business and to the benefit of the business (Bradshaw, 2015).

While an offender as an individual hides occupational crime to enrich himself or herself by abusing corporate resources (Hansen, 2009; Shepherd and Button, 2019), offenders as a group of individuals hide corporate crime to improve business conditions. In both cases, crime is committed by virtue of position and trust in the organization, which prevents monitoring, control, and accountability.

Heath (2008) found that individuals, who are higher up on the ladder in the company, tend to commit larger and more serious occupational crime. The same is probably the case also for corporate crime. Empirical studies show that corporate criminals are older, commit crime for a larger amount of money, and are connected to larger organizations than occupational criminals are. The studies support the assumption that white-collar criminals at the top of the ladder commit financial crime for far larger amounts than what white-collar collar offenders further down the hierarchical ladder do. This finding applies both to occupational and corporate crime.

Corporate crime, often called organizational offenses or business crime (Reed and Yeager, 1996), typically results from actions of several individuals in more or less rooted cooperation. If a business representative commits a crime on behalf of the organization, it is corporate crime. If the same person commits crime for personal gain, it is occupational crime (Shepherd and Button, 2019). At criminal prosecution in the criminal justice system, both occupational crime and corporate crime lead to individuals as defendants, because a company cannot face prosecution and incarceration (Burns and Meitl, 2020; Cohen, 2020). The only relevant punishment for a public or private enterprise is a fine that potentially can ruin the organization (Bookman, 2008). The Norwegian database with 405 convicted white-collar criminals contains 68 offenders (17%) who committed financial crime on behalf of the organization. Corporate crime represents violations of integrity as well as failure to comply with moral standards, as in the example of corruption managed by Siemens in Germany (Eberl et al., 2015).

The organizational dimension implies that the business is the basis for deviant acts. Sometimes the organization is also a victim of crime. In the Norwegian study, 28% of all convicted white-collar criminals victimized their own employers. 19% caused damage to society, for example by tax evasion. 18% caused harm to customers, 15% caused bank losses, and 8% caused loss among shareholders, while 12% hurt others.

The organizational dimension of white-collar crime also becomes evident when several from the same enterprise are involved in offenses (Ashforth et al., 2008), and when the organization is characterized by a criminal mindset (O'Connor, 2005), whether it concerns occupational crime or corporate crime. A single, standalone white-collar criminal can be described as a rotten apple, but when several are involved in crime, and corporate culture virtually stimulates offenses, then it is more appropriate to describe the phenomenon as a basket of rotten apples or as a rotten apple orchard, like Punch (2003: 172) defines them:

> The metaphor of 'rotten orchards' indicate(s) that it is sometimes not the apple, or even the barrel that is rotten but the *system* (or significant parts of the system).

A key characteristic of white-collar crime is opportunism. There must be an opportunity to commit elite crime, and the offender is opportunistic. If opportunities are limited, there will be less crime. This is evident when looking at the gender distribution between women and men. There are far fewer women than men in positions of trust, who are enjoying privileges with little or no control. Therefore, it is not surprising that there are far fewer white-collar offenders among women compared to men. In Norway, women constitute only 7% of white-collar inmates, while the rest are all men.

Opportunity arises out of certain jobs. For example, the opportunity to engage in health care fraud is only possible if one has a job in the health care system. Individuals who are in key positions and involved in networks based on trust have increased access to criminal opportunities. The opportunity perspective is important, because these offenses usually require special business-related access to commit conspiracies, frauds, embezzlements and other kinds of financial crime (Benson and Simpson, 2018).

Offenders take advantage of their positions of power with almost unlimited authority in the opportunity structure (Kempa, 2010). They have legitimate and often privileged access to physical and virtual locations in which crime is committed and concealed, are totally in charge of resource allocations and transaction, and are successful in concealment based on key resources used to hide their crime. Offenders have an economic motivation and opportunity (Huisman and Erp, 2013), linked to an organizational platform and availability, and in a setting of people who do not know, do not care, or do not reveal the individual(s) with behavioral traits who commit crime. Opportunity includes people who are loyal to the criminal either as followers or as silent partners.

Organizational principal agent dynamics

The principal-agent perspective can help illustrate convenience dynamics in the organizational dimension of the theory of convenience. Principal is a term for a person or a body that leaves work to an agent. The agent carries out work for the principal. Typically, the agent provides the principal with some sort of specialized service based on the agents' expertise and availability. The principal may be a board of a company that leaves the corporate management to the CEO. The CEO is then the agent in the relationship (Shen, 2003). The CEO may in turn entrust tasks to other executives, where the CEO becomes the principal, while people in positions such as chief financial officer (CFO), chief operating officer (COO) and chief technology officer (CTO) are agents. Agents perform tasks on behalf of principals.

The agency perspective describes problems that may arise between principal and agent because of diverging preferences and different values, asymmetry in knowledge of activities and performance, and different attitudes to risk. Principals must always suspect that agents make decisions that benefit themselves at the expense of principals. For example, a CEO may cheat and defraud owners (Williams, 2008), and a purchasing manager can fool the CEO when selecting vendors (Chrisman et al., 2007), for example by taking bribes that can cause the company to pay more for inferior quality.

Agency theory applies the assumption of narrow self-interest. The problem arises whenever one party (a principal) employs another (an agent) to carry out a task. The interests of the principal and agent diverge, and the principal has imperfect information about the agent's contribution (Bosse and Phillips, 2016). According to principal-agent analysis, exchanges encourage extraordinary gain (Pillay and Kluvers, 2014). Executives and others in trusted positions are opportunistic agents motivated by utility maximization. Taking an economic model of man that treats human beings as rational actors seeking to maximize utility, when given the opportunity, executives will maximize their utilities at the expense of their principals.

In agency theory, there are three problems: preferences (principal and agent may have conflicting values or goals), risk (principal and agent may not have the same kind of risk aversion or risk willingness), and knowledge (principal and agent may not have the same information and insights). Figure 3.1 illustrates the relevant causal relationships. Preferences, risk, and knowledge are variables on the left-hand side in the diagram. The right-hand side of the diagram is one part of Figure 3.1 that relates to organizational opportunity.

In terms of preferences, the principal's and the agent's best interests may not be in line with each other. Desires and goals of principal and agent may be in conflict. Thus, there is a preference gap as illustrated in Figure 3.1. In terms of risk, the principal and the agent may have different attitudes towards risk. In terms of knowledge, it is difficult or expensive for the principal to verify what the agent is actually doing.

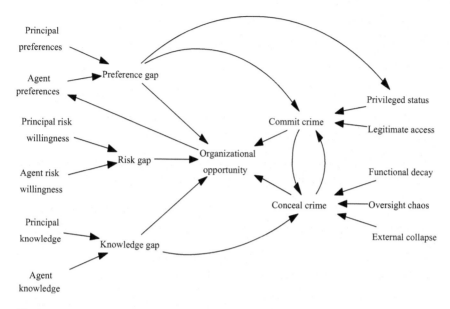

Figure 3.1 Dynamic model of the agency perspective in convenience theory

The model in Figure 3.1 assumes that gaps influence the extent of organizational opportunity for white-collar crime. A larger gap in preferences might restrict organizational opportunity. A larger gap in risk willingness might also restrict organizational opportunity. On the other hand, a larger gap in knowledge can expand the organizational opportunity.

The model in Figure 3.1 introduces some new causal feedback loops. For example, greater organizational opportunity for white-collar crime can influence agent preferences. Change in agent preferences can cause a larger preference gap, which in turn leads to reduced organizational opportunity. The causal loop of organizational opportunity, agent preferences, and preference gap thus represents a negative loop that stabilizes rather than reinforces organizational opportunity.

Another example of a new loop includes preference gap, privileged status, commit crime, organizational opportunity, agent preferences and back to preference gap. If the preference gap increases, the privileged position of the offender might face new limitations and restrictions. Then the convenience of committing crime drops, and organizational opportunity drops accordingly. This feeds back to agent preferences as a correction, thereby reducing the preference gap. This loop started with an increase in preference gap and ended up with a reduction in preference gap. This is thus another negative feedback loop.

Shareholders employ some agents in terms of board members. Board members recruit an agent as chief executive officer. The CEO employs a number of top executives. Top executives recruit middle managers. Thus, principals and agents work at different levels of corporate hierarchy, and some are both in the role of principal in one relationship and in the role of agent in another relationship.

Not only agents can abuse their positions. Principals can also abuse their positions. The model in Figure 3.1 might function also in the study of white-collar crime by principals, for example board members. By causing large gaps in preferences and risks, while reducing the knowledge gap, executives' organizational opportunity drops, while board members themselves can create opportunities for themselves.

Principals expect agents to make decisions in the best interest of the principals. However, due to agency problems, agents may not make decisions in the best interest of principals. On the contrary, agents may be succumbed to self-interest, opportunistic behavior and ignorance of both reasonable and unreasonable requests from principals.

Generally, corruption and other forms of economic crime are in agency theory considered the consequence of the principal's inability to control and prevent the agent from abusing his or her position for personal gain (Li and Ouyang, 2007). However, the principal may as well be the criminal. For example, the CFO may provide inside information to a board member who abuses the information for insider trading. The point here is that the principal and the agent have different roles in an organizational context, where they both have little information about each other's activities.

While occupational crime is an agency problem where the criminal abuses agency roles for personal benefit, corporate crime is a structural problem where the enterprise is to benefit. Most countries' jurisdictions make a similar distinction between a natural person (individual) and a juridical person (organization), and demand criminal liability in terms of prison versus fine.

Agency theory is a management theory often applied to crime, where normally the agent, rather than the principal, is in danger of committing crime. White-collar crime is thus illegal and unethical actions usually by agents of organizations (Vadera and Aguilera, 2015). There is an opportunity for the white-collar offender to carry out the regular job at the same time as crime is committed, because the principal is unable to monitor what the agent is doing, what knowledge the agent applies, and what risk the agent is willing to take (Chrisman et al., 2007; Li and Ouyang, 2007; Williams, 2008). Agency theory argues that the principal is unable to control the agent because of lack of insight and access to activities performed by the agent in roles such as mayor, chairperson or CEO (Eisenhardt, 1985; Jensen and Meckling, 1976; Garoupa, 2007).

Organizational system dynamics models

Dynamic models presented so far in this book derive from system dynamics modeling, where cause-and-effect relationships as well as causal loops determine the extent of financial motive, the extent of organizational opportunity, and the extent of personal willingness for deviant behavior over time. System dynamics is a methodology to frame, understand and discuss complex issues and problems. The methodology can help understand phenomena like white-collar crime occurrences by modeling causes and effects linked to such occurrences. The basis of the system dynamics approach is the recognition that the structure of any system and the many circular, interlocking, and time-delayed relationships among its components determine motives, opportunities and willingness, rather than each component itself (Randers, 2019; Sterman, 2018). Feedback loops are the recursive, repeated and iterative cycles of interactions among factors that influence motive, opportunity, and willingness for white-collar crime.

Organizational dynamics is the interplay among factors that determine organizational behavior over time. Factors create, extend, or modify organizational opportunity for white-collar crime. Organizational dynamics result from continuous changes in a number of interlocked variables (Pitelis and Wagner, 2019). As already mentioned, an organization is a system of coordinated actions among individuals and groups with boundaries and goals (Puranam, 2014). Dynamic performance models propose that opportunity evolves as people's abilities, learning, and other differences change (Christian et al., 2015).

Organizational business dynamics

Convenience dynamics does not only occur because of links between motive, opportunity, and willingness, where changes happen over time in terms of motive rise or fall, opportunity rise or fall, and willingness rise or fall. The context in which white-collar offenses take place is also subject to dynamics, where the business of the organization changes, and where the society in which the organization operates, also changes over time. Such changes will influence the extent of white-collar crime convenience. For example, Lord and Wingerde (2020) described a case for potential altering of dynamics to remove white-collar crime opportunity. There is thus a larger complexity stemming from many relevant variables that interact in multiple ways (Forti and Visconti, 2020: 65):

> The causal loops interconnecting the main features of white-collar crime are strengthened and consolidated within and through corporate organizations, also due to their intersections with institutions of political governance.

Forti and Visconti (2020) conceived all possible dynamic interactions as a system of harms, which – like every system – is more than the sheer sum of single parts. They argue that the elucidation of such a system's dynamics and conditions is much more revealing than any list of single perspectives on white-collar crime.

Dynamics take place at different levels such as the individual, the organizational, and the national levels. Dynamics also take place between these levels. For example, dynamics of state-corporate crime occurs between the national and organizational levels (Bernat and Whyte, 2020: 127):

> This growing body of literature on state-corporate crimes takes as its starting point the mutually reinforcing relationships between state institutions and corporations.

In system dynamics terms, a mutually reinforcing relationship is a positive feedback loop, where increased state involvement in corporate crime will cause increased corporate involvement in state crime. Over time, a positive feedback loop can cause exponential growth in state-corporate crime. The opposite of a positive feedback loop is a negative feedback loop, where for example increased corporate crime causes a reaction in terms of reduced state crime that in turn reduces corporate crime.

Another example of a negative feedback loop might be the relationship between social reaction to, and the fear of, crime, as suggested by Zysman-Quirós (2020). When social reaction becomes tougher, then the fear of crime may decline. There is thus a change in the opposite direction from one variable to the next variable.

Organizational business dynamics take place both in legitimate and criminal organizations, where the former face market dynamics in legal markets while the latter face market dynamics in illegal markets. Criminal organizations will often behave and think according to rational business needs (Huisman, 2020: 142):

> They will consider factors such as new product opportunities, changes in the market, profit margins, competition, and risk management.

Huisman (2020: 143) argued that there is much less research on small and medium-sized enterprises (SMEs), "raising the question whether the findings on complex organizational dynamics as causes of corporate crime are also valid for explaining law-breaking in SMEs".

In addition to the levels of individual, organizational and national activities, there is also transnational activity enabling convenience of white-collar crime. Global companies can easily commit tax evasion in one country with high tax rates by transferring profits to another country with low tax rates. Companies and individuals can use tax havens – offshore countries that offer foreign individuals and businesses little or no tax liability in a politically and economically stable environment – for money laundering (Naheem, 2020). As argued by Huisman (2020: 151),

> ambiguities may be further amplified from a dynamic and transnational perspective, as when regulations and/or morality in business communities or society at large change and/or when laws and regulations and societal morality differ from one country to another.

Similarly, Ezeonu (2020: 402) introduced the transnational perspective in business dynamics when he stated that; "the concept of crimes of globalization (in both its original and its refined formulations) addresses the broader criminal and criminogenic dynamics of the global neoliberal project".

In the same line of reasoning, Wingerde and Lord (2020: 470) stress the relevance of understanding dynamics involving multinational business firms in relation to white-collar crime convenience:

> The dynamics between these firms, governments, and civil society have fundamentally changed over the past two decades. Rather than nation-states, these firms are (and have been for a while) at the center of the economy. In fact, the global economy is increasingly being dominated by complex networks of production, controlled and coordinated by multinational business firms.

Kennedy (2020: 185) referred to research linking white-collar criminogenity to business dynamics:

> Companies operating within industries that are highly dynamic, meaning the industry is seeing rapid fluctuations in demand for its goods, were significantly more likely to engage in illegal behavior. However, firms operating in environments that had low levels of dynamism were also likely to engage in illegal behavior, just not at the same rate as firms in the most dynamic environments. The curvilinear relationships found between illegal corporate behavior, the availability of resources, and a dynamic environment suggest that munificent environments provide just as much motivation for corporate crime as do resource-scarce environments. Additionally, industry-level perceptions of risk and a desire to avoid competitive environments that lead to downward pressure on a company's stock price or financial returns can motivate collusive illegal corporate behavior.

Similarly, Chan and Gibbs (2020: 195) argued that; "crime may be a result of management's reaction to the dynamic environment". Technological advancements are included in the dynamic environment focusing on "the socialization process and structurally created opportunities that reflect changing dynamics in occupational distribution and technological advancements" (Chan and Gibbs, 2020: 200).

Lord and Wingerde (2020: 252) reported research on procedural dynamics in criminal market forces:

> (They) undertook such an analysis when implementing a script analysis to understand the procedural dynamics and mechanics of the market manipulation process. They analyzed the range of interactions between the relevant actors, these actors' behaviors, and the resources essential to allowing the manipulative behaviors to occur.

In the reported study, researchers were able to gain insight into the procedural aspects and organizational dynamics of the manipulations in different scenes of the script. They were able to identify which actors (individual or corporate) were central, and how the actors cooperated across the script. They identified the ways in which regulatory and corporate conditions created opportunities and potential for manipulations (Lord and Wingerde, 2020).

Pathways into convenient white-collar crime

Dynamics at all levels change the extent of convenience in white-collar crime. Dynamics can cause worsening in convenience or improvement in convenience. A large number of pathways through the myriad of interactions can create convenience in white-collar crime. Starting at the state level, a corrupt regime attracts bribes from the private sector. In the private sector, a sales manager then seizes the opportunity to obtain a contract for the company with the state, where the manager in the aftermath might expect a bonus or a promotion. Executives ignore potential controls and guardianships to secure compliance to succeed in delivery of goods and services to the state.

Another example of a potential pathway into convenient white-collar crime could start at the opposite end, at the individual level of narcissistic identification with the organization. The narcissist sees little or no difference between their own money and corporate money. When in need of money, the offender abuses the position to commit embezzlement. Bank accounts are arranged so that lines between private and corporate business become blurred in a collusion of personal and job-related activities.

References

Adler, P.S. and Kwon, S.W. (2002). Social capital: Prospects for a new concept, *Academy of Management Review*, 27 (1), 17–40.

Aguilera, R.V. and Vadera, A.K. (2008). The dark side of authority: Antecedents, mechanisms, and outcomes of organizational corruption, *Journal of Business Ethics*, 77, 431–449.

Ahrne, G. and Brunsson, N. (2011). Organization outside organizations: The significance of partial organization, *Organization*, 18 (1), 83–104.

Ashforth, B.E., Gioia, D.A., Robinson, S.L. and Trevino, L.K. (2008). Re-reviewing organizational corruption, *Academy of Management Review*, 33 (3), 670–684.

Benson, M.L. and Chio, H.L. (2020). Who commits occupational crimes, in: Rorie, M. (editor), *The Handbook of White-Collar Crime*, Hoboken, NJ: John Wiley & Sons, chapter 7, pages 97–112.

Benson, M.L. and Simpson, S.S. (2018). *White-Collar Crime: An Opportunity Perspective*, 3rd edition, New York, NY: Routledge.

Bernat, I. and Whyte, D. (2020). State-corporate crimes, in: Rorie, M.L. (editor), *The Handbook of White-Collar Crime*, Hoboken, NJ: Wiley & Sons, chapter 9, pages 191–208.

Bookman, Z. (2008). Convergences and omissions in reporting corporate and white collar crime, *DePaul Business & Commercial Law Journal*, 6, 347–392.

Bosse, D.A. and Phillips, R.A. (2016). Agency theory and bounded self-interest, *Academy of Management Review*, 41 (2), 276–297.

Bradshaw, E.A. (2015). "Obviously, we're all oil industry": The criminogenic structure of the offshore oil industry, *Theoretical Criminology*, 19 (3), 376–395.

Bucy, P.H., Formby, E.P., Raspanti, M.S. and Rooney, K.E. (2008). Why do they do it? The motives, mores, and character of white collar criminals, *St. John's Law Review*, 82, 401–571.

Burns, R.G. and Meitl, M.B. (2020). Prosecution, defense, and sentencing of white-collar crime, in: Rorie, M.L. (editor), *The Handbook of White-Collar Crime*, Hoboken, NJ: Wiley & Sons, chapter 18, pages 279–296.

Chan, F. and Gibbs, C. (2020). Integrated theories of white-collar and corporate crime, in: Rorie, M.L. (editor), *The Handbook of White-Collar Crime*, Hoboken, NJ: Wiley & Sons, chapter 13, pages 191–208.

Chrisman, J.J., Chua, J.H., Kellermanns, F.W. and Chang, E.P.C. (2007). Are family managers agents or stewards? An exploratory study in privately held family firms, *Journal of Business Research*, 60 (10), 1030–1038.

Christian, M.S., Eisenkraft, N. and Kapadia, C. (2015). Dynamic associations among somatic complaints, human energy, and discretionary behaviors: Experiences with pain fluctuations at work, *Administrative Science Quarterly*, 60 (1), 66–102.

Cohen, M.A. (2020). Punishing corporations, in: Rorie, M.L. (editor), *The Handbook of White-Collar Crime*, Hoboken, NJ: Wiley & Sons, chapter 20, pages 314–333.

Dion, M. (2008). Ethical leadership and crime prevention in the organizational setting, *Journal of Financial Crime*, 15 (3), 308–319.

Dion, M. (2009). Corporate crime and the dysfunction of value networks, *Journal of Financial Crime*, 16 (4), 436–445.

Dodge, M. (2020). Who commits corporate crime? in: Rorie, M. (editor), *The Handbook of White-Collar Crime*, Hoboken, NJ: John Wiley & Sons, chapter 8, pages 113–126.

Eberl, P., Geiger, D. og Assländer, M.S. (2015). Repairing trust in an organization after integrity violations. The ambivalence of organizational rule adjustments, *Organization Studies*, 36 (9), 1205–1235.

Eisenhardt, K.M. (1985). Control: Organizational and economic approaches, *Management Science*, 31 (2), 134–149.

Ezeonu, I. (2020). Market criminology: A critical engagement with primitive accumulation in the petroleum extraction industry in Africa, in: Rorie, M.L. (editor), *The Handbook of White-Collar Crime*, Hoboken, NJ: Wiley & Sons, chapter 25, pages 398–417.

Forti, G. and Visconti, A. (2020). From economic crime to corporate violence: The multifaceted harms of corporate crime, in: Rorie, M.L. (editor), *The Handbook of White-Collar Crime*, Hoboken, NJ: John Wiley & Sons, chapter 5, pages 64–80.

Garoupa, N. (2007). Optimal law enforcement and criminal organization, *Journal of Economic Behaviour & Organization*, 63, 461–474.

Haines, F. (2014). Corporate fraud as misplaced confidence? Exploring ambiguity in the accuracy of accounts and the materiality of money, *Theoretical Criminology*, 18 (1), 20–37.

Hansen, L.L. (2009). Corporate financial crime: Social diagnosis and treatment, *Journal of Financial Crime*, 16 (1), 28–40.

Heath, J. (2008). Business ethics and moral motivation: A criminological perspective, *Journal of Business Ethics*, 83, 595–614.

Holt, T.J. and Kennedy, J.P. (2020). Technology's influence on white-collar offending, reporting, and investigation, in: Rorie, M.L. (editor), *The Handbook of White-Collar Crime*, Hoboken, NJ: Wiley & Sons, chapter 28, pages 451–468.

Huisman, W. (2020). Blurred lines: Collusions between legitimate and illegitimate organizations, in: Rorie, M.L. (editor), *The Handbook of White-Collar Crime*, Hoboken, NJ: Wiley & Sons, chapter 10, pages 139–158.

Huisman, W. and Erp, J. (2013). Opportunities for environmental crime, *British Journal of Criminology*, 53, 1178–1200.

Jensen, M.C. and Meckling, W.H. (1976). Theory of the firm: Managerial behavior, agency costs and ownership structures, *Journal of Financial Economics*, 3 (4), 305–360.

Kawasaki, T. (2020). Review of comparative studies on white-collar and corporate crime, in: Rorie, M.L. (editor), *The Handbook of White-Collar Crime*, Hoboken, NJ: Wiley & Sons, chapter 27, pages 437–447.

Kempa, M. (2010). Combating white-collar crime in Canada: Serving victim needs and market integrity, *Journal of Financial Crime*, 17 (2), 251–264.

Kennedy, J.P. (2020). Organizational and macro-level corporate crime theories, in: Rorie, M.L. (editor), *The Handbook of White-Collar Crime*, Hoboken, NJ: Wiley & Sons, chapter 12, pages 175–190.

Li, S. and Ouyang, M. (2007). A dynamic model to explain the bribery behavior of firms, *International Journal of Management*, 24 (3), 605–618.

Lord, N. and Wingerde, K. (2020). Preventing and intervening in white-collar crimes: The role of law enforcement, in: Rorie, M.L. (editor), *The Handbook of White-Collar Crime*, Hoboken, NJ: Wiley & Sons, chapter 16, 246–261.

McKenndall, M.A. and Wagner, J.A. (1997). Motive, opportunity, choice, and corporate illegality, *Organization Science*, 8, 624–647.

Naheem, M.A. (2020). The agency dilemma in anti-money laundering regulation, *Journal of Money Laundering Control*, published online, https://doi.org/10.1108/JMLC-01-2016-0007.

O'Connor, T.R. (2005). Police deviance and ethics, *part of web cited*, MegaLinks in Criminal Justice. http://faculty.ncwc.edu/toconnor/205/205lect11.htm, downloaded February 19, 2009.

Pickett, K.H.S. and Pickett, J.M. (2002). *Financial Crime Investigation and Control*, New York, NY: John Wiley & Sons.

Pillay, S. and Kluvers, R. (2014). An institutional theory perspective on corruption: The case of a developing democracy, *Financial Accountability & Management*, 30 (1), 95–119.

Pitelis, C.N. and Wagner, J.D. (2019). Strategic shared leadership and organizational dynamic capabilities, *The Leadership Quarterly*, 30, 233–242.

Pontell, H.N., Black, W.K. and Geis, G. (2014). Too big to fail, too powerful to jail? On the absence of criminal prosecutions after the 2008 financial meltdown, *Crime, Law and Social Change*, 61 (1), 1–13.

Punch, M. (2003). Rotten orchards. "Pestilence", police misconduct and system failure, *Policing and Society*, 13 (2), 171–196.

Puranam, P., Alexy, O. and Reitzig, M. (2014). What's "new" about new forms of organizing? *Academy of Management Review*, 39 (2), 162–180.

Randers, J. (2019). The great challenge for system dynamics on the path forward: Implementation and real impact, *System Dynamics Review*, 35 (2), 19–24.

Reed, G.E. and Yeager, P.C. (1996). Organizational offending and neoclassical criminology. Challenging the reach of a general theory of crime, *Criminology*, 34 (3), 357–382.

Rooij, B. and Fine, A.D. (2020). Preventing corporate crime from within: Compliance management, whistleblowing, and internal monitoring, in: Rorie, M.L. (editor), *The Handbook of White-Collar Crime*, Hoboken, NJ: Wiley & Sons, chapter 15, pages 229–245.

Shen, W. (2003). The dynamics of the CEO-board relationship: An evolutionary perspective, *Academy of Management Review*, 28 (3), 466–476.

Shepherd, D. and Button, M. (2019). Organizational inhibitions to addressing occupational fraud: A theory of differential rationalization, *Deviant Behavior*, 40 (8), 971–991.

Sterman, J.D. (2018). System dynamics at sixty: The path forward, *System Dynamics Review*, 34 (1), 5–47.

Trahan, A., Marquart, J. and Mullings, J. (2005). Fraud and the American dream: Toward an understanding of fraud victimization, *Deviant Behavior*, 26 (6), 601–620.

Vadera, A.K. and Aguilera, R.V. (2015). The evolution of vocabularies and its relation to investigation of white-collar crimes: An institutional work perspective, *Journal of Business Ethics*, 128, 21–38.

Valukas, A.R. (2010). *In regard Lehman Brothers Holdings Inc. to United States Bankruptcy Court in Southern District of New York*, Jenner & Block, March 11, 239 pages, www.nysb.uscourts.gov/sites/default/files/opinions/188162_61_opinion.pdf.

Williams, J.W. (2008). The lessons of Enron: Media accounts, corporate crimes, and financial markets, *Theoretical Criminology*, 12 (4), 471–499.

Wingerde, K. and Lord, N. (2020). The elusiveness of white-collar and corporate crime in a globalized economy, in: Rorie, M.L. (editor), *The Handbook of White-Collar Crime*, Hoboken, NJ: Wiley & Sons, chapter 29, pages 469–483.

Zahra, S.A., Priem, R.L. and Rasheed, A.A. (2005). The antecedents and consequences of top management fraud, *Journal of Management*, 31, 803–828.

Zysman-Quirós, D. (2020). White-collar crime in South and Central America: Corporate-state crime, governance, and the high impact of the Odebrecht corruption case, in: Rorie, M.L. (editor), *The Handbook of White-Collar Crime*, Hoboken, NJ: Wiley & Sons, chapter 23, pages 363–380.

4 White-collar convenience evolution

Convenience dynamics in white-collar crime change over time in terms of historical evolution. The question here is whether white-collar crime has become more or less convenient over time. The purpose of this chapter is to discuss how convenience in white-collar crime is relevant to business history research, as the extent of convenience influences the magnitude of financial crime among privileged individuals in the course of their professions. Convenience is savings in time and efforts, as well as avoidance of strain and pain. The theory of convenience suggests that the extent of white-collar crime is dependent on economical motives, organizational opportunities, and personal willingness for deviant behavior. These three dimensions in convenience theory are broken down in this chapter into potential criteria to evaluate whether white-collar crime is more convenient presently compared to the past. Historians are encouraged to apply these criteria in their future studies.

The theory of convenience suggests that a white-collar offender has a financial motive, an organizational opportunity and a personal willingness that make committing and concealing economic crime convenient. A white-collar offender is a privileged individual with high and respectable social status who has access to resources to commit and conceal economic crime in the course of occupational and professional activity (Sutherland, 1939, 1983). A white-collar offender received more than a century ago the label robber baron, who is a wealthy and powerful individual in the upper class of society influencing laws and law enforcement (Spiekermann, 2018).

The purpose of this chapter is to address the following research question: What criteria are relevant to the study of the evolution of white-collar crime? Criteria derive here from convenience theory, where the dimensions of motive, opportunity and willingness influence the extent of convenience. This research is an important contribution to business historians as they continue their studies of the evolution of white-collar crime in business history (Berghoff, 2018; Berghoff and Spiekermann, 2018; Bernsee, 2018; Eberl et al., 2015; Hausman, 2018; Müller, 2018; Pettigrew, 2018; Spiekermann, 2018; Taylor, 2018).

This research is also important because the dominant view globally is that very few white-collar offenders face prosecution (Wingerde and Lord, 2020). "The bigger the crime, the less likely the perpetrator will serve time" (Hausman,

2018: 381). "Corruption only rarely comes to light" (Berghoff, 2018: 423). According to Berghoff and Spiekermann (2018: 290), Sutherland stated that, "the total damages of white-collar crimes were several times higher than those of all other crimes combined". Hausman (2018: 392), who found that offenders present "a long-term danger to the U.S. business climate", emphasized the seriousness of white-collar elite crime. Honest businesspersons – who must have access to capital to succeed – suffer because financial investors, authorities and the public lose faith in business enterprises.

This chapter begins by presenting the concepts of convenience orientation and white-collar convenience. Next, the three dimensions of convenience theory are described, i.e., financial motive, organizational opportunity and personal willingness. Then, some historical perspectives on white-collar crime are subject to review.

White-collar convenience orientation

Convenience is the state of being able to proceed with something with little effort or difficulty, avoiding pain and strain (Mai and Olsen, 2016). The extent to which individuals in privileged positions choose to break the law in difficult situations or tempting situations is dependent on their convenience orientation. Convenience comes at a potential cost to the offender in terms of the likelihood of detection and future punishment. In other worlds, reducing time and effort now entails a greater potential for future cost. Paying for convenience is a way of phrasing this proposition (Farquhar and Rowley, 2009).

Orientation is a function of the mind involving awareness of the situation. This chapter conceptualizes convenience orientation as the value that individuals and organizations in a given situation place on actions with inherent characteristics of saving time and effort. Convenience orientation is a value-like construct that influences behavior and decision-making. Mai and Olsen (2016) measured convenience orientation in terms of a desire to spend as little time as possible on the task, an attitude that the less effort needed the better, and a consideration that it is a waste of time to spend a long time on the task (Sari et al., 2017).

Convenience is a relative concept concerned with the efficiency in time and effort as well as reduction in pain and solution to problems (Engdahl, 2015; Higgins, 1997). A convenient individual is not necessarily bad or lazy. On the contrary, the person is often both smart and rational when choosing a convenient option (Blickle et al., 2006; Sundström and Radon, 2015). As a relative construct, convenience theory is line with the crime-as-choice perspective. This perspective by Shover et al. (2012) suggests that it is a conscious choice among alternatives that leads to law violation. Convenience motivates the choice of action. Convenience is a matter of perception in advance of possible criminal actions. Convenience is a significant variable whose understanding involves complexity in multiple meanings (Sundström and Radon, 2015).

Crime-as-choice leads to opportunity costs. When selecting an illegal path of action, the offender causes costs associated with not selecting a legal path of action. This conceptualization of opportunity cost is crucial to understanding the cost of crime to the potential offender, because the real cost of crime includes shaming, investigation, prosecution, conviction, and incarceration. These cost elements occur when a potential offender is not choosing a legal path of action.

Elite members with a strong convenience orientation favor actions and behaviors with inherent characteristics of saving time and effort (Collier and Kimes, 2012). They have a desire to spend as little time as possible on challenging issues and situations that may occur. They have an attitude that the less effort needed the better, and they think that it will be a waste of time to spend a long time on a problem. They prefer to avoid the problem rather than handle it. They want to avoid discomfort and pain. They want to survive and prosper in the upper echelon of society in the best possible way. Convenience thus motivates the choice of action and behavior (Seiders et al., 2007). An important element is avoiding more problematic, stressful and challenging situations. Because of the overwhelming workload combined with a need to prioritize own time, convenience is often at the core of thinking among chief executives in organizations (Bigley and Wiersma, 2002).

White-collar crime convenience

Convenience orientation towards illegal actions increases as negative attitudes towards legal actions increase. The extent of convenience obviously varies with the mindset. Individual characteristics matter in regard to white-collar crime convenience. Personality traits may facilitate business success at one point in time and white-collar offending at another point in time. Benson (2013) found that narcissistic self-confidence when coupled with drive, ambitiousness, and insensitivity to others may enable some people successfully to undertake risky business endeavors that more prudent and introspective individuals would never attempt. An ambitious and convenient mindset may also permit if not drive these individuals in the single-minded pursuit of their goals to engage in financial crime.

The actual convenience is not important in convenience theory. Rather, the perceived, expected and assumed convenience influences choice of action. Berry et al. (2002) make this distinction explicit by conceptualizing convenience as individuals' time and effort perceptions related to an action. White-collar criminals probably vary in their perceived convenience of their actions. Low expected convenience could be one of the reasons why not more members of the elite commit white-collar offenses. The objective detection risk will be the same in the same situation for everyone, while the subjective detection risk will vary with individual variation in risk perceptions, risk willingness and risk aversion (Berghoff and Spiekermann, 2018: 293):

> Risk-averse people seldom, if ever, violate criminal laws. On the other hand, those who are risk-tolerant or even risk-seeking, i.e. who display fundamental characteristics of entrepreneurial personalities, are much more likely to become criminals.

Convenience in white-collar crime relates to savings in time and effort by privileged and trusted individuals to reach a goal. Convenience is here an attribute of an illegal action. Convenience comes at a potential cost to the offender in terms of the likelihood of detection and future punishment. In other words, reducing time and effort now entails a greater potential for future cost. "Paying for convenience" is a way of phrasing this proposition (Farquhar and Rowley, 2009).

Convenience in the decision-making process is not only concerned with one alternative being more convenient than another alternative. Convenience is also concerned with the extent to which an individual collects information about more alternatives and collects more information about each alternative. Market research indicates that consumers tend to make buying decisions based on little information about few alternatives (Sundström and Radon, 2015). A similar process finds support for white-collar crime where the individual avoids the effort of collecting more information about more alternatives that might have led to a non-criminal rather than a criminal solution to a challenge, opportunity, or problem.

Convenience is of value because time and effort are associated with value. Time is a limited and scarce resource, from a day of 10 or 12 working hours to a person life of 80 or 90 years. Saving time means reallocating time across activities to achieve greater efficiency. Similarly, an effort surplus finds reallocation to create value elsewhere. The more effort people exert on a task, the more outcomes are likely in return (Berry et al., 2002).

Many white-collar criminals have a mindset that will make them stop at nothing to enrich themselves and their organizations. The extent of convenience obviously varies with the mindset. Individual characteristics matter in regard to white-collar crime convenience. The greater benefits of crime and the less costs of crime, the more attractive it is to commit criminal acts. According to Berghoff and Spiekermann (2018: 293), potential white-collar offenders "act on cost-benefit calculations involving the expected utility, the likelihood of being caught, and punishment costs".

While Sutherland introduced white-collar criminal as a term in 1939, other terms such as robber baron emerged several decades earlier. Robber barons are the powerful and wealthy in the upper class of society who define what is right and what is wrong, and who change the laws when they themselves are in danger of breaking the laws (Petrocelli et al., 2003). The rich and mighty people can behave like robber barons because they make the laws and because they control law enforcement. Spiekermann (2018: 363) presents the case of the Spreckels family as an example of robber barons:

> Claus Spreckels (1828–1908) was surely one of the notorious 'robber barons' of the time. . . . When in 1876 the Kingdom of Hawaii and the United States arranged a first reciprocity treaty, which included a bounty for cane sugar imports to the United States, Spreckels took his chance and erected, after corrupting the king and the government, large-scale sugar plantations. Within a few years, Claus Spreckels established a vertically

integrated sugar empire, which not only included plantation and refining but also financing, transport and wholesale trade. Although harshly criticized for exploiting coolie work and corrupting the Sandwich Islands, his political influence in California and Washington, DC generated continuous political support for his business interests.

This book applies the offender-based definition of white-collar crime, which has its origin in the work of Sutherland (1939), who defined white-collar crime based on the social and occupational status of the offender as a crime committed by a person of respectability and high social status in the course of the offender's occupation. The other, offense-based tradition stems from a critique against using offender characteristics as part of the definition. For instance, Shapiro (1990: 347) argues that this "confuse[s] acts with actors, norms with breakers, the modus operandi with the operator". The offense-based tradition is instead concerned with the criminal act in itself, drawing upon legal definitions, motives and means (Piquero and Schoepfer, 2010). Offense-based approaches to white-collar crime emphasize the actions and nature of the illegal act as the defining agent. For example, white-collar crime is typically a non-violent offense (Berghoff and Spiekermann, 2018). Because status is not included in the definition of offense-based approaches, and status is free to vary independently from the definition in most legislations, where an offense-based approach thus allows measures of status to become external explanatory variables.

Berghoff and Spiekermann (2018: 290) are among those emphasizing the importance of Sutherland's work:

> The assessment of the offences committed in the corporate world began to change in light of the theories of sociologist and criminologist Edwin Hardin Sutherland, who not only established the criminological term 'white-collar crime' in 1939, but also made clear that crimes were not exclusively committed by lower-class offenders. Sutherland, who had among other things previously worked on juvenile delinquents in ghettos of recent immigrants, pointed to certain parallels such as the influence of cultural milieus. This concept violated existing prejudices that high-ranking persons would not or only in highly exceptionally circumstances commit crimes and that economic crimes were due to 'merely technical violations', which 'involve no moral culpability'. Sutherland, who is considered one of the most influential criminologists of the twentieth century, vehemently contradicted widespread views that criminality was caused by poverty or biological and psychological factors.

As Agnew (2014: 2) formulates it: "crime is often the most expedient way to get what you want" and "fraud is often easier, simpler, faster, more exciting, and more certain than other means of securing one's ends".

Financial motive convenience

Convenience in the economical dimension of convenience theory focuses on avoidance of threats and exploitation of possibilities by illegal means. The motive for white-collar crime is simply financial gain (Berghoff and Spiekermann, 2018).

Many law-abiding members of the elite use their economic prosperity to climb to the top of Maslow's (1943) hierarchy of needs. Rich people want respect and reputation as well as status and admiration in the community. One way of achieving status is by giving away money through philanthropic behavior. A philanthropist is someone seemingly without self-interest willing to help disadvantaged and ignoring financial gain. Words like status, privileges, recognition, fame and admiration are all associated with both law-abiding as well as criminal white-collar people. White-collar offenders commit economic crime to climb, to remain in or to avoid falling from the pyramid. Hausman (2018: 383) mentions Samuel Insull as a classic philanthropist among white-collar offenders:

> The most visible figure in the holding company movement and its collapse, and indeed, in the entire history of the electric power industry in the United States, was Samuel Insull. . . . He was instrumental in shaping an industry that brought electric power to millions of people and was a noted philanthropist as well.

Exploitation of attractive corporate economic possibilities can cause environmental pollution.

An example is the oil exploitation in the Gulf of Mexico that caused serious environmental pollution. British Petroleum (BP) operating the Deepwater Horizon platform faced criminal charges amounting to US $4 billion because of environmental crime. A federal court in New Orleans sentenced BP to pay the record sum (Müller, 2018).

Organizational opportunity convenience

Convenience in the organizational dimension of convenience theory focuses on opportunities to commit and conceal financial crime in a professional setting.

High social status in privileged positions creates power inequality compared to those without any status in their positions. The perspective of power inequality suggests that, for example, family members in family firms wield significant influence in their firms (Patel and Cooper, 2014). Family members often have legitimate access to firm resources that nonfamily executives in the firm cannot question. Individuals with high social status in privileged positions can cooperate to create a business climate of "organized irresponsibility" (Berghoff, 2018: 425):

> The term implies that management had conspired to prevent efficient controls and therefore facilitated and promoted corruption.

Berghoff and Spiekermann (2018: 291) argue that all economic transactions depend on a certain degree of trust, without which transaction costs would simply be too high for economic activity:

> White-collar criminals abuse the good faith of various stakeholders, from customers to the general public, from shareholders to the authorities. Therefore, white-collar crime often coincides with the breach of trust.

As suggested by Berghoff and Spiekermann (2018: 290), sophisticated concealment is an important factor in white-collar crime:

> The privileged position of white-collar criminals is the result of several factors. Their offences are especially difficult to prosecute because the perpetrators use sophisticated means to conceal them. They can also often afford the best lawyers and have the political clout to influence the legislative process to their advantage and, if need be, to bribe prosecutors and judges. Additionally, the class bias of the courts works to their benefit. The law is often seen as not binding, at least not for and by economic elites.

Berghoff and Spiekermann (2018: 291) found that white-collar crime is often systemic and part of a culture, either of a corporate culture inside the firm or of a culture in the firm's environment:

> In the first case, the corporation's control mechanisms are typically weak, intentionally or unintentionally, which is an obstacle to the prevention and the investigation of economic crimes. Individual responsibility is therefore hard to ascertain. Defendants routinely deny responsibility and point to their superiors who made them commit crimes, or to their inferiors who engaged in shady practices without their knowledge or authorization.

Guardianship, oversight and control become more difficult in times of wrongdoings by misleading attributions. The attribution perspective implies that white-collar offenders are able to attribute causes of crime to everyone else but themselves in the organization. The attribution perspective is about identifying causality predicated on internal and external circumstances (Eberly et al., 2011), where individuals make causal inferences and explanations, dispositional or situational, for the causes of own and others' behaviors (Cianci et al., 2019). External attributions place the cause of a negative event on external factors, absolving the account giver and the privileged individual from personal responsibility. Innocent subordinates receive blame for crime committed by elite members (Lee and Robinson, 2000). According to Sonnier et al. (2015: 10), affective reactions influence blame attribution directly and indirectly by altering structural linkage assessments:

> For example, a negative affective reaction can influence the assessment of causation by reducing the evidential standards required to attribute blame or by increasing the standards of care by which an act is judged.

When the Siemens corruption scandal emerged in the public, top management attempted to blame lower level managers (Berghoff, 2018: 423):

> At first the company defended itself with set phrases like "mishaps of individuals" and isolated offenses committed by a "gang" of criminals, or "This is not Siemens".

Lack of oversight and guardianship was obvious in the Siemens corruption scandal, as phrased by the judge in German court (Berghoff, 2018: 430):

> He compared the Siemens compliance department with "fire fighters, who were equipped with a toothbrush mug to extinguish major fires".

Cartels and corruption networks are important to many global business enterprises (Freiberg, 2020). When the corruption case at Siemens became public knowledge, Murphy and Dacin (2011) found that the business climate encouraged corruption and fraudulent behavior as normal and acceptable. To cope with the scandal, Siemens replaced its management board (Berghoff, 2018: 423):

> Siemens is one of the world's leading electrical engineering corporations. In 2006, a massive corruption scandal erupted, concluded in 2008 with a record fine. For Siemens the largest risk was being barred from government contracts. As a consequence, it replaced virtually its entire managing board, an unprecedented procedure in the history of the company.

However, the criminal market structures did not change. Siemens "thrived in the cozy world of national monopolies and cartels, which guaranteed high margins and no worries about rivals" (Berghoff, 2018: 425). While the new management at Siemens attempted trust repair among stakeholders by introducing updates rules and guidelines, Eberl et al. (2015: 1205) found that the new rules were paradoxical in nature and thus difficult to implement in practice:

> Our findings suggest that tightening organizational rules is an appropriate signal of trustworthiness for external stakeholders to demonstrate that the organization seriously intends to prevent integrity violations in the future. However, such rule adjustments were the source of dissatisfaction among employees since the new rules were difficult to implement in practice. We argue that these different impacts of organizational rules result from their inherent paradoxical nature.

Some members of the elite are simply too powerful to blame. Pontell et al. (2014) found that the financial crisis obviously had its cause in mismanagement in the financial sector, but all in the financial sector avoided serious blame. Status-related factors such as influential positions, upper-class family ties, and community roles often preclude perceptions of blameworthiness (Slyke and Bales, 2012). White-collar offenders "are now regarded as the untouchables, too well-heeled and powerful to lock up" (Hausman, 2018: 381).

Personal willingness convenience

Convenience in the behavioral dimension of convenience theory focuses on the personal willingness for deviant behavior.

The slippery slope perspective suggests that a person can slide over time from legal to illegal activities without really noticing. The small infractions can lead to the larger ones. An organization that overlooks the small infractions of its employees creates a culture of acceptance that may lead to its own demise (Welsh et al., 2014). The slippery slope perspective applies to a number of situations, such as seventeenth-century England, where "unregulated overseas trade was a slippery slope to fraud" (Pettigrew, 2018: 313). Arjoon (2008: 78) explains slippery slope in the following way:

> As commonsense experience tells us, it is the small infractions that can lead to the larger ones. An organization that overlooks the small infractions of its employees creates a culture of acceptance that may lead to its own demise. This phenomenon is captured by the metaphor of the slippery slope. Many unethical acts occur without the conscience awareness of the person who engaged in the misconduct. Specifically, unethical behavior is most likely to follow the path of a slippery slope, defined as a gradual decline in which no one event makes one aware that he or she is acting unethically. The majority of unethical behaviors are unintentional and ordinary, thus affecting everyone and providing support for unethical behavior when people unconsciously lower the bar over time through small changes in their ethical behavior.

A look at Siemens' corporate culture reveals according to Berghoff (2018: 429) an astounding willingness to engage in bribery:

> It was like an unwritten law to go through thick and thin for Siemens. Some employees were proud to have been entrusted with the responsible and at the same time risky task of taking care of organizing bribery. To them it was a token of trustworthiness and importance. Many indeed believed that facilitating bribery was in the best interest of the firm.

As a tribal community and the "Siemens family", the global company has its own peculiar sets of practices in order to preserve and strengthen their cohesion. The rational self-interest found replacement in self-sacrifice to take risks on behalf of the collective. Some privileged individuals even put their behavior on autopilot to serve the organization as they expect to spend the rest of their professional lives at Siemens (Berghoff, 2018).

Rational choice is concerned with benefits of crime exceeding costs (Pratt and Cullen, 2005), where the perceived likelihood of incarceration is a cost element. Another cost element is media exposure, where investigative journalists often are the first to disclose suspected white-collar crime and the offenders. Press reporters' detection of misconduct and crime "represented an important ingredient of the nineteenth-century newspaper" (Taylor, 2018: 346), and this is certainly also the case so far in the twenty-first-century media.

The rational choice approach also applies to the willingness in the behavioral dimension of convenience theory. The rational choice assumption about offending is based on a normative foundation where advantages and disadvantages are subjectively compared (Müller, 2018).

Historical convenience perspectives

In media reports and contemporary debates on white-collar crime, the impression seems often conveyed that law enforcement implicitly is dealing with a relatively new phenomenon (Lord and Wingerde, 2020). While times have changed and so have crime opportunities, this impression nevertheless could not be more erroneous and misleading. Policing white-collar crime has long traditions. Already in the seventeenth and eighteenth centuries, colonial companies suffered from large corruption and embezzlement scandals according to Pettigrew (2018: 307), who suggests that "seventeenth century England offers a distinctive context in which to examine the history of white-collar crime".

As emphasized in the earlier quote from Berghoff and Spiekermann (2018), there are factors that increase convenience and factors that reduce convenience for white-collar crime over time. One additional factor for convenience increase mentioned by them is that with every technological wonder, with every new-fangled financial instrument, or mode of organizing business ventures come bounteous prospects for fraudsters.

One additional factor for convenience reduction was the assessment of financial crime committed by high-level officials in the corporate world that began to change in light of the theory of delinquent association by Sutherland (1939). According to Berghoff and Spiekermann (2018), Sutherland violated existing perceptions that high-ranking persons would not or only in extreme situations commit offenses. Sutherland stated that the total damage of white-collar crime was enormous as it undermined society and its economic systems of markets.

Bernsee (2018: 321) suggests that processes of privatization can lead to dubious or even criminal practices, especially in countries in transition:

> Although the actors involved mostly claim to improve the common good, a remarkable phenomenon is that in many cases, specific groups take extraordinary advantages from them or even enrich themselves in a criminal manner.

He studied privatization in Bavaria and Prussia in the early nineteenth century and found ample evidence of increase in convenience for corruption and other kinds of white-collar crime.

Based on these selected history sources, it seems that a number of factors have increased the convenience of white-collar crime. Some of the factors are new technologies, globalization (Wingerde and Lord, 2020) and other changes, business lawyers finding loopholes in the law and grey areas of unclear legal status, new corporate structures, and new management schools. Factors that reduce the convenience include new laws and regulations, ethics, environmental concerns, public condemnation, and the role of compliance (Biegelman and Bartow, 2012; Graham, 2015; Kawasaki, 2020; Lehman et al., 2019; Marchetti, 2012).

Convenience evaluation criteria

The research question addressed in this chapter is concerned with criteria that one might apply to study the evolution of white-collar crime. We study the evolution of white-collar crime in terms of convenience, where convenience varies in the motivational dimension, the organizational dimension and the behavioral dimension of convenience theory. Illegitimate profits might be a more or less convenient way of satisfying needs and desires. Organizational settings can be more or less convenient to commit and conceal financial crime. Deviant behavior can be more or less convenient for personal willingness.

Within each of the three dimensions of convenience theory, the theory emphasizes certain characteristics that might be relevant in this chapter for criteria to evaluate the evolution of convenience for white-collar offenders over time.

Economical dimension

A distinction exists between occupational crime and corporate crime, where the former mainly benefits a privileged individual, while the latter mainly benefits the organization (Craig and Piquero, 2017). A further distinction exists between threats and possibilities as motives (Langton and Piquero, 2007).

1   *Attractive individual economic possibilities: Are people in privileged professional positions more or less greedy on behalf of themselves and their employers presently compared to the past?* Greed is the most acknowledged motive for financial crime by white-collar offenders. Goldstraw-White (2012) defines greed as socially constructed needs and desires that can never be completely covered or contended. Greed can be a very strong quest to get more and more of something, and there is a strong preference to maximize wealth. To outsiders it may seem strange that rich people have such a strong desire to become even richer that they are willing to break the law. However, as the definition indicates, greedy individuals are never happy with what they have, as they desperately want more all the time. Prosperity is not a means, but a goal for greedy individuals. Greed can grow when the organization does not have an adequate reaction. Both Bucy et al. (2008) and Hamilton and Micklethwait (2006) emphasize greed as the most common cause of criminal acts by white-collar offenders.

2   *Painful individual economic threats: Are people in privileged professional positions more or less strained and stressed in difficult financial situations presently compared to the past?* The strain perspective has become one of the leading theoretical explanations for crime (Langton and Piquero, 2007). The strain perspective argues that a range of factors influence whether individuals cope with strains through crime (Thaxton and Agnew, 2018: 888): "Criminal coping is said to be most likely among those with poor coping skills and resources, little social support, low social control, beliefs favorable to crime, criminal associates, and opportunities for crime". The strain perspective emphasizes strains and stressors that increase the likelihood of crime, the negative emotions (including anger) resulting from those strains that create pressure for corrective action, and the factors that influence or condition the likelihood of criminal coping (Thaxton and Agnew, 2018). Agnew (2005) identified three categories of strain: failure to achieve positively valued goals, the removal of positively valued stimuli, and the presentation of negative stimuli. Crime is one possible action, which seems attractive to some privileged members of the elite as a means to escape from or reduce strains (Froggio and Agnew, 2007).

3   *Attractive corporate economic possibilities: Are business organizations more or less greedy presently compared to the past?* An organization is always looking for attractive corporate economic possibilities. Profit-driven crime is a result of a desire for more gain (Naylor, 2003). In many organizations, ends justify means (Campbell and Göritz, 2014). If ends in terms of ambitions and goals are difficult to realize and achieve in legal ways, illegal means represent an alternative in many organizations (Jonnergård et al., 2010; Welsh and Ordonez, 2014). Among most executives, it is an obvious necessity to achieve goals and objectives, while it is an obvious catastrophe failing to achieve goals and objectives. Dodge (2009: 15) argues that there is tough rivalry that makes executives in the organization commit crime to attain goals: "The competitive environment generates pressures on the organization to violate the law in order to attain goals".

4   *Painful corporate economic threats: Are business organizations more or less strained and stressed in difficult financial situations presently compared to the past?* Threats in the workplace may stem from specific market conditions and market forces. Some business enterprises can be so dominant in an industry that others may only survive through economic crime (Chang et al., 2005; Geest et al., 2017; Leonard and Weber, 1970). The threat of losing everything they have built up working very hard over a long period may cause owners who once were entrepreneurs to intervene and commit VAT fraud and tax evasion in order to prevent their own empire from collapse. The alternative for the former entrepreneurs can be bankruptcy crime by removing all assets before bankruptcy so that creditors receive little or nothing (Box et al., 2019). The purpose is to protect the economic interests of the business (Blickle et al., 2006) and possibly start up again without debts. Threats can create moral panic. Moral panic can characterize

reactions that do not accurately reflect the actual danger of a threat. During a moral panic, sensitization processes generate an escalation in the individual disturbance (Kang and Thosuwanchot, 2017).

5   *Rational self-interest motivation: Are people more or less into weighing up the pros and cons of alternative courses of actions for profit presently compared to the past?* Both individual and corporate responses to possibilities and threats can result from rational self-interest. The economic perspective is concerned with the influence of rational self-interest in explaining the development of white-collar crime (Pillay and Kluvers, 2014). The economic model of rational self-interest is all about weighing up the costs and benefits of alternative courses of actions. The model considers incentives and probability of detection (Welsh et al., 2014). This applies to both private and professional life. Human behavior finds motivation in the self-centered quest for satisfaction and avoidance of suffering (Hirschi and Gottfredson, 1987).

Organizational dimension

The organizational opportunity is concerned with illegal profit that seem more conveniently achieved in an organizational setting where the offender can enjoy power and influence based on position and trust. Opportunity suggests the ability to commit wrongdoing with the expectation that nobody will detect or report it, and the offender will not be punished (Schnatterly et al., 2018). The organizational dimension sets white-collar criminals apart from other financial criminals. White-collar crime can be distinguished from ordinary crime ("street crime") based on the status of the offenders, their access to legitimate occupations, the common presence of an organizational form, and the extent of the costs and harmfulness of such crime. The ability of white-collar offenders to commit and conceal crime links to their privileged position, the social structure, and their orientation to legitimate and respectable careers (Friedrichs et al., 2018).

1   *High social status in privileged positions: Is it more or less possible to blame members of the elite presently compared to the past?* Some members of the elite are simply too powerful to blame. Pontell et al. (2014) found that the financial crisis obviously had its cause in mismanagement in the financial sector, but all in the financial sector avoided serious blame. Status-related factors such as influential positions, upper-class family ties, and community roles often preclude perceptions of blameworthiness (Slyke and Bales, 2012). White-collar offenders "are now regarded as the untouchables, too well-heeled and powerful to lock up" (Hausman, 2018: 381).

2   *Legitimate access to crime resources: Do elite members in privileged professional positions have more or less convenient access to systems to commit and conceal financial crime presently compared to the past?* A white-collar offender has typically legitimate access to resources to commit and conceal crime (Adler and Kwon, 2002). A resource is an enabler applied and used to satisfy human and organizational needs. According to Petrocelli et al. (2003),

access to resources equates access to power. Offenders take advantage of their positions of power with almost unlimited authority in the opportunity structure (Kempa, 2010), because they have legitimate and often privileged access to physical and virtual locations in which crime is committed, are totally in charge of resource allocations and transactions, and are successful in concealment based on key resources used to hide their crime.

3   *Disorganized institutional deterioration: Are business organizations more or less transparent presently compared to the past?* Institutional deterioration can occur conveniently resulting from external legitimacy where deviance is the norm (Rodriguez et al., 2005). Offenders' actions have a superficial appearance of legitimacy also internally, since both legal and illegal actions in the company occur in a manner characterized by disorganization (Benson and Simpson, 2018). Conventional mechanisms of social control are weak and unable to regulate the behavior within organizations (Pratt and Cullen, 2005). In enterprises characterized by instability and heterogeneity, there is reduced likelihood of effective socialization and supervision. The impact of social bonds varies by type of organization and disorganized units negatively affect the ability of social bonds to reduce delinquent behavior (Hoffmann, 2002; Onna and Denkers, 2019).

4   *Lack of oversight and guardianship: Do control functions within business enterprises function better or worse presently, compared to past performance?* As evidenced by many internal investigation reports by fraud examiners after white-collar crime scandals, internal auditors, external auditors, compliance committees and other internal and external control units do not function properly (Biegelman and Bartow, 2012; Graham, 2015; Lehman et al., 2019; Marchetti, 2012). Oversight and control functions tend to be formal units without any insights into the substance of business activities. They tend to review procedures rather than transactions within procedures. Therefore, ineffective control functions are often an important part of the opportunity structure for white-collar crime. For example, at Toshiba Corporation, lack of controls was an important element of the opportunity structure (Deloitte, 2015). Fraud examiners emphasized lack of internal controls by accounting and auditing functions, as well as lack of finance control in each corporate division. At Wells Fargo, corporate control functions were constrained by the decentralized organizational structure (Shearman Sterling, 2017). Fraud examiners excused corporate control functions since they suffered from harm by the decentralized organizational structure and a culture of substantial independence for business units. At Fuji Xerox, CEO Whittaker had gained control over reporting lines to manipulate accounting (Deloitte, 2017). At Danske Bank where money laundering occurred in their Estonian branch, corporate control functions did not work because the branch operated computer systems different from computer systems at the headquarters (Bruun Hjejle, 2018). Telenor executives ignored corruption rumors at VimpelCom since the chief compliance officer and chief legal officer did not know how to handle whistleblowing (Deloitte, 2016).

5   *Criminal market structures: Are cartels and corruption networks more or less conveniently available for business performance presently compared to the past?* While cartels can represent painful corporate economic threats in the economical dimension of convenience theory, a cartel can also represent an opportunity for those enterprises that have joined the cartel (Freiberg, 2020). In many markets, there are cartels that regulate the supply side. Cartel members agree not only on market division but also on prices to various customers (Goncharov and Peter, 2019; Leonard and Weber, 1970). The social exchange perspective aids explanations of how power structures in cartels and corruption networks develop and institutionalize through relationship building and social exchanges among participating enterprises. The perspective suggests that organizational activities are contingent on the actions of other organizations. The successful cartels and networks are dependent on generation of obligations and fulfillment of rewards. Relational efforts in an industry or in a community lead to repeated patterns of interactions that may develop into durable institutions of interdependencies in cartels and networks (Cartier-Bresson, 1997; Cropanzano and Mitchell, 2005; Emerson, 1976; Lawler and Hipp, 2010).

Behavioral dimension

Most research on white-collar crime exists along the behavioral dimension. Researchers have presented numerous suggestions to explain famous people who were willing to commit and conceal financial crime. Some of the most prominent perspectives are differential association (Sutherland, 1939, 1983), lack of self-control (Gottfredson and Hirschi, 1990), slippery slope (Arjoon, 2008), and neutralization techniques (Sykes and Matza, 1957).

1   *The innocent justification offender mind: Do offenders find it more or less convenient to justify misconduct and crime presently compared to the past?* The personal willingness is concerned with the impression that surprisingly few white-collar criminals think they have done anything wrong. Most of them feel innocent and victims of injustice when indicted, prosecuted, convicted, and imprisoned. By application of neutralization techniques (Sykes and Matza, 1957), they deny responsibility, injury, and victim. They condemn the condemners. They claim appeal to higher loyalties and normality of action. They claim entitlement, and they argue the case of legal mistake. They find their own mistakes acceptable. They argue a dilemma arose, whereby they made a reasonable tradeoff before committing the act (Jordanoska, 2018; Kaptein and Helvoort, 2019; Schoultz and Flyghed, 2016, 2019; Siponen and Vance, 2010). Such claims enable offenders to find crime convenient, since they do not consider it a crime, and they do not feel guilty of wrongdoing.

2   *The deviant personality offender mind: Do members of the upper echelon of society view themselves as more or less privileged presently compared to the past?*

Some white-collar offenders are narcissists. Narcissists exhibit an unusual trust in themselves, believing that they are uniquely special and entitled to more benefits than are legitimately available to them (Ouimet, 2010). A particular version of narcissism is narcissistic identification with the organization, where the offender sees little or no difference between self and the business. Then company money is personal money that can be spent whatever way the narcissist prefers (Galvin et al., 2015). A pervasive pattern of grandiosity, need for admiration, and empathy deficits typifies narcissism. While grandiosity and admiration belong to the motivational dimension of convenience theory, empathy deficits belong to the willingness dimension of convenience theory where the offender possesses a sense of entitlement. The offender shows unreasonable expectations to receive and obtain preferential treatments (Zvi and Elaad, 2018).

3   The rational choice offender mind: *Are people more or less into weighing up the pros and cons of alternative behaviors for profit presently compared to the past?* The rational self-interest motivation is part of the economical dimension of convenience theory. The rational choice approach also applies to the willingness in the behavioral dimension of convenience theory. The rational choice assumption about offending is based on a normative foundation where advantages and disadvantages are subjectively compared (Müller, 2018). When there is no perceived likelihood of detection, then there is no deterrence effect to prevent offenses (Comey, 2009). If there is a certain perceived likelihood, then willingness might depend on the perceived consequences. For potential white-collar offenders it can be frightening to think of time in jail or prison. Research has shown that some white-collar offenders suffer from special sensitivity in prison, while others have special resilience in prison (Hunter, 2020; Logan et al., 2019), which means that they cope better with incarceration than other inmates. Deterrence comes from whether or not an offender has to go to prison, rather than the severity of sanction in terms of imprisonment length. Generally, the severity of punishment has shown to have no effect on recidivism (Mears and Cochran, 2018). Rational choice is concerned with benefits of crime exceeding costs (Pratt and Cullen, 2005), where the perceived likelihood of incarceration is a cost element. Another cost element is media exposure, where investigative journalists often are the first to disclose suspected white-collar crime and the offenders. Press reporters' detection of misconduct and crime "represented an important ingredient of the nineteenth-century newspaper" (Taylor, 2018: 346), and this is certainly also the case so far in the twenty-first-century media.

4   The slippery absent offender mind: *Do members of the upper echelon of society suffer from more or less lack of self-control presently compared to the past?* Lack of self-control is a frequent explanation for executive deviance and crime in general (Gottfredson and Hirschi, 1990). While many might be tempted, only those lacking self-control will actually do it. Self-regulation monitors self-control, where self-regulation represents a process of using self-regulatory

resources to control undesirable impulses and override subsequent behavioral responses. As argued by Mawritz et al. (2017), individuals possess varying and limited self-regulatory resources that inhibit responses that may arise from physiological processes, habit, learning, or the strain of the situation. The slippery slope perspective suggests that a person can slide over time from legal to illegal activities without really noticing. The small infractions can lead to the larger ones. An organization that overlooks the small infractions of its employees creates a culture of acceptance that may lead to its own demise (Welsh et al., 2014). The slippery slope perspective applies to a number of situations, such as seventeenth century England, where "unregulated overseas trade was a slippery slope to fraud" (Pettigrew, 2018: 313). Arjoon (2008: 78) explains slippery slope in the following way: "As commonsense experience tells us, it is the small infractions that can lead to the larger ones".

In summary, the purpose of this chapter was to discuss how convenience in white-collar crime might work in business history research, as the extent of convenience influences the magnitude of financial crime among privileged individuals in the course of their professions. Convenience is savings in time and efforts, as well as avoidance of strain and pain. The theory of convenience suggests that the extent of white-collar crime is dependent on economical motives, organizational opportunities, and personal willingness for deviant behavior. These three dimensions in convenience theory were broken down in this chapter into 14 potential criteria to evaluate whether white-collar crime is more convenient presently compared to the past. Historians are encouraged to apply these criteria in their future studies to describe the evolution of white-collar crime.

More convenience dynamics

Figure 4.1 illustrates how financial motive for illegitimate gain, organizational opportunity to commit and conceal white-collar crime, and personal willingness for deviant behavior reinforce each other in the triangle of convenience theory (Braaten and Vaughn, 2019; Chan and Gibbs, 2020; Hansen, 2020). The financial motive is influenced by expected financial gain compared to actual project costs, where a potential offender makes a rational decision of crime-as-choice when benefits exceed costs (Kamerdze et al., 2014; Paternoster et al., 2018; Schnatterly et al., 2018; Shepherd and Button, 2019). The rational choice assumption about offending is based on a normative foundation where advantages and disadvantages are subjectively compared (Müller, 2018). Offenders consider it rational to commit crime if benefits exceed costs. Individual preferences thus determine whether crime is committed (Pratt and Cullen, 2005). The greater benefits of crime and the less costs of crime, the more attractive it is to commit criminal acts. According to Berghoff and Spiekermann (2018: 293), potential white-collar offenders "act on cost-benefit calculations involving the expected utility, the likelihood of being caught, and punishment costs". The assumption

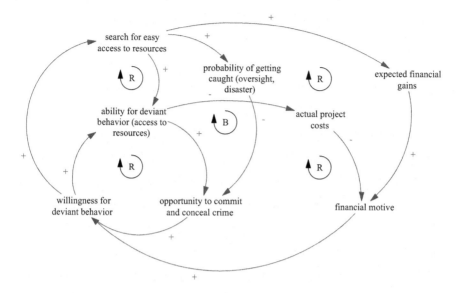

Figure 4.1 Reinforcing loops for convenience in motive, opportunity and willingness

of rational choice is that every crime is chosen and committed for specific reasons. Individuals consciously and deliberately choose criminal behavior of their own free will.

The opportunity to commit and conceal crime in the organizational context depends on the lack of controls, oversight and guardianship as well as the convenient access to crime resources as illustrated in Figure 4.1. Legitimate access to premises and systems (Benson and Simpson, 2018), specialized access in routine activity (Cohen and Felson, 1979), blame game by misleading attribution to others (Eberly et al., 2011), and institutional deterioration (Rodriguez et al., 2005) are some of the perspectives integrated in the opportunity dimension of convenience theory. A typical white-collar offender does not go into hiding as many street criminals do. Rather, the offender conceals financial crime among legal transactions to make illegal transactions seem legitimate, or the offender conceals financial crime by removing certain activities from the books. A typical white-collar offender who has convenient legitimate access to commit crime might spend most of their energy on concealing crime in the professional context.

The personal willingness for deviant behavior depends on both motive and opportunity as illustrated in Figure 4.1. In addition, a number of other factors enhance willingness, such as narcissistic identification (Galvin et al., 2015), acceptable for the elite (Petrocelli et al., 2003), learning from others (Sutherland, 1983), negative events (Engdahl, 2015), application of neutralization techniques (Sykes and Matza, 1957), lack of self-control (Gottfredson and Hirschi, 1990), and sliding on the slippery slope (Welsh et al., 2014).

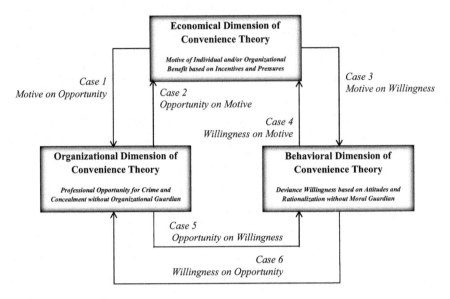

Figure 4.2 Hypothetical links between variables in the triangle of convenience

In the system dynamics terminology (Randers, 2019; Sterman, 2018), financial motive, organizational opportunity, and personal willingness are endogenous variables, as they influence and are influenced by other variables in the dynamic model as well as by each other. Figure 4.2 illustrates the convenience triangle for white-collar crime. There are three variables and six relationships in the triangle. Each relationship represents a causal effect from one variable on the other construct. For example, case 6 is concerned with the influence of willingness on opportunity. When a chief financial officer (CFO) decides to commit embezzlement, for example because of a negative life event, the person will expand organizational opportunities. One avenue for expanding opportunities is to control the work of external auditors in the company, thereby reducing oversight and guardianship.

References

Adler, P.S. and Kwon, S.W. (2002). Social capital: Prospects for a new concept, *Academy of Management Review*, 27 (1), 17–40.

Agnew, R. (2005). *Pressured into Crime: An Overview of General Strain Theory*, Oxford, UK: Oxford University Press.

Agnew, R. (2014). Social concern and crime: Moving beyond the assumption of simple self-interest, *Criminology*, 52 (1), 1–32.

Arjoon, S. (2008). Slippery when wet: The real risk in business, *Journal of Markets & Morality*, Spring, 11 (1), 77–91.

Benson, M.L. (2013). Editor's introduction – White-collar crime: Bringing the offender back in, *Journal of Contemporary Criminal Justice*, 29 (3), 324–330.

Benson, M.L. and Simpson, S.S. (2018). *White-Collar Crime: An Opportunity Perspective*, 3rd edition, New York, NY: Routledge.

Berghoff, H. (2018). "Organised irresponsibility?" The Siemens corruption scandal of the 1990s and 2000s, *Business History*, 60 (3), 423–445.

Berghoff, H. and Spiekermann, U. (2018). Shady business: On the history of white-collar crime, *Business History*, 60 (3), 289–304.

Bernsee, R. (2018). Privatization and corruption in historical perspective: The case of secularization in Bavaria and Prussia in the early nineteenth century, *Business History*, 60 (3), 321–342.

Berry, L.L., Seiders, K. and Grewal, D. (2002). Understanding service convenience, *Journal of Marketing*, 66, 1–17.

Biegelman, M.T. and Bartow, J.T. (2012). *Executive Roadmap to Fraud Prevention and Internal Control: Creating a Culture of Compliance*, London, UK: John Wiley & Sons.

Bigley, G.A. and Wiersma, M.F. (2002). New CEOs and corporate strategic refocusing: How experience as heir apparent influences the use of power, *Administrative Science Quarterly*, 47, 707–727.

Blickle, G., Schlegel, A., Fassbender, P. and Klein, U. (2006). Some personality correlates of business white-collar crime, *Applied Psychology: An International Review*, 55 (2), 220–233.

Box, M., Gratzer, K. and Lin, X. (2019). The asymmetric effect of bankruptcy fraud in Sweden: A long-term perspective, *Journal of Quantitative Criminology*, 35 (2), 287–312.

Braaten, C.N. and Vaughn, M.S. (2019). Convenience theory of cryptocurrency crime: A content analysis of U.S. federal court decisions, *Deviant Behavior*, published online, https://doi.org/10.1080/01639625.2019.1706706.

Bruun Hjejle (2018). *Report on the Non-Resident Portfolio at Danske Bank's Estonian branch*, law firm Bruun Hjejle, https://danskebank.com/-/media/danske-bank-com/file-cloud/2018/9/report-on-the-non-resident-portfolio-at-danske-banks-estonian-branch.pdf, published September 19, downloaded September 25.

Bucy, P.H., Formby, E.P., Raspanti, M.S. and Rooney, K.E. (2008). Why do they do it? The motives, mores, and character of white collar criminals, *St. John's Law Review*, 82, 401–571.

Campbell, J.L. and Göritz, A.S. (2014). Culture corrupts! A qualitative study of organizational culture in corrupt organizations, *Journal of Business Ethics*, 120 (3), 291–311.

Cartier-Bresson, J. (1997). Corruption networks, transaction security and illegal social exchange, *Political Studies*, 45 (3), 463–476.

Chan, F. and Gibbs, C. (2020). Integrated theories of white-collar and corporate crime, in: Rorie, M.L. (editor), *The Handbook of White-Collar Crime*, Hoboken, NJ: Wiley & Sons, chapter 13, pages 191–208.

Chang, J.J., Lu, H.C. and Chen, M. (2005). Organized crime or individual crime? Endogenous size of a criminal organization and the optimal law enforcement, *Economic Inquiry*, 43 (3), 661–675.

Cianci, A.M., Clor-Proell, S.M. and Kaplan, S.E. (2019). How do investors respond to restatements? Reputation and the announcement of corrective actions, *Journal of Business Ethics*, 158, 297–312.

Cohen, L.E. and Felson, M. (1979). Social change and crime rate trends: A routine activity approach, *American Sociological Review*, 44, 588–608.

Collier, J.E. and Kimes, S.E. (2012). Only if it is convenient: Understanding how convenience influences self-service technology evaluation, *Journal of Service Research*, 16 (1), 39–51.

Comey, J.B. (2009). Go directly to prison: White collar sentencing after the Sarbanes-Oxley act, *Harvard Law Review*, 122, 1728–1749.

Craig, J.M. and Piquero, N.L. (2017). Sensational offending: An application of sensation seeking to white-collar and conventional crimes, *Crime & Delinquency*, 63 (11), 1363–1382.

Cropanzano, R. and Mitchell, M.S. (2005). Social exchange theory: An interdisciplinary review, *Journal of Management*, 31 (6), 874–900.

Deloitte (2015). *Investigation Report. Summary Version.* Independent Investigation Committee for Toshiba Corporation. 90 pages, July 20. Ueda, K., Matui, H. Ito, T. and Yamada, K., www.toshiba.co.jp/about/ir/en/news/20150725_1.pdf.

Deloitte (2016). *Review Ownership VimpelCom*, www.telenor.com/wp-content/uploads/2016/04/Deloitte-Report_Telenor_290416_FINAL.pdf.

Deloitte (2017). *Investigation Report*, Independent Investigation Committee, by global auditing firm Deloitte, published June 10, Ito, T., Sato, K. and Nishimura, K., www.fujifilmholdings.com/en/pdf/investors/finance/materials/ff_irdata_investigation_001e.pdf.

Dodge, M. (2009). *Women and White-Collar Crime*, Saddle River, NJ: Prentice Hall.

Eberl, P., Geiger, D. and Assländer, M.S. (2015). Repairing trust in an organization after integrity violations. The ambivalence of organizational rule adjustments, *Organization Studies*, 36 (9), 1205–1235.

Eberly, M.B., Holley, E.C., Johnson, M.D. and Mitchell, T.R. (2011). Beyond internal and external: A dyadic theory of relational attributions, *Academy of Management Review*, 36 (4), 731–753.

Emerson, R.M. (1976). Social exchange theory, *Annual Review of Sociology*, 2, 335–362.

Engdahl, O. (2015). White-collar crime and first-time adult-onset offending: Explorations in the concept of negative life events as turning points, *International Journal of Law, Crime and Justice*, 43 (1), 1–16.

Farquhar, J.D. and Rowley, J. (2009). Convenience: A services perspective, *Marketing Theory*, 9 (4), 425–438.

Freiberg, A. (2020). Researching white-collar crime: An Australian perspective, in: Rorie, M.L. (editor), *The Handbook of White-Collar Crime*, Hoboken, NJ: Wiley & Sons, chapter 26, pages 418–436.

Friedrichs, D.O., Schoultz, I. and Jordanoska, A. (2018). *Edwin H. Sutherland, Routledge Key Thinkers in Criminology*, London, UK: Routledge.

Froggio, G. and Agnew, R. (2007). The relationship between crime and "objective" versus "subjective" strains, *Journal of Criminal Justice*, 35, 81–87.

Galvin, B.M., Lange, D. and Ashforth, B.E. (2015). Narcissistic organizational identification: Seeing oneself as central to the organization's identity, *Academy of Management Review*, 40 (2), 163–181.

Geest, V.R., Weisburd, D. and Blokland, A.A.J. (2017). Developmental trajectories of offenders convicted of fraud: A follow-up to age 50 in a Dutch conviction cohort, *European Journal of Criminology*, 14 (5), 543–565.

Goldstraw-White, J. (2012). *White-Collar Crime: Accounts of Offending Behavior*, London, UK: Palgrave Macmillan.

Goncharov, I. and Peter, C.D. (2019). Does reporting transparency affect industry coordination? Evidence from the duration of international cartels, *The Accounting Review*, 94 (3), 149–175.

Gottfredson, M.R. and Hirschi, T. (1990). *A General Theory of Crime*, Stanford, CA: Stanford University Press.

Graham, L. (2015). *Internal Control Audit and Compliance: Documentation and Testing under the New Coso Framework*, London, UK: John Wiley & Sons.

Hamilton, S. and Micklethwait, A. (2006). *Greed and Corporate Failure: The Lessons from Recent Disasters*, Basingstoke, UK: Palgrave Macmillan.

Hansen, L.L. (2020). Review of the book "Convenience Triangle in White-Collar Crime: Case Studies of Fraud Examinations", *ChoiceConnect*, vol. 57, no. 5, Middletown, CT: Association of College and Research Libraries.

Hausman, W.J. (2018). Howard Hopson's billion dollar fraud: The rise and fall of associated gas & electric company, *Business History*, 60 (3), 381–398.

Higgins, E.T. (1997). Beyond pleasure and pain, *American Psychologist*, 52, 1280–1300.

Hirschi, T. and Gottfredson, M. (1987). Causes of white-collar crime, *Criminology*, 25 (4), 949–974.

Hoffmann, J.P. (2002). A contextual analysis of differential association, social control, and strain theories of delinquency, *Social Forces*, 81 (3), 753–785.

Hunter, B. (2020). The correctional experiences of white-collar offenders, in: Rorie, M.L. (editor), *The Handbook of White-Collar Crime*, Hoboken, NJ: Wiley & Sons, chapter 19, pages 297–313.

Jonnergård, K., Stafsudd, A. and Elg, U. (2010). Performance evaluations as gender barriers in professional organizations: A study of auditing firms, *Gender, Work and Organization*, 17 (6), 721–747.

Jordanoska, A. (2018). The social ecology of white-collar crime: Applying situational action theory to white-collar offending, *Deviant Behavior*, 39 (11), 1427–1449.

Kamerdze, S., Loughran, T., Paternoster, R. and Sohoni, T. (2014). The role of affect in intended rule breaking: Extending the rational choice perspective, *Journal of Research in Crime and Delinquency*, 51 (5), 620–654.

Kang, E. and Thosuwanchot, N. (2017). An application of Durkheim's four categories of suicide to organizational crimes, *Deviant Behavior*, 38 (5), 493–513.

Kaptein, M. and Helvoort, M. (2019). A model of neutralization techniques, *Deviant Behavior*, 40 (10), 1260–1285.

Kawasaki, T. (2020). Review of comparative studies on white-collar and corporate crime, in: Rorie, M.L. (editor), *The Handbook of White-Collar Crime*, Hoboken, NJ: Wiley & Sons, chapter 27, pages 437–447.

Kempa, M. (2010). Combating white-collar crime in Canada: Serving victim needs and market integrity, *Journal of Financial Crime*, 17 (2), 251–264.

Langton, L. and Piquero, N.L. (2007). Can general strain theory explain white-collar crime? A preliminary investigation of the relationship between strain and select white-collar offenses, *Journal of Criminal Justice*, 35 (1), 1–15.

Lawler, E.J. and Hipp, L. (2010). Corruption as social exchange, *Advances in Group Processes*, 27, 269–296.

Lee, F. and Robinson, R.J. (2000). An attributional analysis of social accounts: Implications of playing the blame game, *Journal of Applied Social Psychology*, 30 (9), 1853–1879.

Lehman, D.W., Cooil, B. and Ramanujam, R. (2019). The effects of rule complexity on organizational noncompliance and remediation: Evidence from restaurant health inspections, *Journal of Management*, published online, pages 1–33, https://doi.org/10.1177/0149206319842262.

Leonard, W.N. and Weber, M.G. (1970). Automakers and dealers: A study of criminogenic market forces, *Law & Society Review*, 4 (3), 407–424.

Logan, M.W., Morgan, M.A., Benson, M.L. and Cullen, F.T. (2019). Coping with imprisonment: Testing the special sensitivity hypothesis for white-collar offenders, *Justice Quarterly*, 36 (2), 225–254.

Lord, N. and Wingerde, K. (2020). Preventing and intervening in white-collar crimes: The role of law enforcement, in: Rorie, M.L. (editor), *The Handbook of White-Collar Crime*, Hoboken, NJ: Wiley & Sons, chapter 16, 246–261.

Mai, H.T.X. and Olsen, S.O. (2016). Consumer participation in self-production: The role of control mechanisms, convenience orientation, and moral obligation, *Journal of Marketing Theory and Practice*, 24 (2), 209–223.

Marchetti, A.M. (2012). *Enterprise Risk Management Best Practices: From Assessment to Ongoing Compliance*, Hoboken, NJ: John Wiley & Sons.

Maslow, A.H. (1943). A theory of human motivation, *Psychological Review*, 50 (4), 370–396.

Mawritz, M.B., Greenbaum, R.L., Butts, M.M. and Graham, K.A. (2017). I just can't control myself: A self-regulation perspective on the abuse of deviant employees, *Academy of Management Journal*, 60 (4), 1482–1503.

Mears, D.P. and Cochran, J.C. (2018). Progressively tougher sanctioning and recidivism: Assessing the effects of different types of sanctions, *Journal of Research in Crime and Delinquency*, 55 (2), 194–241.

Müller, S.M. (2018). Corporate behavior and ecological disaster: Dow Chemical and the Great Lakes mercury crisis, 1970–1972, *Business History*, 60 (3), 399–422.

Murphy, P.R. and Dacin, M.T. (2011). Psychological pathways to fraud: Understanding and preventing fraud in organizations, *Journal of Business Ethics*, 101, 601–618.

Naylor, R.T. (2003). Towards a general theory of profit-driven crimes, *British Journal of Criminology*, 43, 81–101.

Onna, J.H.R. and Denkers, A.J.M. (2019). Social bonds and white-collar crime: A two-study assessment of informal social controls in white-collar offenders, *Deviant Behavior*, 40 (10), 1206–1225.

Ouimet, G. (2010). Dynamics of narcissistic leadership in organizations, *Journal of Managerial Psychology*, 25 (7), 713–726.

Patel, P.C. and Cooper, D. (2014). Structural power equality between family and nonfamily TMT members and the performance of family firms, *Academy of Management Journal*, 57 (6), 1624–1649.

Paternoster, R., Jaynes, C.M. and Wilson, T. (2018). Rational choice theory and interest in the "fortune of others", *Journal of Research in Crime and Delinquency*, 54 (6), 847–868.

Petrocelli, M., Piquero, A.R. and Smith, M.R. (2003). Conflict theory and racial profiling: An empirical analysis of police traffic stop data, *Journal of Criminal Justice*, 31 (1), 1–11.

Pettigrew, W.A. (2018). The changing place of fraud in seventeenth-century public debates about international trading corporations, *Business History*, 60 (3), 305–320.

Pillay, S. and Kluvers, R. (2014). An institutional theory perspective on corruption: The case of a developing democracy, *Financial Accountability & Management*, 30 (1), 95–119.

Piquero, N.L. and Schoepfer, A. (2010). Theories of white-collar crime and public policy, in: Barlow, H.D. and Decker, S.H. (editors), *Criminology and Public Policy: Putting Theory to Work*, Philadelphia, PA: Temple University Press.

Pontell, H.N., Black, W.K. and Geis, G. (2014). Too big to fail, too powerful to jail? On the absence of criminal prosecutions after the 2008 financial meltdown, *Crime, Law and Social Change*, 61 (1), 1–13.

Pratt, T.C. and Cullen, F.T. (2005). Assessing macro-level predictors and theories of crime: A meta-analysis, *Crime and Justice*, 32, 373–450.

Randers, J. (2019). The great challenge for system dynamics on the path forward: Implementation and real impact, *System Dynamics Review*, 35 (2), 19–24.

Rodriguez, P., Uhlenbruck, K. and Eden, L. (2005). Government corruption and the entry strategies of multinationals, *Academy of Management Review*, 30 (2), 383–396.

Sari, Y.K., Shaari, Z.H. and Amar, A.B. (2017). Measurement development of customer patronage of petrol station with convenience store, *Global Business and Management Research: An International Journal*, 9 (1), 52–62.

Schnatterly, K., Gangloff, K.A. and Tuschke, A. (2018). CEO wrongdoing: A review of pressure, opportunity, and rationalization, *Journal of Management*, 44 (6), 2405–2432.

Schoultz, I. and Flyghed, J. (2016). Doing business for a "higher loyalty'? How Swedish transnational corporations neutralize allegations of crime, *Crime, Law and Social Change*, 66 (2), 183–198.

Schoultz, I. and Flyghed, J. (2019). From "we didn't do it" to "we've learned our lesson": Development of a typology of neutralizations of corporate crime, *Critical Criminology*, published online doi.org/10.1007/s10612-019-09483-3.

Seiders, K., Voss, G.B., Godfrey, A.L. and Grewal, D. (2007). SERVCON: Development and validation of a multidimensional service convenience scale, *Journal of the Academy of Marketing Science*, 35, 144–156.

Shapiro, S.P. (1990). Collaring the crime, not the criminal: Reconsidering the concept of white-collar crime, *American Sociological Review*, 55, 346–365.

Shearman Sterling (2017). *Independent Directors of the Board of Wells Fargo & Company: Sales Practices Investigation Report*, April 10, 113 pages, Sanger, S.W., Duke, E.A., James, D.M. and Hernandez, E., www08.wellsfargomedia.com/assets/pdf/about/investor-relations/presentations/2017/board-report.pdf.

Shepherd, D. and Button, M. (2019). Organizational inhibitions to addressing occupational fraud: A theory of differential rationalization, *Deviant Behavior*, 40 (8), 971–991.

Shover, N., Hochstetler, A. and Alalehto, T. (2012). Choosing white-collar crime, in: Cullen, F.T. and Wilcox, P. (editors), *The Oxford Handbook of Criminological Theory*, Oxford, UK: Oxford University Press.

Siponen, M. and Vance, A. (2010). Neutralization: New insights into the problem of employee information security policy violations, *MIS Quarterly*, 34 (3), 487–502.

Slyke, S.V. and Bales, W.D. (2012). A contemporary study of the decision to incarcerate white-collar and street property offenders, *Punishment & Society*, 14 (2), 217–246.

Sonnier, B.M., Lassar, W.M. and Lassar, S.S. (2015). The influence of source credibility and attribution of blame on juror evaluation of liability of industry specialist auditors, *Journal of Forensic & Investigative Accounting*, 7 (1), 1–37.

Spiekermann, U. (2018). Cleaning San Francisco, cleaning the United States: The graft prosecutions of 1906–1909 and their nationwide consequences, *Business History*, 60 (3), 361–380.

Sterman, J.D. (2018). System dynamics at sixty: The path forward, *System Dynamics Review*, 34 (1), 5–47.

Sundström, M. and Radon, A. (2015). Utilizing the concept of convenience as a business opportunity in emerging markets, *Organizations and Markets in Emerging Economies*, 6 (2), 7–21.

Sutherland, E.H. (1939). White-collar criminality, *American Sociological Review*, 5 (1), 1–12.

Sutherland, E.H. (1983). *White Collar Crime: The Uncut Version*, New Haven, CT: Yale University Press.

Sykes, G. and Matza, D. (1957). Techniques of neutralization: A theory of delinquency, *American Sociological Review*, 22 (6), 664–670.

Taylor, J. (2018). White-collar crime and the law in nineteenth-century Britain, *Business History*, 60 (3), 343–360.

Thaxton, S. and Agnew, R. (2018). When criminal coping is likely: An examination of conditioning effects in general strain theory, *Journal of Quantitative Criminology*, 34, 887–920.

Welsh, D.T. and Ordonez, L.D. (2014). The dark side of consecutive high performance goals: Linking goal setting, depletion, and unethical behavior, *Organizational Behavior and Human Decision Processes*, 123, 79–89.

Welsh, D.T., Ordonez, L.D., Snyder, D.G. and Christian, M.S. (2014). The slippery slope: How small ethical transgressions pave the way for larger future transgressions, *Journal of Applied Psychology*, 100 (1), 114–127.

Wingerde, K. and Lord, N. (2020). The elusiveness of white-collar and corporate crime in a globalized economy, in: Rorie, M.L. (editor), *The Handbook of White-Collar Crime*, Hoboken, NJ: Wiley & Sons, chapter 29, pages 469–483.

Zvi, L. and Elaad, E. (2018). Correlates of narcissism, self-reported lies, and self-assessed abilities to tell and detect lies, tell truths, and believe others, *Journal of Investigative Psychology and Offender Profiling*, 15, 271–286.

5 Operationalization of convenience

To test the theory of convenience, there is a need to operationalize all the constructs in the structural model in Figure 5.1 as well as develop research hypotheses. The objective of an operationalization is to provide a point of departure for focused empirical research or comparative critical analysis. Friedrichs (2020) distinguishes between operational, typological and polemical levels to organize ideas about white-collar crime. For empirical study, ideas have to move from the polemical via the typological to the operational level.

The overall research proposition is that the tendency to commit white-collar crime increases as a potential offender experiences more of the elements in the model. As the motive becomes stronger, as the opportunity improves, and as the willingness increases, then the theory suggests that the tendency to commit crime rises. Furthermore, the theory suggests that a less likely offender will have a weaker motive, a worse opportunity, and a reduced willingness compared to a more likely offender.

Such a research proposition is not at all easy to test empirically, as there are only three main groups of white-collar people:

1 White-collar people who never commit financial crime.
2 White-collar offenders who never suffer from sanctions because nobody detects their wrongdoing.
3 White-collar offenders who suffer sanctions because of their wrongdoing.

Based on research on the detection rate of white-collar offenses (e.g., Gottschalk and Gunnesdal, 2018), we can assume that group 2 far exceeds the number of people of group 3. We can also assume that most members of the elite in society are law-abiding individuals, and thus assume that group 1 far exceeds the number of people of group 2. The only group, for which there is empirical evidence, is the smallest group 3, where offenders face prosecution and incarceration. As illustrated by a number of case studies in this book, elements of the structural model of convenience theory are easily recognizable.

One empirical approach might be to compare groups 1 and 3, where the research proposition would be that group 1 members have a far lower score on convenience elements than group 3 members. Group 1 members would not

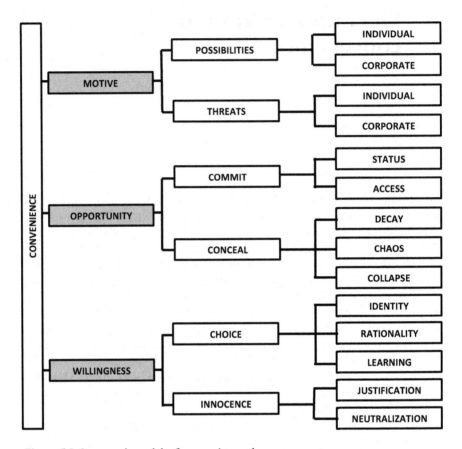

Figure 5.1 Structural model of convenience theory

have a strong motive, would not find many opportunities, and would not perceive a high willingness to commit financial crime.

When empirical research will look for elements of convenience among white-collar people, the research is concerned with both the number of elements and the characteristics of the presence of those elements. Not only will an element be present or not present for a potential offender, it may also play a major or minor role in the overall white-collar convenience for the potential offender. The elements per se will not necessarily be more or less important generally, rather, in each specific case, some elements will be minor while other elements will be major in the overall extent of convenience.

In the following, we imagine that the respondent is a potential or actual white-collar offender. The respondent answers on a scale from "completely disagree" to "completely agree". Statements for group 1 members are first, followed by statements for group 3 members.

Elements of financial motive

Elements of the financial motive represent variables at the individual and the organizational level of analysis. Both individuals and organizations can face possibilities and threats where illegitimate financial gain might serve to explore possibilities and avoid threats.

Motive-possibilities-individual

I have a desire to climb the hierarchy of needs for status and success. I want to realize the American dream of prosperity for myself. I want to satisfy my need for acclaim as a narcissist. I want to restore the perception of equity and equality for me financially compared to others in similar positions. I want to satisfy my desire to help others financially as a social concern.

I had a desire to climb the hierarchy of needs for status and success. I wanted to realize the American dream of prosperity for myself. I wanted to satisfy my need for acclaim as a narcissist. I wanted to restore the perception of equity and equality for me financially compared to others in similar positions. I wanted to satisfy my desire to help others financially as a social concern.

Motive-possibilities-corporate

We need to reach business objectives even when the means are illegal. We need to satisfy greed where nothing is ever enough. We enjoy mutual benefits in exchange relationships, such as corruption. We want to make as much profit as possible since profit is the only goal.

We needed to reach business objectives even when the means were illegal. We needed to satisfy greed where nothing was ever enough. We enjoyed mutual benefits in exchange relationships, such as corruption. We wanted to make as much profit as possible since profit was the only goal.

Motive-threats-individual

It is important to me to avoid loss of self-esteem after organizational failure. It is important to me to remove strain, pain and uncertainty for myself. It is important to me to avoid falling from position in the privileged elite.

It was important to me to avoid loss of self-esteem after organizational failure. It was important to me to remove strain, pain and uncertainty for myself. It was important to me to avoid falling from position in the privileged elite.

Motive-threats-corporate

It is important to us to avoid corporate collapse and bankruptcy. We have to adapt to profitable criminal market forces. We have to join profitable networks and cartels.

It was important to us to avoid corporate collapse and bankruptcy. We had to adapt to profitable criminal market forces. We had to join profitable networks and cartels.

Elements of organizational opportunity

Elements of the organizational opportunity represent variables at the individual as well as the organizational and structural levels of analysis. The status of the offender is at the individual level, while access, decay, and chaos are at the organizational level, and collapse is at the structural level of market structures.

Opportunity-commit-status

I use executive language that people do not understand. I am an elite member too big to fail and too powerful to jail. I apply the blame game by misleading attribution to others. I apply offender humor to distract from deviant behavior. I enjoy power inequality between the elite and others.

I used executive language that people did not understand. I was an elite member too big to fail and too powerful to jail. I applied the blame game by misleading attribution to others. I applied offender humor to distract from deviant behavior. I enjoyed power inequality between the elite and others.

Opportunity-commit-access

I have legitimate access to premises and systems to do whatever I like. I can create opportunities by entrepreneurship. I have specialized access in routine activities. I have legitimate access to strategic resources.

I had legitimate access to premises and systems to do whatever I liked. I could create opportunities by entrepreneurship. I had specialized access in routine activities. I had legitimate access to strategic resources.

Opportunity-conceal-decay

There is institutional deterioration based on legitimacy in the organization. There is inability to control because of social disorganization. There is interference of noise in crime signals. There is misrepresentation in accounting. Auditors report to and are loyal to management rather than the board.

There was institutional deterioration based on legitimacy in the organization. There was inability to control because of social disorganization. There was interference of noise in crime signals. There was misrepresentation in accounting. Auditors reported to and were loyal to management rather than the board.

Opportunity-conceal-chaos

There is lack of control in principal-agent relationships. Sense making of actions in the organization is difficult for outsiders. Costs exceed benefits for whistle-blowers. There is an ethical climate conflict in the organization.

There was lack of control in principal-agent relationships. Sense making of actions in the organization was difficult for outsiders. Costs exceeded benefits for whistle-blowers. There was an ethical climate conflict in the organization.

Opportunity-conceal-collapse

There is rule complexity preventing compliance. Participation in crime networks such as cartels is sometimes required. It is the usual way of doing business in markets with crime forces.

There was rule complexity preventing compliance. Participation in crime networks such as cartels was sometimes required. It was the usual way of doing business in markets with crime forces.

Elements of personal willingness

Elements of personal willingness are all at the individual level of analysis.

Willingness-choice-identity

It is acceptable to have deviant behavior for the elite from social conflict. It is acceptable to have narcissistic identification with the organization. It is acceptable to have a professional deviant identity. Narcissists expect preferential treatment. Reputation is adapted to individual labels. Social ties dwindle with age. Deviant identity labeling occurs.

It was acceptable to have deviant behavior for the elite from social conflict. It was acceptable to have narcissistic identification with the organization. It was acceptable to have a professional deviant identity. Narcissists expected preferential treatment. Reputation was adapted to individual labels. Social ties dwindled with age. Deviant identity labeling occurred.

Willingness-choice-rationality

It is rational behavior when there is a perception of benefits exceeding costs. Behavioral reinforcement of deviance occurs over time. It is important to avoid undesirable impulses in self-regulation. I perceive no deterrence effect. Work-related stress is self-determined. I am sensation seeking to experience adventure.

It was rational behavior when there was a perception of benefits exceeding costs. Behavioral reinforcement of deviance occurred over time. It was important to avoid undesirable impulses in self-regulation. I perceived no deterrence effect. Work-related stress was self-determined. I was sensation seeking to experience adventure.

Willingness-choice-learning

I learn from others by differential association. I take action according to authority as obedience. We have a collectivist value orientation.

I learned from others by differential association. I took action according to authority as obedience. We had a collectivist value orientation.

Willingness-innocence-justification

The act of wrongdoing is morally justifiable. We select information in the upper echelon. Disappointing work context causes entitlement. Negative life events occur. There is a peer pressure.

The act of wrongdoing was morally justifiable. We selected information in the upper echelon. Disappointing work context caused entitlement. Negative life events occurred. There was a peer pressure.

Willingness-innocence-neutralization

I apply neutralization techniques when I do something wrong. I am sometimes sliding on the slippery slope. I lack self-control.

I applied neutralization techniques when I did something wrong. I was sometimes sliding on the slippery slope. I lacked self-control.

Offenders and non-offenders

Formulation of the previous statements for motive, opportunity, and willingness is such that the respondent is either a white-collar person involved in no crime or a white-collar person convicted for crime. It is thus a dichotomous study enabling a statistical comparison of non-offenders with offenders in white-collar crime. To find two suitable samples of non-offenders and offenders is not at all easy. The main hypothesis would be that non-offenders find white-collar crime less convenient compared to offenders.

The dependent variable in empirical study might be group rates of white-collar crime or individual white-collar crime occurrence. Akers (1989: 25) suggests that deviance is an obvious phenomenon, while conformity is the thing that needs an explanation:

> Universal motivation to deviance is assumed, but motivation to conformity is problematic.

Kennedy (2020) suggests that normalization of deviance occurs because organizations are in search of new ways to achieve their goals of efficiency, increased productivity, and economic gains. In some business organizations, executives become subject to evaluation on the following scale, where any action is always better than no action at all:

1   The executive is doing the right thing.
2   The executive is doing the wrong thing.
3   The executive is doing nothing.

For example, a company's operating in resource-scarce environments would be more motivated to engage in deviant corporate acts at level 2, since level 1 seems too difficult, and because level 3 might put the company out of business.

Empirical measurement of the dependent variable is possible as a dichotomy or a scale in which the absence of deviance counts as conformity and its reciprocal counts as deviance.

When reviewing the research literature on the comparison of offenders and non-offenders in other areas than white-collar crime, there are relevant insights available. For example, Eryilmaz (2018) compared offender and non-offender young men, and his research became available in a journal for religion and health. The research findings suggest that offenders tend to have trouble setting life goals when compared to non-offenders. For the research, offenders were from a prison in the capital city of Turkey, Ankara, while the non-offenders were workers in various factories in the vicinity. A statistical t-test comparing responses resulted in significant differences.

Another kind of comparison is experienced offenders versus novice offenders. Carroll and Weaver (2017) studied experienced and novice shoplifters who described their thoughts during consideration of actual crime opportunities in retail stores. The study indicates that novice shoplifters plan and prepare themselves for avoiding detection, while experienced shoplifters were less concerned about detection. Deterrents to shoplifting for novices included fear, guilt and the possibility of detection. Expert shoplifters were more efficient and strategic than novices in their shoplifting considerations (Weaver and Carroll, 1985).

The theory of convenience has elements at the individual, organizational, as well as structural levels. Benson and Simpson (2018: 52) argue that a theory of white-collar crime with a construction in such a way that it applies different levels of analysis is difficult to test empirically:

> Though this kind of approach is comprehensive and provocative, it is also virtually untestable as it is nearly impossible to measure or control for all of the factors that are cited in the explanation.

Ideally, to test convenience theory, variables for motive should be at the individual and organizational level, variables for opportunity should be at the individual, organizational, as well as the structural levels, while variables for willingness need only be at the individual level. Since this is almost impossible, the current research leaves the ideal approach and suggests empirical study at the individual level. The shortcoming of such an approach is that respondents might vary in their views on elements at the organizational and structural levels. For example, various respondents from the same organization might perceive the extent of institutional deterioration in their specific organization differently. Similarly, the extent of corporate motive to explore possibilities and avoid threats by illegitimate financial gain might cause different perceptions by various respondents from the same organization.

Convenience survey statements

A test of convenience theory by survey research will need to distinguish different kinds of organizations. For example, research found that members of religious institutions tend to have weaker personal willingness to commit financial crime, while the organizations themselves offer greater opportunities to commit and conceal financial crime. Other kinds of organizations – such as museums, family-owned enterprises, small and medium-sized business versus multinational corporations, and public organizations – will all have different and special characteristics. Benson and Simpson (2018: 57) suggest that in contrast to for-profit corporations, many other types of organizations, such as hospitals, universities, and government bureaucracies, are not subject to "such a brutally simple and objective measure of their success":

> Like all organizations, they are goal driven, but it is more difficult to tell exactly how well they are doing relative to their goals and to one another. Hence, we expect the leaders of these organizations to be less pressured to break the law to achieve organizational goals.

Ideally, a sample of offenders and non-offenders could lead to breakthrough results when compared in terms of the following convenience statements based on the theory of convenience as structurally modeled in Figure 5.1.

Financial motive

I believe financial crime can help me achieve my personal goals.
   I believe financial crime can help the organization achieve its business goals.
   I believe financial crime can help me avoid personal economic problems.
   I believe financial crime can help the organization avoid bankruptcy.

Organizational opportunity

I believe my status in the organization can make it possible for me to commit financial crime.
   I believe my access to resources in the organization can make it possible for me to commit financial crime.
   I believe my institutional deterioration in the organization can make it possible for me to conceal financial crime.
   I believe lack of control and guardianship in the organization can make it possible for me to conceal financial crime.
   I believe criminal market structure externally can make it possible for me to conceal financial crime.

Personal willingness

I identify so strongly with the organization that I might commit financial crime to save it.

I would consider costs and benefits before committing financial crime.

My inclination to commit crime will increase if others show me how to do it.

I would be willing to commit financial crime if I was able to justify it.

I would be willing to commit financial crime if I had no sense of guilt.

Convenience student survey

Since it is difficult, if not impossible, to access a sample of white-collar offenders and a sample of white-collar non-offenders, the second-best option for empirical study seems to be students in law, criminology and business. Business school students are relevant and interesting because many of them will end up in relevant positions. Either they will have access to resources to commit and conceal financial crime, or they will have access to resources to audit and control financial activities of others in the organization.

Based on responses to the following three statements, empirical research might classify students as potential offenders and potential non-offenders:

1   It is understandable that top executives and other privileged individuals abuse their positions to commit financial crime when they have problems with their personal finances.
2   It is understandable that top executives and other privileged individuals abuse their positions to commit financial crime when the business struggles financially and faces threats such as bankruptcy.
3   It is understandable that chief executives and other privileged individuals abuse their positions to commit financial crime by offering bribes in corrupt countries to obtain business contracts.

The class is divided into two groups, where those with the highest extent of agreement with these statements will serve in the offender group, while those with the highest extent of disagreement with these statements will serve in the non-offender group. Responses are assigned on a scale from strongly agree to strongly disagree. Responses to these three statements represent the dependent variable in statistical analysis using a t-test to distinguish the two groups.

The formulation of statements for the independent variables of motive, opportunity, and willingness might be as follows.

Financial motive

Chief executives and others in privileged positions can benefit from financial crime at work to achieve their personal goals.

Financial crime by top executives and others in privileged positions can help organizations achieve their business goals.

Chief executives and others in privileged positions can benefit from financial crime at work to avoid personal bankruptcy.

Financial crime by top executives and others in privileged positions can help organizations avoid bankruptcy.

Organizational opportunity

Persons in top positions have the opportunity to commit financial crime at work because of their status.

Persons in top positions have the opportunity to commit financial crime at work because of their access to resources.

Persons in top positions have the opportunity to conceal financial crime at work where there is institutional deterioration.

Persons in top positions have the opportunity to conceal financial crime at work where there is lack of oversight and control.

Persons in top positions have the opportunity to conceal financial crime at work where the environment consists of criminal market structures.

Personal willingness

Top executives and others in privileged positions might be willing to commit financial crime at work because they identify too strongly with the business.

Top executives and others in privileged positions might be willing to commit financial crime at work because they make a rational assessment of the pros and cons.

Top executives and others in privileged positions might be willing to commit financial crime at work when they learn criminality from others.

Top executives and others in privileged positions might be willing to commit financial crime at work because they justify their actions.

Top executives and others in privileged positions might be willing to commit financial crime at work because they get rid of guilt.

Oslo research results

In a business school in Oslo, Norway, students can sign up for an elective course on "Leadership and Financial Crime". The course covers two main topics. The first topic is financial crime generally and white-collar crime specifically, where the theory of convenience is introduced. The second topic is fraud examination by financial crime specialists in the private sector, such as local law firms and global auditing firms. The course examination is a term paper where students evaluate a report of investigation by fraud examiners.

Early on in the term, students received the survey instrument during the last lecture hour in class. All students that were present filled in the questionnaire. A total of 111 completed questionnaires were returned before students left the class. Students were only asked about the statements listed previously and not about themselves. Although demographic variables, such as gender (Benson and Gottschalk, 2015; Steffensmeier et al., 2013) might be interesting, they were avoided because of general data protection regulation regarding personal information.

The class had a slight majority of female students, about 60% were women. Since students had chosen this course, rather than elective courses on project management, personal finances or other topics, students were presumably interested in this course. The likely main source of information about the course was previous students, as the class size had grown steadily over the years.

The classifying variable in this research is the extent to which respondents find it understandable that top executives and other privileged individuals abuse their positions to commit financial crime. The variable has three items as listed previously. Each item was measured on a scale from completely agree (1) to completely disagree (5). The offending scale with 3 items has an acceptable reliability score in terms of a Cronbach's alpha of .862.

The average score for the offending scale was 3.061, which means respondents on average agreed slightly to the statements that offending is understandable. This research thus classified respondents with a score lower than 3.061 as offenders, and respondents with a higher score as non-offenders. Out of 111 respondents, 65 were classified as offenders, while 46 were classified as non-offenders. Their average score for each statement in the questionnaire is listed in Table 5.1. Assumed offenders are labeled 1, while assumed non-offenders are labeled 2 in the table. For absolutely all statements in convenience theory, offenders agree more than non-offenders as illustrated with lower scores among the 65 offenders compared to the 46 non-offenders. Offenders thus find crime more convenient than non-offenders in all three dimensions of motive, opportunity, and willingness.

While the differences between offenders and non-offenders are systematically in favor of the research hypothesis that offenders will find white-collar crime more convenient than non-offenders, it is not obvious that all differences are statistically significant. The ideal p-value for statistically different groups is .01 or less. However, p<.05 is a less ambitious threshold often found quite acceptable.

There are only two convenience statements satisfying the ideal p-value requirement in Table 5.2 with a p-value of less than .01. First, with a p-value of .002, there is opportunity-conceal-chaos, where offenders agree significantly more to the statement that persons in top positions have the opportunity to conceal financial crime at work where there is lack of oversight and control. Second, with a p-value of .004, there is motive-threat-corporate, where offenders agree significantly more to the statement that financial crime by top executives and others in privileged positions can help organizations avoid bankruptcy.

As listed in Table 5.2, six more convenience statements are within the acceptable significance threshold of p<.05. There are thus 8 out of 14 statements in the convenience structure in Figure 5.1 that are statistically significant when comparing assumed offenders to assumed non-offenders. The remaining six statements are not statistically significant, but they are indeed different in the suggested direction as listed in Table 5.1.

In conclusion, business students who found it understandable that top executives and others in privileged positions commit white-collar crime were classified as potential offenders, while students who did not find it understandable were

Table 5.1 Mean scores for convenience for assumed offenders (1) versus non-offenders (2)

Convenience statements		N	Mean	Deviation
MOTIVE-POSSIBILITIES-INDIVIDUAL	1,00	65	1,8154	1,21053
	2,00	46	2,3696	1,52547
MOTIVE-POSSIBILITIES-CORPORATE	1,00	65	2,0462	1,26776
	2,00	46	2,5435	1,68268
MOTIVE-THREATS-INDIVIDUAL	1,00	64	1,7969	1,29932
	2,00	46	2,5000	1,69640
MOTIVE-THREATS-CORPORATE	1,00	65	1,7538	1,03124
	2,00	46	2,4565	1,50121
OPPORTUNITY-COMMIT-STATUS	1,00	65	1,9538	1,20456
	2,00	46	2,3913	1,48291
OPPORTUNITY-COMMIT-ACCESS	1,00	65	1,7385	1,07931
	2,00	46	2,2826	1,45546
OPPORTUNITY-CONCEAL-DECAY	1,00	65	2,4308	1,17219
	2,00	45	2,8000	1,19848
OPPORTUNITY-CONCEAL-CHAOS	1,00	65	1,6308	1,05430
	2,00	46	2,4565	1,72184
OPPORTUNITY-CONCEAL-COLLAPSE	1,00	64	2,4219	1,41202
	2,00	46	2,7826	1,28085
WILLINGNESS-CHOICE-IDENTITY	1,00	65	2,3538	1,23023
	2,00	46	2,8696	1,29286
WILLINGNESS-CHOICE-RATIONALITY	1,00	65	2,4000	1,23491
	2,00	46	2,9783	1,46802
WILLINGNESS-CHOICE-LEARNING	1,00	65	2,3538	1,20456
	2,00	45	2,8667	1,42382
WILLINGNESS-INNOCENCE-JUSTIFICATION	1,00	65	2,4308	1,67676
	2,00	46	2,6739	1,41507
WILLINGNESS-INNOCENCE-NEUTRALIZATION	1,00	65	2,8769	1,48437
	2,00	46	3,3261	1,56424

classified as potential non-offenders. The test of convenience theory illustrates that offenders find more motive convenience, opportunity convenience, as well as behavioral convenience by crime when compared to non-offenders.

The presented empirical research is exploratory and not at all satisfactory as evidence for the validity of convenience theory as an integrated explanation for the white-collar crime phenomenon. As discussed in the early parts of this paper, a number of obstacles and study barriers exist that need to be addressed in future empirical research.

Table 5.2 Convenience significance for assumed offenders versus non-offenders

Convenience statements	T-statistic	Significance
MOTIVE-POSSIBILITIES-INDIVIDUAL	2.131	.035
MOTIVE-POSSIBILITIES-CORPORATE	1.776	.079
MOTIVE-THREATS-INDIVIDUAL	2.461	.015
MOTIVE-THREATS-CORPORATE	2.925	.004
OPPORTUNITY-COMMIT-STATUS	1.712	.090
OPPORTUNITY-COMMIT-ACCESS	2.262	.026
OPPORTUNITY-CONCEAL-DECAY	1.609	.110
OPPORTUNITY-CONCEAL-CHAOS	3.128	.002
OPPORTUNITY-CONCEAL-COLLAPSE	1.373	.172
WILLINGNESS-CHOICE-IDENTITY	2.130	.035
WILLINGNESS-CHOICE-RATIONALITY	2.246	.027
WILLINGNESS-CHOICE-LEARNING	2.037	.044
WILLINGNESS-INNOCENCE-JUSTIFICATION	.802	.424
WILLINGNESS-INNOCENCE-NEUTRALIZATION	1.536	.127

Braaten Vaughn convenience study

Braaten and Vaughn (2019) applied convenience theory to an empirical study of cryptocurrency crime based on content analysis of U.S. federal court decisions. Analysis of federal case law revealed patterns and methods of perpetrating illegal cryptocurrency activities, including operating unlicensed money transmitting and money service businesses, commodity fraud, bitcoin scams, including bitcoin exchange fraud and corporate takeover of a credit union to perpetuate illegal bitcoin transactions. The dark web administered other kinds of cryptocurrency crime, which involved selling and purchasing illegal goods and services.

Analysis of U.S. federal district and circuit court cases involving cryptocurrency crime and fraud indicates support for the convenience theory of white-collar crime. The motive for defendants in various schemes was financial gain, because of either threats or possibilities, and either for the company or for personal use. Their roles and positions in the businesses allowed them access to resources that helped them perpetrate fraud against clients, investors, stockholders and other stakeholders. Resources helped them availing of opportunities and favorable circumstances, such as operation of front companies in cases involving unlicensed money transfer and money service business dealing with bitcoins and other virtual currencies. Furthermore, access to resources helped build relationships by defendants and neutralization of blame in cases of commodity fraud, as well as overrepresentation of profits that investors could obtain from purchases of virtual currencies, claiming that tokens were safe and reliable investments, when they were risky.

White-collar offenders overestimated abilities and capacities to provide services promised to investors in securities fraud, and they breached fiduciary duties to their clients and corporate stockholders in bitcoin scams by misappropriating profits and service fees to which they were not entitled. The organizational opportunity structures further enabled them to use the companies for their own personal benefit instead of the stockholders' and investors' benefits. Offenders could engage in dark web transactions as administrators, vendors, and purchasers that guaranteed anonymity and through an online venue that had far reaching and rapid global access. The dark web is neither regulated nor monitored by law enforcement or other government authorities.

Based on court documents, Braaten and Vaughn (2019: 9) found that defendants employed various neutralization techniques to justify their crime, which included allegations of legal mistake and the legality of their actions:

> Defendants also denied injury or harm, denied responsibility, condemned the condemners, appealed to higher loyalties, and presented dilemma trade-offs by weighing various concerns that resulted in the illegal act, including normality of action.

Braaten and Vaughn (2019) classified their cases into four categories. The first category is convenience findings in federal court cases involving unlicensed money transmitting business and money maundering. Table 5.3 lists findings in the three dimensions of convenience theory, i.e., economical dimension in terms of motive, organizational dimension in terms of opportunity, and behavioral dimension in terms of deviance.

The second category is convenience findings in federal court cases involving commodities fraud as listed in Table 5.4. The third category is convenience findings in federal court cases involving securities fraud as listed in Table 5.5. The fourth category is convenience findings in federal court cases involving bitcoin scams, fraud related to bitcoin exchanges, and other illegal activities related to bitcoin as listed in Table 5.6. The fifth and final category is convenience findings in federal cryptocurrency cases involving owners, operators, and vendors on the dark web as listed in Table 5.7.

Table 5.3 Convenience in unlicensed money transfer crime

TITLE OF CASE	ACTS OF DEFENDANT	ECONOMICAL DIMENSION (MOTIVE)	ORGANIZATIONAL DIMENSION (OPPORTUNITY)	BEHAVIORAL DIMENSION (DEVIANCE)
U.S. v. Murgio	Concealed nature of Coin. mx as a Bitcoin exchange through front companies (e.g., Collectables Club)	Greed to profit by millions of dollars from the money laundering of bitcoins through sham companies	Access to money and bitcoin as owner and operator of Coin.mx and Collectible Clubs	Alleged legality of action – actions were not covered by federal or state law regulating money transmitting business

TITLE OF CASE	*ACTS OF DEFENDANT*	*ECONOMICAL DIMENSION (MOTIVE)*	*ORGANIZATIONAL DIMENSION (OPPORTUNITY)*	*BEHAVIORAL DIMENSION (DEVIANCE)*
U.S. v. Faiella	Operated BitInstant on Silk Road	Profits from exchanging cash to bitcoin	Access to money and bitcoin as owner and operator of BitInstant on Silk Road	Claimed no harm or injury because he merely exchanged the cash deposits of his customers to Bitcoins and transferred those funds to client accounts on Silk Road
U.S. v. Budovsky	Operated Liberty Reserve ("LR") as an online money transmitting business for criminals	Profits from a processing fee of 1% of the amounts involved in 55 million separate financial transactions among LR users	Founder of Liberty Reserve; Sole access to funds and computer portals of LR	Alleged legality of action – claimed that acts were not covered by existing laws or regulation; Absence of jurisdiction by U.S. courts
U.S. v. Petix	Operated online exchange of bitcoins	Profits currency exchange of bitcoins	Owner and operator of own business	Alleged legality of action – acts were not unlawful and not covered by existing laws or regulation
U.S. v. Lord	Exchanged approximately $2.6 million for bitcoin	Profits from currency exchange of approximately $2.6 million for bitcoin	Owner and operator of own business	Alleged legality of action – no need for a money service business license because the State of Louisiana does not require virtual currency exchangers to have a state license
U.S. v. Mansy	Operated an unlicensed money transmitting business	Profits from currency exchange of bitcoins	Owner and operator of own business, TV Toyz, LLC.	Alleged legality of action – claimed that acts were not unlawful and not covered by existing laws or regulation
U.S. v. Stetkiw	Operated an unlicensed money transmitting business	Profits from currency exchange of bitcoins	Owner and operator of own business	Condemned the condemners – alleged that the tracking warrant on his vehicle violated the law

Table 5.4 Convenience in commodities fraud

TITLE OF CASE	ACTS OF DEFENDANT	ECONOMICAL DIMENSION (MOTIVE)	ORGANIZATIONAL DIMENSION (OPPORTUNITY)	BEHAVIORAL DIMENSION (DEVIANCE)
Commodity Futures Trading Commission	Fraudulently sold memberships in trading groups that would give virtual currency trading advice to U.S. customers	Profits from membership fees for virtual currency trading advice and transfers of virtual currencies	Chief Technology Officer and sole owner of CabbageTech, Corp. d/b/a Coin Drop Markets	Denial of responsibility – rejected responsibility for the crime and denied leadership role; Blamed his alter-ego personalities
CFTC v. McDonnell	Fraudulently sold memberships in trading groups that would give virtual currency trading advice to U.S. customers	Profits from fees and misappropriation of customers' 660 litecoins worth thousands of dollars to his and his wife's personal accounts	Chief Technology Officer and sole owner of CabbageTech, Corp. d/b/a Coin Drop Markets; Controlled phone numbers, FedEx accounts, email accounts; bank accounts, websites	Denial of responsibility – rejected responsibility for the crime and denied leadership role; Blamed his alter-ego personalities
CFTC v. My Big Coin Pay, Inc.	Fraudulently sold more than $6 million in virtual currency, My Big Coin ("MBC"), and arbitrarily changed the price of MBC to mimic the fluctuations of a legitimate, actively-traded virtual currency	Profits from the fraudulent sale of virtual currency, My Big Coin ("MBC"), amounting to more than $6 million	Operator of MBC coin offering	Alleged legality of action – acts were not unlawful and not covered by existing laws or regulation
Hodges v. Harrison	Solicited investors for the Initial Coin Offering ("ICO") of virtual currencies Monkey Coin and Coeval to raise money for Monkey Capital without registering with the SEC	Profits amounting to approximately $1,170,000 from the ICO of Monkey Coin and Coeval	Manager and operator of Monkey Capital Inc. and Monkey Capital, LLC	Denial of responsibility – shifted blame to others

Table 5.5 Convenience in securities fraud

TITLE OF CASE	ACTS OF DEFENDANT	ECONOMICAL DIMENSION (MOTIVE)	ORGANIZATIONAL DIMENSION (OPPORTUNITY)	BEHAVIORAL DIMENSION (DEVIANCE)
Securities and Exchange Commission	Fraudulently sold BLV tokens during an ICO in exchange for other virtual currencies without registering with the SEC	Profits from the ICO of BLV tokens amounting to $100 million	Founder of Blockvest, LLC	Alleged legality of action – falsely claimed that acts were sanctioned by government regulators
In re Tezos Securities Litigation	Sold unregistered Tezos tokens during an ICO in exchange for $232 million in Bitcoin and Eretheum	Fundraising for corporate projects amounting to approximately $232 million in Bitcoin and Ethereum	Chief Executive Officer and Chief Technology Officer of Dynamic Ledger Solutions and Switzerland-based, non-profit Tezos Foundation (Individual Defendants Arthur and Kathleen Breitman)	Condemned the condemners – U.S. federal court does not have jurisdiction over defendants and U.S. laws do not have extra-territorial application over Swiss defendants
SEC v. PlexCorps	Fraudulently sold at least 81 million unregistered PlexCoin tokens worth $15 million	Personal gain; Profits amounting to $15 million from the sales of about 81 million PlexCoin	Founders of Plex Corps (Individual defendants Lacroix and Paradis-Royer)	Denial of responsibility – rejected responsibility for the crime; Intent to exclude U.S. buyers from ICO
SEC v. PlexCorps	After the court issued the temporary asset freeze order, defendant Lacroix continued spending and dissipating money from several accounts	Personal gain, including leasing a 2018 Mercedes-Benz GLE sports-utility vehicle in Montreal and personal home renovations for a residential property in Quebec	Founders of Plex Corps (Individual defendants Lacroix and Paradis-Royer)	Denial of responsibility – rejected responsibility for the crime; Intent to exclude U.S. buyers from ICO

(Continued)

Table 5.5 (Continued)

TITLE OF CASE	ACTS OF DEFENDANT	ECONOMICAL DIMENSION (MOTIVE)	ORGANIZATIONAL DIMENSION (OPPORTUNITY)	BEHAVIORAL DIMENSION (DEVIANCE)
Balestra v. ATBCOIN LLC	Fraudulently sold digital "ATB Coins" to the general public, including U.S. investors, during an ICO in exchange for other digital assets	Profits amounting to over $20 million from thousands of investors	Co-founders and officers of ATBCOIN LLC	Denied injury from the crime and refuted occurrence of harm; Condemned the condemners – U.S. federal court does not have jurisdiction over defendants
Audet v. Fraser	Fraudulently sold virtual currency physical mining equipment, hardware-hosted mining (ZenMiners), cloud-hosted mining, hashlets, and virtual currency PayCoins	Profits amounting to $19 million of Hashlets to more than 10,000 investors	Defendant Garza was Chief Executive Officer of GAW Miners; Defendant Fraser was de facto Board and financial investor of GAW Miners	Denial of responsibility – rejected responsibility for the crime and shifted blame to co-defendant Garza

Table 5.6 Convenience in bitcoin scams and exchanges

TITLE OF CASE	ACTS OF DEFENDANT	ECONOMICAL DIMENSION (MOTIVE)	ORGANIZATIONAL DIMENSION (OPPORTUNITY)	BEHAVIORAL DIMENSION (DEVIANCE)
Winklevoss Capital Fund, LLC v. Shrem	Shrem received $750,000 from the Winklevaus brothers and the Winklevaus Capital Fund, LLC and purchased 39,876.34 Bitcoin on their behalf – he pocketed the difference in market value of $61,000 equivalent to about 5,000 Bitcoin	Desire for the Winklevaus brothers to invest in BitInstant and to raise the "public profile" of Bitcoin	Founder of BitInstant	Condemned the condemners – U.S. federal court does not have jurisdiction over defendant because the shortfall of $61,000 does not meet the jurisdictional amount of the court
Shin v. Time Squared Global, LLC	Offered non-existent ASIC chips to investors that allegedly would mine bitcoins and give investors daily revenues from mining	Desire for profit	Owner and operator of Time Squared Global, LLC	Denial of injury or harm – alleged that representations that "later in hind site [sic]" were "not carried out, does not constitute a fraud"
Greene v. Mizuho Bank, Ltd.	Mizuho stopped processing international wire withdrawals for bitcoin exchange Mt. Gox but continued accepting deposits from Mt. Gox users, earning revenue from the associated service fees	Corporate profits from service fees on processing of Mt. Gox wire deposits	Japan-based Mizuho	Argued legal mistake and considered infringement irrelevant because of error in the law

(Continued)

Table 5.6 (Continued)

TITLE OF CASE	ACTS OF DEFENDANT	ECONOMICAL DIMENSION (MOTIVE)	ORGANIZATIONAL DIMENSION (OPPORTUNITY)	BEHAVIORAL DIMENSION (DEVIANCE)
U.S. v. Gross	Gross, Chairman of the Helping Other People Excel ("HOPE") Federal Credit Union accepted bribes from Murgio and Lebedev in exchange for: (1) transferring control of HOPE's Board to them (2) obstructing an examination of the National Credit Union Administration ("NCUA") and, (3) making false statements to the NCUA to conceal the activities of Murgio and Lebedev	Bribe money made by corporate officers of Coin. mx and Collectible Clubs	Chairman of the Board of Directors of HOPE	Condemned the condemners – NCUA records are not trustworthy and not admissible as business records because of "evidence of collaboration between the Government and the NCUA"
U.S. v. Brown	Defendant Brown mailed three separate padded envelopes to PricewaterhouseCoopers, and the offices of the Williamson County Republican and Democratic parties demanding $1 million in Bitcoin in exchange for an encryption key to Mitt Romney's unreleased tax returns	Personal gain of $1 million in Bitcoin	N/A	Condemned the condemners – search warrant lacked probable cause and that he was prejudiced by the trial judge's decision to allow questions from the jury

Table 5.7 Convenience in the dark web

TITLE OF CASE	ACTS OF DEFENDANT	ECONOMICAL DIMENSION (MOTIVE)	ORGANIZATIONAL DIMENSION (OPPORTUNITY)	BEHAVIORAL DIMENSION (DEVIANCE)
U.S. v. Ulbricht	Operated Silk Road, an online criminal marketplace, using the Tor software to allow users to transact anonymously using the virtual currency Bitcoin	Corporate profits; Protect credibility of Silk Road among users by ensuring anonymity of transactions and identities	Owner and administrator of Silk Road	Appealed to higher loyalties as a reason for their action – claimed that the person he targeted for murder was "threatening to expose the identities of thousands of my clients that he was able to acquire. . . . [T]his kind of behavior is unforgivable to me. Especially here on Silk Road, anonymity is sacrosanct"
U.S. v. Ulbricht	Operated Silk Road, an online criminal marketplace, using the Tor software to allow users to transact anonymously using the virtual currency Bitcoin	Corporate profits; Protect credibility of Silk Road among users by ensuring anonymity of transactions and identities	Owner and administrator of the dark web Silk Road	Appealed to higher loyalties as a reason for their action – claimed that the person he targeted for murder was "threatening to expose the identities of thousands of my clients that he was able to acquire. . . . [T]his kind of behavior is unforgivable to me. Especially here on Silk Road, anonymity is sacrosanct"
U.S. v. Colldock	Sold methamphetamine, cocaine, and "cash-in-mail" service for bitcoin in Agora and Silk Road	Personal gain	Vendor of illicit drugs in the dark web Agora; Operated a "Fast Cash In Mail For BTC Service"	Condemned the condemners – search warrant lacked probable cause

(Continued)

Table 5.7 (Continued)

TITLE OF CASE	ACTS OF DEFENDANT	ECONOMICAL DIMENSION (MOTIVE)	ORGANIZATIONAL DIMENSION (OPPORTUNITY)	BEHAVIORAL DIMENSION (DEVIANCE)
U.S. v. Vallerius	Moderated the dark web Dream Market	Profits from commissions earned in transactions on the dark web Dream Market	Administrator and Moderator of the dark web Dream Market	Condemned the condemners – alleged the constitutionality and illegality of the search on his person, laptop, phone, and belongings at the Atlanta airport after his arrival from Paris
U.S. v. Donagal	Sold Xanax pills online through Silk Road, Silk Road 2.0, and a personal website and was paid in cash and in the digital currency bitcoin	Personal gain	Leader of an industrial drug manufacturing operation	Presented dilemma trade-off by weighting various concerns that resulted in the illegal act – considered fleeing from crime if arrested because additional time if caught after fleeing would be minimal compared to underlying penalty for illegal act
U.S. v. Reuer	Imported methamphetamine, fentanyl and heroin from Canada and China and payed in Bitcoin	Personal gain	N/A	Argued legal mistake in sentencing guidelines for drug importation and considered infringement irrelevant because of error in the law
U.S. v. Michell	Purchased 100 grams of potassium cyanide on the dark web, paying with Bitcoin	Personal gain	N/A	Alleged normality of action – argued that "mere purchase and possession of potassium cyanide is not a crime"

Virginia research results

In a criminology school in Virginia, United States, students across two upper-level undergraduate criminology courses participated in the survey. Both courses were topics courses that were also electives, one being on white-collar crime and the other being on gender and crime. Although these classes are open to all majors, almost all students attending these courses were criminology and/or sociology majors. Overall the courses were roughly equal in gender composition between male and females, and all students were traditional college aged. Both classes had about 50 students. Because students were free to participate or not (see the following) and there were likely some students in both class who were instructed to only participate once, 71 total students participated in the survey.

The university is a large public institution in the eastern part of the United States. The survey was approved by the University Institutional Review Board. Consistent with privacy and ethical protections, and no student was compelled to participate. A brief summary of the survey and informed consent was explained. Students then filled out the survey in English as students in Oslo had filled it out in Norwegian. Informed consent and surveys were separated and turned in. To further protect student identity no demographic information was obtained. Although demographic variables, such as gender (Benson and Gottschalk, 2015; Steffensmeier et al., 2013) might be interesting, they were avoided because of general data protection regulation regarding personal information.

The classifying variable in this research is the extent to which respondents find it understandable that top executives and other privileged individuals abuse their positions to commit financial crime. The variable has three items as listed at the bottom of the questionnaire. Each item was measured on a scale from completely agree (1) to completely disagree (5). The offending scale with three items has an acceptable reliability score in terms of Cronbach's alpha of .862. The average score for the offending scale is 3.6761, which means that respondents on average disagreed slightly with the statements that offending is understandable. The research classified respondents with a score lower than 3.6761 as potential offenders, and respondents with a higher score as potential non-offenders. Out of 71 respondents, 33 became offenders, while 38 became non-offenders.

Table 5.8 lists respondents' average score for each statement in the survey instrument. Assumed offenders have the 1-label in the table, while assumed non-offenders have the 0-label in the table. For most statements in convenience theory, offenders agree more than non-offenders as illustrated by lower scores among the 33 assumed offenders compared to the 38 assumed non-offenders. For example, on the scale from (1) agree to (5) disagree motive-possibilities-individual have an average score of 2.2424 among offenders and 2.3947 among non-offenders. The only exception is willingness-innocence-justification, where assumed offenders disagree more than non-offenders.

Table 5.8 Mean scores for convenience for assumed offenders (1) versus non-offenders (0)

Convenience statements		N	Mean	Deviation
MOTIVE-POSSIBILITIES-INDIVIDUAL	1	33	2,2424	1,62077
	0	38	2,3947	1,58608
MOTIVE-POSSIBILITIES-CORPORATE	1	33	2,3939	1,63820
	0	38	2,5789	1,74962
MOTIVE-THREATS-INDIVIDUAL	1	33	1,9697	1,42489
	0	38	2,5526	1,60569
MOTIVE-THREATS-CORPORATE	1	33	2,4242	1,60137
	0	38	2,7368	1,62221
OPPORTUNITY-COMMIT-STATUS	1	33	1,6667	1,33853
	0	38	2,0000	1,59391
OPPORTUNITY-COMMIT-ACCESS	1	33	1,4242	1,06155
	0	37	1,8108	1,41102
OPPORTUNITY-CONCEAL-DECAY	1	33	1,9697	1,13150
	0	38	2,0789	1,34328
OPPORTUNITY-CONCEAL-CHAOS	1	33	1,8485	1,20211
	0	38	2,0526	1,50580
OPPORTUNITY-CONCEAL-COLLAPSE	1	33	1,8182	1,23629
	0	38	2,5263	1,63966
WILLINGNESS-CHOICE-IDENTITY	1	33	2,6970	1,53062
	0	38	3,0000	1,43320
WILLINGNESS-CHOICE-RATIONALITY	1	33	2,6970	1,55090
	0	38	3,2105	1,54496
WILLINGNESS-CHOICE-LEARNING	1	33	1,9697	1,26206
	0	38	2,3158	1,47236
WILLINGNESS-INNOCENCE-JUSTIFICATION	1	32	2,4688	1,54470
	0	38	2,2895	1,55803
WILLINGNESS-INNOCENCE-NEUTRALIZATION	1	33	3,0909	1,62718
	0	38	3,5000	1,55529

While the differences between offenders and non-offenders are systematically in favor of the research hypothesis that offenders will find white-collar crime more convenient than non-offenders will, it is not obvious that all differences are statistically significant. The ideal p-value for statistically different groups is .01 or less. However, p < .05 is a less ambitious threshold often found quite acceptable.

There is only one convenience statement satisfying the significance requirement in Table 5.9. Potential offenders agree significantly more to the statement regarding opportunity-conceal-collapse than non-offenders do.

We will compare our research results with a similar study that we conducted in Norway as presented earlier in this chapter. In a business school in Oslo, students can sign up for an elective course on "Leadership and Financial Crime".

Table 5.9 Convenience significance for assumed offenders versus non-offenders

	T-statistic	*Significance*
MOTIVE-POSSIBILITIES-INDIVIDUAL	–,400	,691
MOTIVE-POSSIBILITIES-CORPORATE	–,458	,649
MOTIVE-THREATS-INDIVIDUAL	–1,607	,113
MOTIVE-THREATS-CORPORATE	–,815	,418
OPPORTUNITY-COMMIT-STATUS	–,946	,347
OPPORTUNITY-COMMIT-ACCESS	–1,283	,204
OPPORTUNITY-CONCEAL-DECAY	–,367	,714
OPPORTUNITY-CONCEAL-CHAOS	–,625	,534
OPPORTUNITY-CONCEAL-COLLAPSE	–2,029	,046
WILLINGNESS-CHOICE-IDENTITY	–,861	,392
WILLINGNESS-CHOICE-RATIONALITY	–1,394	,168
WILLINGNESS-CHOICE-LEARNING	–1,055	,295
WILLINGNESS-INNOCENCE-JUSTIFICATION	,481	,632
WILLINGNESS-INNOCENCE-NEUTRALIZATION	–1,082	,283

The course covers two main topics. The first topic is financial crime generally and white-collar crime specifically, where the theory of convenience is introduced. The second topic is fraud examination by financial crime specialists in the private sector, such as local law firms and global auditing firms. The course examination is a term paper where students evaluate a report of investigation by fraud examiners. Early on in the term, students received the survey instrument during the last lecture hour in class. All students that were present filled in the questionnaire. A total of 111 completed questionnaires were returned before students left the class.

The offending scale with 3 items has an acceptable reliability score in terms of a Cronbach's alpha of .862. The average score for the offending scale was 3.061, which means respondents on average disagreed very slightly to the statements that offending is understandable. It is interesting to compare this score with the score of 3.6761. The only two potential explanations for the difference are Norway versus the United States, and sociology students versus business students.

For absolutely all statements in convenience theory, assumed offenders in Norway (business students) agree more than assumed non-offenders (business students) as illustrated with lower scores among the 65 offenders compared to the 46 non-offenders. Offenders thus find crime more convenient than non-offenders in all three dimensions of motive, opportunity, and willingness. Compared to the U.S. sample, where only one significant difference was found, 8 out of 14 statements were significant in the Norwegian sample.

In conclusion, both criminology students in the United States and business students in Norway who found it relatively understandable that top executives and others in privileged positions commit white-collar crime, became classified as potential offenders in our study. Students who did not find it relatively understandable became potential non-offenders. The test of convenience theory illustrates that offenders find more motive convenience, opportunity convenience, as well as behavioral convenience by crime when compared to non-offenders.

The present empirical research is exploratory and not at all sufficient as evidence for the validity of convenience theory as an integrated explanation of the white-collar crime phenomenon. Hopefully, future research will be able to reach more empirical substance to test the theory.

References

Akers, R.L. (1989). A social behaviorist's perspective on integration of theories of crime and deviance, in: Messner, S.F., Krohn, M.D. and Liska, A.E. (editors), *Theoretical Integration in the Study of Deviance and Crime*, Albany, NY: State University of New York Press, pages 23–36.

Benson, M.L. and Gottschalk, P. (2015). Gender and white-collar crime in Norway: An empirical study of media reports, *International Journal of Law, Crime and Justice*, 43, 535–552.

Benson, M.L. and Simpson, S.S. (2018). *White-Collar Crime: An Opportunity Perspective*, 3rd edition, New York, NY: Routledge.

Braaten, C.N. and Vaughn, M.S. (2019). Convenience theory of cryptocurrency crime: A content analysis of U.S. federal court decisions, *Deviant Behavior*, published online, https://doi.org/10.1080/01639625.2019.1706706.

Carroll, J. and Weaver, F. (2017). Shoplifters' perceptions of crime opportunities: A process-tracing study, in: Cornish, D.B. and Clarke, R.V. (editors), *The Reasoning Criminal: Rational Choice Perspectives on Offending*, New York, NY: Routledge.

Eryilmaz, A. (2018). Comparison of offender and non-offender young men to setting goals for life and attributing menaing to life, *Journal of Religion and Health*, 57 (4), 1350–1362.

Friedrichs, D.O. (2020). White collar crime: Definitional debates and the case for a typological approach, in: Rorie, M. (editor), *The Handbook of White-Collar Crime*, Hoboken, NJ: John Wiley & Sons, chapter 2, pages 16–31.

Gottschalk, P. and Gunnesdal, L. (2018). *White-Collar Crime in the Shadow Economy: Lack of Detection, Investigation, and Conviction compared to Social Security Fraud*, London, UK: Springer Publishing/Palgrave Pivot, Palgrave Macmillan.

Kennedy, J.P. (2020). Organizational and macro-level corporate crime theories, in: Rorie, M.L. (editor), *The Handbook of White-Collar Crime*, Hoboken, NJ: Wiley & Sons, chapter 12, pages 175–190.

Steffensmeier, D., Schwartz, J. and Roche, M. (2013). Gender and twenty-first-century corporate crime: Female involvement and the gender gap in Enron-era corporate frauds, *American Sociological Review*, 78 (3), 448–476.

Weaver, F.M. and Carroll, J. (1985). Crime perceptions in a natural setting by expert and novice shoplifters, *Social Psychology Quarterly*, 48 (4), 349–359.

6   White-collar convenience themes

The theory of convenience is an integrated and deductive approach to explaining the white-collar crime phenomenon based on a number of perspectives from criminology, management, sociology, and psychology. There is convenience in the three dimensions of financial motive, organizational opportunity, and deviant behavior. Based on an empirical study of 408 convicted white-collar offenders in Norway, this research identified the frequency of various convenience themes within each dimension. In the financial motive dimension, most convicts committed occupational crime to exploit possibilities (62%). Offenders wanted to climb the hierarchy of needs for status and success. In the organizational opportunity dimension, legitimate access to premises, resources and systems was the most frequent theme (32%). In the deviant behavior dimension, rationality in terms of benefits exceeding costs was the most frequent theme (30%).

The theory of convenience suggests that white-collar crime is dependent on the extent of crime convenience perceived and preferred by offenders (Braaten and Vaughn, 2019; Chan and Gibbs, 2020; Hansen, 2020). Convenience is the state of being able to proceed with something with little effort or difficulty, avoiding pain and strain (Mai and Olsen, 2016). Convenience is savings in time and effort (Farquhar and Rowley, 2009), as well as avoidance of pain and obstacles (Higgins, 1997). Convenience is a relative concept concerned with the efficiency in time and effort as well as reduction in pain and solution to problems (Engdahl, 2015). Convenience is an advantage in favor of a specific action to the detriment of alternative actions. White-collar offenders choose the most convenient path to reach their goals (Wikstrom et al., 2018).

White-collar crime is financial crime committed by individuals in privileged positions in business and public organizations (Sutherland, 1983). White-collar offenders commit and conceal their crime in a professional setting where they have legitimate access to premises, resources and systems (Logan et al., 2019). White-collar crime includes all categories of financial crime, such as fraud, corruption, manipulation and theft (Piquero, 2018).

This chapter presents an empirical study of convicted white-collar offenders in Norway. Convenience themes explored in this study cover the convenience dimensions of motive, opportunity, and willingness as suggested by convenience theory. The chapter addresses the following research question: *What convenience themes dominate among convicted white-collar offenders?* This research is important, as a number of themes are suggested in the research literature, while few of the themes are tested or compared empirically.

Convenience dimensions

The integrated deductive theory of convenience results from a synthesis of perspectives in three dimensions:

- *Convenience in motive.* It is convenient to use illegitimate financial gain to explore possibilities and avoid threats. Climb the hierarchy of needs for status and success (Maslow, 1943), realize the American dream of prosperity (Schoepfer and Piquero, 2006), satisfy the need for acclaim as a narcissist (Chatterjee and Pollock, 2017), and restore the perception of equity and equality (Leigh et al., 2010) are some of the perspectives integrated in the motive dimension of convenience theory. In addition, goal setting is a common practice in the field of organizational behavior, where high performance goals tend to encourage unethical behavior (Welsh and Ordonez, 2014; Welsh et al., 2019). The extra profit from financial crime enables the offender to handle desired possibilities and potential threats. It is mainly the convenience of extra profit, rather than the convenience of illegal profit, that is important in the motive dimension of convenience theory. However, under certain circumstances, there might be some extra benefits from illegal extra profit rather than extra profit in general, since illegal funds avoid the attention of external and internal control mechanisms, including compliance functions (Kawasaki, 2020). Illegitimate financial gain can thus find its ways into exploring possibilities and avoiding threats that recorded funds cannot.
- *Convenience in opportunity.* There is convenient access to resources to commit and conceal financial crime. Legitimate access to premises and systems (Benson and Simpson, 2018), specialized access in routine activity (Cohen and Felson, 1979), blame game by misleading attribution to others (Eberly et al., 2011), and institutional deterioration (Rodriguez et al., 2005) are some of the perspectives integrated in the opportunity dimension of convenience theory. A typical white-collar offender does not go into hiding as many street criminals do. Rather, the offender conceals financial crime among legal transactions to make illegal transactions seem legitimate, or the offender conceals financial crime by removing certain activities from the books. A typical white-collar offender who has convenient legitimate access to commit crime might spend most of the energy on concealing crime in the professional context.
- *Convenience in behavior.* Offenders can conveniently justify crime and neutralize guilt feelings. Application of neutralization techniques (Sykes and Matza, 1957), sliding on the slippery slope (Welsh et al., 2014), lack of self-control (Gottfredson and Hirschi, 1990), narcissistic identification with the organization (Galvin et al., 2015), learning from others by differential association (Sutherland, 1983), and professional deviant identity (Obodaru, 2017) are some of the perspectives integrated in the willingness dimension

of convenience theory. When a white-collar offender justifies crime, then it is obvious to him and her that wrongdoing occurred. However, the offender can claim that the act of wrongdoing is morally justifiable (Schnatterly et al., 2018), and that a negative life event has occurred (Engdahl, 2015). When a white-collar offender denies a guilty mind, then the offender applies neutralization techniques. When a white-collar offender makes crime as a choice, it is convenient based on identity (Galvin et al., 2015), rationality (Pratt and Cullen, 2005), and learning from others (Sutherland, 1983).

The integrated deductive theory of convenience results from synthesis within each of these three dimensions as well as among these three dimensions in the form of up-and-down integration as suggested by Krohn and Eassey (2014). According to Liska et al. (1989), theoretical synthesis requires that the postulation of abstract or general principles that will allow at least fractions of merging theories to be subsumed and interrelated. Effective synthesis can generate additional predictive power not made by the merging theories individually.

Convenience themes

The extent of white-collar crime convenience depends on motive, opportunity and willingness as illustrated in the structural model in Figure 6.1.

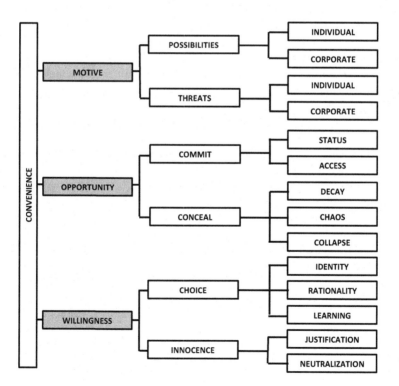

Figure 6.1 Structural model of convenience theory

In the financial motive, profit might be a goal in itself or an enabler to exploit possibilities and to avoid threats. Possibilities and threats exist both for individual members of the organization as well as for the corporation. It is convenient to exploit possibilities and to avoid threats by financial means.

In the organizational opportunity, convenience can exist both to commit white-collar crime and to conceal white-collar crime. Offenders have high social status in privileged positions, and they have legitimate access to crime resources. Disorganized institutional deterioration causes decay, lack of oversight and guardianship causes chaos, and criminal market structures cause collapse.

The personal willingness for deviant behavior is an offender choice or caused by perceived innocence. The choice of crime can be caused by deviant identity, rational consideration, or learning from others. The perceived innocence at crime is possible by means of justification and neutralization. Identity, rationality, learning, justification, and neutralization all contribute to making white-collar crime action a convenient behavior for offenders.

Research method

This research is concerned with convicted white-collar criminals. The collection of our Norwegian sample of white-collar offenders applied the original definition and characteristics of white-collar crime. Our sample thus has the following characteristics: famous individuals in term of high exposed social status and respectability, famous companies in terms of major suppliers in their businesses, surprising stories, important events, substantial consequences, matters of principles, and significant public interest. The two main financial newspapers in Norway are *Dagens Næringsliv* and *Finansavisen*, both of which are conservative-leaning business newspapers. In addition, the business-friendly national daily newspaper *Aftenposten* regularly reports news of white-collar criminals. Left-wing newspapers such as *Klassekampen* very seldom cover specific white-collar criminal cases, although generally report on white-collar crime. The total number of white-collar criminals was 408 reported during those years from 2009 to 2015. We carried out verification of facts in newspaper accounts by obtaining court documents. After registering newspaper accounts as an important indication of white-collar offenders, we compared the contents of newspaper articles and expanded our notes by court sentences, which typically range from 5 to 50 pages in Norwegian district courts, courts of appeal, and the Supreme Court. The term account is used here in the meaning of a statement to explain what has happened.

The research technique applied in this empirical study of archival material is content analysis (Bell et al., 2018; Saunders et al., 2007). Content analysis is any methodology or procedure that works to identify characteristics within texts attempting to make valid inferences (Duriau et al., 2007; Krippendorff, 1980; Patrucco et al., 2017). Content analysis assumes that language reflects both how people understand their surroundings and their cognitive processes.

Cognition refers to what people think and how they think, and cognitive processes affect the way in which people interpret and make sense of what is around them. Therefore, content analysis makes it possible to identify and determine relevant text in a context (McClelland et al., 2010).

Research results

Based on court documents and newspaper coverage of each white-collar crime case, content analysis was applied to identify the financial motive. A distinction is made between occupational crime and corporate crime. Corporate crime is committed to benefit the organization, while occupational crime mainly benefits the offender (Craig and Piquero, 2017; Shepherd and Button, 2019). Self-interested individuals commit occupational crime in their profession against their employers (e.g., embezzlement or receipt of bribes) and other victims. Organizational officials commit corporate crime in the larger interests of an organization, such as bribing potential customers, avoiding taxes by evasion, and misrepresenting accounting to get unjustified government subsidies.

Among all convicts in Norway, most of them committed occupational crime to exploit possibilities (62%), as listed in Table 6.1. Offenders wanted to climb the hierarchy of needs for status and success (Maslow, 1943) and realize the American dream of prosperity (Schoepfer and Piquero, 2006). Some wanted to satisfy the need for acclaim as narcissists (Chatterjee and Pollock, 2017), while others wanted to restore the perception of equity and equality (Leigh et al., 2010). Yet others wanted to satisfy their desire to help others as social concern (Agnew, 2014).

Table 6.1 Frequencies of convenience themes in the dimension of financial motive

FINANCIAL MOTIVE	FREQUENCY	FRACTION
POSSIBILITIES INDIVIDUAL	251	62%
Climb hierarchy of needs, satisfy personal greed		
POSSIBILITIES CORPORATE	102	25%
Reach business objectives, satisfy corporate greed		
THREATS INDIVIDUAL	8	2%
Avoid personal bankruptcy, job loss, strain and pain		
THREATS CORPORATE	47	11%
Avoid corporate collapse, adapt to criminal market forces		
TOTAL	*408*	*100%*

Every fourth convict committed corporate crime to exploit possibilities (25%). Some of them found that reaching business objectives justified illegal means (Jonnergård et al., 2010; Welsh and Ordonez, 2014; Welsh et al., 2019), while others thought it was important to satisfy greed where nothing is ever enough (Goldstraw-White, 2012), and where making as much profit as possible is the only goal (Naylor, 2003). Some enjoyed mutual organizational benefits in exchange relationships (Huang and Knight, 2017).

87% (62% and 25%) committed financial crime to exploit possibilities. Only 13% committed financial crime to avoid threats. Most of those committing crime because of threats did it to rescue the business (11%). Very few did it to rescue their own personal finances (2%). Corporate threats include collapse and bankruptcy (Blickle et al., 2006), and adaption to criminal market forces (Goncharov and Peter, 2019; Leonard and Weber, 1970). Personal threats include avoidance of loss of self-esteem after organizational failure (Crosina and Pratt, 2019), removal of strain, pain and uncertainty (Langton and Piquero, 2007), and avoidance of falling from position in the privileged elite (Piquero, 2012).

Among all convicts in Norway, the most frequent convenience theme in the organizational dimension was access to resources to commit crime (32%), as listed in Table 6.2. For many of the convicts, several convenience themes in the organizational structure were important for their crime convenience. This research identified the most important theme based on content analysis of court documents and media reports. Access to resources to commit crime was thus the most frequent one. As suggested by Benson and Simpson (2018), white-collar offenses manifest the following opportunity properties: (1) the offender has legitimate access to the location in which the crime is committed, (2) the

Table 6.2 Frequencies of convenience themes in the organizational opportunity dimension

ORGANIZATIONAL OPPORTUNITY	FREQUENCY	FRACTION
COMMIT CRIME BASED ON STATUS Too big to fail, blame game, offender humor	71	17%
COMMIT CRIME BASED ON ACCESS Legitimate access to resources, premises, and systems	129	32%
CONCEAL CRIME BASED ON DECAY Institutional deterioration, social disorganization	76	19%
CONCEAL CRIME BASED ON CHAOS Lack of control and guardianship, no whistleblowing	98	24%
CONCEAL CRIME BASED ON COLLAPSE Rule complexity, participate in cartels	34	8%
TOTAL	*408*	*100%*

offender is spatially separate from the victim, and (3) the offender's actions have a superficial appearance of legitimacy.

The second most important convenience theme in Table 6.2 is chaos (24%), where there is no guardianship because of lack of control in the principal-agent relationships (Bosse and Phillips, 2016), costs exceed benefits for whistleblowers (Keil et al., 2010), there are ethical climate conflicts (Victor and Cullen, 1988), and outsiders have a hard time making sense of what is going on internally (Weick, 1995).

The third most important convenience theme in the organizational dimension is decay (19%). Institutional deterioration based on legitimacy occurred (Rodriguez et al., 2005), and oversight functions suffered from inability to control because of social disorganization (Hoffmann, 2002). Furthermore, there was so much interference and noise in crime signals that nobody detected offenses (Karim and Siegel, 1998). Misrepresentation in accounting was the rule rather than the exception (Qiu and Slezak, 2019), and auditors reported to and were controlled by the management rather than the board (Hurley et al., 2019).

Offender status is fourth in the ranking of convenience themes in the organizational dimension (17%). Offenders used an executive language that people did not understand (Ferraro et al., 2005), and offenders as elite members were too big to fail and too powerful to jail (Pontell et al., 2014). Offenders were successful in playing the blame game by misleading attribution of deviance to others (Eberly et al., 2011). Offenders used humor to distract from their own deviant behavior (Yam et al., 2018). There was power inequality between the offender in the elite and others (Patel and Cooper, 2014).

The least frequent convenience theme in the organizational dimension was collapse, where the external environment opened up for more deviant action alternatives. Rule complexity prevented compliance (Lehman et al., 2019), and offenders were able to participate in crime networks such as cartels (Nielsen, 2003). Deviance was the usual way of business in markets with crime forces (Chang et al., 2005). The situational action perspective addresses how environments shape crime opportunities and, subsequently, how modifications in environments can increase criminal opportunities (Huisman and Erp, 2013; Kroneberg and Schulz, 2018; Wikstrom et al., 2018).

Convenience in deviant behavior is the third and final dimension in the theory of convenience for white-collar crime. While several themes apply to most offenders, this research identified the most important willingness theme for each offender. The research found that rationality is the most frequent convenience theme in personal willingness for deviant behavior as listed in Table 6.3. Offenders had a perception of benefits exceeding costs (Pratt and Cullen, 2005) and a perception of no deterrence effect (Comey, 2009). Some made crime a choice as a result of sensation seeking to experience adventure (Craig and Piquero, 2017), while others experienced behavioral reinforcement of deviance over time (Benartzi et al., 2017). There were undesirable impulses in self-regulation (Mawritz et al., 2017), and work-related stress were self-determined (Olafsen et al., 2017).

Table 6.3 Frequencies of convenience themes in the dimension of deviant behavior

PERSONAL WILLINGNESS	FREQUENCY	FRACTION
CHOICE OF CRIME BASED ON IDENTITY Acceptable for the elite, narcissistic identification	37	9%
CHOICE OF CRIME BASED ON RATIONALITY Benefits exceed costs, no perceived deterrence	124	30%
CHOICE OF CRIME BASED ON LEARNING Differential association, obedience, collectivist orientation	92	23%
INNOCENCE IN CRIME BASED ON JUSTIFICATION Negative life events, morally justifiable	72	18%
INNOCENCE IN CRIME BASED ON NEUTRALIZATION Denial of harm, denial of responsibility, denial of victim	83	20%
TOTAL	*408*	*100%*

While rationality accounts for 30% of the offenders, learning accounts for 23%, as listed in Table 6.3. Offenders learned from others by differential association (Sutherland, 1983), and their actions were according to authority as obedience (Baird and Zelin, 2009) and according to collectivist value orientations (Bussmann et al., 2018).

The third most important convenience theme in the behavioral dimension is application of neutralization techniques (20%). Offenders deny harm, deny victim, and deny responsibility (Sykes and Matza, 1957). Some offenders were sliding on the slippery slope (Welsh et al., 2014), and some lacked self-control (Gottfredson and Hirschi, 1990).

Figure 6.2 summarizes the findings in terms of percentage distributions for financial motive (possibilities and threats), organizational opportunity (commit and conceal) and personal willingness (choice and innocence).

Gottschalk and Gunnesdal (2018) estimated that 1 out of 11 white-collar offenders in Norway are detected and brought to justice, which seems supported by an empirical study of bribery detection in Norway by Andresen and Button (2019). Our sample of convicted white-collar criminals is thus only the tip of an iceberg of offenders. What is below the surface in the iceberg metaphor – 10 out of 11 criminals – is completely unknown. We know nothing about distribution of convenience themes among non-convicted white-collar offenders. We might speculate that the reason the large majority of offenders never are brought to justice is because they have different convenience themes from those in the small minority

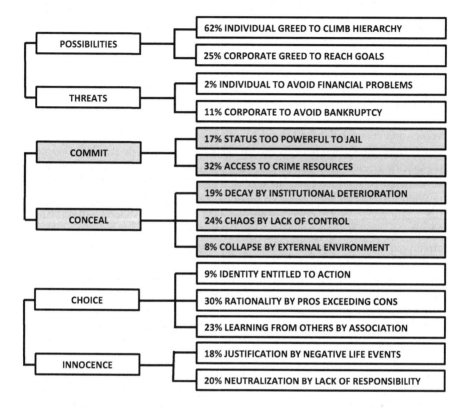

Figure 6.2 Frequency of convenience themes in the sample of convicts

of offenders brought to justice. Therefore, we have no grounds for generalizing our findings from the sample to the population of offenders in Norway.

Nevertheless, it is interesting to note from the sample that most white-collar convicts committed occupational crime, which offenders pursued to obtain illegitimate gain that should enable them personally to climb in the hierarchy of needs. Fewer cases of corporate crime were prosecuted and caused convictions. Especially larger, multinational corporations may have resources to avoid or survive the criminal justice system in a particular jurisdiction such as Norway (Wingerde and Lord, 2020). An example is the Transocean case, where the global offshore drilling contractor avoided taxes in Norway in a spectacular tax evasion scheme. Therefore it is not at all obvious that occupational white-collar crime is more frequent than corporate white-collar crime in Norway.

In the organizational opportunity dimension of convenience, legitimate access is the most frequent characteristic of white-collar offenses. This is no surprise, as white-collar offenders can commit financial crime in their daily routines. Specialized access in the routine activity perspective suggests that crime is convenient since it "directly arises out of the routines of everyday life" (Huisman and Erp, 2013: 1179). A typical white-collar offender does not go into hiding as many street criminals do.

In the dimension of personal willingness for deviant behavior in convenience theory, choice of crime as a rational decision is the most frequent characteristic of white-collar offenses. While some of the rational convicts also applied neutralization techniques to avoid a guilty mind, it is obvious from the archival material that the rationality of comparing advantages and disadvantages – as well as pros and cons – led offenders to commit crime. The rational choice perspective simply states that when benefits exceed costs, we would all do it. The perspective is explicitly a result of the self-regarding preference assumption, where rationality is restricted to self-interested materialism (Paternoster et al., 2018).

While there is an abundance of theories, models and hypotheses that address the white-collar crime phenomenon (e.g., Cullen and Wilcox, 2010; Rorie, 2020), few studies have tested these perspectives empirically. This chapter attempted to test the integrated theory of convenience by classifying 408 convicts in Norway according to their motive, opportunity, and willingness. The most frequent motive was personal gain, the most frequent opportunity characteristic was legitimate access to resources, and the most frequent willingness characteristic was the rational decision of perceiving crime benefits to exceed crime costs.

This chapter addressed a research question concerned with convenience themes that dominate among convicted white-collar offenders. The chapter did not address convenience as such when committing white-collar crime, which would be the basic empirical test of convenience theory. As an emerging theory there are many open avenues for testing it. A recent example is Braaten and Vaughn (2019), who found support for convenience theory when studying cryptocurrency crime.

References

Agnew, R. (2014). Social concern and crime: Moving beyond the assumption of simple self-interest, *Criminology*, 52 (1), 1–32.

Andresen, M.S. and Button, M. (2019). The profile and detection of bribery in Norway and England & Wales: A comparative study, *European Journal of Criminology*, 16 (1), 18–40.

Baird, J.E. and Zelin, R.C. (2009). An examination of the impact of obedience pressure on perceptions of fraudulent acts and the likelihood of committing occupational fraud, *Journal of Forensic Studies in Accounting and Business*, 1 (1), 1–14.

Bell, E., Bryman, A. and Harley, B. (2018). *Business Research Methods*, 2nd edition, New York, NY: Oxford University Press.

Benartzi, S., Beshears, J., Milkman, K.L., Sunstein, C.R., Thaler, R.H., Shankar, M., Tucker-Ray, W., Congdon, W.J. and Galing, S. (2017). Should governments invest more in nudging? *Psychological Science*, 28 (8), 1041–1055.

Benson, M.L. and Simpson, S.S. (2018). *White-Collar Crime: An Opportunity Perspective*, 3rd edition, New York, NY: Routledge.

Blickle, G., Schlegel, A., Fassbender, P. and Klein, U. (2006). Some personality correlates of business white-collar crime, *Applied Psychology: An International Review*, 55 (2), 220–233.

Bosse, D.A. and Phillips, R.A. (2016). Agency theory and bounded self-interest, *Academy of Management Review*, 41 (2), 276–297.

Braaten, C.N. and Vaughn, M.S. (2019). Convenience theory of cryptocurrency crime: A content analysis of U.S. federal court decisions, *Deviant Behavior*, published online, https://doi.org/10.1080/01639625.2019.1706706.

Bussmann, K.D., Niemeczek, A. and Vockrodt, M. (2018). Company culture and prevention of corruption in Germany, China and Russia, *European Journal of Criminology*, 15 (3), 255–277.

Chan, F. and Gibbs, C. (2020). Integrated theories of white-collar and corporate crime, in: Rorie, M.L. (editor), *The Handbook of White-Collar Crime*, Hoboken, NJ: Wiley & Sons, chapter 13, pages 191–208.

Chang, J.J., Lu, H.C. and Chen, M. (2005). Organized crime or individual crime? Endogeneous size of a criminal organization and the optimal law enforcement, *Economic Inquiry*, 43 (3), 661–675.

Chatterjee, A. and Pollock, T.G. (2017). Master of puppets: How narcissistic CEOs construct their professional worlds, *Academy of Management Review*, 42 (4), 703–725.

Cohen, L.E. and Felson, M. (1979). Social change and crime rate trends: A routine activity approach, *American Sociological Review*, 44, 588–608.

Comey, J.B. (2009). Go directly to prison: White collar sentencing after the Sarbanes-Oxley act, *Harvard Law Review*, 122, 1728–1749.

Craig, J.M. and Piquero, N.L. (2017). Sensational offending: An application of sensation seeking to white-collar and conventional crimes, *Crime & Delinquency*, 63 (11), 1363–1382.

Crosina, E. and Pratt, M.G. (2019). Toward a model of organizational mourning: The case of former Lehman Brothers bankers, *Academy of Management Journal*, 62 (1), 66–98.

Cullen, F.T. and Wilcox, P. (2010). *Encyclopedia of Criminological Theory*, Los Angeles, CA: Sage Publications.

Duriau, V.J., Reger, R.K. and Pfarrer, M.D. (2007). A content analysis of the content analysis literature in organization studies: Research themes, data sources, and methodological refinements, *Organizational Research Methods*, 10 (1), 5–34.

Eberly, M.B., Holley, E.C., Johnson, M.D. and Mitchell, T.R. (2011). Beyond internal and external: A dyadic theory of relational attributions, *Academy of Management Review*, 36 (4), 731–753.

Engdahl, O. (2015). White-collar crime and first-time adult-onset offending: Explorations in the concept of negative life events as turning points, *International Journal of Law, Crime and Justice*, 43 (1), 1–16.

Farquhar, J.D. and Rowley, J. (2009). Convenience: A services perspective, *Marketing Theory*, 9 (4), 425–438.

Ferraro, F., Pfeffer, J. and Sutton, R.I. (2005). Economics language and assumptions: How theories can become self-fulfilling, *Academy of Management Review*, 30 (1), 8–24.

Galvin, B.M., Lange, D. and Ashforth, B.E. (2015). Narcissistic organizational identification: Seeing oneself as central to the organization's identity, *Academy of Management Review*, 40 (2), 163–181.

Goldstraw-White, J. (2012). *White-collar Crime: Accounts of Offending Behavior*, London, UK: Palgrave Macmillan.

Goncharov, I. and Peter, C.D. (2019). Does reporting transparency affect industry coordination? Evidence from the duration of international cartels, *The Accounting Review*, 94 (3), 149–175.

Gottfredson, M.R. and Hirschi, T. (1990). *A General Theory of Crime*, Stanford, CA: Stanford University Press.

Gottschalk, P. and Gunnesdal, L. (2018). *White-Collar Crime in the Shadow Economy: Lack of Detection, Investigation, and Conviction Compared to Social Security Fraud*, London, UK: Springer Publishing/Palgrave Pivot, Palgrave Macmillan.

Hansen, L.L. (2020). Review of the book "Convenience Triangle in White-Collar Crime: Case Studies of Fraud Examinations", *ChoiceConnect*, vol. 57, no. 5, Middletown, CT: Association of College and Research Libraries.

Higgins, E.T. (1997). Beyond pleasure and pain, *American Psychologist*, 52, 1280–1300.

Hoffmann, J.P. (2002). A contextual analysis of differential association, social control, and strain theories of delinquency, *Social Forces*, 81 (3), 753–785.

Huang, L. and Knight, A.P. (2017). Resources and relationships in entrepreneurship: An exchange theory of the development and effects of the entrepreneur-investor relationship, *Academy of Management Review*, 42 (1), 80–102.

Huisman, W. and Erp, J. (2013). Opportunities for environmental crime, *British Journal of Criminology*, 53, 1178–1200.

Hurley, P.J., Mayhew, B.W. and Obermire, K.M. (2019). Realigning auditors' accountability: Experimental evidence, *The Accounting Review*, 94 (3), 233–250.

Jonnergård, K., Stafsudd, A. and Elg, U. (2010). Performance evaluations as gender barriers in professional organizations: A study of auditing firms, *Gender, Work and Organization*, 17 (6), 721–747.

Karim, K.E. and Siegel, P.H. (1998). A signal detection theory approach to analyzing the efficiency and effectiveness of auditing to detect management fraud, *Managerial Auditing Journal*, 13 (6), 367–375.

Kawasaki, T. (2020). Review of comparative studies on white-collar and corporate crime, in: Rorie, M.L. (editor), *The Handbook of White-Collar Crime*, Hoboken, NJ: Wiley & Sons, chapter 27, pages 437–447.

Keil, M., Tiwana, A., Sainsbury, R. and Sneha, S. (2010). Toward a theory of whistle-blowing intentions: A benefit-cost differential perspective, *Decision Sciences*, 41 (4), 787–812.

Krippendorff, K. (1980). *Content Analysis: An Introduction to its Methodology*, Beverly Hills, CA: Sage.

Krohn, M.D. and Eassey, J.M. (2014). Integrated theories of crime, in: Miller, J.M. (editor), *The Encyclopedia of Theoretical Criminology*, Chichester, UK: John Wiley & Sons, pages 458–463.

Kroneberg, C. and Schulz, S. (2018). Revisiting the role of self-control in situational action theory, *European Journal of Criminology*, 15 (1), 56–76.

Langton, L. and Piquero, N.L. (2007). Can general strain theory explain white-collar crime? A preliminary investigation of the relationship between strain and select white-collar offenses, *Journal of Criminal Justice*, 35 (1), 1–15.

Lehman, D.W., Cooil, B. and Ramanujam, R. (2019). The effects of rule complexity on organizational noncompliance and remediation: Evidence from restaurant health inspections, *Journal of Management*, published online, pages 1–33, https://doi.org/10.1177/0149206319842262.

Leigh, A.C., Foote, D.A., Clark, W.R. and Lewis, J.L. (2010). Equity sensitivity: A triadic measure and outcome/input perspectives, *Journal of Managerial Issues*, 22 (3), 286–305.

Leonard, W.N. and Weber, M.G. (1970). Automakers and dealers: A study of criminogenic market forces, *Law & Society Review*, 4 (3), 407–424.

Liska, A.E., Krohn, M.D. and Messner, S.F. (1989). Strategies and requisites for theoretical integration in the study of crime and deviance, in: Messner, S.F., Krohn, M.D. and Liska, A.E. (editors), *Theoretical Integration in the Study of Deviance and Crime*, Albany, NY: State University of New York Press, pages 1–20.

Logan, M.W., Morgan, M.A., Benson, M.L. and Cullen, F.T. (2019). Coping with imprisonment: Testing the special sensitivity hypothesis for white-collar offenders, *Justice Quarterly*, 36 (2), 225–254.

Mai, H.T.X. and Olsen, S.O. (2016). Consumer participation in self-production: The role of control mechanisms, convenience orientation, and moral obligation, *Journal of Marketing Theory and Practice*, 24 (2), 209–223.

Maslow, A.H. (1943). A theory of human motivation, *Psychological Review*, 50 (4), 370–396.

Mawritz, M.B., Greenbaum, R.L., Butts, M.M. and Graham, K.A. (2017). I just can't control myself: A self-regulation perspective on the abuse of deviant employees, *Academy of Management Journal*, 60 (4), 1482–1503.

McClelland, P.L., Liang, X. and Barker, V.L. (2010). CEO commitment to the status quo: Replication and extension using content analysis, *Journal of Management*, 36 (5), 1251–1277.

Naylor, R.T. (2003). Towards a general theory of profit-driven crimes, *British Journal of Criminology*, 43, 81–101.

Nielsen, R.P. (2003). Corruption networks and implications for ethical corruption reform, *Journal of Business Ethics*, 42 (2), 125–149.

Obodaru, O. (2017). Forgone, but not forgotten: Toward a theory of forgone professional identities, *Academy of Management Journal*, 60 (2), 523–553.

Olafsen, A.H., Niemiec, C.P., Halvari, H., Deci, E.L. and Williams, G.C. (2017). On the dark side of work: A longitudinal analysis using self-determination theory, *European Journal of Work and Organizational Psychology*, 26 (2), 275–285.

Patel, P.C. and Cooper, D. (2014). Structural power equality between family and nonfamily TMT members and the performance of family firms, *Academy of Management Journal*, 57 (6), 1624–1649.

Paternoster, R., Jaynes, C.M. and Wilson, T. (2018). Rational choice theory and interest in the "fortune of others", *Journal of Research in Crime and Delinquency*, 54 (6), 847–868.

Patrucco, A.S., Luzzini, D. and Ronchi, S. (2017). Research perspectives on public procurement: Content analysis of 14 years of publications in the Journal of Public Procurement, *Journal of Public Procurement*, 16 (2), 229–269.

Piquero, N.L. (2012). The only thing we have to fear is fear itself: Investigating the relationship between fear of falling and white-collar crime, *Crime and Delinquency*, 58 (3), 362–379.

Piquero, N.L. (2018). White-collar crime is crime: Victims hurt just the same, *Criminology & Public Policy*, 17 (3), 595–600.

Pontell, H.N., Black, W.K. and Geis, G. (2014). Too big to fail, too powerful to jail? On the absence of criminal prosecutions after the 2008 financial meltdown, *Crime, Law and Social Change*, 61 (1), 1–13.

Pratt, T.C. and Cullen, F.T. (2005). Assessing macro-level predictors and theories of crime: A meta-analysis, *Crime and Justice*, 32, 373–450.

Qiu, B. and Slezak, S.L. (2019). The equilibrium relationships between performance-based pay, performance, and the commission and detection of fraudulent misreporting, *The Accounting Review*, 94 (2), 325–356.

Rodriguez, P., Uhlenbruck, K. and Eden, L. (2005). Government corruption and the entry strategies of multinationals, *Academy of Management Review*, 30 (2), 383–396.

Rorie, M. (2020). *The Handbook of White-Collar Crime*, Hoboken, NJ: Wiley & Sons.

Saunders, M., Lewis, P. and Thornhill, A. (2007). *Research Methods for Business Students*, 5th edition, London, UK: Pearson Education.

Schnatterly, K., Gangloff, K.A. and Tuschke, A. (2018). CEO wrongdoing: A review of pressure, opportunity, and rationalization, *Journal of Management*, 44 (6), 2405–2432.

Schoepfer, A. and Piquero, N.L. (2006). Exploring white-collar crime and the American dream: A partial test of institutional anomie theory, *Journal of Criminal Justice*, 34 (3), 227–235.

Shepherd, D. and Button, M. (2019). Organizational inhibitions to addressing occupational fraud: A theory of differential rationalization, *Deviant Behavior*, 40 (8), 971–991.

Sutherland, E.H. (1983). *White Collar Crime: The Uncut Version*, New Haven, CT: Yale University Press.

Sykes, G. and Matza, D. (1957). Techniques of neutralization: A theory of delinquency, *American Sociological Review*, 22 (6), 664–670.

Victor, B. and Cullen, J.B. (1988). The organizational bases of ethical work climates, *Administrative Science Quarterly*, 33, 101–125.

Weick, K.E. (1995). *Sensemaking in Organizations*, Thousand Oaks, CA: Sage.

Welsh, D., Bush, J., Thiel, C. and Bonner, J. (2019). Reconceptualizing goal setting's dark side: The ethical consequences of learning versus outcome goals, *Organizational Behavior and Human Decision Processes*, 150, 14–27.

Welsh, D.T. and Ordonez, L.D. (2014). The dark side of consecutive high performance goals: Linking goal setting, depletion, and unethical behavior, *Organizational Behavior and Human Decision Processes*, 123, 79–89.

Welsh, D.T., Ordonez, L.D., Snyder, D.G. and Christian, M.S. (2014). The slippery slope: How small ethical transgressions pave the way for larger future transgressions, *Journal of Applied Psychology*, 100 (1), 114–127.

Wikstrom, P.O.H., Mann, R.P. and Hardie, B. (2018). Young people's differential vulnerability to criminogenic exposure: Bridging the gap between people- and place-oriented approaches in the study of crime causation, *European Journal of Criminology*, 15 (1), 10–31.

Wingerde, K. and Lord, N. (2020). The elusiveness of white-collar and corporate crime in a globalized economy, in: Rorie, M.L. (editor), *The Handbook of White-Collar Crime*, Hoboken, NJ: Wiley & Sons, chapter 29, pages 469–483.

Yam, K.C., Christian, M.S., Wei, W., Liao, Z. and Nai, J. (2018). The mixed blessing of leader sense of humor: Examining costs and benefits, *Academy of Management Journal*, 61 (1), 348–369.

7 Social security fraud

White-collar offenders and social security fraudsters are two groups who both commit financial crime. In a perspective of critical criminology, white-collar offenders belong to the elite in society with certain mechanisms of protection and often privileged treatment in the criminal justice system, while social security offenders are treated like street criminals with less protection and almost automated treatment in the criminal justice system. When miscarriage of justice occurs, a white-collar convict can receive a large financial compensation from the government. This chapter presents the case of miscarriage of justice against 36 individuals who were wrongfully convicted of social security fraud and incarcerated. The case is discussed in the perspectives of social conflict theory, blame game hypothesis, and executive destiny from organizational accounts.

A scandal is a publicized instance of transgression that runs counter to social norms, typically resulting in condemnation and discredit and other consequences such as bad press, disengagement of key constituencies, the severance of network ties, and decrease in key performance indicators (Piazza and Jourdan, 2018). Slyke and Bales (2012) suggest that individuals with high social status and privileged positions – such as chief executives – cannot avoid detection and blame. Executives might lose in the blame game (Eberly et al., 2011; Lehman et al., 2019: Schnatterly et al., 2018). On the other hand, Pontell et al. (2014) suggest that the accused might simply be too powerful to blame. Depending on how accounts of a scandal evolve over time, shifts in attribution of blame and scapegoating might occur (Lee and Robinson, 2000; Resodihardjo et al., 2015; Xie and Keh, 2016). The blamed individual will typically deny responsibility based on the neutralization technique of disclaiming wrongdoing (Sykes and Matza, 1957).

This chapter presents a case study to illustrate chief executive destiny caused by changing accounts of events and changing attributions of blame. This research is important, as chief executives are in a principal-agent relationship (Khanna et al., 2015; Zahra et al., 2005; Williams, 2008), where opportunistic behavior is motivated by individual utility maximization (Bosse and Phillips, 2016; Pillay and Kluvers, 2014).

The scandal in this case is concerned with wrongful prosecution and conviction of individuals who received social security benefits (Meldalen and Lofstad, 2019;

NTB, 2019). The case is concerned with miscarriage of justice. Misleading interpretations of laws caused conviction and incarceration of innocent individuals for social security fraud (Larsen, 2019; Lofstad, 2019). The scandal is particularly interesting in the social conflict perspective, where white-collar offenders may feel entitled to violate and then modify the law, while social security fraudsters are at the bottom of social status and have to accept whatever happens to them (Petrocelli et al., 2003; Schwendinger and Schwendinger, 2014).

The social security scandal is first presented in this chapter. Then there follows discussion of the case in the perspective of social conflict and finally in the perspective of the blame game hypothesis.

Social security scandal

The Norwegian Labor and Welfare Administration, NAV, was embroiled in a controversy after it incorrectly interpreted rules from the European Union (EU). While not being a member of EU, Norway is part of the European Economic Area (EEA) that cooperates with the EU on legal and other matters. The controversy quickly developed into a serious scandal with demands made for the authority's chief executive, Sigrun Vågeng, to resign. Politicians were also quickly critical, with left-wing Red party leader Bjørnar Moxnes calling for the case of a scandal where the minister in charge of labor and social issues in the Norwegian government, Anniken Hauglie, should resign. Socialist party leader Audun Lysbakken described it as a catastrophe, while prime-minister Erna Solberg said that it was incredibly unfair and should not happen in Norway (NTB, 2019). State prosecutor Tor-Aksel Busch asked all law enforcement agencies to review recent social security fraud cases (Meldalen and Lofstad, 2019).

NAV is responsible for around a third of Norway's state budget. The authority administers social security programs including unemployment benefits, pensions and child benefits. Compared to other countries, the welfare benefits in Norway are quite good. For example, sick leave and unemployment only cause minimal reductions in income and thus marginal reductions in standard of living for the benefit receivers.

On Monday, October 29, 2019, the authority admitted it had made comprehensive errors in its interpretation of sickness benefits, which is support for people who need medical treatment or other activities to help them get back to work. Sickness benefits are called work assessment allowances in Norway that also include support for people who are unable to work due to a sick child's care needs. At least 48 individuals had been wrongly convicted of social security fraud, out of which 36 individuals had served time in jail (Lofstad, 2019).

The issue specifically affected people who received benefits while living in Norway, but were staying temporarily in another EEA country. NAV practiced rules for being on work assessment allowances or other care benefits incorrectly. NAV thought that benefit receivers had to stay in Norway when on benefits. However, as an EEA country, not only the flow of capital, but also the flow of people is encouraged within Europe. EU regulations made this explicit for social security in 2012, when it was documented that receivers of social security benefits could travel and stay wherever they like within EEA.

Thirty-six receivers of social security benefits were not just in a difficult situation in their lives, they were denied further benefits, they had to pay back received money, and they had to serve time in jail, because they had stayed temporarily abroad. They were victims of a miscarriage of justice, which is considered extremely serious in Norway. When people are asked how many guilty persons should be free to avoid incarcerating an innocent person, people tend to say at least 100. In the Norwegian culture, it is an extremely serious wrongdoing to punish innocent persons (Larsen, 2019).

Sigrun Vågeng was born in 1950 and thus entitled to retire the following year 2020 at the age of 70 years. She holds a master's of business administration (MBA) degree and became chief executive at NAV in 2015. Four years later, the social security scandal became public. Then she said she would retire anyway next year.

Both government minister Hauglie and chief executive Vågeng promised to conduct independent investigations of the scandal. They would hire fraud examiners from local law firms or global auditing firms to conduct internal investigations. Research has shown that it can be a smart move to be the client for a fraud examination as fraud examiners can help move attention away from the client.

Social conflict theory

Both social security fraud and white-collar offenses represent serious forms of financial crime causing harm and victims in society. The police have limited resources to investigate economic crime and have to prioritize their resources by dropping a large portion of cases (Brooks and Button, 2011). The two types of cases are in many ways two extremes on the scale of economic criminals (Gottschalk and Gunnesdal, 2018). While social security fraud is committed by people who basically need financial help from the community to live decent lives, white-collar crime is committed by individuals in the upper echelons of society who abuse their positions to enrich themselves or the organizations they are associated with.

A number of situations are viewed as social security fraud, including misuse of benefits, making false statements on claims, and buying or selling social security cards. Concealing information that affects eligibility for benefits is also considered to be fraud. People who represent social security recipients commit fraud if they misuse the benefits they are entrusted with (Lensvelt-Mulders et al., 2006). It is considered fraud when people knowingly provide inaccurate information when they apply for social security benefits. Anyone receiving social security disability benefits must inform the social security administration if they also receive workers' compensation benefits form their organizations where they are or were employed.

The social conflict theory suggests that the powerful and wealthy in the upper class of society define what is right and what is wrong. The rich and mighty can behave like "robber barons" because they make the laws. Therefore, the ruling class does not consider a white-collar offense as a regular crime, and certainly not one similar to street crime or social security fraud (Michel, 2016).

Social conflict theory holds that laws and law enforcement are used by dominant groups in society to minimize threats to their interests posed by those whom they perceive as dangerous and greedy (Petrocelli et al., 2003). Crime is defined by legal codes and sanctioned by institutions of criminal justice to secure order in society. The ruling class secures order in the ruled class by means of laws and law enforcement. Conflicts and clashes between interest groups are restrained and stabilized by law enforcement.

In addition, particularly in Scandinavian countries, conflicts and clashes are restrained also by the minimum standard of living provided by social security benefits. Sick people, disabled people, refugees and others suffering from negative life events are very well taken care in terms of a reasonable standard of living. However, when there is suspicion of benefit abuse, NAV quickly report cases to the police, the police quickly deliver cases to the prosecution, prosecutors quickly show up in court, and judges quickly sentence offenders to jail. The defendants are incapable of defend themselves effectively with the help of second-rate attorneys. The criminal justice system seems to work almost automatically in social security cases (Gottschalk and Gunnesdal, 2018). The best attorneys work for white-collar defendants.

According to the social conflict theory, the justice system is biased and designed to protect the wealthy and powerful (Arrigo and Bernard, 1997; Schoultz and Flyghed, 2019). It is not designed to protect the poor and powerless. The losers in society are to be taken care of in a way determined by the winners (Michel, 2016). If the losers deviate from arrangements determined by the winners, then they are quickly sanctioned in countries such as Norway (Gottschalk and Gunnesdal, 2018).

Blame game hypothesis

Internally at NAV, a blame game started. The first loser in the blame game was announced on December 4, 2019, which was one month after the scandal became public. One of the senior executives reporting to Vågeng resigned from her position. The media reported (Ruud and Spence, 2019):

> Kjersti Monland will be the first to step down as a result of the social security scandal. She will quit her job Monday, December 9.

NAV published a press release about Monland's resignation:

> Over the past few weeks, Nav has received heavy criticism for its handling of the EEA regulations related to cash benefits. Confidence in Nav is greatly weakened and many Nav employees have a difficult working day.
>
> – I have respect and understanding for Kjersti's decision, but I am also happy that she will continue to use her expertise and capacity to the best

of our organization's development work. Kjersti is also available to contribute clarification and knowledge about the coming work on the EEA case, says Sigrun Vågeng.

– I have come to the conclusion that it is both necessary and appropriate to appoint a new leader who can continue this important work, as well as strengthen the power of the department in this critical phase. All tasks in the department and the line must be able to be filled satisfactorily, both in relation to government ministries, the management of Nav and the outside world says benefits director Kjersti Monland.

Kjersti Monland became an obvious scapegoat as many commented in the Norwegian media after the announcement of her resignation from the position of benefits director. Scapegoating is a form of denial of responsibility accompanied with placement of blame on an individual or group of individuals (Lee and Robinson, 2000; Resodihardjo et al., 2015; Xie and Keh, 2016).

Moland's resignation occurred less than a week before an internal audit report was due. Vågeng had asked the internal audit function at Nav to conduct a review as the scandal broke. Being the client for the audit review, Vågeng decided on the mandate. This is in line with many famous internal reviews, where being the client for the review can protect the client from negative attention.

As the social security scandal reached the headlines in all media in December 2019, the blame game expanded from the social security service Nav to a number of other actors in the criminal justice system. The police received blame for simply trusting cases from Nav without conducting independent criminal investigations. The prosecution received blame for simply trusting cases from the police without conducting independent evaluation of presented evidence and application of the law. District courts received blame for simply trusting the prosecution and not helping defendants tell their stories. Judges received blame for sentencing defendants to jail even when the amount was only the equivalent of US$ 10,000.

This blame game caused a fear "in the top legal expertise to be drawn into the scandal" (Spence and Ruud, 2019). While all actors in the criminal justice system were attacked by blame attribution, each actor could point at the other actors to reduce own blameworthiness.

After more than a month of public attention, most suspected actors in the scandal had successfully distributed blame in the media, where confusion occurred among politicians and others about who to really blame.

By successfully playing the blame game, the offender will attribute blame for wrongdoing to someone else (DeScioli and Bokemper, 2014; Eberly et al., 2011; Hurrell, 2016; Keaveney, 2008; Lee and Robinson, 2000; Sonnier et al., 2015), thereby reducing the perceived violation of trust.

Essentially, in the blame-game hypothesis, all involved persons attempt to pass the blame on, absolving themselves of the responsibility for the negative event. Lack of causal accounts increases disapproval ratings of the harm carried out by placing the blame of harmful acts on others. For example, by attributing corruption to an executive in the organization as a rotten apple, the suspect will feel betrayed by other executives who, in their opinion, belong to a rotten apple basket in terms of a criminogenic business culture.

External attribution is obviously the preference by most to avoid internal attribution. External attributions place the cause of a negative event on external factors, absolving executives from personal responsibility. However, unstable attributions suggest that the cause of a negative event is unlikely to persist over time, and as such mitigate the severity of the predicament. Uncontrollable attributions suggest that the cause of the event is not within the control of the attributor, further removing any blame or responsibility for unjust act from the account giver (Lee and Robinson, 2000).

Self-blame is rare and often non-existent. Nobody will blame oneself for a negative event. Self-blame is attributing a negative event to one's behavior or disposition (Lee and Robinson, 2000).

Some are too powerful to blame. Pontell et al. (2014) found that the financial crisis obviously had its cause in mismanagement in the financial sector, but all in the financial sector avoided serious blame. The investigation of the collapse at Lehman Brothers is a typical example (Jenner Block, 2010). Status-related factors such as influential positions, upper-class family ties, and community roles often preclude perceptions of blameworthiness (Slyke and Bales, 2012).

Chief executive destiny

In attempting to respond to and manage scandals, private and public organizations and their executives develop and publicize explanations (Bundy and Pfarrer, 2015; Whyte, 2016) as accounts of events (Albrecht, 1996; Hearit, 2006), since media coverage is critical in shaping opinions (Gamache and McNamara, 2019). Accounts are statements made by an actor to explain unanticipated or untoward behavior that is subject to some sort of evaluative inquiry by other actors (Scott and Lyman, 1968). Initial accounts are typically supportive of top management by claiming that mistakes and deviant behavior occurred in various functions in the organization.

Chief executive Vågeng received such a message from the first internal report, where chief auditor Klepp (2019: 4) claimed in the executive summary of the report that; "responsibilities and tasks for arrangements abroad are spread across several units both in-line and between-lines".

However, as a scandal evolves, a key part of the evolution of accounts seems to be the divergence of interests between the organizational entity and individual top leaders (Bandura, 1999; Schoultz and Flyghed, 2016; Schnatterly et al., 2018). The interests of the organization diverge from those of the individuals who first responded to the crisis.

Reports of investigations by fraud examiners are an important source of information regarding executive destiny in organizations. Unfortunately, most client organizations keep reports secret and are not willing to make them available for research (Gottschalk and Tcherni-Buzzeo, 2017). It was possible to find and retrieve 13 reports from Canada, Denmark, Japan, New Zealand, Nigeria, Norway, Sweden, and most from the United States:

> In the reports, we searched for corporate accounts as communicated excuses and justifications for wrongdoings. We found that denial of knowledge and denial of responsibility are frequent corporate excuses, while claiming higher loyalties and claiming entitlement to action are frequent justifications. We were also interested in the destiny of executives who received blame for deviance. Seven out of thirteen executives received blame in investigation reports and received termination from their companies. Three executives found themselves terminated since the companies went bankrupt.

More and more commentators in the media, professors in academics, politicians in parliament and others called for the resignation of chief executive Vågeng and government minister Hauglie. But they did not resign. Vågeng replied to her critics that she would restore trust in Nav before she retired the following year. Hauglie replied to her critics that an investigation committee appointed by the government would present its report in the following year. However, in January 2020, both governmental minister Hauglie and chief executive Vågeng were forced to resign (Alnes, 2020).

In conclusion, white-collar offenders and social security fraudsters are two groups who both commit financial crime. In a perspective of critical criminology, white-collar offenders belong to the elite in society with certain mechanisms of protection and often privileged treatment in the criminal justice system, while social security offenders are treated like street criminals with less protection and almost automated treatment in the criminal justice system. When miscarriage of justice occurs, a white-collar convict can receive a large financial compensation from the government. This chapter presented the case of miscarriage of justice against 36 individuals who were wrongfully convicted of social security fraud and incarcerated. The case study supports the social conflict theory, where miscarriage of justice against social security fraudsters is less serious than miscarriage of justice against white-collar fraudsters. The case study also supports the blame game hypothesis where nobody is willing to take on the blame for the scandal, but instead is willing to attribute blame to others. As a consequence, executive destiny became less traumatic or non-existent.

References

Albrecht, S. (1996). *Crisis Management for Corporate Self-Defense: How to Protect Your Organization in a Crisis: How to Stop a Crisis Before It Starts.* New York, NY: American Management Association.

Alnes, E. (2020). Sigrun Vågeng sluttar som Nav-sjef (Sigrun Vågeng quits as Nav-chief), public Norwegian broadcasting corporation *NRK*, www.nrk.no, published January 31.

Arrigo, B.A. and Bernard, T.J. (1997). Postmodern criminology in relation to radical and conflict criminology, *Critical Criminology*, 8 (2), 39–60.

Bandura, A. (1999). Moral disengagement in the perpetration of inhumanities, *Personality and Social Psychology Review*, 3 (3), 193–209.

Bao, D., Kim, Y., Mian, G.M. and Su, L. (2019). Do managers disclose or withhold bad news? Evidence from short interest, *The Accounting Review*, 94 (3), 1–26.

Bosse, D.A. and Phillips, R.A. (2016). Agency theory and bounded self-interest, *Academy of Management Review*, 41 (2), 276–297.

Brooks, G. and Button, M. (2011). The police and fraud investigation and the case for a nationalized solution in the United Kingdom, *The Police Journal*, 84, 305–319.

Bundy, J. and Pfarrer, M.D. (2015). A burden of responsibility: The role of social approval at the onset of a crisis, *Academy of Management Review*, 40 (3), 345–369.

DeScioli, P. and Bokemper, S. (2014). Voting as a counter-strategy in the blame game, *Psychological Inquiry*, 25, 206–214.

Eberly, M.B., Holley, E.C., Johnson, M.D. and Mitchell, T.R. (2011). Beyond internal and external: A dyadic theory of relational attributions, *Academy of Management Review*, 36 (4), 731–753.

Gamache, D.L. and McNamara, G. (2019). Responding to bad press: How CEO temporal focus influences the sensitivity to negative media coverage of acquisitions, *Academy of Management Journal*, 62 (3), 918–943.

Gottschalk, P. and Gunnesdal, L. (2018). *White-Collar Crime in the Shadow Economy: Lack of Detection, Investigation, and Conviction compared to Social Security Fraud*, London, UK: Springer Publishing/Palgrave Pivot, Palgrave Macmillan.

Gottschalk, P. and Tcherni-Buzzeo, M. (2017). Reasons for gaps in crime reporting: The case of white-collar criminals investigated by private fraud examiners in Norway, *Deviant Behavior*, 38 (3), 267–281.

Hearit, K.M. (2006). *Crisis Management by Apology: Corporate Responses to Allegations of Wrongdoing*, Mahwah, NJ: Lawrence Erlbaum Associates.

Hurrell, S.A. (2016). Rethinking the soft skills deficit blame game: Employers, skills withdrawal and the reporting of soft skills gaps, *Human Relations*, 69 (3), 605–628.

Jenner Block (2010). *In regard Lehman Brothers Holdings Inc. to United States Bankruptcy Court in Southern District of New York*, law firm Jenner & Block, A.R. Valukas, https://jenner.com/lehman/VOLUME%203.pdf, downloaded September 23, 2018.

Keaveney, S.M. (2008). The blame game: An attribution theory approach to marketer-engineer conflict in high-technology companies, *Industrial Marketing Management*, 37, 653–663.

Khanna, V., Kim, E.H. and Lu, Y. (2015). CEO connectedness and corporate fraud, *The Journal of Finance*, 70, 1203–1252.

Klepp, T. (2019). *Spesialoppdrag – D2019-10. Kartlegging av fakta i EØS-saken. Internrevisjon (Special assignment – D2019–10. Documentation of facts in the EEA case)*, Arbeids- og velferdsetaten (Norwegian Labor and Welfare Administration), December 11, 74 pages.

Larsen, M.H. (2019). NAV-svindel straffes hardere enn hvitsnippforbrytelser (NAV fraud punished harder than white-collar crime), daily Norwegian newspaper *Aftenposten*, www.aftenposten.no, published November 1.

Lee, F. and Robinson, R.J. (2000). An attributional analysis of social accounts: Implications of playing the blame game, *Journal of Applied Social Psychology*, 30 (9), 1853–1879.

Lehman, D.W., Cooil, B. and Ramanujam, R. (2019). The effects of rule complexity on organizational noncompliance and remediation: Evidence from restaurant health inspections, *Journal of Management*, published online, pages 1–33, https://doi.org/10.1177/0149206319842262.

Lensvelt-Mulders, G.J.L.M., Heijden, P.G.M. and Laudy, O. (2006). A validation of a computer-assisted randomized response survey to estimate the prevalence of fraud in social security, *Journal of the Royal Statistical Society*, 69, 305–318.

Lofstad, R. (2019). Hentet ut av fengsel etter ni dager (Brought out of jai lafter nine days), daily Norwegian newspaper *Dagbladet*, www.dagbladet.no, published October 30.

Meldalen, S.G. and Lofstad, R. (2019). Måtte selje leilighet etter feilaktig NAV-dom (Had to sell apartment after incorrect NAV judgment, daily Norwegian newspaper *Dagbladet*, www.dagbladet.no, published October 30.

Michel, C. (2016). Violent street crime versus harmful white-collar crime: A comparison of perceived seriousness and punitiveness, *Critical Criminology*, 24, 127–143.

NTB (2019). SV og Rødt vurderer mistillit – krever klare NAV-svar fra Hauglie (SV and Red assess distrust – require clear NAV answers from Hauglie, daily Norwegian business newspaper *Dagens Næringsliv*, www.dn.no, published November 4.

Petrocelli, M., Piquero, A.R. and Smith, M.R. (2003). Conflict theory and racial profiling: An empirical analysis of police traffic stop data, *Journal of Criminal Justice*, 31 (1), 1–11.

Piazza, A. and Jourdan, J. (2018). When the dust settles: The consequences of scandals for organizational competition, *Academy of Management Journal*, 61 (1), 165–190.

Pillay, S. and Kluvers, R. (2014). An institutional theory perspective on corruption: The case of a developing democracy, *Financial Accountability & Management*, 30 (1), 95–119.

Pontell, H.N., Black, W.K. and Geis, G. (2014). Too big to fail, too powerful to jail? On the absence of criminal prosecutions after the 2008 financial meltdown, *Crime, Law and Social Change*, 61 (1), 1–13.

Resodihardjo, S.L., Carroll, B.J., Eijk, C.J.A. and Maris, S. (2015). Why traditional responses to blame games fail: The importance of context, rituals, and sub-blame games in the face of raves gone wrong, *Public Administration*, 94 (2), 350–363.

Ruud, S. and Spence, T. (2019). Kjersti Monland går av som ytelsesdirektør i Nav (Kjerti Monland resigns as benefits director at Nav), daily Norwegian newspaper *Aftenposten*, www.aftenposten.no, published December 4.

Schnatterly, K., Gangloff, K.A. and Tuschke, A. (2018). CEO wrongdoing: A review of pressure, opportunity, and rationalization, *Journal of Management*, 44 (6), 2405–2432.

Schoultz, I. and Flyghed, J. (2016). Doing business for a "higher loyalty"? How Swedish transnational corporations neutralize allegations of crime, *Crime, Law and Social Change*, 66 (2), 183–198.

Schoultz, I. and Flyghed, J. (2019). From "we didn't do it" to "we've learned our lesson": Development of a typology of neutralizations of corporate crime, *Critical Criminology*, published online, https://doi.org/10.1007/s10612-019-09483-3.

Schwendinger, H. and Schwendinger, J. (2014). Defenders of order or guardians of human rights? *Social Justice*, 40 (1/2), 87–117.

Scott, M.B and Lyman, S.M. (1968). Accounts, *American Sociological Review*, 33 (1), 46–62.

Slyke, S.V. and Bales, W.D. (2012). A contemporary study of the decision to incarcerate white-collar and street property offenders, *Punishment & Society*, 14 (2), 217–246.

Sonnier, B.M., Lassar, W.M. and Lassar, S.S. (2015). The influence of source credibility and attribution of blame on juror evaluation of liability of industry specialist auditors, *Journal of Forensic & Investigative Accounting*, 7 (1), 1–37.

Spence, T. and Ruud, S. (2019). Jusprofessor ber Stortinget nedsette egen granskingskommisjon av trygdeskandalen (Law professor asks the parliament to establish its own investigation committee for the social security scandal), daily Norwegian newspaper *Aftenposten*, www.aftenposten.no, published December 28.

Sykes, G. and Matza, D. (1957). Techniques of neutralization: A theory of delinquency, *American Sociological Review*, 22 (6), 664–670.

Whyte, D. (2016). It's common sense, stupid! Corporate crime and techniques of neutralization in the automobile industry, *Crime, Law and Social Change*, 66 (2), 165–181.

Williams, J.W. (2008). The lessons of Enron: Media accounts, corporate crimes, and financial markets, *Theoretical Criminology*, 12 (4), 471–499.

Xie, Y. and Keh, H.T. (2016). Taming the blame game: Using promotion programs to counter product-Hhrm crises, *Journal of Advertising*, 45 (2), 211–226.

Zahra, S.A., Priem, R.L. and Rasheed, A.A. (2005). The antecedents and consequences of top management fraud, *Journal of Management*, 31, 803–828.

8 Case study
FIFA bidding process

On December 2, 2010, the executive committee of the international football association FIFA, using an anonymous voting procedure, determined the hosts for the 2018 and 2022 FIFA world cup tournaments. Allegations of corruption related to the voting process had surfaced even before the final vote that December day in Zürich in Switzerland. Ever since, there have been persistent allegations of misconduct with respect to the selection process. In 2017, British newspaper The Guardian reported that a FIFA official took bribes to back Qatar's 2022 world cup bid (Laughland, 2017):

> Julio Grondona, who died in 2014, told witness Alejandro Burzaco he was owed money for vote, Burzaco testifies amid corruption investigation. A senior FIFA official took at least $1m in bribes to vote for Qatar to host the 2022 World Cup, a witness testified in court on Tuesday, as part of a broad investigation into corruption at FIFA. Julio Grondona, a senior vice-president at FIFA and head of the Argentinian football association until his death in 2014, allegedly told the witness, Alejandro Burzaco, an Argentinian sports marketing executive, that he was owed the money in exchange for his vote, which helped Qatar secure the lucrative tournament.

Three years earlier, in 2014, the Garcia report was completed. The Garcia (2014) report was an investigation produced by Michael Garcia and Cornel Borbély into allegations of corruption in world association football. Garcia and Borbély were appointed in 2012 to investigate ethical breaches at FIFA, which is world football's governing body. The two examiners quickly focused on persistent public accusations of bribery in the 2018 and 2022 world cup bids, which had been won in 2010 by Russia and Qatar respectively. The Garcia report was kept secret for several years before it was leaked to a German newspaper and subsequently released by FIFA in 2017.

Denial of criminal wrongdoing

In this book's perspective of evolving accounts as scandals arrive at the attention of stakeholders and the public, the FIFA scandal is a typical example (Hundt and Horsch, 2019; Naheem, 2020). It was persistent public accusations of bribery and corruption that forced top officials at FIFA to initiate an investigation. Initially, the Swiss Joseph Blatter, president of FIFA since 1998, denied any wrongdoing. However, Blatter had to resign in 2015 when the Swiss attorney general announced criminal proceedings against him regarding criminal mismanagement and misappropriation. Seven FIFA officials were arrested at hotel Baur au Lac in Zürich. Other FIFA officials were arrested and charged in the United States (Viswanatha et al., 2015).

When Garcia and Borbély handed in their investigation report to FIFA in 2014, FIFA officials attempted to keep it secret forever. Hans-Joachim Eckert, the FIFA's head of adjudication on ethical matters, refused to publish the report, when citing various legal grounds. Instead of releasing the report of 350 pages, Eckert chose to publish his own 42-page summary late in 2014. Eckert's summary was then heavily criticized in the media as a whitewash, which is similar to money laundering, where traces of wrongdoing are supposed to disappear after washing and laundering information. Rumors and suspicions concerning FIFA corruption led in 2015 Europe's footballing nations to meet to discuss an alternative location to Russia for the world cup in 2018 (Wallace, 2015).

Garcia criticized Eckert's summary as materially incomplete. After unsuccessfully appealing for the FIFA to publish the complete 350-page report, Garcia resigned from the position of chairperson at the investigative branch of FIFA's ethics committee (Roan, 2017). Over the following years, there was much speculation in the media regarding the contents of the report, particularly which aspects Eckert had left out of his summary and Garcia had felt were serious enough to warrant his resignation (Laughland, 2017; Wallace, 2015). In June 2017, the German newspaper Bild announced that it had obtained a leaked copy of the report and planned to publish it (Roan, 2017). FIFA released the report on the following day, preempting the newspaper coverage. The German Eckert, who has previously been a judge in the regional Munich court, had now to resign from his position as chairperson of the adjudicatory chamber of FIFA (Das, 2017).

Bidding investigation process

The investigation into the bidding by 9 teams composed of 11 different countries – a process that in its formal phase covered more than a year – required significant commitment of time and resources. The inquiry into the bidding process involved interviewing representatives of each of the bid teams, current and former executive committee members and FIFA officials (Garcia, 2014: 7):

> In addition, other football officials who were believed to have relevant information were called upon to assist in establishing the facts of the case. Third parties, although not subject to the cooperation requirements of the FCE (FIFA Code of Ethics), were also approached and asked for cooperation. In all, more than 75 interviews were conducted, either in person with an audio recording for the record or through written questions. Investigatory

team members traveled to ten countries to conduct interviews, including the United States, Italy, Holland, Spain, Japan, Australia, England, Malaysia, Switzerland, Oman, and the Netherlands. Witnesses who could not appear for interviews were sent written questions. In many cases, follow up questions were sent.

Interviewers taped all oral interviews, and copies of the transcripts were later provided to the interviewees or their attorneys with an opportunity to propose corrections. The tapes, transcripts and any comments or additions by witnesses became parts of the investigation record.

The fraud examiners announced early on that they would listen to anyone who believed they had relevant information, and that such information would be duly evaluated (Garcia, 2014: 7):

> It was a message aimed at making public an opportunity to assist for those interested in making this review as complete as possible. Many, including several media outlets, took advantage of that opportunity to provide information helpful in clarifying the facts.

Corruption allegations and accusations were widespread and varied. Some were presented in the media, and some were reported directly to the fraud examiners. Still others were uncovered in the course of reviewing the materials collected and produced during the investigation (Garcia, 2014: 8):

> With each issue, and with every witness, the same procedure was followed, namely a process designed to address the significant allegations in as thorough and efficient a manner possible while treating fairly all parties to that process.

FIFA president Joseph Blatter

FIFA president Joseph 'Sepp' Blatter is mentioned 81 times in the 350-page report. Fraud examiners conclude that Blatter was responsible for mismanagement, but not fraud (Garcia, 2014: 336):

> President Blatter's responsibility for the myriad issues that developed over the course of the bidding process or were uncovered by this inquiry merits consideration. As a preliminary matter, it must be made clear that evidence in the record does not establish a prima facie case that President Blatter violated the FCE. The one concrete allegation against the President, concerning an account purportedly held in his name at a U.S. bank, was demonstrably false. As head of FIFA, however, President Blatter bears some responsibility for a flawed process that engendered deep public skepticism, and for presiding over an Executive Committee whose culture of entitlement contributed to many of the issues this Report identifies.

Fraud examiners argue that Blatter must take responsibility for the failures that occurred on his watch. He made himself accessible on a selective basis, giving the impression that individuals such as Peter Hargitay were insiders afforded preferential treatment, including freedom to speak to high-ranking FIFA officials about inappropriate topics, such as quality of competing bids, in a manner that was not tolerated by others. Hargitay was in the business of lobbying and campaign strategies. He worked as a consultant to several of the nine bidding teams composed of 11 different countries.

One of the failures mentioned by the fraud examiners was FIFA payments of $200,000 in bonus to Adamu and Temarii, who had both been banned as devils of the sport (Garcia, 2014: 338):

> Messrs. Adamu and Temarii were prohibited from voting because they were found, pursuant to FIFA's own internal governance procedures, to have committed misconduct related to the bidding process.

Adamu and Temarii were not allowed anymore to attend executive committee meetings at FIFA because they had accepted bribes in the world cup bidding process. Nevertheless, Blatter allowed the payment of bonuses to all executive committee members including the two members labeled devils of the sport (Garcia, 2014: 338):

> As the leader of FIFA, responsibility for these failings and for positive steps taken to reform the organization resides with President Blatter.

Initially, the Swiss Sepp Blatter, president of FIFA since 1998, denied any wrongdoing documented in the Garcia report in 2014. However, Blatter had to resign the following year in 2015 when the Swiss attorney general announced criminal proceedings against him regarding criminal mismanagement and misappropriation.

FIFA executive committee

FIFA consists of the following branches: the congress (legislative), the committee (executive), and the secretariat (administrative). Given the crucial role played by the executive committee, and given the already terminated committee members Adamu and Temarii, Garcia (2014) discuss the authority of the committee in some detail. The committee is responsible for making decisions regarding allocation of world cup tournaments. There are 23 members on the committee.

Garcia (2014) attempted to interview a number of committee members including former German top football player Franz Beckenbauer. By letter dated March 6, 2014, fraud examiners requested Beckenbauer's cooperation in establishing the facts relevant to their inquiry. Specifically, the investigators asked him to provide dates when he would be available to meet for a witness interview. He did not respond until March 24, telling that he was busy and asking for questions in writing. Accordingly, the investigators sent Beckenbauer a letter with 21 questions on April 8. The letter noted Beckenbauer's obligation to cooperate with the investigation. One month later, Beckenbauer replied by asking to have the questions translated from English to German. Accordingly, the investigators sent Beckenbauer a German translation on May 16. A case developed against Beckenbauer for the conduct of failure to cooperate.

Franz Beckenbauer is among several FIFA executive committee members whose behaviors are described in detail by Garcia (2014). Beckenbauer is mentioned 149 times in the 350-page report, for example on page 248:

> Qatar bid team members repeatedly denied that Mr. Bin Hammam had a direct relationship to or role on the Qatar bid team. For example in October 2009, Messrs. Bin Hammam, Beckenbauer and Radmann met wit the Emir of Qatar in Doha. According to Mr. Beckenbauer, the purpose of the meeting was to discuss the Qatar bid, and the Emir tried to convince Mr. Beckenbauer of the merits of the Qatar bid. Email correspondence from Mr. Bin Hammam's assistant indicates that Mr. Bin Hammam arranged the meeting with the Emir.

Other executive committee members frequently mentioned by Garcia (2014) as not cooperating with the investigation include Jack Warner (provisional ban and resignation), Ricardo Teixeira (resigned from all football-related activity), and Mohamed Bin Hammam (banned for life from all football-related activity). Chuck Blazer (provisional ban) and Nicholás Leoz (resigned from all football-related activity) are also mentioned together with some more.

According to the investigation report by Garcia (2014), Mohamed Bin Hammam was an active briber who bribed a number of FIFA executive committee members. Hammam was a FIFA vice president and held formal positions in the football association in Qatar. On behalf of Qatar as one of the 11 bidders for the FIFA world cup, Hammam was involved in corruption to enable Qatar to win the bidding competition for the FIFA world cup in 2022.

Hammam was banned for life from all football-related activity (Garcia, 2014: 231):

> The Ethics Committee conducted proceedings against Mr. Bin Hammam in 2011 and 2012. Mr. Bin Hammam was interviewed and provided written statements and documents during those and related matters. In a final report submitted with the supporting evidence to the Adjudicatory Chamber and to Mr. Bin Hammam on December 3, 2012 (the "December 2012 Bin Hammam Report"), the Investigatory Chamber concluded that "Mr. Bin Hammam has engaged in a pattern of misconduct" in violation of the FCE. Based on that report, the Adjudicatory Chamber banned Mr. Bin Hammam from football-related activity for life. Mr. Bin Hammam, who had appealed a previous lifetime ban from the Ethics Committee in 2011 to CAS and secured a reversal, did not appeal the December 2012 ban.

Australia and Qatar whistleblowers

Whistleblowing is the disclosure by an individual in an organization or in society of deviant practices to someone who can do something about it. Whistleblowing is an action by current and former employees who believe that their business or colleague(s) are involved in activities of misconduct or crime, cause unnecessary harm, violate human rights or contribute to otherwise immoral offenses. Whistleblowing is the disclosure by an organizational member of deviant practices to someone who can help solve the problem. Whistleblowers stand out as a group of reporters who have made observations and who are willing to disclose what they have observed.

In May 2013, a source suggested that the investigation team contact an anonymous whistleblower in Australia. The person was a former member of the Australia 2022 bid team. The person had been the head of corporate and public affairs at Australia 2022. The whistleblower noted during her initial communications with the examiners that providing information might violate non-disclosure or confidentiality obligations that she owed her former employer under the terms of her severance agreement. Accordingly, upon examiners' request, the football federation of Australia provided a release statement. Examiners subsequently interviewed the whistleblower twice, in New York in November 2013 and in Australia in April 2014.

The whistleblower told examiners that Australia 2022 was involved in corruption to win the FIFA 2022 world cup. For example, Australia 2022 bought an expensive pearl necklace as a gift for the wife of FIFA executive committee member Jack Warner. However, stories from the Australian whistleblower (AW) were not supported by evidence from the whistleblower (Garcia, 2014: 59):

> While AW provided some useful information regarding possible issues for the Investigatory Chamber to examine, the evidence – including evidence she provided – often did not support her specific recollections and allegations. For example, the Investigatory Chamber asked about a highly publicized 2009 incident in which Australia 2022 reportedly bought a pearl necklace as a gift for the wife of FIFA Executive Committee member Jack Warner. AW said she sent Australia 2022 Chairman Frank Lowy and CEO Ben Buckley an email at the time expressing concerns that the gift violated bidding rules.

Another whistleblower mentioned in the investigation report was from Qatar. Allegations by an insider on the Qatari bid team came to light soon after Qatar was awarded the rights to host the 2022 world cup tournament. Accusations of corruption by a former Qatar bid team employee began circulating in the global press almost immediately after Qatar's victory (Garcia, 2014: 250):

> A few days later, President Blatter received a letter from British politician Ivan Lewis – Member of Parliament and Shadow Secretary of State for

Culture, Media and Sport – "regarding serious allegations which have been made with regard to corruption associated with the bidding process for the 2022 World Cup."

Both FIFA president Blatter and secretary general Valcke denied the allegations by claiming that there was no supportive evidence, and they responded to Lewis that FIFA was not in a position to intervene. Similarly, fraud examiners ended up not believing the Qatar whistleblower (Garcia, 2014: 272):

> Accordingly, the Investigatory Chamber has not relied on any information or material it received from QW (Qatar whistleblower) in reaching any conclusions in this Report.

Misconduct investigation conclusions

In the conclusion section of the Garcia (2014) report, fraud investigators suggest to open formal proceedings against certain individuals on the executive committee of FIFA:

- Angel Maria Llona violated FIFA rules of conduct by intimidating the investigation and interfering with the investigation by threatening to recuse fraud examiners.
- Michel D'Hooghe received a valuable painting from a member of the Russian bidding team.
- Worawi Makudi had a conflict of interest where a large contract with Qatar was negotiated during the bidding process.
- Franz Beckenbauer was suspected of involving himself with the Australian bid team as he had a conflict of interest.
- Chung Mong-Joon wrote letters to other committee members indicating improper offers or promises of benefits in order to influence the world cup vote.
- Amos Adamu caused the Qatar bidding team to be the sponsor of an event for his son where the son would personally benefit from the sponsorship.
- Reynald Temarii received more than Euro 300,000 from Bin Hammam for "legal fees" shortly after announcing he would pursue his appeal of the FIFA ethics committee decision to ban Hammam from football.
- Jack Warner requested benefits from the Australian and English bid teams.
- Ricardo Texeira accepted lavish accommodations and other benefits provided to him in Doha, and he arranged contracts for the Brazilian federation's commercial rights.
- Mohamed Bin Hammam paid Temarii more than Euro 300,000 immediately after Temarii's decision to appeal a ban imposed by the FIFA ethics committee.
- Nicholás Leoz requested a substantial personal benefit – namely, a knighthood – from England's bid team.

- Julio Grondona was suspected of wrongdoing, but he died before the release of the Garcia (2014) report.

Several of the named executive committee members mentioned previously are not accused of corruption or other kinds of financial misconduct. Instead, they are accused of not cooperating with the fraud examiners. This kind of accusation is problematic, since several of the approaches by the investigators seem confrontational rather than cooperative. Therefore, there might have been acceptable reasons why individuals such as Llona and Beckenbauer did not cooperate with the investigators. If Garcia and the other examiners had approached suspects and witnesses in a more professional manner, they might have succeeded in obtaining relevant and complete statements. Therefore, the report gives the impression that investigators rather than informants are to blame when the investigation failed in obtaining statements from relevant persons on the executive committee of FIFA. It seems that the tradition of public prosecutors in the United States of blaming witnesses for not cooperating and then prosecuting witnesses for lack of cooperation as an offense has been transferred into a European context where the courts are quite unfamiliar with such a perspective. For example, Garcia (2014: 333) suggests that "Mr. Beckenbauer's actions in response to the Investigatory Chamber's efforts to seek his assistance are already the subject of formal investigative proceedings".

References

Das, A. (2017). FIFA moves to replace ethics committee leaders, *The New York Times*, www.nytimes.com, published May 9.

Garcia, M.J. (2014). *Report on the Inquiry into the 2018/2022 FIFA World Cup Bidding Process*, Investigatory Chamber with Cornel Borbély, FIFA Ethics Committee, 350 pages.

Hundt, S. and Horsch, A. (2019). Sponsorship of the FIFA world cup, shareholder wealth, and the impact of corruption, *Applied Economics*, 51 (23), 2468–2491.

Laughland, O. (2017). FIFA official took bribes to back Qatar's 2022 world cup bid, court hears, *The Guardian*, www.theguardian.com, published November 15.

Naheem, M.A. (2020). The agency dilemma in anti-money laundering regulation, *Journal of Money Laundering Control*, published online, https://doi.org/10.1108/JMLC-01-2016-0007.

Roan, D. (2017). World cup 2022: Claims of corruption in Qatar bid published in Germany, *BBC*, www.bbc.com, published June 27.

Viswanatha, A., Robinson, J., Morse, A. and Matthews, C.M. (2015). FIFA rocked as U.S. charges 14 in corruption investigation, *The Wall Street Journal*, www.wsj.com, published May 27.

Wallace, S. (2015). FIFA corruption: Europe plots to stage an 'alternative World Cup' I place of Russia 208, *Independent*, www.independent.co.uk, published June 2.

9 Filling the governance gap

Reviewed literature indicates that there is a growing gap between public government and private governance when it comes to prevention and detection of misconduct and crime in organizations. This chapter suggests that investigative journalists in the media and fraud examiners in private investigations have the potential of filling some of this gap. Based on the theory of crime signal detection, this chapter suggests that investigative journalists are in the position of detecting white-collar crime scandals as they rely on tips and whistleblowing. Empirical evidence from Norway documents that the media disclose a significant fraction of crime stories that later result in prosecution and conviction of white-collar offenders. Empirical evidence from Norway does not document any significant contribution from fraud examiners, as they typically conclude with misconduct, but no crime.

Gottschalk and Gunnesdal (2018) have estimated a detection rate for white-collar crime of less than 1 out of 12 offenders in Norway, which seems supported by an empirical study of bribery detection in Norway by Andresen and Button (2019). The detection rate in the United States seems even lower based on estimates of the magnitude of white-collar crime by the National White-Collar Crime Center (Huff et al., 2010) and the Association of Certified Fraud Examiners (ACFE, 2008, 2014, 2016) between $300 and $660 billion (Wall-Parker, 2020). Offenders tend to move under the radar (Williams, 2019). As argued by Walburg (2020: 343), too little insight exists about the extent, structures, and development of white-collar crime and its multifaceted varieties, especially when it comes to corporate crime:

> this is largely explicable by the well-known and persistent difficulties of measuring undetected acts of corporate wrongdoing

Kourula et al. (2019) argue that there is a gap between government and governance, where neither public authorities nor self-regulating bodies involve themselves in detection of corruption and other forms of financial crime. Actors in the criminal justice system seem to have a preference towards street criminals rather than white-collar criminals (Michel, 2016). Prevention and control of crime are two of the primary objectives and functions of the criminal justice system.

Actors in auditing and compliance functions in business and public enterprises seem to have a preference towards formal rules and guidelines in the form of window-dressing rather than detection of potential offenders (Desai, 2016). Alon et al. (2019) argue that accounting and auditing functions have undergone a legitimacy crisis in recent years.

Kourula et al. (2019: 1109) suggest, "Civil society was perceived to be left to fill the gaps that other sectors did not address", because "growing private regulation often put civil society in the driver's seat in 'policing' business activities" as "privatization of authority" has occurred. Furthermore, Kourula et al. (2019: 1110) suggest, "Governments are losing power", and "Governments lack enforcement capacity to impact multinational companies".

This chapter suggests that investigative journalists in the media and fraud examiners at global auditing firms and local law firms seem to fill some of the gap between public government and private governance when it comes to detection of white-collar offenders (Button and Gee, 2013; Schneider, 2006; Williams, 2005, 2008, 2014). Press reporters' detection of misconduct and crime "represented an important ingredient of the nineteenth-century newspaper" (Taylor, 2018: 346), and this is certainly also the case so far in the twenty-first-century media.

This chapter raises the question of the contribution of private actors, such as journalists and fraud examiners, in detecting white-collar crime. The role of journalists in exposing white-collar crime seems to be an underdeveloped area of study. In that context, this chapter is an important addition to research. It provides a detailed assessment of a large number of white-collar crime cases in Norway and their resolution, including the role of journalists.

Government or governance

Eberlein (2019) argues, "Globalization opens markets for corporations but outstrip the capacity of states to regulate cross-border business conduct for the public good". He found that there is no zero-sum constellation of substitution between government and governance, which would imply that regulatory authority shifts from governments to corporations willing to step in and fill the gap in responsibility for crime prevention and detection. Corporations are not willing or able fully to accept public responsibilities. Corporate social responsibility activities have their obvious limitations in practice.

Similarly, Schneider and Scherer (2019: 1147) argue, "The extent to which state authorities can regulate the externalities and the behavior of multinational corporations is limited", and "Gaps in governance abound in today's globalized world". There is an erosion of state power and a shift towards private regulation. National governments collectively are taking limited initiatives through the OECD, European Union, United Nations and other multinational organizations. One problem in state cooperation is that they do not agree on what should be legal and illegal activities, as exemplified by Boghossian and Marques (2019).

Maher et al. (2019) found that governments not just in global business, but also in local business are reluctant to intervene. They observed an ambiguity of the state to involve itself. This is in line with the observation by Pontell et al. (2014) that some companies are too big to fail, and some white-collar offenders are too powerful to jail. The researchers observed an absence of criminal prosecutions after the 2008 financial meltdown in the United States.

A potential avenue to fill the gap between government and governance might be to strengthen business-government interactions. However, Hamann (2019) found that business-government interactions result in corporate social irresponsibility, where a process of dynamic deterioration leads to passivity in both government and governance.

Kourula et al. (2019: 1103) define government as those public actors, which have exclusive authority over legitimate force in a specific territory:

> In our contemporary world, governments defined in this way are generally coextensive with nation-states. By virtue of this unique mode of authority, the "sine qua non" of state power, governments have the capacity, within their jurisdictions, to impose legally binding constraints and sanctions over non-governmental actors, whether in politics, society, or markets.

When there is suspicion of corporate white-collar crime, the government branch typically involved is the national criminal justice system. The police have the task of investigating suspicions by reconstructing past events and sequences of events. If the police find sufficient evidence of law violation, then the case moves to the prosecution. The defendant faces the prosecutor in court, where a jury or a judge decides whether the suspected criminal is guilty of law violation.

Kourula et al. (2019: 1104) define governance as those private actors, which direct behaviors in business conduct by rulemaking, enforcement and sanctioning:

> By "governance" we refer not to corporate governance, but to the wider concept of societal governance, that of the collective means to give "direction to society" which we take to include direction to society's politics and markets.

When there is suspicion of corporate white-collar crime, the governance branch typically involved is the compliance function, potentially cooperating with internal and external auditors as well as various controllers. Internal or external fraud examiners have the task of investigating suspicions by reconstructing past events and sequences of events. If fraud examiners find sufficient evidence of law violation, then the case stops, moves internally or moves externally to the national criminal justice system. If secrecy to protect corporate reputation is the main concern, then the case typically stops and remains internal (Gottschalk and Tcherni-Buzzeo, 2017).

Over time, there is less government and more governance in many countries. This is a kind of privatization, where privatization is the transfer of organizations or capacities that were once in the public sector to private ownership or management. In the area of criminal justice, privatization represents a form of self-policing (Kourula et al., 2019).

This chapter has chosen governance to locate some of the context for the following research. It needs mentioning, however, that private policing is sometimes linked to governance, where private policing is concerned with both prevention and detection of crime (Brooks and Button, 2011; Button, 2019; Button et al., 2007a, 2007b; Button and Gee, 2013; Gottschalk and Tcherni-Buzzeo, 2017; Schneider, 2006; Williams, 2005, 2014).

Corporate crime detection

This chapter applies the offender-based definition of white-collar crime, which has its origin in the work of Sutherland (1939), who defined white-collar crime based on the social and occupational status of the offender as a crime committed by a person of respectability and high social status in the course of the offender's occupation. In the theory of convenience, status is an internal variable to explain white-collar crime occurrence. As Agnew (2014: 2) formulates it: "crime is often the most expedient way to get what you want" and "fraud is often easier, simpler, faster, more exciting, and more certain than other means of securing one's ends".

The theory of crime signal detection is relevant to the study of white-collar crime detection. Signal detection theory is concerned with the ability of individuals to understand pieces of information that can come from various sources. The theory emphasizes individuals' varying signal discrimination processes. Discrimination processes include the sensitivity towards signals in general as well as the separation of real signals from noise signals.

Signal detection theory is a model for how humans detect signals in a background of interference or noise. The theory assumes that the human observer behaves like a rational economic decision-maker, and attempts to balance costs and benefits to arrive at an optimal solution. There are four possibilities in the decision matrix of the observer of potential misconduct and crime (Karim and Siegel, 1998: 368):

- The observer notices a noise when it is a signal (called a miss).
- The observer notices a signal when it is a signal (called a hit).
- The observer notices a noise when it is a noise (called a correct identification).
- The observer notices a signal when it is a noise (called a false alarm).

The observer needs to make a decision concerning the event and classify it either as a signal or as noise. In an organizational context – where less powerful individuals suspect powerful individuals of wrongdoing – the less powerful will conveniently prefer to think of the event as a noise rather than as a signal.

Signal detection theory may shed some light into why some actors discover and disclose more white-collar crime than other potential observers disclose. Signal detection theory holds that the detection of a stimulus depends on both the intensity of the stimulus and the physical and psychological state of the individual. A detector's ability or likelihood to detect some stimulus is affected by the intensity of the stimulus (e.g., how loud a signal is) and the physical and psychological state of the detector (e.g., how alert the person is). Perceptual sensitivity depends upon the perceptual ability of the observer to detect a signal or target or to discriminate signal from non-signal events (Szalma and Hancock, 2013). There might be dysfunctional cognitive style and lack of achievement motivation (Martinsen et al., 2016).

Furthermore, detecting persons may have varying ability to discern between information-bearing recognition (called pattern) and random patterns that distract from information (called noise).

According to the theory of signal detection, there are a number of determinants of how a person will detect a signal (Huff and Bodner, 2013). In addition to signal intensity, signal alertness and pattern recognition, there are other factors such as personal competence (including knowledge, skills and attitude), experience, and expectations. These factors determine the threshold level. Low signal intensity, low signal alertness and limited pattern recognition, combined with low competence, lack of experience and lack of expectations will lead to a high threshold level, meaning that the individual will not detect white-collar crime.

Signal alertness is not a stable mindset over time. Rather, the extent of signal alertness by an observer varies with other concerns that the person may have (Qiu and Slezak, 2019).

Signal detection theory implies that persons make decisions under conditions of uncertainty. The theory assumes that the decision-maker is not a passive receiver of information, but an active decision-maker who makes difficult perceptual judgments under conditions of uncertainty. Whether a stimulus is present or absent, whether a stimulus is perceived or not perceived, and whether an observer ignores a perceived stimulus will influence the decision in terms of detecting or not detecting white-collar crime.

Gomulya and Mishina (2017: 557) introduced the term signal susceptibility since signals may be differently susceptible to potential errors and manipulation:

> This could be due to a variety of possible reasons, including whether the signal is self- or other-reported, whether it is verifiable, or whether it is a "stock" or a "flow" signal. Self-reported signals should on average be more susceptible to manipulations by the focal signaler (i.e., the one who can benefit from a positive signal) compared to signals reported by third parties.

Given this definition, signal susceptibility can be included as an aspect of signal intensity, where signal intensity deteriorates at suspicion of errors and manipulation increases. Similarly, noise in general will reduce signal intensity. Gomulya and Mishina (2017: 555) distinguish between two sources of noise during signaling – noise from the signal itself and noise from the behavior of the signaler.

Another term introduced by Gomulya and Mishina (2017: 55) is signal reliance, where reliance on different types of signals is based on the credibility of the signaler, and "thus a similar signal is likely to have different effects for credible versus less credible" signalers. Given this perspective, signal reliance can be included as an aspect of signal alertness, where less credible signalers cause lower alertness to the signal.

Gomulya and Mishina (2017) discuss pattern recognition in terms of screening theory where the receiver prioritizes among possible types of signals. The focus is on how receivers place differential value on signals that may come from different senders such as documents, accounts, and individuals. Screening theory posits that receivers screen by focusing on signals that they believe are highly correlated with unobservable characteristics of interest.

Signal detection theory characterizes the activity of an individual's discrimination as well as psychological factors that bias his or her judgment. The theory is concerned with the individual's discriminative capacity, or sensitivity that is independent of the judgmental bias or decision criterion the individual may have had when the discrimination took place in the head of the observer.

Whistleblowers are often important actors in the discovery of white-collar misconduct and crime for both investigative journalists and fraud examiners. Whistleblowing is the disclosure by an individual in an organization or in society of deviant practices to someone who can do something about it (Bjørkelo et al., 2011). Whistleblowing is an action by employees who believe that their business or colleague(s) are involved in activities of misconduct and crime, cause unnecessary harm, violate human rights, or contribute to otherwise immoral offenses (Mpho, 2017). However, one mechanism preventing many potential whistleblowers is the fear of retaliation and reprisals (Miceli and Near, 2013; Park et al., 2020; Rehg et al., 2009). This chapter is not concerned with whistleblowing as such and refers thus only to relevant research on the phenomenon (Alleyne et al., 2013; Andrade, 2015; Culiberg and Mihelic, 2017; Dyck et al., 2010).

Research method

This research is concerned with detection of white-collar criminals. The collection of our Norwegian sample of white-collar offenders applied the original definition and characteristics of white-collar crime. Our sample thus has the following characteristics: famous individuals in term of high exposed social status and respectability, famous companies in terms of major suppliers in their businesses, surprising stories, important events, substantial consequences, matters of principles, and significant public interest. The two main financial newspapers in

Norway are *Dagens Næringsliv* and *Finansavisen*, both of which are conservative-leaning business newspapers. In addition, the business-friendly national daily newspaper *Aftenposten* regularly reports news of white-collar criminals. Left-wing newspapers such as *Klassekampen* very seldom cover specific white-collar criminal cases, although generally report on white-collar crime. The total number of white-collar criminals was 408 reported during those years from 2009 to 2015. We carried out verification of facts in newspaper accounts by obtaining court documents. After registering newspaper accounts as an important indication of white-collar offenders, we compared the contents of newspaper articles and expanded our notes by court sentences, which typically range from 5 to 50 pages in Norwegian district courts, courts of appeal, and the Supreme Court. The term account is here used in the meaning of a statement to explain what has happened.

The collection of our Norwegian sample of fraud examination reports took place again by reading the same newspapers and then identifying client organizations for the investigations. Client organizations in the public and private sector hire investigators from law firms and auditing firms to conduct fraud examinations. Contacting client organizations often led to refusal of insight based on privacy issues and other matters. After several years of contacting client organizations, 130 reports became the basis for this research.

Investigative journalists

Norwegian courts convicted 405 white-collar offenders to prison from 2009 to 2016. Table 9.1 lists sources of detection for these criminals. We find journalists occupy the top position, followed by crime victims, bankruptcy lawyers, internal auditors, tax authority clerks, bank employees, external auditors, and police officers.

Table 9.1 Detection of white-collar crime

#	Crime detection source	Sum	%
1	Journalists investigating tips from readers	101	25 %
2	Crime victims suffering financial loss	52	13 %
3	Bankruptcy lawyers identifying misconduct	45	11 %
4	Internal auditors controlling transactions	45	11 %
5	Tax authority clerks carrying out controls	25	6 %
6	Bank employees controlling accounts	18	4 %
7	External auditors controlling clients	18	4 %
8	Police officers investigating financial crime	9	2 %
9	Controlling shareholders	4	1 %
10	Other knowledge workers as detection sources	88	23 %
	TOTAL	405	100 %

A real example of the contribution of an investigative journalist to uncover white-collar crime in Norway is relevant to provide here. Seven decommissioned Norwegian naval vessels ended up in the hands of a warlord in Nigeria. The 2012 sale took a surprising turn when an investigative journalist in a Norwegian daily newspaper (Egeberg, 2014, 2015) revealed that the vessels were serving, two years later, in the private flotilla of a former Nigerian rebel (Evans, 2017; Tufts, 2018). Nigeria is rich on oil resources where the rebels fight for control (Ezeonu, 2020; PwC, 2015; Reporter, 2013). The news about the six demilitarized missile torpedo boats and one naval support vessel triggered both an internal fraud examination by PwC (2014, 2015) for the Ministry of Defense in Norway and a police investigation by Økokrim (Norwegian national authority for investigation and prosecution of economic and environmental crime).

The police investigation led to the conviction in May 2017 of one Norwegian official on bribery charges and the revelation of the role played by a UK intermediary, CAS-Global Ltd. The firm applied for export licenses in Norway and for a re-export license for the naval support vessel from the UK, telling the Norwegians that the ships would support an official West African mission, and the British that the ships should serve the Nigerian government (Tufts, 2018).

The Norwegian official appealed the conviction in a district court in Norway in May 2017 via a court of appeals and further to the Supreme Court (Oslo tingrett, 2017; NTB, 2019). The Supreme Court confirmed in May 2019 the sentence in Borgarting court of appeals from October 2018 of 4 years and 3 years in prison for the former commander Bjørn Stavrum in the Norwegian navy (Borgarting, 2018; Eriksen, 2019; Høyesterett, 2019).

Table 9.2 presents an exploratory attempt to describe signal detection features of observers who have noticed and discover white-collar crime. Signal intensity, signal alertness, pattern recognition and personal experience from signal detection theory are characteristics of detection ability.

Table 9.2 Characteristics of stimulus in detection of white-collar crime

#	Crime detection	Signal intensity	Signal alertness	Pattern recognition	Personal knowledge	Score
1	Media journalists	High	High	Low	Medium	9
2	Crime victims	High	Low	Medium	Low	7
3	Bankruptcy lawyers	Low	Low	Medium	Medium	6
4	Internal auditors	Low	Medium	Medium	Medium	7
5	Tax clerks authority	Low	Medium	Low	Medium	6
6	Bank employees	Low	Medium	Low	Low	5
7	External auditors	Low	Medium	Medium	Low	6
8	Police officers	Low	Medium	High	Low	7
9	Stock clerks	Low	Low	Medium	Low	5
10	Other sources	–	–	–	–	–

Pattern recognition is a matter of sensemaking and contextualization. Contextualization captures the ongoing process of understanding and explaining relationships between information elements. High gives a score of three, medium a score of two, and low a score of one.

We argue that signal intensity for tips to journalists normally is high, as whistleblowers tend to be upset and want to get attention (Andresen and Button, 2019). Furthermore, we suggest that signal alertness is high among journalists, as they are dependent on tips in their daily work to cover news stories. The issue of pattern recognition is not obvious for journalists, since they often present fragments on a publishing basis, rather than a complete and consistent story of events. Personal experience will vary among journalists who may or may not have been writing about white-collar crime before, depending on the extent of specialization among journalists in the newspaper.

The idea of Table 9.2 is to apply four characteristics of signal detection theory to detection of white-collar crime. At this stage, the items and values represent exploratory research that need further study to be trustworthy. Selection of characteristics as well as judgment along these characteristics for each crime detection source requires multiple raters to enable inter-rater reliability in future research.

One reason for the high signal alertness among journalists is their complete dependence on external tips to produce news stories. Journalists always need sources to which they have no access unless the sources cooperate with the media. By being polite and receptive, journalists increase the likelihood that whistleblowers and others will contact the media when they learn of potential misconduct and crime (Andresen and Button, 2019). There seems to be a lot to learn from investigative media and their journalists. Rather than formal procedures often applied on a routine basis by auditors and internal controllers, information sources in terms of persons in networks seem to be a more fruitful approach to detection of white-collar crime.

Fraud examiners

Fraud examiners at global auditing firms and local law firms are in the business of reconstructing past events and sequences of events when there is suspicion of white-collar crime in client organizations. They contribute to the detection of offenders. Table 9.3 lists 130 reports of investigations in Norway, which were available for research. The investigated organization is the client for the examination, such as nursing home Adecco, hospital Ahus, municipality Andebu, traffic station Arendal, etc. The investigating firm is the fraud examiner, such as local law firm Wiersholm, auditing firm PwC, auditing firm BDO, an internal audit function, etc. The suspected white-collar crime included fraud, corruption, embezzlement, etc.

The final column in Table 9.3 lists crime detection source where white-collar offenders became defendants in court and convicted to prison. As the list indicates very few of the fraud examination reports resulted in convictions. Most

Table 9.3 Characteristics of fraud examinations at suspicion of white-collar crime

#	Investigated organization	Investigating firm	Suspicion of white-collar crime	Detected by
1	Adecco nursing home	Wiersholm *law firm* 2011	*Fraud in employment contracts*	
2	Ahus *hospital*	PwC *audit firm 2013*	*Fraud when charging mapping services*	
3	Andebu municipality	BDO *audit firm 2014*	*Abuse of mayor position in procurement*	
4	Arendal traffic station	*Internal audit function 2017*	*Corruption for illegal vehicle permits*	
5	Askøy *municipality*	BDO *audit firm 2018*	*Public procurement from family members*	
6	Bergen *municipality*	*Internal control function 2018*	*Building permit to friends without control*	
7	Bergen havn *port authority*	Havarikommisjon commission 2019	*Accident from maintenance cost savings*	
8	Bergensklinikkene *private health clinic*	Ernst & Young *audit firm 2019*	*Subsidy fraud by false number of addicts*	
9	Betanien *foundation*	BDO *audit firm 2014*	*Embezzlement by chief executive (CEO)*	Victim
10	Briskeby *public sports arena*	Lynx *law firm 2011*	*Fraud in public construction funds*	
11	Bærum *municipality*	G-partner *law firm 2007*	*Corruption at public procurement*	Media
12	Bårlidalen *public water waste site*	Svendby *consulting firm 2016*	*Fraud by overbilling the municipality*	
13	Dale *property development*	Komrev. Rogaland *public audit 2015*	*Public funds spent on private vacations*	
14	Danske Bank *banking*	Bruun & Hjejle *law firm 2018*	*Money laundering in Estonian branch*	
15	Demokratene *political party*	Partirevisjon *internal control function 2016*	*Illegitimate government subsidy*	
16	DNB *banking*	Hjort *law firm 2016*	*Tax evasion in wealth management*	
17	Drammen municipality	Deloitte *audit firm 2017*	*Corruption in building permits*	Media
18	Eckbo *foundations*	Thommessen *law firm 2009*	*Chairperson fraud in foundation funds*	
19	Fadderbarna foundation	BDO *audit firm 2011*	*Fake documents hiding fraud*	

#	Investigated organization	Investigating firm	Suspicion of white-collar crime	Detected by
20	FilmCamp *public fund for productions*	Komrev. Nord *public audit 2016*	*Fraud by abuse of public funding*	
21	Fjell *municipality*	Deloitte *audit firm 2017*	*Corruption in construction permits*	
22	Flyktningtjenesten *public refugee funding*	Buunk et al. *internal audit 2015*	*Embezzlement by refugee services manager*	
23	Forsvaret military contracts	Dalseide *special committee 2006*	*Corruption in military computer contracts*	
24	Forsvaret *military logistics*	PwC *audit firm 2014*	*Corruption in military sales unit*	Media
25	Forsvaret *department of defense routines*	PwC *audit firm 2015*	*Illegal profits from sale of discarded equipment*	Media
26	Fredrikstad *municipality*	PwC *audit firm 2018*	*VAT fraud by public company*	
27	Fredrikstad *municipality*	Simonsen *law firm 2018*	*VAT fraud by public company*	
28	Fretex *Salvation Army*	Grette *law firm 2017*	*Financial targets to remove executive*	
29	Furuheim *foundation nursing home*	Hald *law firm 2006*	*Fraud in foundation construction*	
30	Fyrlykta *foundation child care*	Deloitte *audit firm 2017*	*Fraud of public funds for excessive salaries*	
31	Fyrlykta *foundation child care*	Stiftelsestilsynet *public examination 2018*	*Fraud of public funds for excessive salaries*	
32	Gartnerhallen *fruits and vegetables*	Wiersholm *law firm 2018*	*Fraud by farmers demanding repay*	Audit
33	Gassnova *public projects*	BDO *audit firm 2013*	*Corruption in public procurement*	
34	Grimstad *municipality*	BDO *audit firm 2016*	*Corruption in public procurement*	
35	Grimstad *municipality*	Hjort *law firm 2018*	*Corruption in public procurement*	
36	Grimstad *municipality*	Tinia *consulting firm 2018*	*Fraud against caretaker of handicapped person*	
37	Hadeland *broadband mobile company*	PwC *audit firm 2014*	*Embezzlement by chief financial officer (CFO)*	Police

(Continued)

Table 9.3 (Continued)

#	Investigated organization	Investigating firm	Suspicion of white-collar crime	Detected by
38	Hadeland *energy supply company*	PwC *audit firm 2014*	*Embezzlement by chief financial officer (CFO)*	Police
39	Halden *municipality skating hall*	KPMG *audit firm 2012*	*Fraud in construction project*	
40	Halden *municipality buildings*	Hjort *law firm 2013*	*Corruption in building permits*	
41	Hedmark *municipality*	Wiersholm *law firm 2007*	*Illegal benefits for executives*	
42	Helse Nord *hospital*	PwC *audit firm 2018*	*Fraud at executive removal from position*	
43	Hordaland *police department*	Wiersholm *law firm 2015*	*Whistleblower financial retaliation*	
44	Hordaland *police department*	Stamina *consulting firm 2019*	*Corruption in public procurement*	
45	Jondal *municipality*	SBDL *law firm 2018*	*Corruption and private enterprise*	
46	Karasjok *municipality*	Vest-Finnmark *public audit 2018*	*Friends got illegitimate favors*	
47	Karolinska *hospital*	Setterwalls *law firm 2018*	*Public procurement of consulting without tender*	
48	Kjøpsvik *municipality*	Komrev. Nord *public audit 2015*	*Fraud by property developer*	
49	Klengstua *kindergarten*	Halden *municipal internal audit 2019*	*Fraud in subsidies from municipality*	
50	Kommunal-departement *department of interior*	BDO *audit firm 2018*	*Fraud in subsidies for kindergartens*	
51	Kraft & Kultur *energy enterprise*	Ernst & Young *audit firm 2012*	*Accounting fraud by misrepresentation*	Media
52	Kragerø *shipping*	Deloitte *audit firm 2012*	*Compensation for leader without contract*	
53	Kristiansand *municipality*	Komrev. Agder *public audit 2016*	*Private property developer abused political position*	
54	Kristiansand *municipality*	Tofte *law firm 2018*	*Harassment for financial benefit*	
55	Kvalsund *municipality*	Vest-Finnmark *public audit 2012*	*Fraudulent consulting fees*	
56	Kvam Auto *car dealer*	Wikborg *law firm 2015*	*Majority shareholder fraudulent behavior*	

#	Investigated organization	Investigating firm	Suspicion of white-collar crime	Detected by
57	Kvinnherad *municipality*	Deloitte *audit firm* 2019	*Fraud in chief executive retirement compensation*	
58	Langemyhr *building company*	PwC *audit firm* 2008	*Fraudulent working hours invoicing*	
59	Larvik havn *port authority*	Komrev. Telemark *public audit* 2018	*Corruption in container terminal*	
60	Larvik *municipality*	Komrev. Telemark *public audit* 2017	*Corruption in building permits*	
61	Leksvik *municipality*	Midt-Norge *audit organization* 2017	*Illegal benefits to chief executive*	
62	Lenvik *municipality*	KomRev *audit organization* 2018	*Fraud by executive*	
63	Lunde *transportation company*	Vierdal *law firm* 2012	*Bankruptcy fraud*	Bank-ruptcy
64	Lyoness-Lyconet *gambling enterprise*	Stiftelsestilsynet *public examination* 2018	*Pyramid play similar to Ponzi scheme*	
65	Moskvaskolen *school in Moscow*	Ernst & Young *audit firm* 2013	*Paid teachers without teaching*	
66	NAV *social security authority*	Wiersholm *law firm* 2016	*Employees illegal abuse of information for gain*	
67	NDLA *public learning software*	Deloitte *audit firm* 2015	*Private abuse of public funds*	
68	NFF *football players association*	Lynx *law firm* 2012	*Fraud in player transfers*	
69	NIF *sports association*	BDO *audit firm* 2014	*Association president bribed*	
70	Nordea *banking*	Mannheimer Swartling *law firm* 2016	*Tax evasion in wealth management*	
71	Norsk Tipping *public betting*	Deloitte *audit firm* 2010	*CEO private property served*	
72	Norwegian Poker Team *private gambling*	Aftenposten *media investigation* 2018	*Money laundering at poker game*	
73	Næringsdepartement *department of industry*	PwC *audit firm* 2016	*Corruption in state-owned enterprises*	
74	Næringsdepartement *department of industry*	Ernst & Young *audit firm* 2018	*Embezzlement by executive in aid program*	
75	Orange *health services provider*	Bergen *municipality audit function* 2016	*Fraud by executive compensation*	
76	Oslo Boligbygg *municipal housing*	BDO *audit firm* 2017	*Corruption in public procurement*	Media

(Continued)

Table 9.3 (Continued)

#	Investigated organization	Investigating firm	Suspicion of white-collar crime	Detected by
77	Oslo Boligbygg *municipal housing*	Deloitte *audit firm* 2018	*Corruption in public procurement*	Media
78	Oslo Boligbygg *municipal housing*	Komrev. Oslo *public audit* 2018	*Corruption at procurement of facilities*	Media
79	Oslo Bymiljø *municipal parks*	Ernst & Young *audit firm* 2019	*Fraud by fake invoicing of park works*	Media
80	Oslo Lindeberg *nursing home*	Kommunerevisjon *public audit* 2013	*Fraud in employment contracts*	
81	Oslo Omsorgsbygg *housing administration*	PwC *audit firm* 2009	*Abuse of Norwegian public funds in Spain*	
82	Oslo Omsorgsbygg *housing administration*	Komrev. Oslo *public audit* 2018	*Chief executive employed family members*	
83	Oslo Omsorgsbygg *housing administration*	PwC *audit firm* 2019	*Chief executive employed family members*	
84	Oslo Renovasjon *public garbage collection*	Deloitte *audit firm* 2017	*Fraud in employm ent contracts*	Media
85	Oslo Samferdsel *public transportation*	PwC *audit firm* 2007	*Corruption in public procurement*	
86	Oslo *municipal school buildings*	Kommunerevisjon *public audit* 2006	*Project manager bribed in corruption*	Bank
87	Oslo *municipal school buildings*	Kommunerevisjon *public audit* 2006	*Property manager bribed in corruption*	Bank
88	Oslo Unibuss *public transportation*	Wiersholm *law firm* 2012	*Corruption in public procurement*	Media
89	Oslo Vei *public transportation firm*	Kvale *law firm* 2013	*Bankruptcy fraud*	
90	Politiets utlending *police department*	KPMG *audit firm* 2016	*Executive abuse of overtime compensation*	
91	Rana *municipality*	PwC *audit firm* 2008	*Corruption in public investment fund*	
92	Re *municipality*	Komrev. Vestfold *public audit* 2015	*Insurance fraud by putting a building on fire*	
93	Region Syddanmark *public authority*	Kromann Reumert *law firm* 2015	*Fraud by abuse of public position*	
94	Romanifolket *foundation*	Stiftelsestilsynet *public examination* 2017	*Fraud in abuse of public subsidies*	
95	Romerike Vannverk *public waterworks*	Distriktsrevisjon *public audit* 2007	*Fraud in privatization of public property*	Media

#	Investigated organization	Investigating firm	Suspicion of white-collar crime	Detected by
96	Sandefjord municipality	Tenden *law firm 2017*	Abuse of executive position for family benefit	
97	Siva *state funding of industries*	Wikborg *law firm 2018*	Chief executive funded his own company	
98	Skien *municipality*	BDO *audit firm 2017*	Fraudulent removal of sand from public property	
99	Skjervøy municipality	KomRev *public audit* 2015	Public funds allocated to personal property	
100	Stangeskovene *forest company*	Ernst & Young *audit firm 2013*	Private stock exchange excluding bidders	
101	Statoil *energy*	Hagen et al. *internal controllers 2013*	Cost savings in security measures causing accident	
102	Statoil *energy*	Saure et al. *internal controllers 2016*	Cost savings in security measures causing accident	
103	Statoil *energy*	Østby et al. *internal controllers 2017*	Cost savings in security measures causing accident	
104	Stavanger municipality	PwC *audit firm 2013*	Kidnapping fraud in public child care	
105	Sykehusapotekene *hospital pharmacies*	Moberg Segrov *consulting firm 2019*	Harassment for corporate profits	
106	Sykehusbygg *hospital buildings*	Kluge *law firm 2017*	Executive benefit from harassment of subordinate	
107	Sykehuset Innlandet *hospital*	Haavind *law firm 2011*	Fraudulent abuse of chief executive position	
108	Telenor *VimpelCom mobile company*	Deloitte *audit firm* 2016	Corruption to obtain licenses in Uzbekistan	
109	Tennisforbundet *tennis association*	Lewis et al. *consulting firm 2018*	Fraudulent arrangements of game results	
110	Tidal *music streaming service*	NTNU *research group* 2018	Fraudulent manipulation of streaming accounting	
111	Tjøme *municipality*	BDO *audit firm 2017*	Corruption in building permits at the seaside	

(Continued)

Table 9.3 (Continued)

#	Investigated organization	Investigating firm	Suspicion of white-collar crime	Detected by
112	Tolga *municipality*	Fylkesman *public examination 2019*	*Fraudulent diagnoses for retarded inhabitants*	
113	Tomter *shopping center association*	Holmen *audit firm 2014*	*Fraud in deregulation of shopping area*	
114	Transocean *oil rig company*	Riksadvokaten *public prosecutor 2017*	*Tax evasion*	
115	Trendtech *investment securities*	Finanstilsynet *public audit 2016*	*Misrepresentation of investor figures*	
116	Troms Kraft *energy company*	Norscan *consulting firm 2013*	*Fraudulent abuse of company funds*	
117	Universitetssykehuset Nord *hospital*	Arbeidsrettsadvokatene *law firm 2015*	*Economic exploitation of work force*	
118	Uppsala *municipality*	KPMG *audit firm 2018*	*Manipulation of audited numbers*	
119	Utenriksdepartement *state department*	Duane Morris *law firm 2016*	*Fraud in housing rental for diplomats*	
120	Utenriksdepartement *state department*	Kontrollenhet *internal audit 2016*	*Fraud in financing of development project*	
121	Utenriksdepartement *state department*	Kontrollenhet *internal audit 2017*	*Fraud in financing of development project*	
122	Utlendings-direktoratet *foreign affairs*	Deloitte *audit firm 2016*	*Subsidy fraud at return of refugees*	
123	Verdibanken *banking*	Wiersholm *law firm 2012*	*Insider trading in bank shares*	
124	Vestre Viken *hospital*	PwC *audit firm 2018*	*Fraudulent diagnoses to obtain more state funding*	
125	Vestvågøy *municipality*	Komrev. Nord *public audit 2018*	*Illegal procurement*	
126	Videoforhandlere *series production*	BDO *audit firm 2013*	*Abuse of state subsidies*	
127	Vistamar *rehabilitation center*	Komrev. Trondheim *public audit 2018*	*Embezzlement by chief executive*	
128	Vitalegruppen *private nursing*	BDO *audit firm 2017*	*Fraud in municipal subsidies*	
129	World Ventures *gaming company*	Stiftelsestilsynet *public examination 2014*	*Illegal pyramid of Ponzi scheme*	
130	Zachariasbryggen *property development*	Selmer *law firm 2014*	*Fraud in transfer of property rights*	

of the reports of investigations resulted in blame for misconduct and wrongdoing, and some resulted in sanctioning where individuals had to leave the organization. Some reports concluded that suspicions of white-collar crime were unfounded and accusations were unjust.

Among the few investigations that lead to cases in the criminal justice system, media journalists detected most of the crime. We have thus the following distribution based on Table 9.3:

- 12 conviction cases detected by investigative journalists.
- 2 conviction cases detect by bank employees.
- 2 conviction cases detected by the police.
- 1 conviction case detected by a victim.
- 1 conviction case detected by a bankruptcy lawyer.
- 1 conviction case detected by an auditor.
- 111 suspicion cases categorized by fraud examiners as no misconduct, or misconduct, but no crime.

The biggest category in the final column in Table 9.3 is blank entries. Unfortunately, we do not know the outcomes of all these cases. What we know is that none of the cases led to prosecution and conviction. This result is in itself interesting for two main reasons. First, fraud examiners hired by client organizations tend to deliver what clients expect in terms of descriptions of misconduct and suggestions for preventive actions in the future. Clients prefer fraud examiners to avoid indications of crime in terms of law violations (Gottschalk and Tcherni-Buzzeo, 2017). Second, miscarriage of justice should be avoided at all costs in the Norwegian culture (Holmes et al., 2020). If there is any doubt at all, a suspected offender should never be prosecuted. Therefore, a large number of guilty persons are never on trial to avoid that an innocent person ever ends up on trial. If Norway would have the same incarceration rate as the United States relative to the national population, Norway would have 38,000 individuals rather than the current 3,800 individuals in prison. There is thus a ten times difference, which is explained by a number of factors, including the fear of miscarriage of justice.

While Table 9.3 lists a total of 130 fraud investigation reports, which is a large sample, we have no way of telling whether the sample is in any way representative of all fraud examination reports in Norway. As emphasized by Gottschalk and Tcherni-Buzzeo (2016), most reports are kept secret and never disclosed to either the public or the police. Our sample can thus be biased in some unknown direction. Nevertheless, it is interesting to note that the most frequent fraud examiner is a local law firm (33 cases), which is followed by public audit (27 cases). The distribution among global auditing firms is 15 cases by PwC, 13 cases by BDO, 11 cases by Deloitte, 6 cases by Ernst & Young, and 3 cases by KPMG.

One of the main problems with detecting many forms of white-collar crime is that they are not obvious. Indeed, the perpetrators often deliberately design the offenses so that they appear to be legitimate business practices. Thus, unlike most ordinary forms of street crime, outsiders do not often recognize white-collar offenses, at least not for some time. Piecing together evidence that a white-collar crime has actually occurred is always much more difficult than it is for other types of offenses. This means that detecting and interpreting signals of a white-collar offense is indeed a problem, and perhaps signal detection theory can find a useful application in this context.

In conclusion, this chapter first reviewed literature on public government versus private governance in regulating business conduct in organizations. Next, the theory of signal detection illustrated factors that influence detection of white-collar crime signals. Two empirical studies from Norway followed, where one is a sample of convicted white-collar offenders, and the other is a sample of investigations by fraud examiners. While investigative journalists disclose a significant fraction of crime stories that later result in prosecution and conviction of white-collar offenders, few fraud examiners make similar contributions to fill the gap between government and governance.

While miscarriage of justice is a top priority in Norwegian society with less than six million inhabitants, crime detection and evidence development seem more at the core of investigative journalism compared to fraud examination. An avenue for future research is to study mandates in fraud examinations and competence of fraud examiners. Maybe auditing and legal knowledge are less relevant compared to competence in psychology, sociology, and management.

References

ACFE (2008). *2008 Report to the Nation – On Occupational Fraud & Abuse*, Association of Certified Fraud Examiners, Austin, Texas, USA.

ACFE (2014). *Report to the Nations on Occupational Fraud and Abuse, 2014 Global Fraud Study*, Association of Certified Fraud Examiners, Austin, Texas, USA.

ACFE (2016). *CFE Code of Professional Standard*, Association of Certified Fraud Examiners, www.acfe.com/standards/

Agnew, R. (2014). Social concern and crime: Moving beyond the assumption of simple self-interest, *Criminology*, 52 (1), 1–32.

Alleyne, P., Hudaib, M. and Pike, R. (2013). Towards a conceptual model of whistle-blowing intentions among external auditors, *The British Accounting Review*, 45 (1), 10–23.

Alon, A., Mennicken, A. and Samsonova-Taddei, A. (2019). Dynamics and limits of regulatory privatization: Reorganizing audit oversight in Russia, *Organization Studies*, 40 (8), 1217–1240.

Andrade, J. (2015). Reconceptualising whistleblowing in a complex world, *Journal of Business Ethics*, 128 (2), 321–335.

Andresen, M.S. and Button, M. (2019). The profile and detection of bribery in Norway and England & Wales: A comparative study, *European Journal of Criminology*, 16 (1), 18–40.

Bjørkelo, B., Einarsen, S., Nielsen, M.B. and Matthiesen, S.B. (2011). Silence is golden? Characteristics and experiences of self-reported whistleblowers, *European Journal of Work and Organizational Psychology*, 20 (2), 206–238.

Boghossian, J. and Marques, J.C. (2019). Saving the Canadian fur industry's hide: Government's strategic use of private authority to constrain radical activism, *Organization Studies*, 40 (8), 1241–1268.

Borgarting (2018). Case number 17-108216AST-BORG/02, *Borgarting lagmannsrett (Borgarting Court of Appeals)*, Oslo, Norway, October 10.

Brooks, G. and Button, M. (2011). The police and fraud investigation and the case for a nationalized solution in the United Kingdom, *The Police Journal*, 84, 305–319.

Button, M. (2019). The "new" private security industry, the private policing of cyberspace and the regulatory questions, *Journal of Contemporary Criminal Justice*, published online, https://doi.org/10.1177/1043986219890194.

Button, M. and Gee, J. (2013). *Countering Fraud for Competitive Advantage: The Professional Approach to Reducing the Last Great Hidden Cost*, Chichester, UK: John Wiley & Sons.

Button, M., Frimpong, K., Smith, G. and Johnston, L. (2007a). Professionalizing counter fraud specialists in the UK: Assessing progress and recommendations for reform, *Crime Prevention and Community Safety*, 9, 92–101.

Button, M., Johnston, L., Frimpong, K. and Smith, G. (2007b). New directions in policing fraud: The emergence of the counter fraud specialists in the United Kingdom, *International Journal of the Sociology of Law*, 35, 192–208.

Culiberg, B. and Mihelic, K.K. (2017). The evolution of whistleblowing studies: A critical review and research agenda, *Journal of Business Ethics*, 146 (4), 787–803.

Desai, V.M. (2016). Under the radar: Regulatory collaborations and their selective use to facilitate organizational compliance, *Academy of Management Journal*, 59 (2), 636–657.

Dyck, A., Morse, A. and Zingales, L. (2010). Who blows the whistle on corporate fraud? *The Journal of Finance*, 65 (6), 2213–2253.

Eberlein, B. (2019). Who fills the global governance gap? Rethinking the roles of business and government in global governance, *Organization Studies*, 40 (8), 1125–1146.

Egeberg, K. (2014). Norske krigsskip havnet i Nigeria – Langt i fra hva som var avtalen, sier Forsvaret (Norwegian warships ended up in Nigeria – Far from what was the agreement, the Military Defense says), daily Norwegian newspaper *Dagbladet*, www.dagbladet.no, published June 14.

Egeberg, K. (2015). *Nigeria-båtene: Metoderapport til Skup-prisen 2014 (The Nigeria Boats: Methods Report to the Skup Prize 2014)*, Dagbladet, Oslo, Norway.

Eriksen, N. (2019). Rettskraftig korrupsjonsdom i Nigeriabåt-saken (Enforceable corruption verdict in Nigeria boat case), daily Norwegian newspaper *Dagbladet*, www.dagbladet.no, published May 15.

Evans, R. (2017). Anti-corruption police investigate UK firm over ex-Nigerian warlord deal, *The Guardian*, www.theguardian.com, published May 14.

Ezeonu, I. (2020). Market criminology: A critical engagement with primitive accumulation in the petroleum extraction industry in Africa, in: Rorie, M.L. (editor), *The Handbook of White-Collar Crime*, Hoboken, NJ: Wiley & Sons, chapter 25, pages 398–417.

Gomulya, D. and Mishina, Y. (2017). Signaler credibility, signal susceptibility, and relative reliance on signals: How stakeholders change their evaluative processes after violation of expectations and rehabilitative efforts, *Academy of Management Journal*, 60 (2), 554–583.

Gottschalk, P. and Gunnesdal, L. (2018). *White-Collar Crime in the Shadow Economy: Lack of Detection, Investigation, and Conviction Compared to Social Security Fraud*, London, UK: Springer Publishing/Palgrave Pivot, Palgrave Macmillan.

Gottschalk, P. and Tcherni-Buzzeo, M. (2017). Reasons for gaps in crime reporting: The case of white-collar criminals investigated by private fraud examiners in Norway, *Deviant Behavior*, 38 (3), 267–281.

Hamann, R. (2019). Dynamic de-responsibilization in business-government interactions, *Organization Studies*, 40 (8), 1193–1216.

Holmes, M.C.S., Huuse, C.F., Engen, R.V. and Kristiansen, T. (2020). Kallmyr i NAV høring: En annen type justismord (Kallmyr in NAV hearing: Another kind of miscarriage of justice), daily Norwegian newspaper *VG*, www.vg.no, published January 13.

Høyesterett (2019). Dom avsagt 13. mai 2019 i anke over Borgarting lagmannsretts dom 23. oktober 2018 (Verdict announced May 13, 2019 regarding appeal for Borgarting court's verdict October 23, 2018), *Høyesterett (Norwegian Supreme Court)*, Oslo, Norway.

Huff, M.J. and Bodner, G.E. (2013). When does memory monitoring succeed versus fail? Comparing item-specific and relational encoding in the DRM paradigm, *Journal of Experimental Psychology: Learning, Memory, and Cognition*, 39 (4), 1246–1256.

Huff, R., Desilets, K. and Kane, J. (2010). *The National Public Survey on White Collar Crime*, Fairmont, WV: National White Collar Crime Center, www.nw3c.org.

Karim, K.E. and Siegel, P.H. (1998). A signal detection theory approach to analyzing the efficiency and effectiveness of auditing to detect management fraud, *Managerial Auditing Journal*, 13 (6), 367–375.

Kourula, A., Moon, J., Salles-Djelic, M.L. and Wicker, C. (2019). New roles of government in the governance of business conduct: Implications for management and organizational research, *Organization Studies*, 40 (8), 1101–1123.

Maher, R., Valenzuela, F. and Böhm, S. (2019). The enduring state: An analysis of governance-making in three mining conflicts, *Organization Studies*, 40 (8), 1169–1192.

Martinsen, Ø.L., Furnham, A. and Hærem, T. (2016). An integrated perspective on insight, *Journal of Experimental Psychology*, 145 (10), 1319–1332.

Miceli, M.P. and Near, J.P. (2013). An international comparison of the incidence of public sector whistle-blowing and the prediction of retaliation: Australia, Norway, and the US, *Australian Journal of Public Administration*, 72 (4), 433–446.

Michel, C. (2016). Violent street crime versus harmful white-collar crime: A comparison of perceived seriousness and punitiveness, *Critical Criminology*, 24, 127–143.

Mpho, B. (2017). Whistleblowing: What do contemporary ethical theories say? *Studies in Business and Economics*, 12 (1), 19–28.

NTB (2019). En del av Nigeriabåt-saken opp i Høyesterett (Part of the Nigerian boat case in the Supreme Court), daily Norwegian newspaper *Dagbladet*, www.dagbladet.no, published May 1.

Oslo tingrett (2017). Verdict 16-110357MED-OTIR/04, judge Lise Bogen Behrens, *Oslo tingrett (Oslo District Court)*, May 16.

Park, H., Bjørkelo, B. and Blenkinsopp, J. (2020). External whistleblowers' experiences of workplace bullying by superiors and colleagues, *Journal of Business Ethics*, 161, 591–601.

Pontell, H.N., Black, W.K. and Geis, G. (2014). Too big to fail, too powerful to jail? On the absence of criminal prosecutions after the 2008 financial meltdown, *Crime, Law and Social Change*, 61 (1), 1–13.

PwC (2014). *Forsvarets logistikkorganisasjon: Rapport etter gjennomgang av salg av fartøy (Military Logistic Organization: Report after Review of Sales of Vessels)*, auditing firm PricewaterhouseCoopers, October 31, Oslo, Norway.

PwC (2015). *Auditor-General for the Federation. Investigative Forensic Audit into the Allegations of Unremitted Funds into the Federation Accounts by the NNPC*, engagement leader Pedro Omontuemhen, PricewaterhouseCoopers, Lagos, Nigeria, www.premiumtimesng.com/docs_download/Full%20report – 20billion%20 dollars%20missing%20oil%20money.pdf?cf=1, downloaded September 2, 2018.

Qiu, B. and Slezak, S.L. (2019). The equilibrium relationships between performance-based pay, performance, and the commission and detection of fraudulent misreporting, *The Accounting Review*, 94 (2), 325–356.

Rehg, M.T., Miceli, M.P., Near, J.P. and Scotter, J.R.V. (2009). Antecedents and outcomes of retaliation against whistleblowers: Gender differences and power relationships, *Organization Science*, 19 (2), 221–240.

Reporter (2013). Nigerians yawn over missing billions, *The Sun*, December 31, https:// infoweb.newsbank.com/apps/news/document-view?p=AWNB&t=&sort=YMD_dat e%3AD&maxresults=20&f=advanced&val-base-0=NNPC&fld-base-0=alltext&bln-base-1=and&val-base-1=oil%20revenues&fld-base-1=alltext&bln-base-2=and&val-base-2=2013&fld-base-2=YMD_date&docref=news/14C0EF3456A37C88, retrieved November 3, 2018.

Schneider, A. and Scherer, A.G. (2019). State governance beyond the 'shadow of hierarchy': A social mechanisms perspective on governmental CSR policies, *Organization Studies*, 40 (8), 1147–1168.

Schneider, S. (2006). Privatizing economic crime enforcement: Exploring the role of private sector investigative agencies in combating money laundering, *Policing & Society*, 16 (3), 285–312.

Sutherland, E.H. (1939). White-collar criminality, *American Sociological Review*, 5 (1), 1–12.

Szalma, J.L. and Hancock, P.A. (2013). A signal improvement to signal detection analysis: Fuzzy SDT on the ROCs, *Journal of Experimental Psychology: Human Perception and Performance*, 39 (6), 1741–1762.

Taylor, J. (2018). White-collar crime and the law in nineteenth-century Britain, *Business History*, 60 (3), 343–360.

Tufts (2018). *CAS-Global Ltd. and the Private Nigerian Coast Guard Fleet*, Compendium of Arms Trade Corruption, World Peace Foundation, The Fletcher School, Tufts University, www.sites.tufts.edu/corruptarmsdeals/.

Walburg, C. (2020). White-collar and corporate crime: European perspectives, in: Rorie, M.L. (editor), *The Handbook of White-Collar Crime*, Hoboken, NJ: Wiley & Sons, chapter 21, pages 337–346.

Wall-Parker, A. (2020). Measuring white collar crime, in: Rorie, M.L. (editor), *The Handbook of White-Collar Crime*, Hoboken, NJ: John Wiley & Sons, chapter 3, pages 32–44.

Williams, J.W. (2005). Reflections on the private versus public policing of economic crime, *British Journal of Criminology*, 45, 316–339.

Williams, J.W. (2008). The lessons of Enron: Media accounts, corporate crimes, and financial markets, *Theoretical Criminology*, 12 (4), 471–499.

Williams, J.W. (2014). The private eyes of corporate culture: The forensic accounting and corporate investigation industry and the production of corporate financial security, in: Walby, K. and Lippert, R.K. (editors), *Corporate Security in the 21st Century: Theory and Practice in International Perspective*, Hampshire, Houndmills, UK: Palgrave Macmillan, pages 56–77.

Williams, M.L., Levi, M., Burnap, P. and Gundur, R.V. (2019). Under the corporate radar: Examining insider business cybercrime victimization through an application of routine activities theory, *Deviant Behavior*, 40 (9), 1119–1131.

10 Case study
Movie piracy

The theory of convenience suggests that characteristics of white-collar offenders include motive, opportunity, and willingness for deviant behavior. This chapter discusses the case offenders developing and supporting the software platform Popcorn Time. The motive seems to be sensation seeking with a deviant identity. The opportunity seems to be unknown and anonymous identity of offenders based on the lack of oversight and guardianship on the Internet. The willingness seems to be lack of self-control as well as disclaim of responsibility for violations of intellectual property rights.

Popcorn Time is a software platform to access and view video streaming without paying for it (Stone, 2015). The legality of the software depends on the jurisdiction. A website created in Norway explained and provided access Popcorn Time. Both the software and the website are illegal violations of intellectual property laws in Norway (NTB, 2018). A court order revoked the domain name for the website to the Norwegian state by court order, after hearings in the court of appeals (Borgarting, 2019) and the Supreme Court (Høyesterett, 2019).

The Norwegian National Authority for Investigation and Prosecution of Economic and Environmental Crime (Økokrim) prosecuted the case in court. Both courts defined the perpetrator as unknown (Borgarting, 2019; Høyesterett, 2019). Therefore, no individual could appear as defendant in court. The organization behind the website in Norway was making money on advertising in the legal form of an independent association. The chairperson of the association witnessed in court, but he was never prosecuted (NTB, 2018). Similarly, the developers of Popcorn Time remained anonymous and unknown (Stone, 2015).

The case study in this chapter analyzes the court verdicts in Norway based on convenience theory. The theory of convenience suggests that white-collar crime occurs when there is a financial motive, an organizational opportunity, and a personal willingness for deviant behavior (Chan and Gibbs, 2020; Hansen, 2020; Braaten and Vaughn, 2019).

White-collar convenience

Convenience is the state of being able to proceed with something with little effort or difficulty, avoiding pain and strain (Mai and Olsen, 2016). Convenience is savings in time and effort (Farquhar and Rowley, 2009), as well as avoidance of pain and obstacles (Higgins, 1997). Convenience is a relative concept concerned with the efficiency in time and effort as well as reduction in pain and solution to problems (Engdahl, 2015). Convenience is an advantage in favor of a specific action to the detriment of alternative actions. White-collar offenders choose the most convenient path to reach their goals (Wikstrom et al., 2018).

White-collar crime is non-violent crime committed by individuals in competent positions (Piquero, 2018). White-collar offenders commit and conceal their crime in a professional setting where they have legitimate access to premises, resources and systems (Logan et al., 2019). The benefit from white-collar crime might be financial gain, personal adventure or some other desired outcome (Craig and Piquero, 2017; Sutherland, 1983).

The theory of convenience suggests that white-collar misconduct and crime occurs when there is a motive benefiting an individual or n organization, professional opportunity to commit and conceal crime, and personal willingness for deviant behavior (Chan and Gibbs, 2020; Hansen, 2020; Braaten and Vaughn, 2019). The theory of convenience is an umbrella term for many well-known perspectives from criminology, strategy, psychology, and other schools of thought. Motive, opportunity and willingness are the three dimensions in convenience theory. Since convenience is a relative concept, convenience theory is a crime-as-choice theory. Shover et al. (2012) suggest that it is a conscious choice among alternatives that leads to law violation.

Figure 10.1 illustrates again the structure of white-collar convenience. The extent of white-collar crime convenience manifests itself by motive, opportunity and willingness.

The personal willingness for deviant behavior manifests itself by offender choice and perceived innocence. The choice of crime can be caused by deviant identity, rational consideration, or learning from others. The perceived innocence at crime manifests itself by justification and neutralization. Identity, rationality, learning, justification, and neutralization all contribute to making white-collar crime action a convenient behavior for offenders (Craig and Piquero, 2017; Engdahl, 2015; Sutherland, 1983; Sykes and Matza, 1957).

Popcorn case description

"Too Good to Be Legal" was the heading of an article in Blomberg Businessweek, where Stone (2015: 31) described Popcorn Time as making piracy easier than ever:

> In the past year, a program called Popcorn Time has become the kinder, gentler face of piracy online, taming BitTorrent to make it far more user-friendly and less obviously sketchy. Free incarnations for PCs, phones, and tablets look pretty much like Netflix, Hulu, or Amazon Instant Video.

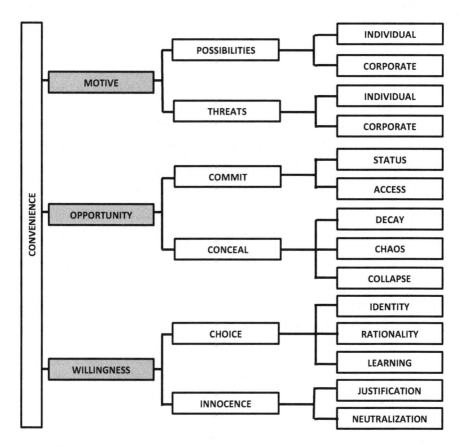

Figure 10.1 Structural model of convenience theory

The daily Norwegian newspaper "Aftenposten" told the story under the article heading, "Norwegians violated the law by watching movies through Popcorn Time" (NTB, 2018):

> Hundreds of thousands of Norwegians have broken the law after watching movies and TV shows through the free service Popcorn Time, Follo district court states in a recent verdict.
>
> Popcorn Time is a free service that offers streaming of movies and TV shows in the same manner as other suppliers on the market, such as Netflix. The difference is that Popcorn Time neither pays the licensees nor has obtained permission to show the contents.
>
> – A special feature of this technology is that parts of the file are retrieved from an infinitely large number of users. Users who watch movies and TV

shows through Popcorn Time will usually contribute to this file sharing by allowing others to retrieve parts of the file from them while watching movies. It is this kind of availability by the users that Follo district court says is undoubtedly in violation of the intellectual property law says Dahl.

Licensees in Norway may have lost as much as NOK 500 million, Willy Johansen said in court. He is the head of the Rights Alliance and secretary general of the Norwegian Videogram Association. It was also referred to an article in Aftenposten in May 2015, where a survey by TNS Gallup showed that 315,000 Norwegians used Popcorn Time weekly.

– Users of illegal file sharing services cannot subsequently claim that they were unaware of the actions being illegal and will hopefully result in more users abstaining from such offenses. Generally, Økokrim does not comment on the cases that we will investigate, but it is clear that users of Popcorn Time can, in principle, be prosecuted, says Dahl.

While Popcorn Time has provided a quick and easy way to download and view movies and TV shows that are copyrighted material, the Norwegian domain has reinforced the opportunity of illegal use, the court states.

It is stated in the verdict about Popcorn Time, among other things, that the service cannot be considered to have any function or purpose other than providing access to protected films and TV shows, without the licensees' consent, says police lawyer Dahl.

The verdict in Norwegian courts (Borgarting, 2019; Høyesterett, 2019) is in line with the statement that "if you are seen as encouraging people to infringe, then you have a copyright problem" (Stone, 2015: 32).

Defense attorney Ola Tellesbø had argued in the court for dismissal of the case (Borgarting, 2019: 5):

Popcorn Time is software that integrates several features including a browser, a BitTorrent client and a player. The software and technology behind it is not in itself illegal, as the prosecution has acknowledged. Nor is the Bit-Torrent technology, which enables efficient file sharing, illegal. The fact that the software can be used to share copyrighted material cannot lead to criminal liability for those behind the Norwegian domain. Based on the content of popcorn-time.no, it is most natural to compare the website with a technology blog. This cannot be confused with the software Popcorn Time and possible copyright infringements when using it.

The main purpose of the domain has been to sell advertisements and VPN solutions, not to facilitate or contribute to copyright infringement. This is substantiated by the fact that there was a disclaimer on the website, as well as information that use and downloading might be illegal and is done at the user's own risk.

The contents of the Norwegian domain also have protection under the Norwegian Constitution (§ 100) and the European Convention on Human Rights (Article 10), which protect the freedom of expression and information.

The prosecuting authority has not established a causal link between the content of the Norwegian domain and alleged copyright infringements. There is a clear weakness in the investigation that it has not been investigated how many users (if any) have visited the Norwegian domain, possibly clicked further on from the Norwegian site and downloaded the software, and then used the software for copyright infringements. The fraction of legal material in the directories that the software's search features are linked to is also not examined.

There is no basis for concluding that physical or mental involvement has taken place. The decisive factor in the scope of the responsibility is the relevance of penalty for the actions. The Napster sentence and Filmspeler case from the European Court of Justice do not apply as comparable cases and are irrelevant to determine the extent of participation.

Napster was a piracy site hosting infringing files. Pirate Bay did not host such files, nor link to them. Instead, Pirate Bay hosted trackers, that is, files which tell users of individual BitTorrent apps which other BitTorrent users to link to in order to download large files. Nevertheless, the European Court of Justice ruled that Pirate Bay was infringing copyright (Hern, 2017).

The reference to Filmspeler at the European Court of Justice was a case where the Dutch citizen Jack Wullens sold a multimedia device online called the Filmspeler. The device acts as a medium between an audiovisual data source and a TV. Wullems' player made it possible for users to watch free programming on their TVs regardless of copyright protection. The court noted that the sole purpose of the device was intentionally to access copyrighted work, where Wullens made money on sale of his device while depriving the rights holders of their economic benefit (Dotinga, 2017).

Convenience case study

The unknown perpetrator referred to in the Norwegian court documents (Borgarting, 2019; Høyesterett, 2019) is the team of anonymous developers of Popcorn Time (Stone, 2015: 32):

> Creating a less cumbersome wrapper for BitTorrent was the primary objective of Popcorn Time's anonymous developers, a group of friends in Argentina, ways a Dutch blogger who goes by Ernesto van der Sar and runs TorrentFreak, a news site that covers file sharing. The creators abandoned Popcorn Time just a few weeks after its launch, writing on their website that they needed to "move on with our lives" . . .
>
> Popcorn Time survived. Its code is open-source, so several other groups of coders quickly released versions after the site shut down. "We were users of the original and were sad to watch it go", wrote a developer of one of the spinoff versions, who answered an e-mail sent through his group's website and insisted on communicating through anonymous Internet chat software to protect his identity. "The amount of attention this project has

been receiving is HUGE, ground breaking and way above anything we expected when we first picked it up".

In the motive dimension of convenience theory, sensation seeking seems to be an important driving force for anonymous and unknown developers of piracy software such as Popcorn Time. Sensation seeking to experience adventure is a common characteristic of some white-collar offenses (Craig and Piquero, 2017). Sensation seeking is a psychological trait where the offender seeks excitement. The offender seeks variation, novelty, complexity and intensity. The offender may be willing to take physical, social, legal and financial risks for the sake of such experiences. Even when the sensation seeking is not particularly strong, many white-collar crime acts may involve sensations that some find exciting.

Sensation seeking does not necessarily represent anti-social behavior. For example, bribing a potential customer during contract negotiations can be both social and exciting. When executives from the German bus manufacturer MAN bribed public officials from a Norwegian transportation agency, they went for a walk in a German forest where the Germans handed over envelopes containing euros to the Norwegians (Solem and Kleppe, 2014). For both briber and bribed, the forest tour in itself might have been exciting. The memory of the Black Forest (Schwarzwald) at night will probably remain with the participants. Long and boring meetings, reading volumes of documents, and writing minutes of meetings, on the other hand, might be activities that participants soon forget.

Craig and Piquero (2017: 1367) mention other examples where individuals can be sensation seeking:

> Those qualities could fit a business man adding false charges to his expense account to make some extra money just to see if he can get away with it. These factors may also describe a retail employee stealing money from the cash drawer, or an individual committing an elaborate Ponzi scheme that requires complex planning and intense pressure.

Sensation seekers such as hackers and pirates attempt to avoid boredom by replacing repetitive activities such as status meetings in software projects, computer operations monitoring and documentation of applications with thrill and adventures. They search out risky and exciting activities and have distaste for monotonous situations.

Figure 10.2 illustrates the convenience theme of sensation seeking as a possibility for the individual piracy developer.

In their empirical study involving students, Craig and Piquero (2017) included embezzlement and credit card fraud. Stealing money from an employer by embezzlement is risky not only because of legal implications but also because of the probable job loss. Abusing a roommate's credit card cannot only result in legal punishment but also an interpersonal cost if caught. At the same time, the offender can perceive both embezzlement and credit card abuse as thrilling adventures in a situation characterized by boredom. These offenses can also

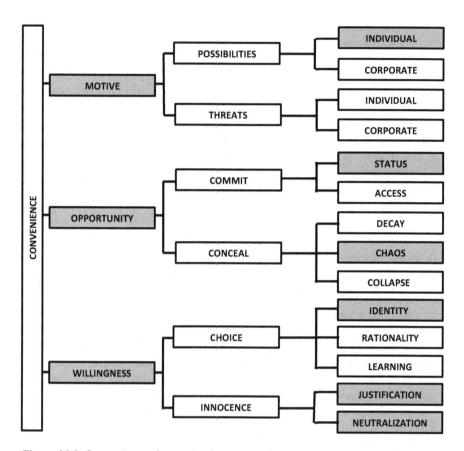

Figure 10.2 Convenience themes in the case study

represent acts involving new and intense experiences. To claim to be the roommate is a fraudulent behavior that the offender may perceive as a high-pressure event.

In their empirical study involving students, Craig and Piquero (2017) made a distinction between socialized sensation seeking and un-socialized sensation seeking. While thrill and adventure seeking represents social experience, disinhibition and boredom avoidance represents unsocial experience. The researchers found that unsocial – but not social – sensation seeking was a positive predictor of intentions to engage in shoplifting, embezzlement and credit card fraud.

In the opportunity dimension of convenience theory, being an anonymous and unknown perpetrator makes it possible to rescue software and avoid detection (Stone, 2015: 32):

> The anonymous Popcorn Time developer says the added pressure is motivating him and his colleagues to finish a version of the software that operates

entirely by connecting viewers' computers and doesn't rely at all on central servers. "When we release this, there will be nothing to be taken down again", he says.

Figure 10.2 indicates the high social status among insiders when committing piracy crime as white-collar crime (Slyke and Bales, 2012). Status-related factors such as influential positions in the technological underworld make offenders untouchable (Hausman, 2018).

Figure 10.2 indicates that lack of oversight and guardianship against pirates on the Internet is another element of the opportunity structure characterized by chaos when it comes to policing the Internet. The climate encourages deviant behavior as normal and acceptable among hackers and pirates (Murphy and Dacin, 2011). Offenders can play the blame game to avoid attention (Eberly et al., 2011; Lee and Robinson, 2000).

Deviant behavior willingness

In the willingness dimension of convenience theory, lack of self-control (Gottfredson and Hirschi, 1990) seems related to sensation seeking in that willingness for sensation seeking increases with deterioration of self-control. Low self-control individuals give in more easily to their impulsive desires.

Lack of self-control is a frequent explanation for executive deviance and crime in general (Gottfredson and Hirschi, 1990). While many might be tempted, only those lacking self-control will actually do it. Self-regulation monitors self-control, where self-regulation represents a process of using self-regulatory resources to control undesirable impulses and override subsequent behavioral responses. As argued by Mawritz et al. (2017), individuals possess varying and limited self-regulatory resources that inhibit responses that may arise from physiological processes, habit, learning, or the strain of the situation. When resources that regulate self-control are depleted, individuals struggle to constrain their urges and engage in behavior almost unwittingly, using quick, thoughtless responses. They move down the slippery slope from the right side of the law to the wrong side of the law (Arjoon, 2008). Self-control processes deplete self-regulatory resources and impair one's ability to control subsequent inappropriate responses.

Kroneberg and Schulz (2018: 59) link lack of self-control (Gottfredson and Hirschi, 1990) to the situational action perspective, when they find that "personal moral rules play a crucial role in the process of perception of action alternatives, whereas self-control matters only in the subsequent process of choice should actors start to deliberate on whether or not to break the law". While the perception of action alternatives belongs to the organizational opportunity dimension of white-collar offending, the subsequent lack of self-control belongs to the personal willingness dimension of white-collar offending. The situational action perspective addresses how environments shape crime opportunities and, subsequently, how modifications in environments can increase criminal opportunities

(Huisman and Erp, 2013). When the situational action perspective by Wikstrom et al. (2018) distinguishes between three stages, (1) perception of action alternatives (legal alternatives, illegal alternatives), (2) process of choice (habit, rational deliberation), and (3) action, then Kroneberg and Schulz (2018) conceptualize lack of self-control as well as lack of deterrence on the axis from (2) to (3). The situational action perspective aims to integrate personal and environmental explanatory perspectives within the framework of a situation.

Lack of self-control as described by Gottfredson and Hirschi (1990), combined with sensation seeking as described by Craig and Piquero (2017), can substantially increase the level of willingness among potential white-collar offenders. The researchers also found that unsocial as well as social sensation seeking correlates positively with low self-control.

In addition to lack of self-control, justification of action and neutralization of guilt are typical sources of willingness in deviant behavior. The developers of Popcorn Time thought they did nothing wrong (Stone, 2015: 32):

> The developers don't call themselves pirates. Asked about consequences of making illicit file sharing easier, the anonymous developer claims Popcorn Time doesn't break any laws because it's just an index of other BitTorrent sites and doesn't host any pirated material. "The torrent world was here with millions of users way before us and will be here BILLIONS of users way after us", he wrote.

The neutralization technique of disclaiming responsibility for crime is relevant here (Sykes and Matza, 1957), where piracy developers claim not being responsible for what happens. They argue that the responsibility for obeying copyright laws should fall to users. Generally, when applying this neutralization technique, the offender claims that one or more of the conditions of responsible agency did not occur. The person committing a deviant act defines himself or herself as lacking responsibility for his or her actions. In this technique, the person rationalizes that the action in question is beyond his or her control. The offender views himself as a billiard ball, helplessly propelled through different situations. He denies responsibility for the event or sequence of events (Jordanoska, 2018; Kaptein and Helvoort, 2019; Schoultz and Flyghed, 2019; Siponen and Vance, 2010).

Robert Red English, a developer of a separate Popcorn Time spinoff who communicated over Skype Instant Messenger from Ontario with Stone (2015: 32), also argued that the responsibility for obeying copyright laws should fall to users:

> "I'm not going to justify it", he wrote. "If it's stealing or not varies by country and each user is given the choice to use the program, and warned we use torrents. It's up to them to choose if they wish to continue".
>
> That's common defense among people who collect links to pirated videos, but judicial precedent doesn't back it up. The founders of Pirate Bay, a popular BitTorrent hub, made similar arguments in Swedish court and

received prison sentences. Older file-sharing networks such as Napster and Grokster shut down, because U.S. courts ruled that they were emboldening users to break laws.

Figure 10.2 indicates that deviant identity might also be a cause of willingness among piracy developers. Some white-collar offenders take on a professional deviant identity (Obodaru, 2017). The identity perspective suggests that individuals develop professional identities where they commit to a chosen identity. It is a process of generating possible selves, selecting one, and discarding the others. Professional identity is how an individual sees himself or herself in relation to work. The self-concept is a complex cognitive structure containing all of a person's self-representations. According to the identity perspective, roles and identities are interdependent concepts. Identity enactment refers to acting out an identity, or claiming the identity by engaging in behaviors that conform to role expectations and that allow the identity to become manifest. Deviant behavior finds an anchor in a person's professional identity, where the deviant leader must claim and assume a leader identity by their followers.

Labeling can influence the deviant personality offender mind. The labeling perspective suggests that individuals adapt to the reputation created by others. The labeling perspective argues that the deviant reputation stigmatizes a person into a stereotype. Formal societal reaction to the individual can be a stepping-stone in the development of a criminal career. The deviant label is over time embedded in the individual. The labeled person is increasingly likely to become involved in social groups that consist of social deviants and unconventional others without feeling any doubt or regret since the behavior is in accordance with the label glued to the person by others (Bernburg et al., 2006).

In conclusion, this chapter has illustrated how the convenience theory applies to hackers and pirates on the Internet. The theory of convenience suggests that characteristics of white-collar offenders include motive, opportunity, and willingness for deviant behavior. This chapter discussed the case offenders developing and supporting the software platform Popcorn Time. The motive seems to be sensation seeking with a deviant identity. The opportunity seems to be unknown and anonymous identity of offenders based on the lack of oversight and guardianship on the Internet. The willingness seems to be lack of self-control as well as a disclaiming of responsibility for violations of intellectual property rights.

References

Arjoon, S. (2008). Slippery when wet: The real risk in business, *Journal of Markets & Morality*, Spring, 11 (1), 77–91.

Bernburg, J.G., Krohn, M.D. and Rivera, C.J. (2006). Official labeling, criminal embeddedness, and subsequent delinquency, *Journal of Research in Crime and Delinquency*, 43 (1), 67–88.

Borgarting (2019). Court case 17-170796AST-BORG/01, *Borgarting lagmannsrett (Borgarting Court of Appeals)*, February 1, judges Mats Wilhelm Ruland, Marit

Bjørånesset Frogner and Bjørn E. Engstrøm. Prosecutor Esben Kyhring, defense attorney Christian Fredrik Bonnevie Hjort.

Braaten, C.N. and Vaughn, M.S. (2019). Convenience theory of cryptocurrency crime: A content analysis of U.S. federal court decisions, *Deviant Behavior*, published online, https://doi.org/10.1080/01639625.2019.1706706.

Chan, F. and Gibbs, C. (2020). Integrated theories of white-collar and corporate crime, in: Rorie, M.L. (editor), *The Handbook of White-Collar Crime*, Hoboken, NJ: Wiley & Sons, chapter 13, pages 191–208.

Craig, J.M. and Piquero, N.L. (2017). Sensational offending: An application of sensation seeking to white-collar and conventional crimes, *Crime & Delinquency*, 63 (11), 1363–1382.

Dotinga, W. (2017). EU court finds copyright issues with streaming player, *Courthouse News Service*, www.courthousenews.com, published April 26.

Eberly, M.B., Holley, E.C., Johnson, M.D. and Mitchell, T.R. (2011). Beyond internal and external: A dyadic theory of relational attributions, *Academy of Management Review*, 36 (4), 731–753.

Engdahl, O. (2015). White-collar crime and first-time adult-onset offending: Explorations in the concept of negative life events as turning points, *International Journal of Law, Crime and Justice*, 43 (1), 1–16.

Farquhar, J.D. and Rowley, J. (2009). Convenience: A services perspective, *Marketing Theory*, 9 (4), 425–438.

Gottfredson, M.R. and Hirschi, T. (1990). *A General Theory of Crime*, Stanford, CA: Stanford University Press.

Hansen, L.L. (2020). Review of the book "Convenience Triangle in White-Collar Crime: Case Studies of Fraud Examinations", *ChoiceConnect*, vol. 57, no. 5, Middletown, CT: Association of College and Research Libraries.

Hausman, W.J. (2018). Howard Hopson's billion dollar fraud: The rise and fall of associated gas & electric company, *Business History*, 60 (3), 381–398.

Hern, A. (2017). European court of justice rules Pirate Bay is infringing copyright, *The Guardian*, www.theguardian.com, published June 15.

Higgins, E.T. (1997). Beyond pleasure and pain, *American Psychologist*, 52, 1280–1300.

Høyesterett (2019). Dom avsagt 13. mai 2019 i anke over Borgarting lagmannsretts dom 23. oktober 2018 (Verdict announced May 13, 2019 regarding appeal for Borgarting court's verdict October 23, 2018), *Høyesterett (Norwegian Supreme Court)*, Oslo, Norway.

Huisman, W. and Erp, J. (2013). Opportunities for environmental crime, *British Journal of Criminology*, 53, 1178–1200.

Jordanoska, A. (2018). The social ecology of white-collar crime: Applying situational action theory to white-collar offending, *Deviant Behavior*, 39 (11), 1427–1449.

Kaptein, M. and Helvoort, M. (2019). A model of neutralization techniques, *Deviant Behavior*, 40 (10), 1260–1285.

Kroneberg, C. and Schulz, S. (2018). Revisiting the role of self-control in situational action theory, *European Journal of Criminology*, 15 (1), 56–76.

Lee, F. and Robinson, R.J. (2000). An attributional analysis of social accounts: Implications of playing the blame game, *Journal of Applied Social Psychology*, 30 (9), 1853–1879.

Logan, M.W., Morgan, M.A., Benson, M.L. and Cullen, F.T. (2019). Coping with imprisonment: Testing the special sensitivity hypothesis for white-collar offenders, *Justice Quarterly*, 36 (2), 225–254.

Mai, H.T.X. and Olsen, S.O. (2016). Consumer participation in self-production: The role of control mechanisms, convenience orientation, and moral obligation, *Journal of Marketing Theory and Practice*, 24 (2), 209–223.

Mawritz, M.B., Greenbaum, R.L., Butts, M.M. and Graham, K.A. (2017). I just can't control myself: A self-regulation perspective on the abuse of deviant employees, *Academy of Management Journal*, 60 (4), 1482–1503.

Murphy, P.R. and Dacin, M.T. (2011). Psychological pathways to fraud: Understanding and preventing fraud in organizations, *Journal of Business Ethics*, 101, 601–618.

NTB (2018). Nordmenn Brøt Loven ved å se Filmer gjennom Popcorn Time (Norwegians violated the law by watching movies through Popcorn Time), daily Norwegian newspaper *Aftenposten*, www.aftenposten.no, published January 19.

Obodaru, O. (2017). Forgone, but not forgotten: Toward a theory of forgone professional identities, *Academy of Management Journal*, 60 (2), 523–553.

Piquero, N.L. (2018). White-collar crime is crime: Victims hurt just the same, *Criminology & Public Policy*, 17 (3), 595–600.

Schoultz, I. and Flyghed, J. (2019). From "we didn't do it" to "we've learned our lesson": Development of a typology of neutralizations of corporate crime, *Critical Criminology*, published online doi.org/10.1007/s10612-019-09483-3.

Shover, N., Hochstetler, A. and Alalehto, T. (2012). Choosing white-collar crime, in: Cullen, F.T. and Wilcox, P. (editors), *The Oxford Handbook of Criminological Theory*, Oxford, UK: Oxford University Press.

Siponen, M. and Vance, A. (2010). Neutralization: New insights into the problem of employee information security policy violations, *MIS Quarterly*, 34 (3), 487–502.

Slyke, S.V. and Bales, W.D. (2012). A contemporary study of the decision to incarcerate white-collar and street property offenders, *Punishment & Society*, 14 (2), 217–246.

Solem, L.K. and Kleppe, M.K. (2014). Seks Dømt for Korrupsjon i Unibuss-Saken (Six convicted in the Unibuss Case), daily Norwegian business newspaper *Dagens Næringsliv*, www.dn.no/korrupsjon/unibuss/kriminalitet/seks-domt-for-korrupsjon-i-unibuss-saken/1-1-5245586, published December 3.

Stone, B. (2015). Too good to be legal, *Bloomberg Businessweek* March 2–March 8, pages 31–33.

Sutherland, E.H. (1983). *White Collar Crime: The Uncut Version*, New Haven, CT: Yale University Press.

Sykes, G. and Matza, D. (1957). Techniques of neutralization: A theory of delinquency, *American Sociological Review*, 22 (6), 664–670.

Wikstrom, P.O.H., Mann, R.P. and Hardie, B. (2018). Young people's differential vulnerability to criminogenic exposure: Bridging the gap between people- and place-oriented approaches in the study of crime causation, *European Journal of Criminology*, 15 (1), 10–31.

11 Stage model for offenders

This chapter presents convenience dynamics in white-collar crime in terms of steps, levels, and stages over time. This chapter applies again the offender-based perspective concerned with individuals in white-collar crime. The chapter presents a five-stage model for white-collar offenders, where crime might result mainly from opportunity, motive, justification, choice, or strategy. At each of these five levels, a case describes a convicted offender from Norway, Japan, Germany, Sweden, and the United States respectively. Classification of offenders at different stages can enable researchers to study different categories of white-collar offenders and their potential paths over time. This chapter applies again the emerging theory of convenience, which suggests that the state of being able to proceed with something with little effort and difficulty, and avoiding pain and strain, is contributing to white-collar crime occurrences.

Stage models define discrete levels to study individual and organizational phenomena over time. Stage models represent a theoretical approach to phenomena where stages, steps or levels are (1) sequential in nature, (2) occur as a hierarchical progression that is not easily reversed, and (3) involve a broad range of individual or organizational activities and structures (Gottschalk and Dean, 2010; Gottschalk and Markovic, 2016; Röglinger et al., 2012; Solli-Sæther and Gottschalk, 2015). Stage models serve the purpose of capturing characteristics of single instances as well as determine the paths that observed entities might follow over time.

This chapter applies the concept of stage models to white-collar offenders by application of convenience theory. White-collar offenders are members of the elite in society who commit financial crime in the course of their occupations in business, government or other organizational settings (Sutherland, 1983). The theory of convenience suggests that the financial motive, the organizational opportunity, and the personal willingness for deviant behavior determine the tendency to commit white-collar crime on behalf of individuals or behalf of the organization. Convenience is the state of being able to proceed with something with little effort or difficulty, avoiding pain and strain (Mai and Olsen, 2016). Convenience is savings in time and effort (Farquhar and Rowley, 2009), as well as avoidance of pain and obstacles (Higgins, 1997). Convenience is a relative concept concerned with the efficiency in time and effort as well as reduction in pain and solution to problems (Engdahl, 2015). Convenience is an advantage in favor of a specific action to the detriment of alternative actions. White-collar offenders choose the most convenient path to reach their goals (Wikstrom et al., 2018).

This chapter introduces a five-stage model where opportunity, motive, justification, choice, and strategy are labels for the five stages. Then case studies from Norway, Japan, Germany, Sweden, and the United States illustrate the application of the stages. This research represents an important novel approach to distinguishing financial crime occurrences in the elite in society, which might prove helpful in crime prevention and crime detection in investigative psychology and offender profiling.

Development of the stage model

Ideally, stage models need to be both theoretically sound and empirically testable. Researchers have proposed a number of multistage models, which assume that predictable patterns exist in the development of individual and organizational behavior, and that these patterns unfold as discrete periods of time best thought of as stages, steps or levels. These models have different distinguishing characteristics. Stages are the result of a desire to explore and exploit possibilities, or as a response to external or internal crises. Some models suggest that the unit of analysis progresses through stages while others implicitly argue that there may be multiple paths through the stages. Therefore, a stage model may need to allow for multiple paths through levels as long as they follow a unidirectional pattern. These models find application in management research, where the assumption is that predictable patterns exist that conceptualize in terms of stages, steps or levels.

Stage models can have varying number of stages, and each stage needs a label according to the issue at hand. Here we suggest the following five stages for white-collar crime offenders as illustrated in Figure 11.1:

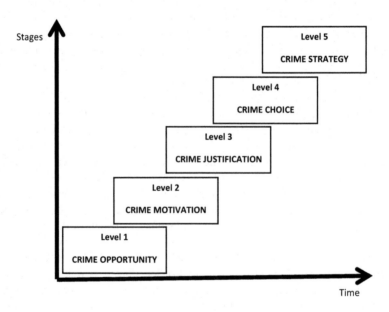

Figure 11.1 Stage model for white-collar offenders

1   *Crime opportunity*: White-collar crime is resulting from an opportunity that simply is so attractive that the advantage deserves exploitation. The offender knows that it is wrong and that it is bad, but the opportunity is so attractive that violating the law is an obvious choice to the offender. The offender uses a kind of executive language that people do not understand (Ferraro et al., 2005), and nobody questions the deviant behavior since there is power inequality between the elite and others (Baird and Zelin, 2009; Patel and Cooper, 2014), and because the offender uses humor to distract attention from deviant behavior (Yam et al., 2018). Institutional deterioration (Rodriguez et al., 2005), social disorganization (Hoffmann, 2002; Sampson and Laub, 1993), and noise in crime signals (Karim and Siegel, 1998) are important elements in the opportunity structure. Furthermore, lack of control in principal-agent relationships (Bosse and Phillips, 2016), difficult or impossible to make sense for outsiders (Weick, 1995), lack of whistle-blowing (Keil et al., 2010), and ethical climate conflict (Victor and Cullen, 1988) are additional elements in the opportunity structure. This first stage of crime opportunity is a reactive behavior where crime intention emerges from detection of an attractive opportunity.

2   *Crime motivation*: White-collar crime is resulting from a motive of exploiting possibilities and avoiding threats. The offender is attracted to the American dream of prosperity (Schoepfer and Piquero, 2006), and hopes to satisfy the need for acclaim as a narcissist (Chatterjee and Pollock, 2017). The offender wants to satisfy greed where nothing is ever enough (Goldstraw-White, 2012). Making as much profit as possible is the only important goal (Naylor, 2003; Welsh and Ordonez, 2014). It is important not to lose self-esteem after organizational failure (Crosina and Pratt, 2019; Olafsen et al., 2017). It is also important to remove strain, pain and uncertainty (Langton and Piquero, 2007). This second stage of crime motivation is a proactive behavior where a financial motive leads to the search for opportunities.

3   *Crime justification*: There is a reason for crime that justifies the offense. The act of wrongdoing is morally justifiable (Schnatterly et al., 2018). The offender finds it necessary to restore the perception of equity and equality (Leigh et al., 2010; Nichol, 2019). The offender needs to satisfy his or her desire to help others as social concern (Agnew, 2014). In the case of corruption, both briber and bribed can enjoy mutual benefits in exchange relationships (Huang and Knight, 2017). Elite members are simply too big to fail and too powerful to jail (Pontell et al., 2014; Sutherland, 1983), since laws are not for the elite to follow (Bussmann et al., 2018; Gamache and McNamara, 2019; Petrocelli et al., 2003; Welsh et al., 2014). The blame for harm deserves attribution to others (Bernburg et al., 2006; Eberly et al., 2011; Mingus and Burchfield, 2012). Rule complexity justifies lack of compliance (Lehman et al., 2019), and the offender is entitled to action (Galvin et al., 2015; Obodaru, 2017; Zvi and Elaad, 2018). On the other hand, negative life events (Engdahl, 2015) and peer pressure (Gao and

Zhang, 2019) can justify white-collar crime. This third stage of crime justification is an intended deviant behavior that is conveniently possible to carry out because of excuses and justifications.

4   *Crime choice*: The offender makes a rational choice of committing crime. There is a perception of benefits exceeding costs as rational (Pratt and Cullen, 2005), and behavioral reinforcement of deviance takes place over time (Benartzi et al., 2017; Comey, 2009; Mawritz et al., 2017). The offender has chosen to climb the hierarchy of needs for status and success (Maslow, 1943). Business goals and objectives are mandatory at any costs (Jonnergård et al., 2010). Falling from position in the privileged elite is unthinkable (Piquero, 2012). The choice of crime is convenient by application of neutralization techniques (Sykes and Matza, 1957) and lack of self-control (Gottfredson and Hirschi, 1990). This fourth stage of crime choice is a deliberate choice of crime to the detriment of alternative actions.

5   *Crime strategy*: The offender has a strategy of committing crime whenever it is convenient. Corporate collapse and bankruptcy should never be an option (Blickle et al., 2006). Adaption to profitable criminal market forces is quite natural and obvious (Chang et al., 2005; Leonard and Weber, 1970), and joining profitable criminal networks and cartels is a desirable avenue for the offender (Goncharov and Peter, 2019; Nielsen, 2003). The offender has legitimate access to premises, systems and other resources for wrongdoing (Adler and Kwon, 2002; Benson and Simpson, 2018; Cohen and Felson, 1979), and the offender can apply entrepreneurial skills (Ramoglou and Tsang, 2016) to seek sensation and experience adventure (Craig and Piquero, 2017). The fifth stage of crime strategy is an explicit inclusion of illegal acts and behaviors within the arsenal of possible business options to reach strategic objectives for the enterprise.

Research method of case study

This research retrieved secondary material to identify relevant white-collar offenders for case study research. Five secondary sources are applied. First, organizations hire fraud examiners at global auditing firms and local law firms to conduct internal investigations in the organizations when there is suspicion of misconduct and crime. Some reports of investigations by fraud examiners are publicly available (BDO, 2014; Deloitte, 2011; Ernst & Young, 2012; Nergaard, 2013). Second, some convicted white-collar offenders write and publish their autobiographies (Belfort, 2008; Benulic, 2018; Middelhoff, 2017). Third, court documents can be available and obtainable (Drammen tingrett, 2015). Fourth, media typically cover white-collar crime cases as they involve famous people and major organizations (Buanes, 2015; Ellingsen, 2015; Gustafsson, 2015; Inagati, 2015; Johansen, 2015; Johnsen, 2013; Mo, 2018; Nakling, 2015; Nakamoto, 2011; Neate, 2012; Patsiaouras and Fitchett, 2011; Storbeck, 2018; Weidermann, 2017). Finally, student thesis can serve as references (Riis and Øverland, 2018).

The research method applied in these empirical case studies of executive deviance is content analysis (Bell et al., 2018; Saunders et al., 2007). Content analysis is any methodology or procedure that works to identify characteristics within texts attempting to make valid inferences (Duriau et al., 2007; Krippendorff, 1980; Patrucco et al., 2017). Content analysis assumes that language reflects both how people understand their surroundings and their cognitive processes. Cognition refers to what people think and how they think, and cognitive processes affect the way in which people interpret and make sense of what is around them. Therefore, content analysis makes it possible to identify and determine relevant text in a context (McClelland et al., 2010).

Case study research findings

Stage 1: Are Blomhoff at Betanien in Norway

Are Blomhoff was a priest in the Methodist church in Norway. In addition to theological training, Blomhoff had also received education in business administration. He worked for the Betanien Foundation, which belonged to the Methodist church. The foundation runs nursing homes, kindergartens and other social services. Blomhoff quickly climbed in the ranks at Betanien as he was able to obtain government funding for a number of projects and received international recognition as he collaborated on projects in Israel, Estonia and other places. He was well known and well respected in many religious institutions (Ellingsen, 2015; Johnsen, 2013).

The Betanien foundation made a decision to establish a nursing home in Spain for elderly from Norway, both because the climate is much more attractive, especially in the winter season, and because the operating costs would be lower in Spain compared to Norway. Blomhoff took on the task of buying a piece of land in Spain and hiring a construction firm to build the nursing home.

Money for the construction project originated at Betanien's bank account in Norway and ended up in Betanien's bank account in Spain. Blomhoff was in charge at both sides, as he initiated transfers of money and confirmed receipt of money. While auditors in Norway thought auditors in Spain would review money transfers, auditors in Spain believed auditors in Norway would review accounts. Nobody else but Blomhoff was involved in financial matters regarding the Spanish project (Riis and Øverland, 2018).

Blomhoff faced an opportunity for white-collar crime in the form of embezzlement. There was an opportunity that simply invited Blomhoff to take advantage of his privileges while in Spain. He knew that it was wrong and that it was bad, but the opportunity was so attractive that violating the law became an obvious choice for him as an offender.

At first, he embezzled some money as he bought himself a private apartment in Spain, where the embezzled money helped finance his apartment. Next, he arranged parties that looked more and more like orgies, where he recruited prostitutes to participate. He developed a drinking problem, but stayed at work (Buanes, 2015).

When he returned to Norway on business trips, he was sober and behaved like a priest, executive and family man. He developed two different kinds of lifestyle, one for Norway and another one for Spain.

Two employees at Betanien observed Blomhoff's wrongdoing and wanted to blow the whistle on him. They got in touch with the chairperson at the foundation, Christian Hysing-Dahl, but he would simply not believe them. When the whistleblowers threatened to tell investigative journalists in a major Norwegian newspaper (Gustafsson, 2015), Hysing-Dahl hired auditing firm BDO (2014) to conduct a fraud examination. At the same time, Hysing-Dahl confronted Blomhoff with the allegations, and Blomhoff confessed a minor amount that he had embezzled (Johansen, 2015; Riis and Øverland, 2018). As fraud examiners from BDO (2014) detected larger amounts, then Blomhoff confessed those as well. In 2015, Blomhoff received a sentence in a Norwegian district court of three years in prison for embezzlement (Drammen tingrett, 2015). Two months later, Hysing-Dahl resigned from the chair of the board together with most of the other board members (Johansen, 2015; Nakling, 2015).

Stage 2: Tsuyhoshi Kikukawa at Olympus in Japan

Tsuyhoshi Kikukawa was the chief executive officer and then the chairperson of the board at Olympus Corporation in Japan. He had a strong motive to avoid threats for the business as well as to achieve recognition as one of the most successful business people in Japan. He received in the end the blame as the main architect of the fraud scheme at Olympus from fraud examiners at Deloitte (2011). For Kikukawa, the threat of decline or even collapse in the stock market valuation of Olympus was unacceptable, while all measures of avoidance were acceptable.

Kikukawa introduced the tobashi scheme, where losses seem to disappear by shifting losses between portfolios. Received funds did end up on Olympus' consolidated financial statements. A tobashi scheme is a financial fraud through accounting manipulation where the corporation's losses apparently disappear by shifting them between external portfolios. The loss separation scheme to dispose of unrealized losses on financial assets made it look like Olympus had substantial financial claims (Inagati, 2015; Nakamoto, 2011).

Kikukawa had been the CEO before Michael Woodford took on the position. Shortly after taking on the position, Woodford blew the whistle on fraud (Neate, 2012): "Former Olympus chief executive tells of the risks he ran in exposing fraud scandal at the digital camera company". Kikukawa thus resigned in 2011, and he was in 2013 sentenced to three years in jail.

British newspaper The Guardian interviewed former Olympus chief executive Michael Woodford as the man who blew the whistle on a fraud of one billion pounds (Neate, 2012):

> He first got wind of the claims just weeks after taking over as chief executive – the first foreigner, or *gaijin*, to run the company, and only the fourth at any major Japanese company – when a friend emailed him a

translation of "amazingly detailed" claims published in Facta, a local magazine with a campaigning remit similar to Private Eye. "When I got to the office I expected everyone to be talking about it. But no one mentioned it". By lunchtime he summoned two of his most trusted colleagues and asked them if they had read it. They had, but said that Tsuyoshi Kikukawa, Olympus's previous CEO and then chairman, had "told them not to tell me". Eventually Woodford demanded a meeting with Kikukawa and Hisashi Mori, then deputy president and "Kikukawa's permanent sidekick".

Kikukawa ousted Woodford and denied any wrongdoing. The initial corporate account was that they denied telling any details, and only generally admitting to weak corporate governance (Nakamoto, 2011). A similar response occurred some years later at Toshiba Corporation where irregularities "had come to light" and "the company declined to provide further details" (Inagati, 2015).

Stage 3: Thomas Middelhoff at Alstrom in Germany

Thomas Middelhoff was on the board of directors of Bertelsmann from 1990 to 2002, being the chief executive officer (CEO) from 1998. From 2004 to 2009, Middelhoff was chair on the supervisory board of retailer Arcandor (previously KarstadQuelle AG) and CEO of the company (Weidermann, 2017). In 2014, Middelhoff received a conviction on charges of fraud related to his activities while head of Arcandor, and the court passed a sentence of three years in jail. The criminal court in Essen found him guilty of misusing corporate funds at the Arcandor, which had collapsed in 2009 a few months after he left as chief executive.

When Middelhoff received the verdict, he was surprised and said that; "I thought certain rules did not apply to me" (Storbeck, 2018: 12). This is in line with the crime justification perspective, where elite members believe that they are simply too big to fail and too powerful to jail, since laws are not for the elite to follow.

The court in Germany found Middelhoff guilty of embezzlement and related tax fraud (Storbeck, 2018: 12):

> One offense was making Arcandor pay the bulk of a costly birthday present for a longtime mentor. The other was to expense 27 private flights, among them helicopter lifts between his home and Arcandor's headquarters 150 kilometers away, to avoid the notorious traffic jams on the motorway. The financial damage stands at about Euro 500 000.

Middelhoff (2017: 227) justifies his actions for which he received a prison sentence, as in his opinion the verdict was only about a publication, a symposium and an anniversary:

> Das Urteil: Eine Festschrift, ein Symposium und ein prominenter Jubilar.

While justifying his actions, he also illustrates his convenient opportunities to do whatever he liked. In the case of a publication, he suggests in his autobiography that he informed some board members who "happened to be present" when he told them. He was thus able to spend company money – in a company that soon after was to file for bankruptcy – on a private idea of a publication and party for a friend.

He justifies his private plane trips by citing bomb threats in regular passenger planes. However, nobody had approved his excessive travel expenses. He hired charter airplanes for himself at the expense of the company. He argued that it was not out of convenience, but for timesaving, flexibility and for security reasons he chartered planes (Middelhoff, 2017: 232):

> Nicht aus Bequemlichkeit, sondern aus Zeitoptimierungs-, Flexibilitäts- und eben auch aus Sicherheitsgründen.

Middelhoff was very well connected and met with the chancellor in Germany. He writes in his book about an incident of personal conversation with the then federal chancellor Gerhard Schröder, in which he had informed the chancellor in his capacity as chair of the supervisory board at KarstadtQuelle about the crisis and its causes (Middelhoff, 2017: 231):

> nach einem persönlichen Gespräch mit dem damaligen Bundeskanzler Gerhard Schröder, in welchem ich ihn in meiner Funktion als Aufsichtsratsvorsitzender über die Krise bei KarstadtQuelle, ihre Ursachen und das Sanierungskonzept informiert hatte.

Thomas Middelhoff was convinced he had done nothing wrong. He starts his autobiography by telling about the morning where he was to testify in the court of appeals, when family, friends and travelers for days had been firmly convinced of a positive verdict, including himself (Middelhoff, 2017: 11):

> Familie, Freunde und Weggefährte sind seit Tagen fest von einem positiven Urteilsspruch überzeugt. Auch ich glaube das.

He was so convinced of acquittal, that he had already invited friends and family to a celebration the same evening in his house (Middelhoff, 2017: 12):

> Dann soll der Freispruch gefeiert werden, so haben wir es geplant.

Stage 4: Boris Benulic at Kraft & Kultur in Sweden

Boris Benulic was the chief executive officer (CEO) at energy company Kraft & Kultur in Sweden, which was a subsidiary of the Norwegian energy corporation Troms Kraft (Nergaard, 2013). It seems that Benulic made the choice of crime based on a perception of benefits exceeding costs as rational, and it seems that behavioral reinforcement of deviance took place over time. His salary increased substantially over time, as board members believed they observed growth in sales and profits, especially growth in financial contributions to the group and parent company, and the board paid him bonuses for seemingly successful entrepreneurship (Benulic, 2018).

Troms Kraft hired fraud examiners from global auditing firm Ernst & Young (2012) to conduct an internal investigation at Kraft & Kultur. They were surprised to find a series of emails from Benulic instructing accountants to manipulate figures in such ways that the bottom lines in terms of profits would result in predetermined numbers. For example, in an email dated June 5, 2008, Benulic wrote that the electricity income had to be set in such a way that the income from electricity would result in a sum that made the firm complete at 16,1 million Swedish kroner in profits after tax (Ernst & Young, 2012: 10):

> Elintäkterna – ta en summa där som gör at vi landar på 16,1 MSEK i resultat etter skatt.

In 2018, the Supreme Court in Sweden upheld the final verdict of three and a half years in prison for Boris Benulic for accounting fraud (Mo, 2018).

Stage 5: Jordan Belfort at Stratton Oakmont in the United States

Jordan Belfort founded Stratton Oakmont brokerage firm in 1989 in the United States. Belfort (2008: 270) suggests in his autobiography entitled "The Wolf of Wall Street" that "money makes people do strange things". Jordan Belfort admits all kinds of wrongdoings, and explains his illegal actions with self-irony. He denies no guilt, and he justifies or excuses no actions. It is a fascinating and frightening book that later became a major motion picture. Belfort admits being the offender through all the deviant behaviors described in his book. For example, Belfort (2008: 151) admits having involved family members in money laundering from the United States to a Swiss bank in Europe:

> Plausible deniability was obviously an international obsession among white-collar criminals. . . . "But to answer your question, I'm planning to use a family member with a different last name than mine. She's from my wife's side, and she's not even a U.S. citizen, she's British. I'm flying to London tomorrow morning, and I can have her back here the day after tomorrow – passport in hand – ready to open an account at your bank".

Jordan Belfort is a very different autobiographer who does not apply neutralization techniques at all. Belfort seems proud of all the eccentric endeavors he undertook both privately and as the founder and CEO of the brokerage firm Stratton Oakmont. He had a strategy of committing crime whenever it was convenient. He adapted his firm to profitable criminal market forces and found it quite natural, obvious and attractive. He explored possibilities for illegitimate individual as well as corporate gain. In addition to greed and the American dream, Belfort was also out for adventure. He was sensation seeking to experience adventure by being on the wrong side of the law. He made his employees join and enjoy new, intense, and sensational introductions of firms to the stock exchange by defrauding stockowners.

At Stratton Oakmont, they all attempted to avoid boredom by replacing repetitive activities such as regular meetings with thrill and adventures. They searched risky and exciting activities and had distaste for monotonous situations (Patsiaouras and Fitchett, 2011: 217):

> The feelings of monotony, repetition of tasks and long working hours are neutralized and counteracted by the extravagant purchase and display of status symbols, in order to enhance owner's social position, and also through unlimited resources to pleasures offered by the services of prostitutes. Throughout his book, Belfort highlights how his insatiable sexual appetite has been satisfied through paid sex with numerous "high class" hookers.

The court convicted Belfort to prison because he had defrauded more than 1000 clients. He spent two years in prison.

In conclusion, the concept of stage models serves the purpose of distinguishing white-collar crime cases as well as illustrating escalation in seriousness over time. The stage model in this chapter suggests that it is much more serious with crime as a strategy at level five compared to crime as an opportunity at level one. Crime as an opportunity is avoidable when the opportunity structure declines. Crime as a strategy, on the other hand, is a choice where nobody might interfere before eventually evidence of crime ends up in front of the courts. This exploratory conceptualization to classify white-collar offenders into categories of crime seriousness might serve as a starting point for other researchers as well as for law enforcement in developing new insights into the phenomenon of elite financial crime.

References

Adler, P.S. and Kwon, S.W. (2002). Social capital: Prospects for a new concept, *Academy of Management Review*, 27 (1), 17–40.

Agnew, R. (2014). Social concern and crime: Moving beyond the assumption of simple self-interest, *Criminology*, 52 (1), 1–32.

Baird, J.E. and Zelin, R.C. (2009). An examination of the impact of obedience pressure on perceptions of fraudulent acts and the likelihood of committing occupational fraud, *Journal of Forensic Studies in Accounting and Business*, 1 (1), 1–14.

BDO (2014). *Gransking av Stiftelsen Betanien i Bergen (Examination of the Foundation Betanien in Bergen) – Anonymisert og revidert sammendrag (Anonymised and Revised Summary)*, auditing firm BDO, Oslo, Norway.

Belfort, J. (2008). *The Wolf of Wall Street: How Money Destroyed a Wall Street Superman*, London, UK: Hodder & Stoughton.

Bell, E., Bryman, A. and Harley, B. (2018). *Business Research Methods*, 2nd edition, New York: Oxford University Press.

Benartzi, S., Beshears, J., Milkman, K.L., Sunstein, C.R., Thaler, R.H., Shankar, M., Tucker-Ray, W., Congdon, W.J. and Galing, S. (2017). Should governments invest more in nudging? *Psychological Science*, 28 (8), 1041–1055.

Benson, M.L. and Simpson, S.S. (2018). *White-Collar Crime: An Opportunity Perspective*, 3rd edition, New York, NY: Routledge.

Benulic, B. (2018). *Inte mitt krig (Not My War)*, Sweden: Cultura Aetatis Publishing.

Bernburg, J.G., Krohn, M.D. and Rivera, C.J. (2006). Official labeling, criminal embeddedness, and subsequent delinquency, *Journal of Research in Crime and Delinquency*, 43 (1), 67–88.

Blickle, G., Schlegel, A., Fassbender, P. and Klein, U. (2006). Some personality correlates of business white-collar crime, *Applied Psychology: An International Review*, 55 (2), 220–233.

Bosse, D.A. and Phillips, R.A. (2016). Agency theory and bounded self-interest, *Academy of Management Review*, 41 (2), 276–297.

Buanes, F. (2015). Aktor krever fire års fengsel for tidligere Stavanger-pastor (The prosecutor requires four years in prison for previous Stavanger pastor), daily Norwegian newspaper *Stavanger Aftenblad*, www.aftenbladet.no, published January 27.

Bussmann, K.D., Niemeczek, A. and Vockrodt, M. (2018). Company culture and prevention of corruption in Germany, China and Russia, *European Journal of Criminology*, 15 (3), 255–277.

Chang, J.J., Lu, H.C. and Chen, M. (2005). Organized crime or individual crime? Endogeneous size of a criminal organization and the optimal law enforcement, *Economic Inquiry*, 43 (3), 661–675.

Chatterjee, A. and Pollock, T.G. (2017). Master of puppets: How narcissistic CEOs construct their professional worlds, *Academy of Management Review*, 42 (4), 703–725.

Cohen, L.E. and Felson, M. (1979). Social change and crime rate trends: A routine activity approach, *American Sociological Review*, 44, 588–608.

Comey, J.B. (2009). Go directly to prison: White collar sentencing after the Sarbanes-Oxley act, *Harvard Law Review*, 122, 1728–1749.

Craig, J.M. and Piquero, N.L. (2017). Sensational offending: An application of sensation seeking to white-collar and conventional crimes, *Crime & Delinquency*, 63 (11), 1363–1382.

Crosina, E. and Pratt, M.G. (2019). Toward a model of organizational mourning: The case of former Lehman Brothers bankers, *Academy of Management Journal*, 62 (1), 66–98.

Deloitte (2011). *Investigation Report. Olympus Corporation. Third Party Committee.* Kainaka, T., Nakagome, H., Arita, T., Sudo, O., Katayama, E. and Takiguchi, K., www.olympus-global.com/en/common/pdf/if111206corpe_2.pdf, published December 6, retrieved September 10, 2018.

Drammen tingrett (2015). Dom avsagt 02.02.2015 i Drammen tingrett med saksnummer 15–002674ENE-DRAM (Sentence announced on February 2, 2015 in Drammen district court with case number 15-002674ENE-DRAM), *Drammen tingrett (Drammen District Court)*, Drammen, Norway.

Duriau, V.J., Reger, R.K. and Pfarrer, M.D. (2007). A content analysis of the content analysis literature in organization studies: Research themes, data sources, and methodological refinements, *Organizational Research Methods*, 10 (1), 5–34.

Eberly, M.B., Holley, E.C., Johnson, M.D. and Mitchell, T.R. (2011). Beyond internal and external: A dyadic theory of relational attributions, *Academy of Management Review*, 36 (4), 731–753.

Ellingsen, K.A. (2015). *Gud med oss (God with us): Tilsynsmennenes rapport til årskonferansen I Halden 2015 (Trustee Report to the Annual Conference in Halden)*, Metodistkirken i Norge (The Methodist Church in Norway), www.metodistkirken. no, published June 16.

Engdahl, O. (2015). White-collar crime and first-time adult-onset offending: Explorations in the concept of negative life events as turning points, *International Journal of Law, Crime and Justice*, 43 (1), 1–16.

Ernst & Young (2012). *Troms Kraft AS – Gransking av Kraft & Kultur i Sverige AB (Troms Kraft Inc. – Investigation of Kraft & Kultur in Sweden Inc.)*, global auditing firm Ernst & Young, Norway.

Farquhar, J.D. and Rowley, J. (2009). Convenience: A services perspective, *Marketing Theory*, 9 (4), 425–438.

Ferraro, F., Pfeffer, J. and Sutton, R.I. (2005). Economics language and assumptions: How theories can become self-fulfilling, *Academy of Management Review*, 30 (1), 8–24.

Galvin, B.M., Lange, D. and Ashforth, B.E. (2015). Narcissistic organizational identification: Seeing oneself as central to the organization's identity, *Academy of Management Review*, 40 (2), 163–181.

Gamache, D.L. and McNamara, G. (2019). Responding to bad press: How CEO temporal focus influences the sensitivity to negative media coverage of acquisitions, *Academy of Management Journal*, 62 (3), 918–943.

Gao, P. and Zhang, G. (2019). Accounting manipulation, peer pressure, and internal control, *The Accounting Review*, 94 (1), 127–151.

Goldstraw-White, J. (2012). *White-Collar Crime: Accounts of Offending Behavior*, London, UK: Palgrave Macmillan.

Goncharov, I. and Peter, C.D. (2019). Does reporting transparency affect industry coordination? Evidence from the duration of international cartels, *The Accounting Review*, 94 (3), 149–175.

Gottfredson, M.R. and Hirschi, T. (1990). *A General Theory of Crime*, Stanford, CA: Stanford University Press.

Gottschalk, P. and Dean, G. (2010). Stages of knowledge management systems in policing financial crime, *International Journal of Law, Crime and Justice*, 38 (3), 94–108.

Gottschalk, P. and Markovic, V. (2016). Transnational criminal organizations (TCOs): The case of combating criminal biker gangs, *International Journal of Criminal Justice Sciences*, 11 (1), 30–44.

Gustafsson, K. (2015). Tviler på at styret ikke visste (Doubts that the board did not know), Norwegian web newspaper *Dagen*, www.dagen.no, published March 17.

Higgins, E.T. (1997). Beyond pleasure and pain, *American Psychologist*, 52, 1280–1300.

Hoffmann, J.P. (2002). A contextual analysis of differential association, social control, and strain theories of delinquency, *Social Forces*, 81 (3), 753–785.

Huang, L. and Knight, A.P. (2017). Resources and relationships in entrepreneurship: An exchange theory of the development and effects of the entrepreneur-investor relationship, *Academy of Management Review*, 42 (1), 80–102.

Inagati, K. (2015). Toshiba scraps dividend after finding accounting irregularities, *Financial Times*, May 8, https://infoweb.newsbank.com/apps/news/document-view?p=AWNB&t=&sort=YMD_date%3AD&page=43&maxresults=20&f=advanc

ed&val-base-0=toshiba&fld-base-0=alltext&bln-base-1=and&val-base-1=account-ing%20scandal&fld-base-1=alltext&bln-base-2=and&val-base-2=2015&fld-base-2=YMD_date&docref=news/1553B56CCE48DC40, retrieved November 3, 2018.

Johansen, L. (2015). Hele styret trekker seg etter pastor-skandalen (The whole board resigns after pastor scandal), daily Norwegian newspaper *VG*, www.vg.no, published April 14.

Johnsen, L. (2013). Drammensprest siktet for underslag av nesten 15 millioner (Drammen priest charged for embezzlement of nearly 15 million), daily Norwegian newspaper *Drammens Tidende*, www.dt.no, published November 21.

Jonnergård, K., Stafsudd, A. and Elg, U. (2010). Performance evaluations as gender barriers in professional organizations: A study of auditing firms, *Gender, Work and Organization*, 17 (6), 721–747.

Karim, K.E. and Siegel, P.H. (1998). A signal detection theory approach to analyzing the efficiency and effectiveness of auditing to detect management fraud, *Managerial Auditing Journal*, 13 (6), 367–375.

Keil, M., Tiwana, A., Sainsbury, R. and Sneha, S. (2010). Toward a theory of whistle-blowing intentions: A benefit-cost differential perspective, *Decision Sciences*, 41 (4), 787–812.

Krippendorff, K. (1980). *Content Analysis: An Introduction to its Methodology*, Beverly Hills, CA: Sage.

Langton, L. and Piquero, N.L. (2007). Can general strain theory explain white-collar crime? A preliminary investigation of the relationship between strain and select white-collar offenses, *Journal of Criminal Justice*, 35 (1), 1–15.

Lehman, D.W., Cooil, B. and Ramanujam, R. (2019). The effects of rule complexity on organizational noncompliance and remediation: Evidence from restaurant health inspections, *Journal of Management*, published online, pages 1–33, https://doi.org/10.1177/0149206319842262.

Leigh, A.C., Foote, D.A., Clark, W.R. and Lewis, J.L. (2010). Equity sensitivity: A triadic measure and outcome/input perspectives, *Journal of Managerial Issues*, 22 (3), 286–305.

Leonard, W.N. and Weber, M.G. (1970). Automakers and dealers: A study of crimi-nogenic market forces, *Law & Society Review*, 4 (3), 407–424.

Mai, H.T.X. and Olsen, S.O. (2016). Consumer participation in self-production: The role of control mechanisms, convenience orientation, and moral obligation, *Journal of Marketing Theory and Practice*, 24 (2), 209–223.

Maslow, A.H. (1943). A theory of human motivation, *Psychological Review*, 50 (4), 370–396.

Mawritz, M.B., Greenbaum, R.L., Butts, M.M. and Graham, K.A. (2017). I just can't control myself: A self-regulation perspective on the abuse of deviant employees, *Academy of Management Journal*, 60 (4), 1482–1503.

McClelland, P.L., Liang, X. and Barker, V.L. (2010). CEO commitment to the status quo: Replication and extension using content analysis, *Journal of Management*, 36 (5), 1251–1277.

Middelhoff, T. (2017). *Der Sturz: Die Autobiografie von Thomas Middelhoff (The Fall: The Autobiography of Thomas Middelhoff)*, Stuttgart, Germany: LangenMuller in der F.A. Herbig Verlagsbuchhandlung.

Mingus, W. and Burchfield, K.B. (2012). From prison to integration: Applying modi-fied labeling theory to sex offenders, *Criminal Justice Studies*, 25 (1), 97–109.

Mo, M.L. (2018). Nå må Boris Benulic sone i fengsel (Now Boris Benulic must be jailed), online newspaper *iTromsø*, www.itromso.no, published May 8.

Nakamoto, M. (2011). Olympus turns focus on Japan's governance, *Financial Times*, November 8, https://infoweb.newsbank.com/apps/news/document-view?p=AWNB&t=&sort=YMD_date%3AD&maxresults=20&f=advanced&val-base-0=tobashi&fld-base-0=alltext&bln-base-1=and&val-base-1=olympus&fld-base-1=alltext&bln-base-2=and&val-base-2=fraud&fld-base-2=alltext&bln-base-3=and&val-base-3=2011&fld-base-3=YMD_date&docref=news/13AE854CE15B17D0, retrieved October 31, 2018.

Nakling, A. (2015). Lærdomen frå Betanien (Lessons learned from Betanien), daily Norwegian newspaper *Bergens Tidende*, www.bt.no, published March 20.

Naylor, R.T. (2003). Towards a general theory of profit-driven crimes, *British Journal of Criminology*, 43, 81–101.

Neate, R. (2012). Michael Woodford: The man who blew whistle on £1bn fraud, *The Guardian*, www.theguardian.com, published November 23, retrieved July 2, 2019.

Nergaard, L.L. (2013). *Sammendrag av granskingsrapport – Troms Kraft AS (Summary of Investigation Report – Troms Kraft Inc.)*, Norscan Partners, Norway.

Nichol, J.E. (2019). The effects of contract framing on misconduct and entitlement, *The Accounting Review*, 94 (3), 329–344.

Nielsen, R.P. (2003). Corruption networks and implications for ethical corruption reform, *Journal of Business Ethics*, 42 (2), 125–149.

Obodaru, O. (2017). Forgone, but not forgotten: Toward a theory of forgone professional identities, *Academy of Management Journal*, 60 (2), 523–553.

Olafsen, A.H., Niemiec, C.P., Halvari, H., Deci, E.L. and Williams, G.C. (2017). On the dark side of work: A longitudinal analysis using self-determination theory, *European Journal of Work and Organizational Psychology*, 26 (2), 275–285.

Patel, P.C. and Cooper, D. (2014). Structural power equality between family and nonfamily TMT members and the performance of family firms, *Academy of Management Journal*, 57 (6), 1624–1649.

Patrucco, A.S., Luzzini, D. and Ronchi, S. (2017). Research perspectives on public procurement: Content analysis of 14 years of publications in the Journal of Public Procurement, *Journal of Public Procurement*, 16 (2), 229–269.

Patsiaouras, G. and Fitchett, G. (2011). The wolf of Wall Street: Re-imagining Veblen for the 21st century, *Advances in Consumer Research – European Conference Proceedings*, 9, 214–218.

Petrocelli, M., Piquero, A.R. and Smith, M.R. (2003). Conflict theory and racial profiling: An empirical analysis of police traffic stop data, *Journal of Criminal Justice*, 31 (1), 1–11.

Piquero, N.L. (2012). The only thing we have to fear is fear itself: Investigating the relationship between fear of falling and white-collar crime, *Crime and Delinquency*, 58 (3), 362–379.

Pontell, H.N., Black, W.K. and Geis, G. (2014). Too big to fail, too powerful to jail? On the absence of criminal prosecutions after the 2008 financial meltdown, *Crime, Law and Social Change*, 61 (1), 1–13.

Pratt, T.C. and Cullen, F.T. (2005). Assessing macro-level predictors and theories of crime: A meta-analysis, *Crime and Justice*, 32, 373–450.

Ramoglou, S. and Tsang, E.W.K. (2016). A realist perspective of entrepreneurship: Opportunities as propensities, *Academy of Management Review*, 41, 410–434.

Riis, C. and Øverland, K.J. (2018). *Økonomisk kriminalitet i religiøse miljøer: Hva er spesielle kjennetegn ved mulighet, motiv og villighet når økonomisk kriminalitet begås av hvitsnipper i religiøse miljøer? (Economic Crime in Religious Environments: What Are Special Characteristics of Opportunity, Motive and Willingness When Economic Crime is Committed by White-Collars in Religious Environments?)*, Master thesis, BI Norwegian Business School, Oslo, Norway.

Rodriguez, P., Uhlenbruck, K. and Eden, L. (2005). Government corruption and the entry strategies of multinationals, *Academy of Management Review*, 30 (2), 383–396.

Röglinger, M., Pöppelbuss, J. and Becker, J. (2012). Maturity model in business process management, *Business Process Management Journal*, 18 (2), 328–346.

Sampson, R.J. and Laub, J.H. (1993). *Crime in the Making: Pathways and Turning Points Through Life*, Cambridge, MA: Harvard University Press.

Saunders, M., Lewis, P. and Thornhill, A. (2007). *Research Methods for Business Students*, 5th edition, London, UK: Pearson Education.

Schnatterly, K., Gangloff, K.A. and Tuschke, A. (2018). CEO wrongdoing: A review of pressure, opportunity, and rationalization, *Journal of Management*, 44 (6), 2405–2432.

Schoepfer, A. and Piquero, N.L. (2006). Exploring white-collar crime and the American dream: A partial test of institutional anomie theory, *Journal of Criminal Justice*, 34 (3), 227–235.

Solli-Sæther, H. and Gottschalk, P. (2015). Stages-of-growth in outsourcing, offshoring and backsourcing: Back to the future? *Journal of Computer Information Systems*, 55 (2), 88–94.

Storbeck, O. (2018). Lunch with the FT Thomas Middelhoff: 'I thought certain rules did not apply to me', *Financial Times*, Sunday, May 13, 12–13.

Sutherland, E.H. (1983). *White Collar Crime: The Uncut Version*, New Haven, CT: Yale University Press.

Sykes, G. and Matza, D. (1957). Techniques of neutralization: A theory of delinquency, *American Sociological Review*, 22 (6), 664–670.

Victor, B. and Cullen, J.B. (1988). The organizational bases of ethical work climates, *Administrative Science Quarterly*, 33, 101–125.

Weick, K.E. (1995). *Sensemaking in Organizations*, Sage, CA: Thousand Oaks.

Weidermann, V. (2017). Wie Thomas Middelhoff sein Leben umdichtet (How Thomas Middelhoff rewrote his life), German magazine *Der Spiegel*, Ausgabe 37, www.spiegel.de.

Welsh, D.T. and Ordonez, L.D. (2014). The dark side of consecutive high performance goals: Linking goal setting, depletion, and unethical behavior, *Organizational Behavior and Human Decision Processes*, 123, 79–89.

Welsh, D.T., Ordonez, L.D., Snyder, D.G. and Christian, M.S. (2014). The slippery slope: How small ethical transgressions pave the way for larger future transgressions, *Journal of Applied Psychology*, 100 (1), 114–127.

Wikstrom, P.O.H., Mann, R.P. and Hardie, B. (2018). Young people's differential vulnerability to criminogenic exposure: Bridging the gap between people- and place-oriented approaches in the study of crime causation, *European Journal of Criminology*, 15 (1), 10–31.

Yam, K.C., Christian, M.S., Wei, W., Liao, Z. and Nai, J. (2018). The mixed blessing of leader sense of humor: Examining costs and benefits, *Academy of Management Journal*, 61 (1), 348–369.

Zvi, L. and Elaad, E. (2018). Correlates of narcissism, self-reported lies, and self-assessed abilities to tell and detect lies, tell truths, and believe others, *Journal of Investigative Psychology and Offender Profiling*, 15, 271–286.

12 Crisis-response dynamics

Corporations sometimes hire fraud examiners from local law firms and global auditing firms when financial crime scandals emerge. Fraud examination reports tend to remain confidential at client organizations. We were able to find and retrieve 12 reports from Denmark, Japan, New Zealand, Norway, Sweden, and the United States. We compare fraud examiners' accounts of potential misconduct and crime with initial corporate statements and determine the extent of match or mismatch over time in terms of denial, justification, excuse, apology or other responses. Based on exploratory research into the crisis-response match, we find that 7 out of 12 responses were outside the match zone.

This chapter is concerned with corporate scandals that threaten corporate social approval, legitimacy, reputation, and even survival (Greer and McLaughlin, 2017; Fisse and Braithwaite, 1988; Goldstraw-White, 2012; Piazza and Jourdan, 2018). For example, cartels (Goncharov and Peter, 2019), tax evasion (Balakrishnan et al., 2019; Dyreng et al., 2019; Guenther et al., 2019), misleading disclosure to investors (Jennings, 2019), or other forms of misrepresentation in accounting (Qiu and Slezak, 2019) can cause financial crime scandals. There was obviously a lack of corporate social responsibility (Davidson et al., 2019), and scandals are often revealed after whistleblowing (Gao et al., 2015; Gao and Zhang, 2019).

In attempting to respond to and manage scandals, corporations and their executives develop and publicize explanations (Bundy and Pfarrer, 2015; Scott and Lyman, 1968; Whyte, 2016) as corporate accounts (Albrecht, 1996; Hearit, 2006), since media coverage is critical in shaping stakeholder opinions (Gamache and McNamara, 2019). We address the following research question: What is the extent of crisis-response match following corporate white-collar crime scandals?

This chapter starts by reviewing response strategies after scandals as suggested by Bundy and Pfarrer (2015). It is to be expected that corporate accounts evolve over time as more information about the event come to light and as the corporation assesses external reactions. Furthermore, Bao et al. (2019) found that managers withhold bad news in general. A key part of the evolution of corporate accounts seems to be the divergence of interests between the corporate entity and individual corporate leaders (Bandura, 1999; Schoultz and Flyghed, 2016; Schnatterly et al., 2018).

We apply the framework developed by Bundy and Pfarrer (2015) to our 12 cases and suggest how their theoretical framework can be explored empirically to analyze patterns in the development and consequences that follow actual corporate scandals.

Scandal response strategies

An account is a statement made by an actor to explain unanticipated or untoward behavior that is subject to some sort of evaluative inquiry by other actors (Scott and Lyman, 1968). An account can take the form of a justification, excuse, or apology or some other explanatory perspective (Goffman, 1971). Techniques of neutralization influence accounts. Examples include the denial of responsibility technique, the appeal to higher loyalties technique, as well as the claim of rule complexity technique (Benson, 1985; Lehman et al., 2019; Maruna and Copes, 2005; Schoultz and Flyghed, 2019; Sykes and Matza, 1957). Corporations have social and economic power to survive harmful consequences that follow the exposure of wrongdoing (Cohen, 2001).

Bundy and Pfarrer (2015: 347) define social approval as "perception of general affinity toward an organization", legitimacy as "assessment of an organization's appropriateness", and reputation as "assessment of an organization's ability to deliver value". Bundy and Pfarrer (2015) suggest that a response strategy should accept crisis responsibility to the extent expected from the environment to avoid a crisis-response mismatch.

Response strategies range on a continuum from defensive to accommodative (Bundy and Pfarrer, 2015). A defensive response strategy attempts to avoid social approval loss by eliminating an organization's suggested association with a crisis. Examples range from outright denial of responsibility, via attacking accusers and shifting blame onto other entities, to presenting the organization as a victim of an incident. In contrast, an accommodative response strategy attempts to manage social approval loss by acknowledging an organization's role in a crisis and hoping that appearing to be honest and contrite will reduce external negative perceptions of the company. Thus, Bundy's and Pfarrer's (2015) accommodative strategy is what the theory of accounts would call an apology. Examples range from outright acceptance of responsibility to the communication of regrets and apologies. None of the cases examined here initially used an entirely accommodative response strategy. Rather, at first the companies attempted to reframe how external observers judged a crisis, while the companies neither completely accepted nor denied responsibility.

All crises are uncertain events that generate initial negative reactions. Bundy and Pfarrer (2005: 352) argue that an effective response strategy matches external observers' situational attributions of the crisis to prevent cognitive dissonance among observers:

> A crisis with higher situational attributions of responsibility should be matched with a response strategy that accepts more responsibility, and a

crisis with lower situational attributions of responsibility should be matched with a response strategy that accepts less responsibility. . . . An organization that is underconforming by being defensive in response to a crisis with higher situational attributions risks being perceived as unethical and manipulative.

Thus, as argued by Bundy and Pfarrer (2015: 363), "in the latter stages of a crisis, a truly misleading defensive strategy may offer few benefits". When we compare corporations' initial reactions to exposure of wrongdoings, we have to keep in mind that much more information might be available at later stages. Uniformed individuals deliver their initial accounts with their own reputational interests in mind. What is later contained in internal reports of investigations that are commissioned by corporate leaders normally has a much more solid information base compared to the onset of a crisis. The interests of the organization may have diverged from those of the individuals who first responded to the crisis. Complete knowledge of responsibility is rare at the onset of a crisis, and it may take a long time before an organization and stakeholders agree on the facts. In the beginning, there are mainly rumors, allegations, and perceptions of what happened, how it happened, who did what to make it happen or not happen, and why it happened. Uncertainty decreases over time and consequently the space for making sense of events is reduced (Bundy and Pfarrer, 2015: 364): "An organization therefore may switch its response strategy based on new information and feedback from evaluators".

A later corporate account that is significantly different from an early account – sometimes leading to dismissal of executives and board directors (Ghannam et al., 2019) – is not necessarily a result of manipulation or other unethical communication strategies. It might as well be the case that new information gave reason to communicate an updated corporate account. The release of authoritative information that conflicts with an organization's initial response can trigger a switch in a corporate account (Bundy and Pfarrer, 2015: 364): "Because such information is difficult to contest, it is likely that any organization would alter its message to be consistent with the message evaluators will perceive as more credible".

Nevertheless, an organization may face extreme reactions to its switching response strategies, especially when a switch comes as a major surprise. A non-consistent response throughout a scandal can itself increase the loss of social approval for the organization. In contrast, consistent corporate accounts throughout the scandal might create trust in the organizational handling of the crisis. Our investigation is designed to determine how the accounts of corporations mired in scandals actually do change over time.

However, as we show in what follows initial accounts sometimes appeared more as obfuscations rather than as denials, justifications, excuses, or apologies. By obfuscation, we mean that the initial public statements neither admit nor deny that anything untoward has happened. Rather, the statement vaguely suggests that something may have happened but nobody knows for sure because details of the event are missing.

Examination reports and news

Our data come from two sources. First, we found reports issued by external examiners who were hired by companies to investigate scandals and document their findings. Private and public organizations sometimes hire investigators from global auditing firms or law firms to investigate suspicions of executive deviance related to white-collar crime suspicions (Brooks and Button, 2011; Button et al., 2007a, 2007b; Button and Gee, 2013; Schneider, 2006; Williams, 2005, 2014). At the end of their inquiry, a report is typically produced and given to the client organization as their property. Unfortunately, most clients keep reports secret (Gottschalk and Tcherni-Buzzeo, 2017). Only a few reports are publicly available, and they are often hard to find. Via Internet searches, we were able to identify and retrieve 20 reports written in English, but 7 of the reports focused on individual wrongdoing and 1 involved a political squabble in a Canadian municipality rather than corporate wrongdoing. Thus, these 8 cases were excluded. The remaining 12 reports focused on corporate scandals and serve as our data source for the final account developed by each corporation:

1　Fuji Xerox in New Zealand investigated by Deloitte (2017) after aggressive sales practices and inappropriate accounting scandal.
2　The national petroleum company in Nigeria (NNPC) investigated by PwC (2015) after missing crude oil revenues to the government scandal.
3　Lehman Brothers in the US investigated by Jenner Block (2010) after bankruptcy scandal.
4　WorldCom in the US investigated by PwC (2003) after bankruptcy scandal.
5　Enron Corporation in the US investigated by Wilmer Cutler Pickering (2003) after bankruptcy scandal.
6　Danske Bank in Denmark investigated by Bruun Hjejle (2018) after money laundering scandal in the Estonian branch.
7　Toshiba Corporation in Japan investigated by Deloitte (2015) after accounting fraud scandal.
8　Olympus Corporation in Japan investigated by Deloitte (2011) after financial instruments scandal.
9　General Motors in the US investigated by Jenner Block (2014) after ignition switch scandal.
10　Telenor in Norway investigated by Deloitte (2016) after corruption scandal at VimpelCom where Telenor was a major shareholder.
11　Nordea Bank in Sweden investigated by Mannheimer Swartling (2016) after bank transaction scandal in tax havens.
12　Wells Fargo's Community Bank investigated by Shearman Sterling (2017) after deviant sales practices scandal.

Our second data source is news stories that appeared in various news outlets when a scandal first came to public attention for the 12 corporations. Initial accounts are important, because stakeholders as well as the public quickly begin to associate a scandal with the organization (Bundy and Pfarrer, 2015). An organization's initial response may be influential because it may anchor first impressions externally. To trace how corporate communications about the scandals change, we started with the first media coverage of the scandal that included any explanation or account of the scandal that a corporate insider delivered. To identify initial accounts we used the online database 'Newsbank' and the function Access World News (AWN), which archives stories from thousands of U.S. and global news sources. The stories form a written history of an event as it occurs (Newsbank, 2018). From the investigative reports, it was possible to identify approximately when reports of the scandal first appeared in the news media.

The analytic method applied in this study is content analysis of initial news reports and final investigation reports. Content analysis is any methodology or procedure that works to identify characteristics within texts in order to make valid inferences (Krippendorff, 1980; Patrucco et al., 2017). The goal of content analysis is to identify and determine relevant text in a context that will permit one to address relevant theoretical questions (Hsieh and Shannon, 2005; McClelland et al., 2010).

Corporate scandal responses

In Table 12.1, we present a condensed version of how the accounts for our 12 cases changed from initial exposure to the final investigative report. For the sake of insight, the cases showing similar initial accounts are grouped together, starting with denial of wrongdoing, followed by obfuscation and denial of responsibility.

Table 12.1 presents in qualitative terms the evolution of the initial corporate accounts to the final investigation accounts. We assume that initial corporate accounts represent a response strategy from the organization in which it is attempting to prevent or limit the loss of social approval, legitimacy, and reputation, while the accounts produced in the final report are intended to terminate speculations and restore or at least begin to restore the loss of public social approval, now that the corporation has a clearer understanding of what happened and how it has been perceived by external evaluators.

To extend our analysis, we build upon the suggestion of Bundy and Pfarrer (2015) that corporate responses to scandals will be most successful in terms of avoiding loss of social approval when the corporations response strategy matches situational attributions of responsibility as illustrated in Figure 12.1.

We attempted to operationalize scales for both corporate initial response strategies and situational attributions based, respectively, on the initial public response from the corporation and then the final investigative report. Corporate response can range from 1 (corporation denies any responsibility for the event) to 5 (corporation acknowledges full and complete responsibility for the event). Situational attribution can range from 1 (the investigative reports concludes that the corporation has no responsibility for the event) to 5 (the report concludes

Table 12.1 Initial accounts and investigation accounts after scandals

#	BUSINESS	INITIAL CORPORATE ACCOUNTS	INVESTIGATION ACCOUNTS
1	New Zealand: Fuji Xerox in New Zealand involved in inappropriate sales and accounting practices.	**Denial of wrongdoing:** "Fuji Xerox New Zealand managing director Gavin Pollard said the company had always been confident there were no grounds for any action, and it was pleased the matter was closed" (Hamish, 2016).	**Admission of wrongdoing and scapegoating:** "In the interviews in this Investigation, a number of interviewees (APO-related people) said the pressure from FX to attain business results (especially to achieve sales) was very intense" (Deloitte, 2017).
2	Nigeria: National petroleum company NNPC in Nigeria withheld transfers of oil revenues to the government.	**Denial of wrongdoing:** "The NNPC claimed that the country's chief banker was ignorant on matters of oil earnings and remittances. It accused Mr. Sanusi of Nigeria's version of the capital sin: Playing politics" (Reporter, 2013).	**Admission but minimization of wrongdoing:** "For the period reviewed, we identified possible errors in the computation of crude oil prices at the NNPC that resulted in a $3.6 million shortfall in incomes to the Federation account" (PwC, 2015).
3	U.S.: Lehman Brothers went bankrupt because of alleged risky management.	**Denial of wrongdoing:** Lehman's shares fell $7.51, or 19%, to $31.75 after Chief Executive Officer Richard Fuld said in a statement that the Federal Reserve's decision to lend to brokers and accept securities as collateral "improves the liquidity picture and, from my perspective, takes the liquidity issue for the entire industry off the table" (Onaran, 2008).	**Denial of wrongdoing and scapegoating:** "The business decisions that brought Lehman to its crisis of confidence may have been in error but were largely within the business judgment rule" (Jenner Block, 2010).
4	U.S.: WorldCom went bankrupt after inappropriate accounting.	**Denial of wrongdoing:** "In a conference call with investors and analysts, Ebbers and other executives sought to dismiss concerns about WorldCom's accounting practices, debt load and cash flow. The CEO also said he will not sell WorldCom shares to pay down his personal debt" (Porretto, 2002).	**Admission of wrongdoing:** "Numerous individuals – most of them in financial and accounting departments, at many levels of the Company and in different locations around the world – became aware in varying degrees of senior management' s misconduct" (PwC, 2003).

(Continued)

Table 12.1 (Continued)

#	BUSINESS	INITIAL CORPORATE ACCOUNTS	INVESTIGATION ACCOUNTS
5	U.S.: Enron Corporation went bankrupt after inappropriate accounting practices.	**Denial of wrongdoing:** "'Absolutely no accounting issue', Lay told analysts, 'no trading issue, no reserve issue, no previously unknown problem issues' are behind the departure. There will be 'no change in the performance or outlook of the company going forward', he added" (Deseret News, 2001).	**Admission of wrongdoing and scapegoating:** "Individually, and collectively, Enron's Management failed to carry out its substantive responsibility for ensuring that the transactions were fair to Enron – which in many cases they were not – and its responsibility for implementing a system of oversight and controls over the transactions" (Wilmer Cutler Pickering, 2003).
6	Denmark: Danske Bank's Estonian branch involved in money laundering scandal.	**Obfuscation of wrongdoing:** "The Danish bank has admitted to 'major deficiencies in control and governance' at its Estonian branch" (Moscow Times, 2017).	**Denial of responsibility and scapegoating**: "With regard to the Non-Resident Portfolio, it has been found that, from 2007 through 2017, a number of former and current employees, both at the Estonian branch and at Group level, did not comply with legal obligations forming part of their employment with the bank. Most of these employees are no longer employed by the bank" (Bruun Hjejle, 2018).
7	Japan: Toshiba Corporation in Japan involved in inappropriate accounting practices.	**Obfuscation of wrongdoing:** "Toshiba withdrew its earnings guidance and scrapped its year-end dividend payout on Friday, saying it had found improper accounting on some of its infrastructure projects" (Inagati, 2015).	**Acceptance of responsibility and scapegoating:** "For some projects, it has been found that certain members of top management were aware of the intentional overstating of apparent current-period profits and the postponement of recording expenses and losses, or the continuation thereof, but did not give instructions to stop or correct them" (Deloitte, 2015).

#	BUSINESS	INITIAL CORPORATE ACCOUNTS	INVESTIGATION ACCOUNTS
8	Japan: Olympus Corporation in Japan involved in inappropriate accounting practices scandal.	**Obfuscation of wrongdoing:** "Olympus' admission that it had covered up losses on securities investments dating back to the 1990s by booking them as acquisition fees of up to $1.4bn between 2006 and 2008 has once again thrown the spotlight on the weak corporate governance of Japanese companies" (Nakamoto, 2011).	**Admission of responsibility:** "Olympus used SG Bond Plus Fund for 'tobashi' of part of the losses it suffered as the result of failures in financial management techniques in the 1990s. To cover up losses to which 'tobashi' had been used, Olympus and OFUK purchased warrants attached to FA and dividend preferred shares in association with the Gyrus acquisition; ultimately Olympus planned to use Funds for back-flow of funds" (Deloitte, 2011).
9	U.S.: General Motors' reluctant to correct ignition switch failure for financial reasons.	**Obfuscation of wrongdoing:** "'All of these crashes occurred off-road and at high speeds, where the probability of serious or fatal injuries was high regardless of air bag deployment', GM spokesman Alan Adler said" (Shepardson and Burden, 2014).	**Admission of responsibility:** "From the outset, the Cobalt ignition switch had significant problems that were known to GM personnel" (Jenner Block, 2014).
10	Norway: Telenor in Norway had ownership in VimpelCom in the Netherlands that was involved in corruption in Uzbekistan.	**Denial of responsibility:** "'We are a minority shareholder in VimpelCom, so it's up to VimpelCom to take responsibility for answering any questions that relate to their operations', Telenor communications head Glenn Mandelid told AFP" (Agence France, 2014).	**Admission of responsibility and scapegoating:** "In due consideration to what is stated above, we are notwithstanding of the opinion that certain employees at Telenor at certain point in time should have handled the 2011 concerns differently. The individuals in question are senior employees of Telenor and with high-ranking leadership positions and/or with professional education and experience" (Deloitte, 2016).

(Continued)

Table 12.1 (Continued)

#	BUSINESS	INITIAL CORPORATE ACCOUNTS	INVESTIGATION ACCOUNTS
11	Sweden: Nordea in Sweden had a subsidiary in Luxembourg revealed by the Panama Papers in backdating documents.	**Denial of responsibility:** "Nordea, the Nordic region's biggest bank, says it doesn't help wealthy customers evade taxes in response to reports linking it to the Panamanian law firm at the center of a media investigation into offshore accounts" (Associated Press, 2016).	**Admission of wrongdoing:** "The investigation has found deficiencies in the procedures regarding renewal of Powers of Attorney (POA). In at least seven cases investigation has shown that backdated documents have been requested or provided during the last six years, which is illegal when it aims at altering the truth" (Mannheimer Swartling, 2016).
12	U.S.: Wells Fargo's Community Bank had inappropriate sales practices.	**Denial of responsibility:** "Wells Fargo has said it fired 5,300 employees for secretly opening unauthorized deposit and credit card accounts – conduct that resulted in $185 million in fines announced Thursday – but the bank isn't providing many details" (Rothacker, 2016).	**Admission of wrongdoing and scapegoating:** "Wells Fargo's decentralized corporate structure gave too much autonomy to the Community Bank's senior leadership, who were unwilling to change the sales model or even recognize it as the root cause of the problem" (Shearman Sterling, 2017).

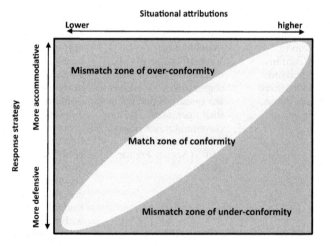

Figure 12.1 The crisis-response match

Source: (adapted from Bundy and Pfarrer, 2015)

that the corporation carries full and complete responsibility for the event). Subtracting the number assigned to the initial corporate response strategy from the number assigned to the final investigative report shows the extent of match for each case in Table 12.2. Zero is the ultimate match, while four is a complete mismatch. The negative number for Lehman Brothers indicates that the initial corporate response was more accommodative than the final report. Lehman Brothers' executives were later studied by Crosina and Pratt (2019) in terms of organizational mourning.

It is important to note that the initial responses listed in Table 12.1 have a general character, while responses here in Table 12.2 are rated specifically in terms of responsibility.

Figure 12.2 illustrates in a graphical manner the data presented in Table 12.2, and suggests that 4 out of the 12 corporate accounts were within the match zone of conformity. The figure suggests that all response strategies were defensive while most situational attributions tended to be more accommodative. The figure illustrates the idea suggested by Bundy and Pfarrer (2015) that an accommodative response

Table 12.2 Results of simple rating of response-attribution match

#	*Business*	*Response*	*Attribution*	*Match*
1	Fuji Xerox Corporation in New Zealand (Deloitte, 2017)	3	4	1
2	Nigerian National Petroleum Corporation in Nigeria (PwC, 2015)	1	2	1
3	Lehman Brothers in the U.S. (Jenner Block, 2010)	3	2	−1
4	WorldCom Corporation in the U.S. (PwC, 2003)	2	5	3
5	Enron Corporation in the U.S. (Wilmer Cutler Pickering, 2003)	1	5	4
6	Danske Bank in Denmark (Bruun Hjejle, 2018)	2	5	3
7	Toshiba Corporation in Japan (Deloitte, 2015)	2	4	2
8	Olympus Corporation in Japan (Deloitte, 2011)	1	4	3
9	General Motors in the U.S. (Jenner Block, 2014)	2	5	3
10	VimpelCom by Telenor in Norway (Deloitte, 2016)	2	3	1
11	Nordea bank in Sweden (Mannheimer Swartling, 2016)	2	4	2
12	Wells Fargo's Community Bank in the U.S. (Shearman Sterling, 2017)	1	4	3

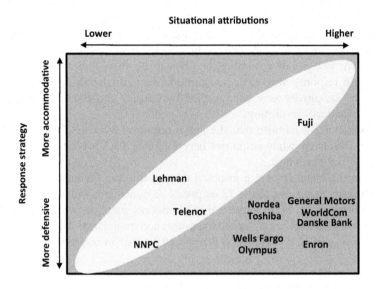

Figure 12.2 The crisis-response match for our sample based on simple rating

strategy as such is of no value. The response strategy has to be adapted to the situational attributions to be successful. Corporate accounts that match external expectations can minimize the loss of social approval, legitimacy, and reputation.

We can expand our empirical study by including the variable of information increase followed by a subsequent uncertainty reduction. As argued by Bundy and Pfarrer (2015), initial corporate accounts occur at the onset of a crisis, where a high level of uncertainty both internally and externally is common. As a crisis evolves and the scandal grows in size, more information will almost always emerge. An organization may therefore switch its response, especially when more credible information becomes available. The report prepared by external investigators hired by the company presents the kind of credible and authoritative information that might conflict with an organization's initial framing of the event. If the investigators have detected information that the organization had no way of knowing, then it is information shortage rather than deception that caused the initial response to be different from examiners' conclusions.

We introduced this information in our analysis by reviewing the investigation reports to determine whether new significant information emerged after the initial exposure of the scandal. Our content analysis here is focused on determining whether the reports use information from sources, such as documents, accounts, and interviews, that was not known to the corporation at first. We introduce the new information variable in Table 12.3. A zero in the column for new information indicates that no significant new information

Table 12.3 Effect of information correction on response-attribution match

#	Business	Scandal response match	New examination information	Revised response match
1	Fuji Xerox Corporation in New Zealand (Deloitte, 2017)	1	0	1
2	Nigerian National Petroleum Corporation in Nigeria (PwC, 2015)	1	1	0
3	Lehman Brothers in the U.S. (Jenner Block, 2010)	−1	0	−1
4	WorldCom Corporation in the U.S. (PwC, 2003)	3	0	3
5	Enron Corporation in the U.S. (Wilmer Cutler Pickering, 2003)	4	0	4
6	Danske Bank in Denmark (Bruun Hjejle, 2018)	3	1	2
7	Toshiba Corporation in Japan (Deloitte, 2015)	2	0	2
8	Olympus Corporation in Japan (Deloitte, 2011)	3	0	3
9	General Motors in the U.S. (Jenner Block, 2014)	3	0	3
10	VimpelCom by Telenor in Norway (Deloitte, 2016)	1	1	0
11	Nordea bank in Sweden (Mannheimer Swartling, 2016)	2	1	1
12	Wells Fargo's Community Bank in the U.S. (Shearman Sterling, 2017)	3	1	2

is present in a report. A one in the column indicates that some new information emerges. The third column indicates a corrected crisis-response match where the new information number is subtracted from the initial crisis-response match.

Based on available information from investigation reports and the media, the analysis shows that significant new information emerged in 5 of our 12 cases. As a consequence, the response match improves for these cases as illustrated in Figure 12.3. This result suggests that in at least some of the cases examined here, the initial response from corporate agents was in some way deceptive. In other words, at some level of the organization, the nature of the scandal was understood, but corporate agents did not necessarily know and

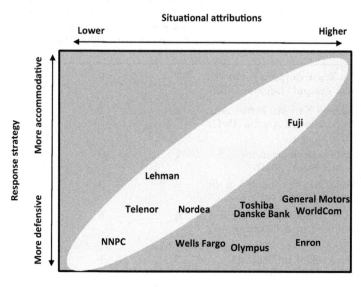

Figure 12.3 Corrected crisis-response match for our sample based on simple rating

chose to engage in impression management and present the scandal in such a way that its potential negative effects on the organization's reputation would be minimized.

It is important to emphasize that the assessments presented in Table 12.3 and Figure 12.3 are exploratory and are shown to illustrate the possibility of analyzing corporate responses to scandals by comparing responses at two different points in time, first by corporate agents and later by their investigators respectively. Future research needs to verify the underlying assumption suggested in a research proposition by Bundy and Pfarrer (2015: 357):

> The more an organization's response strategy matches evaluators' situational attributions of crisis responsibility, the lower the mean and variance of social approval loss.

The research article by Bundy and Pfarrer (2015) is a purely theoretical paper presenting four research propositions. This chapter demonstrates a potential path to conduct an empirical test of their crisis-response match in Figures 12.2 and 12.3.

Convenience theory perspectives

We have presented and analyzed accounts from 12 corporate scandals based on Bundy and Pfarrer's (2015) zones of conformity. 5 out of 12 crises were caused by accounting scandals that seem to satisfy Hurley et al.'s (2019: 233) description of audit quality dependent on who hires the auditor:

> Our design shifts auditors' accountability from managers, who have directional goal preferences, to investors, who prefer judgment accuracy. We find that removing auditors' economic accountability to managers and replacing it with psychological accountability to investors significantly increases audit quality.

What emerges from our empirical study of 12 scandals is the impression of convenience, when corporations attempt to tackle an evolving scandal in their communications. Convenience is a term used to describe the potential savings in time and effort, as well as the potential avoidance of suffering and pain (Engdahl, 2015). Convenience is the state of being able to proceed with something with little effort or difficulty, avoiding pain and strain (Mai & Olsen, 2016). A convenience-oriented person or organization is one who seeks to accomplish a task in the shortest time with the least expenditure of human energy and organizational resources (Berry et al., 2002).

Convenience orientation varies among entities, as some are more concerned than others about time saving, effort reduction, and pain avoidance (Higgins, 1997). Convenience comes at a potential cost to the entity in terms of the likelihood of detection of more serious wrongdoing over time. In other worlds, reducing time and effort now entails a greater potential for future cost. Paying for convenience is a way of phrasing this proposition (Farquhar and Rowley, 2009).

Convenience is a phenomenon that can be observed in many aspects of human life. For example, convenience stores and convenience shopping is associated with easy access to goods and services (Sari et al., 2017). A theory of convenience can be applied to a number of areas where people prefer alternatives that are associated with savings in time and effort, and also with avoidance of pain and problems. For example, a convenience theory of cheating suggests that cheating is a preferred alternative in certain situations. Convenience orientation is a potential explanation for white-collar crime, where convenience can be found in the financial motive (Nichol, 2019), the organizational opportunity (Pontell et al., 2014), and the personal willingness for deviant behavior (Schnatterly et al., 2018).

Sundström and Radon (2015) argue that a convenient individual or organization is not necessarily bad or lazy. On the contrary, it can be seen as smart and rational to be convenient. From a resource matching perspective, convenience directly relates to the amount of time and effort (resources) that must be dedicated to accomplishing a task. However, convenience is a more comprehensive construct than simply examining ease of use perceptions that also addresses the amount of effort in an interaction such as accounts after a scandal. Ease of use is the degree to which an alternative action is free of effort. Convenience addresses the time and effort exerted before, during, and after an action or avoidance of action (Collier and Kimes, 2012).

As a relative construct, convenience is in line with decision-making among alternatives, where accounts can imply denial, justification, excuse or apology. What is considered most convenient is decided by the corporation. Because of the overwhelming workload combined with a need to prioritize own time, convenience is often at the core of thinking among chief executives in organizations (Bigley and Wiersma, 2002). A suggestion for future research is to explore the convenience perspective in scandal response strategies (Chan and Gibbs, 2020; Hansen, 2020; Nolasco and Vaughn, 2019; Vasiu and Podgor, 2019).

In conclusion, this chapter has studied the match or mismatch between situational attributions and response strategies during the scandals. When correcting for new and significant information emerging, only 5 out of 12 companies found themselves in the match zone of conformity. The remaining seven companies can be found in the mismatch zone of under-conformity as far as we could determine based on our exploratory research.

We did not link the extent of match or mismatch to executive destiny since our sample is so small. However, it is interesting to mention that the two executive survivors who experienced no negative consequences for themselves both belonged to companies in the match zone of conformity (NNPC and Nordea). Only future research can tell whether there is a link between corporate accounts and executive destiny.

References

Agence France (2014). Telenor involved in Uzbek corruption case: Report, *Agence France-Presse*, https://infoweb.newsbank.com/apps/news/document-view?p=AWNB&t=&sort=YMD_date%3AD&maxresults=20&f=advanced&val-base-0=telenor&fld-base-0=alltext&bln-base-1=and&val-base-1=VimpelCom&fld-base-1=alltext&bln-base-2=and&val-base-2=2014&fld-base-2=YMD_date&bln-base-3=and&val-base-3=corruption&fld-base-3=alltext&docref=news/151A057C74610AD8.

Albrecht, S. (1996). *Crisis Management for Corporate Self-Defense: How to Protect Your Organization in a Crisis: How to Stop a Crisis Before It Starts*. New York: American Management Association.

Associated Press (2016). The latest: Ex-PM for Georgia said to have 'nothing to hide', *The Associated Press*, April 4, https://infoweb.newsbank.com/apps/news/document-view?p=AWNB&t=&sort=YMD_date%3AD&page=8&maxresults=20&f=advanced&val-base-0=nordea&fld-base-0=alltext&bln-base-1=and&val-base-1=panama%20papers&fld-base-1=alltext&bln-base-3=and&val-base-3=2016&fld-base-3=YMD_date&docref=news/15C0ADA08E6FFBE0.

Balakrishnan, K., Blouin, J.L. and Guay, W.R. (2019). Tax aggressiveness and corporate transparency, *The Accounting Review*, 94 (1), 45–69.

Bandura, A. (1999). Moral disengagement in the perpetration of inhumanities, *Personality and Social Psychology Review*, 3 (3), 193–209.

Bao, D., Kim, Y., Mian, G.M. and Su, L. (2019). Do managers disclose or withhold bad news? Evidence from short interest, *The Accounting Review*, 94 (3), 1–26.

Benson, M.L. (1985). Denying the guilty mind: Accounting for involvement in a white-collar crime, *Criminology*, 23 (4), 583–607.

Berry, L.L., Seiders, K. and Grewal, D. (2002). Understanding service convenience, *Journal of Marketing*, 66, 1–17.

Bigley, G.A. and Wiersma, M.F. (2002). New CEOs and corporate strategic refocusing: How experience as heir apparent influences the use of power, *Administrative Science Quarterly*, 47, 707–727.

Brooks, G. and Button, M. (2011). The police and fraud investigation and the case for a nationalized solution in the United Kingdom, *The Police Journal*, 84, 305–319.

Bruun Hjejle (2018). *Report on the Non-Resident Portfolio at Danske Bank's Estonian branch*, law firm Bruun Hjejle, https://danskebank.com/-/media/danske-bank-com/file-cloud/2018/9/report-on-the-non-resident-portfolio-at-danske-banks-estonian-branch.pdf.

Bundy, J. and Pfarrer, M.D. (2015). A burden of responsibility: The role of social approval at the onset of a crisis, *Academy of Management Review*, 40 (3), 345–369.

Button, M. and Gee, J. (2013). *Countering Fraud for Competitive Advantage: The Professional Approach to Reducing the Last Great Hidden Cost*, Chichester, UK: John Wiley & Sons.

Button, M., Frimpong, K., Smith, G. and Johnston, L. (2007a). Professionalizing counter fraud specialists in the UK: Assessing progress and recommendations for reform, *Crime Prevention and Community Safety*, 9, 92–101.

Button, M., Johnston, L., Frimpong, K. and Smith, G. (2007b). New directions in policing fraud: The emergence of the counter fraud specialists in the United Kingdom, *International Journal of the Sociology of Law*, 35, 192–208.

Chan, F. and Gibbs, C. (2020). Integrated theories of white-collar and corporate crime, in: Rorie, M.L. (editor), *The Handbook of White-Collar Crime*, Hoboken, NJ: Wiley & Sons, chapter 13, pages 191–208.

Cohen, S. (2001). *States of Denial: Knowing about Atrocities and Suffering*, Cambridge, UK: Polity Press.

Collier, J.E. and Kimes, S.E. (2012). Only if it is convenient: Understanding how convenience influences self-service technology evaluation, *Journal of Service Research*, 16 (1), 39–51.

Crosina, E. and Pratt, M.G. (2019). Toward a model of organizational mourning: The case of former Lehman Brothers bankers, *Academy of Management Journal*, 62 (1), 66–98.

Davidson, R.H., Dey, A. and Smith, A.J. (2019). CEO materialism and corporate social responsibility, *The Accounting Review*, 94 (1), 101–126.

Deloitte (2011). *Investigation Report. Olympus Corporation. Third Party Committee*. Kainaka, T., Nakagome, H., Arita, T., Sudo, O., Katayama, E. and Takiguchi, K., www.olympus-global.com/en/common/pdf/if111206corpe_2.pdf, published December 6.

Deloitte (2015). *Investigation Report. Summary Version*. Independent Investigation Committee for Toshiba Corporation. 90 pages, July 20. Ueda, K., Matui, H. Ito, T. and Yamada, K., www.toshiba.co.jp/about/ir/en/news/20150725_1.pdf.

Deloitte (2016). *Review Ownership VimpelCom*, www.telenor.com/wp-content/uploads/2016/04/Deloitte-Report_Telenor_290416_FINAL.pdf.

Deloitte (2017). *Investigation Report*, Independent Investigation Committee, by global auditing firm Deloitte, published June 10, Ito, T., Sato, K. and Nishimura, K., www.fujifilmholdings.com/en/pdf/investors/finance/materials/ff_irdata_investigation_001e.pdf.

Deseret News (2001). Enron's CEO resigns, *Deseret News*, August 11, https://
infoweb.newsbank.com/apps/news/document-view?p=AWNB&t=&sort=YMD_
date%3AA&page=8&maxresults=20&f=advanced&val-base-0=enron&fld-base-
0=alltext&bln-base-2=and&val-base-2=accounting&fld-base-2=alltext&bln-base-
3=and&val-base-3=2001&fld-base-3=YMD_date&docref=news/0F369D49A9F0
C1F4.

Dyreng, S.D., Hanlon, M. and Maydew, E.L. (2019). When does tax avoidance result
in tax uncertainty? *The Accounting Review*, 94 (2), 179–203.

Engdahl, O. (2015). White-collar crime and first-time adult-onset offending: Explorations in the concept of negative life events as turning points, *International Journal
of Law, Crime and Justice*, 43 (1), 1–16.

Farquhar, J.D. and Rowley, J. (2009). Convenience: A services perspective, *Marketing
Theory*, 9 (4), 425–438.

Fisse, B. and Braithwaite, J. (1988). The allocation of responsibility for corporate crime:
Individualism, collectivism and accountability, *Sydney Law Review*, 11, 468–513.

Gamache, D.L. and McNamara, G. (2019). Responding to bad press: How CEO
temporal focus influences the sensitivity to negative media coverage of acquisitions,
Academy of Management Journal, 62 (3), 918–943.

Gao, J., Greenberg, R. and Wong-On-Wing, B. (2015). Whistleblowing intentions of
lower-level employees: The effect of reporting channel, bystanders, and wrongdoing, *Journal of Business Ethics*, 126 (1), 85–99.

Gao, P. and Zhang, G. (2019). Accounting manipulation, peer pressure, and internal
control, *The Accounting Review*, 94 (1), 127–151.

Ghannam, S., Bugeja, M., Matolcsy, Z.P. and Spiropoulos, H. (2019). Are qualified
and experienced outside directors willing to join fraudulent firms and if so, why?
The Accounting Review, 94 (2), 205–227.

Goffman, E. (1971). *Relations in Public: Microstudies of the Public Order*. New York:
Basic Books.

Goldstraw-White, J. (2012). *White-Collar Crime: Accounts of Offending Behavior*,
London, UK: Palgrave Macmillan.

Goncharov, I. and Peter, C.D. (2019). Does reporting transparency affect industry
coordination? Evidence from the duration of international cartels, *The Accounting
Review*, 94 (3), 149–175.

Gottschalk, P. and Tcherni-Buzzeo, M. (2017). Reasons for gaps in crime reporting:
The case of white-collar criminals investigated by private fraud examiners in Norway,
Deviant Behavior, 38 (3), 267–281.

Greer, C. and McLaughlin, E. (2017). Theorizing institutional scandal and the regulatory state, *Theoretical Criminology*, 21 (2), 112–132.

Guenther, D.A., Wilson, R.J. and Wu, K. (2019). Tax uncertainty and incremental tax
avoidance, *The Accounting Review*, 94 (2), 229–247.

Hamish, M. (2016). SFO closes Fuji Xerox probe, *The Press*, December 24, https://
infoweb.newsbank.com/apps/news/document-view?p=AWNB&t=&sort=YMD_
date%3AD&maxresults=20&f=advanced&val-base-0=fuji%20xerox&fld-base-0=
alltext&bln-base-2=and&val-base-2=new%20zealand&fld-base-2=alltext&bln-base-
3=and&val-base-3=2016&fld-base-3=YMD_date&docref=news/16175F5693A0B
FF0.

Hansen, L.L. (2020). Review of the book "Convenience Triangle in White-Collar
Crime: Case Studies of Fraud Examinations", *ChoiceConnect*, vol. 57, no. 5,
Middletown, CT: Association of College and Research Libraries.

Hearit, K.M. (2006). *Crisis Management by Apology: Corporate Responses to Allegations of Wrongdoing*, Mahwah, NJ: Lawrence Erlbaum Associates.

Higgins, E.T. (1997). Beyond pleasure and pain, *American Psychologist*, 52, 1280–1300.

Hsieh, H. and Shannon, S.E. (2005). Three Approaches to Qualitative Content Analysis, *Qualitative Health Research*, 15 (9), 1277–1288.

Hurley, P.J., Mayhew, B.W. and Obermire, K.M. (2019). Realigning auditors' accountability: Experimental evidence, *The Accounting Review*, 94 (3), 233–250.

Inagati, K. (2015). Toshiba scraps dividend after finding accounting irregularities, *Financial Times*, May 8, https://infoweb.newsbank.com/apps/news/documentview?p=AWNB&t=&sort=YMD_date%3AD&page=43&maxresults=20&f=advanced&val-base-0=toshiba&fld-base-0=alltext&bln-base-1=and&val-base-1=accounting%20scandal&fld-base-1=alltext&bln-base-2=and&val-base-2=2015&fld-base-2=YMD_date&docref=news/1553B56CCE48DC40.

Jenner Block (2010). *In regard Lehman Brothers Holdings Inc. to United States Bankruptcy Court in Southern District of New York*, law firm Jenner & Block, A.R. Valukas, https://jenner.com/lehman/VOLUME%203.pdf.

Jenner Block (2014). *Report to the Board of Directors of General Motors Company Regarding Ignition Switch Recalls*, law firm Jenner & Block, A.R. Valukas, www.beasleyallen.com/webfiles/valukas-report-on-gm-redacted.pdf.

Jennings, J. (2019). The role of sell-side analysts after accusations of managerial misconduct, *The Accounting Review*, 94 (1), 183–203.

Krippendorff, K. (1980). *Content Analysis: An Introduction to its Methodology*, Beverly Hills, CA: Sage.

Lehman, D.W., Cooil, B. and Ramanujam, R. (2019). The effects of rule complexity on organizational noncompliance and remediation: Evidence from restaurant health inspections, *Journal of Management*, published online, pages 1–33, https://doi.org/10.1177/0149206319842262.

Mai, H.T.X. and Olsen, S.O. (2016). Consumer participation in self-production: The role of control mechanisms, convenience orientation, and moral obligation, *Journal of Marketing Theory and Practice*, 24 (2), 209–223.

Mannheimer Swartling (2016). *Report on Investigation of Nordea Private Banking in Relation to Offshore Structures*, www.nordea.com/Images/33-125429/Report-on-investigation-of-Nordea-Private-Banking-in-relation-to-offshore-structures.pdf.

Maruna, S. and Copes, H. (2005). What have we learned from five decades of neutralization research? *Crime and Justice*, 32, 221–320.

McClelland, P.L., Liang, X. and Barker, V.L. (2010). CEO commitment to the status quo: Replication and extension using content analysis, *Journal of Management*, 36 (5), 1251–1277.

Moscow Times (2017). Danske Bank under investigation for Russian fraud, *Moscow Times*, October 16, https://infoweb.newsbank.com/apps/news/documentview?p=AWNB&t=&sort=YMD_date%3AD&maxresults=20&f=advanced&val-base-0=danske%20bank&fld-base-0=alltext&bln-base-1=and&val-base-1=money%20laundering&fld-base-1=alltext&bln-base-2=and&val-base-2=Estonian%20branch&fld-base-2=alltext&bln-base-3=and&val-base-3=2017&fld-base-3=YMD_date&docref=news/1679489633293E88.

Nakamoto, M. (2011). Olympus turns focus on Japan's governance, *Financial Times*, November 8, https://infoweb.newsbank.com/apps/news/documentview?p=AWNB&t=&sort=YMD_date%3AD&maxresults=20&f=advanced&

val-base-0=tobashi&fld-base-0=alltext&bln-base-1=and&val-base-1=olympus&fld-base-1=alltext&bln-base-2=and&val-base-2=fraud&fld-base-2=alltext&bln-base-3=and&val-base-3=2011&fld-base-3=YMD_date&docref=news/13AE854CE15B17D0.

Newsbank (2018). *Newsbank* partners with 9.000 publishers worldwide, www.newsbank.com.

Nichol, J.E. (2019). The effects of contract framing on misconduct and entitlement, *The Accounting Review*, 94 (3), 329–344.

Nolasco, C.A. and Vaughn, M.S. (2019). Convenience theory of cryptocurrency crime: A content analysis of U.S. Federal Court decisions, *Deviant Behavior*, published online, https://doi.org/10.1080/01639625.2019.1706706.

Onaran, Y. (2008). Lehman stock falls hard despite CEO's confidence, *The Virginian Pilot*, March 18, https://infoweb.newsbank.com/apps/news/document-view?p=AWNB&t=&sort=YMD_date%3AD&page=46&maxresults=20&f=advanced&val-base-0=lehman%20brothers%20bankruptcy&fld-base-0=alltext&bln-base-1=and&val-base-1=bankruptcy&fld-base-1=alltext&bln-base-2=and&val-base-2=Fuld&fld-base-2=alltext&bln-base-3=and&val-base-3=2008&fld-base-3=YMD_date&docref=news/11F82EF876C656C0.

Patrucco, A.S., Luzzini, D. and Ronchi, S. (2017). Research perspectives on public procurement: Content analysis of 14 years of publications in the Journal of Public Procurement, *Journal of Public Procurement*, 16 (2), 229–269.

Piazza, A. and Jourdan, J. (2018). When the dust settles: The consequences of scandals for organizational competition, *Academy of Management Journal*, 61 (1), 165–190.

Pontell, H.N., Black, W.K. and Geis, G. (2014). Too big to fail, too powerful to jail? On the absence of criminal prosecutions after the 2008 financial meltdown, *Crime, Law and Social Change*, 61 (1), 1–13.

Porretto, J. (2002). WorldCom profit falls but company says finances are solid, *Associated Press*, February 7, https://infoweb.newsbank.com/apps/news/document-view?p=AWNB&t=&sort=YMD_date%3AA&maxresults=20&f=advanced&val-base-0=worldcom&fld-base-0=alltext&bln-base-1=and&val-base-1=scandal&fld-base-1=alltext&bln-base-2=and&val-base-2=accounting%20scandal&fld-base-2=alltext&bln-base-3=and&val-base-3=2002&fld-base-3=YMD_date&bln-base-4=and&val-base-4=ebbers&fld-base-4=alltext&docref=news/0F86C5B0DB8FBDD4.

PwC (2003). *Report of Investigation by the Special Investigative Committee of the Board of Directors of WorldCom Inc.*, Wilmer Cutler Pickering, www.concerned-shareholders.com/CCS_WCSpecialReportExc.pdf.

PwC (2015). *Auditor-General for the Federation. Investigative Forensic Audit into the Allegations of Unremitted Funds into the Federation Accounts by the NNPC*, engagement leader Pedro Omontuemhen, PricewaterhouseCoopers, Lagos, Nigeria, www.premiumtimesng.com/docs_download/Full%20report – 20billion%20dollars%20missing%20oil%20money.pdf?cf=1.

Qiu, B. and Slezak, S.L. (2019). The equilibrium relationships between performance-based pay, performance, and the commission and detection of fraudulent misreporting, *The Accounting Review*, 94 (2), 325–356.

Reporter. (2013). Nigerians yawn over missing billions, *The Sun*, December 31, https://infoweb.newsbank.com/apps/news/document-view?p=AWNB&t=&sort=YMD_date%3AD&maxresults=20&f=advanced&val-base-0=NNPC&fld-base-0=alltext&bln-base-1=and&val-base-1=oil%20revenues&fld-base-1=alltext&bln-base-2=and&v-

al-base-2=2013&fld-base-2=YMD_date&docref=news/14C0EF3456A 37C88.

Rothacker, R. (2016). Banking – Wells Fargo gives few details about firings, *Charlotte Observer*, published September 10, https://infoweb.newsbank.com/apps/news/document-view?p=AWNB&t=&sort=YMD_date%3AD&maxresults=20&f=advanced&val-base-0=rothacker&fld-base-0=Author&bln-base-1=and&val-base-1=wells%20fargo&fld-base-1=alltext&bln-base-2=and&val-base-2=eshet&fld-base-2=alltext&docref=news/15F5B3B95E914970.

Sari, Y.K., Shaari, Z.H. and Amar, A.B. (2017). Measurement development of customer patronage of petrol station with convenience store, *Global Business and Management Research: An International Journal*, 9 (1), 52–62.

Schnatterly, K., Gangloff, K.A. and Tuschke, A. (2018). CEO wrongdoing: A review of pressure, opportunity, and rationalization, *Journal of Management*, 44 (6), 2405–2432.

Schneider, S. (2006). Privatizing economic crime enforcement: Exploring the role of private sector investigative agencies in combating money laundering, *Policing & Society*, 16 (3), 285–312.

Schoultz, I. and Flyghed, J. (2016). Doing business for a "higher loyalty"? How Swedish transnational corporations neutralize allegations of crime, *Crime, Law and Social Change*, 66 (2), 183–198.

Schoultz, I. and Flyghed, J. (2019). From "we didn't do it" to "we've learned our lesson": Development of a typology of neutralizations of corporate crime, *Critical Criminology*, published online doi.org/10.1007/s10612-019-09483-3.

Scott, M.B and Lyman, S.M. (1968). Accounts, *American Sociological Review*, 33 (1), 46–62.

Shearman Sterling (2017). *Independent Directors of the Board of Wells Fargo & Company: Sales Practices Investigation Report*, April 10, 113 pages, Sanger, S.W., Duke, E.A., James, D.M. and Hernandez, E., www08.wellsfargomedia.com/assets/pdf/about/investor-relations/presentations/2017/board-report.pdf.

Shepardson, D. and Burden, M. (2014). GM recalls 778K cars to replace ignition switches after fatal crashes, *Detroit News*, February 13, https://infoweb.newsbank.com/apps/news/document-view?p=AWNB&t=&sort=YMD_date%3AA&maxresults=20&f=advanced&val-base-0=ignition%20switch%20failure&fld-base-0=alltext&bln-base-1=and&val-base-1=GM&fld-base-1=alltext&bln-base-2=and&val-base-2=cobalt&fld-base-2=alltext&bln-base-3=and&val-base-3=2014&fld-base-3=YMD_date&bln-base-4=and&val-base-4=learned&fld-base-4=alltext&docref=news/14BF79CC1AB3B180.

Sundström, M. and Radon, A. (2015). Utilizing the concept of convenience as a business opportunity in emerging markets, *Organizations and Markets in Emerging Economies*, 6 (2), 7–21.

Sykes, G. and Matza, D. (1957). Techniques of neutralization: A theory of delinquency, *American Sociological Review*, 22 (6), 664–670.

Vasiu, V.I. and Podgor, E.S. (2019). Organizational opportunity and deviant behavior: Convenience in white-collar crime, in: *Criminal Law and Criminal Justice Books*, New Brunswick, NJ: Rutgers, the State University of New Jersey, July, www.clcjbooks.rutgers.edu.

Whyte, D. (2016). It's common sense, stupid! Corporate crime and techniques of neutralization in the automobile industry, *Crime, Law and Social Change*, 66 (2), 165–181.

Williams, J.W. (2005). Reflections on the private versus public policing of economic crime, *British Journal of Criminology*, 45, 316–339.

Williams, J.W. (2014). The private eyes of corporate culture: The forensic accounting and corporate investigation industry and the production of corporate financial security, in: Walby, K. and Lippert, R.K. (editors), *Corporate Security in the 21st Century: Theory and Practice in International Perspective*, Hampshire, Houndmills, UK: Palgrave Macmillan, pages 56–77.

Wilmer Cutler Pickering (2003). *Report of Investigation by the Special Investigative Committee of the Board of Directors of Enron Corp.*, William C. Powers, Raymond S. Troubh, Herbert S. Winokur, law firm Wilmer, Cutler & Pickering, http://i.cnn.net/cnn/2002/LAW/02/02/enron.report/powers.report.pdf, downloaded September 23, 2018.

Conclusion

Institutional collapse is just one kind of organizational dynamics that make it possible for white-collar crime to occur more frequently. According to institutional theory, the organizational context, behaviors and processes may support white-collar crime. Organizational behaviors reflect a culture that evolves over time and that becomes legitimized within an organization (Itzkovich and Heilbrunn, 2016). Corruption and other kinds of financial crime become entrenched by the legitimizing process (Pillay and Kluvers, 2014; Rostami et al., 2015).

While the theory of institutional collapse is concerned with breakdown caused in interaction with external forces (Shadnam and Lawrence, 2011), the theory of social disorganization is concerned with collapse caused only by internal forces. Social disorganization leads to the breakdown of conventional social norms. The gradual erosion of conventional relationships weakens the organization and makes it unable to satisfy the needs of its members. The organization gradually loses the ability to control the behavior of its members. There is no functional authority over potential white-collar criminals in the organization (Wood and Alleyne, 2010). As result of social disorganization, organizational opportunity to commit white-collar crime increases (Hoffmann, 2002; Swart and Kinnie, 2003).

Slippery slope theory is a third theoretical perspective on organizational dynamics as an enabler of white-collar crime. Slippery slope means that a person slides over time from legal to illegal activities. Arjoon (2008: 78) explains slippery slope in the following way:

> As commonsense experience tells us, it is the small infractions that can lead to the larger ones. An organization that overlooks the small infractions of its employees creates a culture of acceptance that may lead to its own demise. This phenomenon is captured by the metaphor of the slippery slope. Many unethical acts occur without the conscience awareness of the person who engaged in the misconduct. Specifically, unethical behavior is most likely to follow the path of a slippery slope, defined as a gradual decline in which no one event makes one aware that he or she is acting unethically. The majority of unethical behaviors are unintentional and ordinary, thus affecting everyone and providing support for unethical behavior

when people unconsciously lower the bar over time through small changes in their ethical behavior.

Welsh et al. (2014) argue that many recent scandals seem resulting from a slippery slope in which a series of small infractions gradually increase over time. Committing small indiscretions over time may gradually lead people to complete larger unethical acts that they otherwise would have judged to be impermissible.

The slippery slope theory is in contrast to individual theories such as the standard economic model of rational choice theory as described in the economic dimension. Psychological and organizational processes shape moral behavior, where individuals are motivated to view themselves in a positive manner that corresponds with their moral values. Individuals tend to rationalize minor unethical acts so that they may derive some benefit without feeling forced negatively to update their self-concept. For example, a minor transgression such as taking a pen home from the office may seem permissible, whereas taking money out of the company cash drawer may more clearly emerge as stealing (Welsh et al., 2014).

A fourth theoretical perspective on organizational dynamics as enabler of white-collar crime is neutralization theory (Sykes and Matza, 1957). For example, in religious organizations, there is evidence that misconduct and crime find rationalization by higher loyalties. When the Catholic Church in Norway had a long list of individuals who were not members of the church, they refused to pay back subsidies to the government. Tjørholm (2016: 12), a professor of religion at a university in Norway, argued that in some situations, the Catholic Church seems to decouple itself from the common moral and social obligations:

> The prosecutor recently announced the indictment against Oslo Catholic Diocese. The prosecutor accused the chief financial officer in the church of serious fraud, with a maximum possible prison sentence of six years. On the part of Oslo Catholic Diocese, the allegation involves a fine of one million Norwegian kroner. Bishop Bernt Eidsvig avoided indictment because adequate evidence of guilt does not exist. Management in Oslo Catholic Diocese has undoubtedly adopted reprehensible methods when members forced to register served as a basis for allocation of state subsidies.

A fifth and final example of a dynamic perspective is dynamics created by differential association. The essence of differential association is that criminal behavior is learned, and the main part of learning comes from within important personal groups. Exposure to the attitudes of members of the organization that either favor or reject legal codes influences the attitudes of the individual. The individual will go on to commit crime if the person experiences more attitudes that favor law violation than attitudes that favor abiding by the law (Hoffmann, 2002; Sutherland, 1983; Wood and Alleyne, 2010).

Chan and Gibbs (2020) describe the theory of convenience, which is the basis for convenience dynamics, as an integrated theory of white-collar and corporate crime that conducts a cross level up and down integration. They suggest that the theory is a deductive and parsimonious integration by unifying concepts from macro-economic, meso-organizational, and micro-behavioral perspectives. All these concepts are glued together by the overarching concept of convenience.

The table here lists four cases from Germany, the United States, and Japan that might illustrate convenience dynamics in white-collar crime. Middelhoff expanded his organizational opportunities for misconduct and crime as he rose to higher levels in German enterprises. He might have slid down the slippery slope without really noticing that he ended up on the wrong side of the law. The slippery slope perspective suggests that a person can slide over time from legal to illegal activities without really noticing. The small infractions can lead to the larger ones. An organization that overlooks the small infractions of its employees creates a culture of acceptance that may lead to its own demise (Welsh et al., 2014). The slippery slope perspective applies to a number of situations, such as seventeenth-century England, where "unregulated overseas trade was a slippery slope to fraud" (Pettigrew, 2018: 313). Arjoon (2008: 78) explains slippery slope in the following way:

> As commonsense experience tells us, it is the small infractions that can lead to the larger ones. An organization that overlooks the small infractions of its employees creates a culture of acceptance that may lead to its own demise. This phenomenon is captured by the metaphor of the slippery slope. Many unethical acts occur without the conscience awareness of the person who engaged in the misconduct. Specifically, unethical behavior is most likely to follow the path of a slippery slope, defined as a gradual decline in which no one event makes one aware that he or she is acting unethically. The majority of unethical behaviors are unintentional and ordinary, thus affecting everyone and providing support for unethical behavior when people unconsciously lower the bar over time through small changes in their ethical behavior.

The second offender in the following table is Kerik in the United States. His convenience dynamics resembles the application of neutralization techniques (Sykes and Matza, 1957) as well as the blame game (Eberly et al., 2011). His willingness increased as he found he did nothing wrong. When his willingness increased, then the motive for illegitimate gain increased. He said in his autobiography that; "I had lived a version of the American dream" (Kerik, 2015: 146). The American dream of prosperity and success is a strong motive for white-collar crime (Schoepfer and Piquero, 2006). As Kerik felt innocence, he could expand his illegitimate involvement driven by the American dream.

The third offender in the table is Belfort in the United States. Rather than continue his work as a stockbroker for others on the Wall Street, he created convenience dynamics by setting up his own firm. By hiring young people eager

Table 13.1 Convenience theory applied to offenders in Germany, the United States, and Japan

White-collar criminal	Convenient economical motive	Convenient organizational opportunity	Convenient personal willingness
Middelhoff (2017)	The American dream of prosperity and success (Schoepfer and Piquero, 2006)	Sensemaking of actions difficult for outsiders (Weick, 1995)	Professional deviant identity (Obodaru, 2017)
Kerik (2015)	Removal of strain and pain (Langton and Piquero, 2007)	Too big to fail, too powerful to jail (Pontell et al., 2014)	Lack of self-control (Gottfredson and Hirschi, 1990)
Belfort (2008)	Greed where nothing is ever enough (Goldstraw-White, 2012)	Inability to control because of social disorganization (Hoffmann, 2002)	Sensation seeking to experience adventure (Craig and Piquero, 2017)
Kikukawa (Deloitte, 2011)	Avoid threats from investors (Logan et al., 2019)	Access to crime resources (Berghoff and Spiekermann, 2018)	Blaming others for misconduct (Slyke and Bales, 2012)

to make money, he created new opportunities by entrepreneurship (Ramoglou and Tsang, 2016). He used a language that few of the young ones understood (Ferraro et al., 2005), while he knew that they would all be loyal to him. Belfort created a deviant collectivist value orientation (Bussmann et al., 2018), where deviant identity labeling occurred (Mingus and Burchfield, 2012).

The fourth and final offender in the table is Kikukawa in Japan. He had climbed the hierarchy of needs for status and success (Maslow, 1943) to become the CEO and later the chairperson at Olympus Corporation. He seems to have supported the idea that business ends justify means in goal orientation (Jonnergård et al., 2010), where stable profits reported to investors is the overarching goal. When Olympus' performance declined, they found ways to compensate by implementing the loss separation scheme of tobashi. Kikukawa's convenience dynamics consisted of increased willingness from declining business performance, which caused an opportunity expansion in the organizational setting by the loss separation scheme.

References

Arjoon, S. (2008). Slippery when wet: The real risk in business, *Journal of Markets & Morality*, Spring, 11 (1), 77–91.

Belfort, J. (2008). *The Wolf of Wall Street: How Money Destroyed a Wall Street Superman*, London, UK: Hodder & Stoughton.

Berghoff, H. and Spiekermann, U. (2018). Shady business: On the history of white-collar crime, *Business History*, 60 (3), 289–304.

Bussmann, K.D., Niemeczek, A. and Vockrodt, M. (2018). Company culture and prevention of corruption in Germany, China and Russia, *European Journal of Criminology*, 15 (3), 255–277.

Chan, F. and Gibbs, C. (2020). Integrated theories of white-collar and corporate crime, in: Rorie, M.L. (editor), *The Handbook of White-Collar Crime*, Hoboken, NJ: Wiley & Sons, chapter 13, pages 191–208.

Craig, J.M. and Piquero, N.L. (2017). Sensational offending: An application of sensation seeking to white-collar and conventional crimes, *Crime & Delinquency*, 63 (11), 1363–1382.

Deloitte (2011). *Investigation Report. Olympus Corporation. Third Party Committee.* Kainaka, T., Nakagome, H., Arita, T., Sudo, O., Katayama, E. and Takiguchi, K., www.olympus-global.com/en/common/pdf/if111206corpe_2.pdf, published December 6.

Eberly, M.B., Holley, E.C., Johnson, M.D. and Mitchell, T.R. (2011). Beyond internal and external: A dyadic theory of relational attributions, *Academy of Management Review*, 36 (4), 731–753.

Ferraro, F., Pfeffer, J. and Sutton, R.I. (2005). Economics language and assumptions: How theories can become self-fulfilling, *Academy of Management Review*, 30 (1), 8–24.

Goldstraw-White, J. (2012). *White-Collar Crime: Accounts of Offending Behavior*, London, UK: Palgrave Macmillan.

Gottfredson, M.R. and Hirschi, T. (1990). *A General Theory of Crime*, Stanford, CA: Stanford University Press.

Hoffmann, J.P. (2002). A contextual analysis of differential association, social control, and strain theories of delinquency, *Social Forces*, 81 (3), 753–785.

Itzkovich, Y. and Heilbrunn, S. (2016). The role of co-workers' solidarity as an antecedent of incivility and deviant behavior in organizations, *Deviant Behavior*, 37 (8), 861–876.

Jonnergård, K., Stafsudd, A. and Elg, U. (2010). Performance evaluations as gender barriers in professional organizations: A study of auditing firms, *Gender, Work and Organization*, 17 /6), 721–747.

Kerik, B.B. (2015). *From Jailer to Jailed: My Journey from Correction and Police Commissioner to Inmate #84888-054*, New York, NY: Threshold Editions.

Langton, L. and Piquero, N.L. (2007). Can general strain theory explain white-collar crime? A preliminary investigation of the relationship between strain and select white-collar offenses, *Journal of Criminal Justice*, 35 (1), 1–15.

Logan, M.W., Morgan, M.A., Benson, M.L. and Cullen, F.T. (2019). Coping with imprisonment: Testing the special sensitivity hypothesis for white-collar offenders, *Justice Quarterly*, 36 (2), 225–254.

Maslow, A.H. (1943). A theory of human motivation, *Psychological Review*, 50 (4), 370–396.

Middelhoff, T. (2017). *Der Sturz: Die Autobiografie von Thomas Middelhoff (The Fall: The Autobiography of Thomas Middelhoff)*, Stuttgart, Germany: LangenMuller in der F.A. Herbig Verlagsbuchhandlung.

Mingus, W. and Burchfield, K.B. (2012). From prison to integration: Applying modified labeling theory to sex offenders, *Criminal Justice Studies*, 25 (1), 97–109.

Obodaru, O. (2017). Forgone, but not forgotten: Toward a theory of forgone professional identities, *Academy of Management Journal*, 60 (2), 523–553.

Pettigrew, W.A. (2018). The changing place of fraud in seventeenth-century public debates about international trading corporations, *Business History*, 60 (3), 305–320.

Pillay, S. and Kluvers, R. (2014). An institutional theory perspective on corruption: The case of a developing democracy, *Financial Accountability & Management*, 30 (1), 95–119.

Pontell, H.N., Black, W.K. and Geis, G. (2014). Too big to fail, too powerful to jail? On the absence of criminal prosecutions after the 2008 financial meltdown, *Crime, Law and Social Change*, 61 (1), 1–13.

Ramoglou, S. and Tsang, E.W.K. (2016). A realist perspective of entrepreneurship: Opportunities as propensities, *Academy of Management Review*, 41, 410–434.

Rostami, A., Melde, C. and Holgersson, S. (2015). The myth of success: The emergence and maintenance of a specialized gang unit in Stockholm, Sweden, *International Journal of Comparative and Applied Criminal Justice*, 39 (3), 199–217.

Schoepfer, A. and Piquero, N.L. (2006). Exploring white-collar crime and the American dream: A partial test of institutional anomie theory, *Journal of Criminal Justice*, 34 (3), 227–235.

Shadnam, M. and Lawrence, T.B. (2011). Understanding widespread misconduct in organizations: An institutional theory of moral collapse, *Business Ethics Quarterly*, 21 (3), 379–407.

Slyke, S.V. and Bales, W.D. (2012). A contemporary study of the decision to incarcerate white-collar and street property offenders, *Punishment & Society*, 14 (2), 217–246.

Sutherland, E.H. (1983). *White Collar Crime: The Uncut Version*, New Haven, CT: Yale University Press.

Swart, J. and Kinnie, N. (2003). Sharing knowledge in knowledge-intensive firms, *Human Resource Management Journal*, 13 (2), 60–75.

Sykes, G. and Matza, D. (1957). Techniques of neutralization: A theory of delinquency, *American Sociological Review*, 22 (6), 664–670.

Tjørholm, O. (2016). Det katolske medlemsjukset er fortsatt juks (Catholic membership cheating is still fraud), daily Norwegian newspaper *Aftenposten*, December 5, pages 12–13.

Weick, K.E. (1995). *Sensemaking in Organizations*, Sage, CA: Thousand Oaks.

Welsh, D.T., Ordonez, L.D., Snyder, D.G. and Christian, M.S. (2014). The slippery slope: How small ethical transgressions pave the way for larger future transgressions, *Journal of Applied Psychology*, 100 (1), 114–127.

Wood, J. and Alleyne, E. (2010). Street gang theory and research: Where are we now and where do we go from here? *Aggression and Violent Behavior*, 15, 100–111.

Index

Note: Page locators in **bold** indicate a table. Page locators in *italics* indicate a figure.

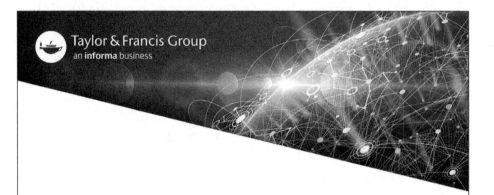

Taylor & Francis Group
an **informa** business

Taylor & Francis eBooks

www.taylorfrancis.com

A single destination for eBooks from Taylor & Francis
with increased functionality and an improved user
experience to meet the needs of our customers.

90,000+ eBooks of award-winning academic content in
Humanities, Social Science, Science, Technology, Engineering,
and Medical written by a global network of editors and authors.

TAYLOR & FRANCIS EBOOKS OFFERS:

A streamlined
experience for
our library
customers

A single point
of discovery
for all of our
eBook content

Improved
search and
discovery of
content at both
book and
chapter level

REQUEST A FREE TRIAL
support@taylorfrancis.com

 Routledge
Taylor & Francis Group

 CRC Press
Taylor & Francis Group

Printed in the United States
by Baker & Taylor Publisher Services